Christ Consciousness

Norman Paulsen

The Builders Publishing Co.
P. O. Box 2278
Salt Lake City, Utah 84110

First Printing, 1980, as *SUNBURST: Return of the Ancients*
© Copyright 1980, by Norman Paulsen
Library of Congress Catalog Card #79-66005
ISBN 0-941848-00-0

Revised and Reprinted as *Christ Consciousness*
© Copyright 1984, by Norman Paulsen
Library of Congress Catalog Card #84-72066
ISBN 0-941848-03-5 Cloth Edition
ISBN 0-941848-04-3 Paperback

Cover artwork and design by Craig Hanson and Donna Wright Kiddie

Printed in the United States of America
by The Builders Publishing Company
P. O. Box 2278
Salt Lake City, Utah 84110

Acknowledgements

I wish to thank all the brothers and sisters who have remained faithful in their efforts to support our family and the acquisition of Christ Consciousness for all the races of humanity. It has been through their love, devotion and support that I have been able to compile and write this book.

I wish to extend a personal thank you to Sandi De Silva, Tricia Mayes Dunham, Craig Hanson and John & Donna Kiddie for their special contributions. To Daya Mata, Sister Janaki, and Sister Sharana, of Self-Realization Fellowship, for their loving energy and their sensitive editorial suggestions. Also to Judy Paller for her further editorial help and to Elke Firth of Dzierzon & Associates for typesetting a very difficult manuscript.

I also would like to express my great love, admiration and appreciation to my dear friend and companion, Patty, who has dedicated long days and nights of work compiling all the material of this book into a presentable form. Her tireless, selfless contribution has made this book possible in a form I feel will be acceptable to all.

Brother Norman

Table of Contents

Illustrations

Photographs

Drawings

Maps

Richard Bucke, author of *Cosmic Consciousness*

Dedication

I wish to express my deep appreciation to Richard Bucke, the author of *Cosmic Consciousness*, and his unparalleled contribution to humanity in compiling and writing this great work. His book arrived at a time in my life when I most needed confirmation of my own unique experiences. It has been my constant companion for more than twenty years. In his volume I found many friends at a time in my life when I had few.

In Bucke's book one finds the companionship of many spirits whose lives have been filled with the New Sense, Christ Consciousness; all in varying degrees of expression but all, in essence, stating the same divine truths that the New Sense conveys. Through his book entitled *Leaves of Grass*, Walt Whitman has also greatly influenced my life and discoveries regarding the Christ or Cosmic Sense.

As I write these words today I am seated at the headquarters ranch house on Big Springs Ranch, near Wells, Nevada, in the northeastern corner of the state. Looking through the window across twenty-five miles of open grassland, Pilot Peak climbs upward in the distance to the elevation of 10,716 feet. Pilot Peak is one of the navigational landmarks used by the pioneers moving from Salt Lake City westward to Donner Pass. Johnson Springs, which I can hear running in the distance, was a stopping point for weary travelers and animals on their westward journey. Richard Bucke himself once drank from Johnson Springs on his journey westward from Salt Lake City.

This is my first attempt at writing and I have been encouraged to write this volume by many friends who feel the story should be told. I feel justified in doing so for the following reasons: (1) that this book might be an inspiration to others, like myself, who seek answers to divine truths; (2) that others, like myself, who will accept nothing short of a face-to-face meeting with the Divine Spirit, might have some direction on their journey; (3) that whosoever seeks to serve and try to fulfill divine will might have some ideas of what might transpire in their lives.

Bucke's book does not describe in detail actual events of any particular life that lead up to the dawning of the Cosmic Sense. I have tried to put into words in this volume the inspiration and events which led me to Christ Consciousness. I humbly submit this narrative about the evolution of the New Sense as it occurred in my life and in the lives of others I know about. I feel the true gospel of Christ is the Cosmic or Christ Sense now in evidence in many cases across the face of the earth. I also wish to express my great love and admiration for Paramhansa Yogananda, who provided inspiration, direction, and the Baptism of Fire for me at an early age. His discipline and example set my feet upon the path Homeward.

I have attempted to set down in this book some of the experiences I have had in my lifetime. I do not expect the reader to believe or disbelieve, but only to examine them in the light of his or her own understanding. Incredible as some of them may seem, they are absolutely true and I have tried to express them as they have actually happened. Perhaps this book is far ahead of its time, but surely there will be those who will recognize the truths contained herein.

May Divine Spirit descend upon you on your journey through this life and bless you with discovery of Christ Consciousness within you and around you.

— Brother Norman

THIS BOOK IS DEDICATED TO THE BUILDERS
AND ALL WHO SEEK TO KNOW THEM

White Bear, co-author of the *Book of the Hopi*

Foreword

Christ Consciousness will reveal the true spiritual interpretation of our past worlds. It will also give, to those who search, spiritual confidence — what the Good Book should have revealed in the beginning.

Norman Paulsen's writing will prove to mankind his great spiritual courage to write this book, especially when it will conflict with scientific interpretations of our world's knowledge.

Mankind has searched for a greater understanding of himself in many spiritual institutions, either through ancient beliefs or in modern creeds or cults.

Man was given divine intelligence when created, but in due time, man forgot his Creator. This was the beginning of his downfall. Worldly concepts were man's only ambition. He was given freedom of thought, but with warning. The warning has now brought all nations to "the Point of No Return." Nations' compromise with their Creator is at an end.

For those who have an opportunity to read this book, the truth is now open. Someone said: "If you know the truth, the truth shall set you free."

— White Bear
Hopi Tribe, Arizona

N. D. Paulsen, the author

Introduction to Christ Consciousness

Christ Consciousness or Cosmic Consciousness is a higher state of consciousness than self-consciousness, or simple-consciousness, which pervades the races of humanity on this planet today. Christ Consciousness is, in fact, 180 degrees away from self-consciousness and exists upon the highest plane of reality. In humanity, there are three states of consciousness in evidence today.

The first is simple-consciousness, which is possessed by human beings and also higher forms of the animal kingdom. In this state the entity is aware of its body, its needs, and the fact that it is separate from all other forms of life around it. Simple-consciousness is driven by instinct (Mother's and Father's nature), to go and acquire food, shelter, and bodily comforts. Simple-consciousness groups together for survival and procreation.

Self-consciousness is all of this and more. Self-consciousness begins to fully express selfishness, for it distinctly sees the physical body as totally separated from the creation which surrounds it. Self-consciousness begins to store mental images of all which it beholds and now desires to possess. These mental images are expressed in verbal languages and writings (i.e., the arts, crafts, sciences and religions). These self-conscious abilities raise the creature human far above the highest state of simple-conscious expression. In fact, an enormous distance separates the two.

Christ or Cosmic Consciousness is the third state and is as far above self-consciousness, as self-consciousness is beyond simple-consciousness. In this state the creature human is now aware of the two former states of consciousness, as both are still functioning within Christ Consciousness. Therefore, full understanding of all life-forms and images is now available. Christ or Cosmic Consciousness implies an illumination or understanding of the whole cosmos, the expanding Sphere of Creation.

Along with this tremendous enlightenment comes the intellectual illumination, the incredible ability to speak and describe all which it sees as if from the center of all created images and thought-forms. The creature human has now become a member of a new species on earth. Along with this exalted state comes the awareness of moral exaltation, a state of ever-new joy and elation, accompanied by the feeling of great expansion and freedom from bodily confines. There is a quickening of the moral sense which is a contribution to the whole human race along with the enhanced intellectual powers; the most profound of all is the soul's sense of immortality, the consciousness of eternal life. This is not a conviction that one shall have this, but the absolute consciousness that one already has it! Only one's own personal experience of this state, or the continued study and meditation on those who have attained it, can ever enable us to realize what this Cosmic- or Christ-Conscious sense really is.

It is my belief that humanity on this planet is now standing on the threshold of this divine evolution of consciousness. I further believe that anyone can be a candidate and that intelligent contact with Christ-Conscious minds assists self-conscious beings toward the higher goal. I therefore hope to bring about, through the instrument of this book, inspiration and desire in individuals to seek out this great truth and take the most important steps toward it. The future of humanity, I think, is extremely hopeful. The New Sense of which we speak, if possessed by the multitudes, would literally create a new heaven and a new earth. Old concepts would be done away with; all would become new!

In the light of Christ Consciousness, all religions will disappear like phantom images on the cosmic screen; the human spirit will be revolutionized. "Not my will, Father, but rather thy will be done on earth." The word "religion" will not exist, for the light of truth will dominate the lives of everyone. There will be no dependence on tradition, or the verbal expounding of priests. This truth will not dwell in churches and prayers, hymns and discourses, nor depend on special revelations from the mouths of so-called gods who come to teach. One's own divine revelations from within will suffice.

There will be no efforts to save men from their sins, nor any promises of a heavenly abode after death. The sense of immortality will exist along with the other five senses as absolute knowledge from the well of eternal experiences. There will be no doubt of the Absolute Godhead, as every spirit shall see the Absolute face to face. Discourses between man and his Creator will no longer need intermediaries; he shall receive direct communication with divine will. The sense of sin will no longer exist in the minds of the races, nor the worry of death, or the future to come. Each spirit will now know its oneness with all of life and the spheres of creation.

This planet, populated by men and women possessing Christ Consciousness, will be so far removed from the societies of today, there will be absolutely no comparison. The 180 degrees between self-conscious societies and Cosmic-Conscious societies will again bring heaven on earth.

The savior of humanity is Christ or Cosmic Consciousness — in Paul's language, the Christ. The Cosmic Sense, whenever it appears, destroys selfishness in the individual spirit, along with the sense of sin, shame, guilt, and fear.

The Evolution of Christ Consciousness

The divine faculty called Christ Consciousness once predominated the societies on this planet at a time when the Sons and Daughters of God were on earth. The following biblical quotations are taken from the Holy Bible, Oxford Annotated Edition; printed by New York Oxford University Press, 1962. Quotes on the Sons of God and the Nephilim (Nefilim) substantiate the existence of a race of divine physical beings who were on earth before and after the creation of man in the biblical Genesis account. I feel this evidence is very important to the fundamental theme of this writing. Who were the Sons of God who were present when man was created? And where are they today? Was there a great division among the Sons of God millenniums ago, which resulted in the biblical reference to Fallen Angels? I will attempt to answer these ancient questions in this volume.

> When men began to multiply on the face of the ground, and daughters were born to them, the sons of God saw that the daughters of men were fair; and they took to wife such of them as they chose. The Nephilim were on the earth in those days, and also afterward, when the sons of God came in to the daughters of men, and they bore children to them. These were the mighty men that were of old, the men of renown.
>
> — Genesis 6:1, 2 & 4

> So they brought to the people of Israel an evil report of the land which they had spied out, saying... "and all the people that we saw in it are men of great stature. And there we saw the Nephilim (the sons of Anak, who come from the Nephilim) and we seemed to ourselves like grasshoppers, and so we seemed to them."
>
> — Numbers 13:32-33

> ...And we turned and went in the direction of the wilderness of Moab. And the Lord said unto me, "Do not harass Moab or contend with them in battle, for I will not give you any of their land for a possession, because I have given Ar to the sons of Lot for a possession." The Emin formerly lived there, people great and many, and tall as the Anakim they are also known as Rephaim, but the Moabites call them Emim. (Deuteronomy 2:9-10.) Men of great stature, whose

xxi

super-human power was thought to result from divine human marriages, the Anakim are also referred to as the Anunnaki by Zecharia Sitchin, in *The 12th Planet* .

— The Author

Then God said, "Let us make man in our image after our likeness; . . ." (Genesis 1:26.) The plural *us* and *our* appears to refer to the divine beings who surround God in his heavenly court; the Sons of God.

— The Author

Then the Lord God said, "Behold the man has become like one of us, knowing good and evil and now, lest he put forth his hand and take also of the tree of life, and eat and live forever. . . ."

— Genesis 3:22

Come let us go down and there confuse their language that they may not understand one another's speech.

— Genesis 11:7

The fall of some of the angels of heaven and the great wars which ensued are a matter of record in all the ancient texts still to be found existing on earth. This planet once hosted a super civilization of divine beings who constructed a great network of cities which belted the whole earth. The evidence thereof is still to be seen today in the Eastern and Western Hemispheres. What, indeed, happened? That is the question long asked.

If at one time Christ Consciousness prevailed here on earth, then why did it depart? And beyond that, will it return again? I believe it is here now in isolated cases which are becoming more and more apparent. Now let us examine what is known about this ancient, and now again very New Sense.

I wish to state to the reader that in this introduction I have used some material directly from Richard Bucke's *Cosmic Consciousness*. It is my feeling that I cannot enlarge much upon the quality of the presentation and description of the Christ or Cosmic Sense as written by Dr. Bucke. I have therefore paraphrased Bucke's words freely. I hope the reader will also examine Dr. Bucke's work. It is the first and only book of its kind, describing the appearance of the old, but New Sense, in and around mankind on earth, and its manifestation in many of the world's greatest leaders.

— The Author

By examination we find the New Sense does not appear by chance in this person or that. It seems in the past it was necessary for some exalted personality to appear and supply the pre-conditions for its birth. In the known past cases, the personage has been of exceptional physique, health, and beauty, possessing handsome features accompanied by a humble nature expressing strong magnetism. This divine faculty has many names but they have not been understood or in most cases recognized.

In the case of Siddhartha Gautama, the Buddha, it has been named *Nirvana*. The reason for this is that it is said to eliminate lower mental states such as the sense of fear, sin, and shame, and the fear of death. Accompanying this, the desire for wealth is also subjugated. The word *Nirvana* is defined as the state to which the Buddhist saint is to aspire as the highest aim and the highest good. Jesus called the Cosmic Sense the *Kingdom of Heaven*, whereas Paul called it *the Christ*. He spoke of himself as a man in Christ, of "them that are in Christ." He also called it *the Spirit of God*.

Paul later describes another individuality that lived within him. This entity he called *Christ, the divinely sent deliverer*, identifying it not so much with Jesus, the man, as with the deliverer who was to be sent in his person. In this instance Paul referred to Jesus, the man, as well as Jesus, the Messiah, the herald and exemplar of the new and higher race yet to come. The dual personality of men and women possessing Christ Consciousness is a constant and recurring phenomenon. Mohammed called the New Sense *Gabriel*, and looked upon it as a distinct and separate person who dwelt in him and spoke to him. Dante called the faculty *Beatrice*. Balzac called the New Sense *Specialism;* Shakespeare addressed the New Sense in his sonnets as *a young friend* of his. Whitman called it *My Soul* and spoke of it as another entity.

To further illustrate the objectification of this subjective phenomena, it must be remembered that to the entity possessing the Cosmic Sense, the terms objective and subjective lose their old meaning, and objects gross and the unseen soul become one. Here is a poem written, no doubt, from the essence of the Cosmic Sense.

> So mused a traveler on the earthly plane
> Being in himself a type of all mankind.
> For aspirations dim at first possessed
> Him only, rising vaguely in his dreams,
> Till in ripe years his early musings changed
> To inspiration and the light of the soul,
> Then vision came, and in the light he saw
> What he had hoped now openly revealed;
> And much besides — the inmost soul of things,
> And "beauty" as the crown of life itself,
> Ineffable, transcending mortal form;
> For robed in light, no longer fantasy,
> Before his gaze the true "ideal" stood,
> Sublimely fair, beyond conception, clothed
> In beauty and divinest symmetry.

Yet pined he not like him of Latmos when
In dreaming ecstasy upon the hills
Beneath the moon he saw his love unveiled;
For well he knew the crowning of his life
Was in that vision and would be fulfilled.
Nay, was fulfilled, for henceforth by his side
A radiant being stood, his guiding light
And polar star, that as a magnet held
Him in the hold of ever-during love! . . .
— William Sharpe, *The Dual Image*

Vision of The Great Central SöN-SüN (to be pronounced as one syllable, "sun") — O spark which started all, and endless chain of things. The divine expanding Sphere of Creation, ever moving outward, filled with images and infinite light, projecting all from within thyself. As in a mirror, all faces become your own. I see myself in all things constantly.

Christ Consciousness as defined in three stages:

1. He who sees another SöN-SüN rise on the horizon at midnight (that is, the Magi).

2. He who sees another SöN-SüN, as in a swoon, face to face, and hears the voice thereof.

3. He who sees another SöN-SüN face to face and experiences so-called physical death, enters that light, sees all which life and light have become (the expanding Sphere of Creation), and returns to reclaim his mortal form after minutes, hours, or days. Henceforth, this spirit has become a true Son or Daughter of the Living Light, a Christed being.

Upon the plane of Christ Consciousness, it must be understood that all cases are not of the same degree. As we observe self-conscious expression, we find a wide range of diversification. Where some rise to prominence in science, art, literature, law, and religion, others occupying the same planes do not. If we are to imagine a world peopled by Cosmic-Conscious beings, we would find the same variety of expression as exists in the self-conscious world of today. Here also, they would vary in intellectual ability and moral and spiritual elevation. This condition would again contribute to wide ranges of character, even exceeding the self-conscious world of expression today. Yes, here one being might well appear a god while others might pass unnoticed.

The Christ-Conscious being is strengthened and purified by the New Sense and is immediately raised far above the highest planes of self-consciousness. A person possessing the Cosmic Sense permanently would be infinitely higher and nobler than the person existing on the highest self-conscious levels of existence. Any person who has experienced this illumination of Christ Consciousness, for only a moment, would probably never again descend to the level of the merely self-conscious individual. For years afterward they would feel the purifying and exalting effect of that Divine Illumination. That person undoubtedly would be recognized as possessing a spiritual stature above and beyond the average individual.

The hypothesis I have adopted requires that cases of Christ or Cosmic Consciousness should become more and more numerous and apparent in the immediate years following A.D. 1930. This will be accompanied by a great surge of cases of illumination among young and old alike shortly before the year 2000.

Looking back to the time of Siddhartha Gautama, the greatest known cases stand out in human memory in such a manner as to never fade away entirely until some distant future time. Listed as such they are: Siddhartha Gautama, Moses, Jesus, Krishna, Paul, Plotinus, Mohammed, Dante, St. Catherine Laboure, St. John of the Cross, Francis Bacon, St. Teresa of Avila, Jacob Behmen, William Blake, William Shakespeare, Joseph Smith, Walt Whitman, Richard Bucke, Ramakrishna, Paramhansa Yogananda, and more.

We are aware that at the present time there are many lesser cases than these noted above and that the number of similar cases in the past cannot be compared, due to the fact that they are not recorded correctly or have been lost through time. It must be remembered that the cases listed above are only perhaps a small fraction of the cases which have occurred since the time of Gautama. Also, the greater cases in past histories may not be recorded due to the fact that the works which bring about remembrance were not carried through entirely. However, enough volumes do exist for us to read in both the East and the West to contribute remembrance to those who are not mentioned here.

Looking at the life of Jesus, we find he set down no writings known to us. Had it not been for Paul, who quickly followed in his footsteps and recorded all, would we today remember him as we do? Even among those who wrote their works down, memories of them have often died and their writings have been lost. Looking quickly at Shakespeare, all of his writings might have been destroyed in a great fire which occurred, and the world would have been deprived forever of the Shakespearean drama. Either the spoken or written word of these past cases of illumination can only, by the nature of things, be appreciated by a select few of their contemporaries, and in almost every case, are exceedingly liable to be forgotten.

Cosmic or Christ Consciousness has dwelt among us for millenniums but, for the most part, has been unrecognized. The appearance of isolated cases, both in the East and the West, has contributed to all of the world's known religions. The greater majority of civilized men and women around the world bow before those teachers who have possessed it. It can be said that all inspired teachers of today derived the lessons they transmit directly or indirectly from the few cases of Divine Illumination existing now or in the past.

The impact of Christ or Cosmic Consciousness on the individual usually creates apprehension in the beginning. The person may well believe the New Sense is a symptom or form of insanity. Mohammed seemed alarmed; Paul certainly was, and others most certainly have been. The first impact upon the self-conscious individual is the transparency of all formerly known objects. The former realities fade away like mists, revealing the presence of another reality which seemingly penetrates matter from within and without. The self-conscious ego reels under the vision which begins to break down mental concepts at an alarming rate. How then shall we know that this is a New Sense being added to our other senses, and not a form of insanity and delusion?

By comparison, the former expresses a moral degree far beyond anything ever known before, whereas the latter experience is amoral and of a distinctly negative nature. The experience of Christ Consciousness is moral to the highest degree, and of a nature so positive it supports the fabric of creation. If it were other than this, all known world religions would be deep delusions, as they have sprung forth from the very individuals possessing this very unique sense. Reason and great love, the mental fabric of this sense, tell us otherwise. Even though the objective universe and the subjective universe are seemingly joined (i.e., the microcosm to the macrocosm), one possessing the New Sense sees the reality of created objects and also the reality of that which created them, existing side by side, so to speak. Objects gross and the unseen soul are one.

The profound reality of this vision eventually dispels all fear in the individual, and a total sense of freedom and immortality dawn within the consciousness. If, indeed, Cosmic or Christ Consciousness is a form of insanity, we are confronted with the fact (were it not an absurdity), that our societies, including all of our greatest religions of today, must rest on delusion. Far from granting or entertaining such an awful alternative, reason tells us, functioning through our five senses, that an ocean is still an ocean; a mountain is still in evidence, as before. All functions of the senses are normal with the exception that one sees the interior of all objects in a new light of reality.

The absolute proof of this statement can be found in the lives of the persons here cited as examples. It is certain that modern civilizations rest largely on the teachings of the Cosmic or Christ Sense. The masters were taught by it, as was the rest of the world through their books, followers, and disciples. Cosmic Consciousness is aware of its own existence in other individuals and recognizes other cases as true brothers and sisters of a divine race of beings, just as self-consciousness recognizes intellectual powers and the presence of virtue in others around it. In just this way, the New Sense sees its life in other illumined beings.

By example, three self-conscious entities would describe a horse basically the same way but each would vary in its complete description as to color, size, and shape. All cases of Christ Consciousness basically state the same facts: (1) The vision of the incredible brilliance, much akin to our own physical sun; (2) The face-to-face meeting with a divine intelligence which permeates the whole vessel of the creation; (3) The absolute knowing that one is immortal and that any further pursuit of salvation is unnecessary, as one already has it; (4) The elimination of the sense of sin, and the full understanding of the law of cause and effect which binds thoughts and images together in the creation.

It is my opinion that all cases of Christ Consciousness agree with each other in their descriptions of it, and that all world religions are, in essence, offsprings of the Cosmic Sense. As it has been said, Siddhartha Gautama and Jesus, the Christ, taught much the same doctrine. It has already been implied that a candidate for Christ Consciousness must belong to the higher planes of the world of self-consciousness. Extraordinary intellect is not a real requirement but complements the aspirant on this path, as do a good physique, good health, an exalted moral nature, love and a devotion to the divine image held by the seeker, as well as courage, and the will to never give up, coupled with self-sacrifice, service, and humility. The act of meditation on the Divine Nature (seen in all natural images) early in youth, hastens one's pursuit of it. All of this being granted, and the aspirant having reached the top of the self-conscious mental stratum, Christ Consciousness eventually dawns. First, the clear horizon before sunrise is seen from within, and then the full-blown SöN-SüN disc rises in a sky that is clear to the beholder. The inner vision eclipses the ordinary sense of sight.

As in a swoon, one instant,
Another sun, ineffable full-dazzles me,
And all the orbs I knew, and brighter, unknown orbs
One instant of the future land, Heaven's land.

— Walt Whitman

Day seemed to be added to day
As if he who is able had adorned the heavens
with another sun.

— Dante

This is called the Baptism of Fire, which Paul beheld on the road to Damascus, and in which brilliance thereof he was converted, "Oh, King Agrippa, I saw a light above the brightness of the noonday sun." (Acts 26:13.)

The by-product of Christ Consciousness is ecstasy beyond description. This is the ecstasy that exists far beyond the self-conscious mind and its perimeters of experience. It is divine in all respects, transcending states produced by the five senses. It is indeed the complete experience of the New Sense, and that which all writers and poets have tried to capture in words. Following this ecstatic state comes the illumination of the intellect, again quite impossible to describe.

Gautama preserved it in the *sutras;* Jesus in the parables; Paul in his epistles; Dante at the end of the *Purgatorio* and in the beginning of *Paradiso;* Shakespeare in his sonnets; Balzac in *Seraphita;* Whitman in *Leaves of Grass;* and Edward Carpenter in *Towards Democracy.*

In that great flash of light, that moment when divine rays penetrate the realms of the self-conscious mind, all is known — or should we say, all is comprehended. The very essence of life force which created all images is now dwelling, completely exposed, within and around the self-conscious ego. This penetrating force shatters all previous concepts held by the self-conscious mind concerning God, the visible and invisible universe, and life itself. One no longer sees planets, suns, and galaxies as inert, lifeless matter, but rather the contrary. All visible images now become alive and are pulsating with the rhythms of eternal energy combinations. God himself now becomes visible to the beholder within and surrounding all images.

In an instant, one learns more than many self-conscious existences could ever contribute. The infinite floodgate is breached, and that flood never ceases in this life or hereafter. Above and beyond this, the greatest realization is experienced. God himself is a state of ever-new joy and ever-new and expanding love which rests, as it were, on the surface of eternal peace. The vision reveals that the very keelson of the creation is itself, love. Ten, twenty, thirty, fifty years afterwards, the flood of divine wisdom comes pouring down on the newborn being, the Christ Child. For lack and want of words, how can one express this divine state, this pearl of great price? Only you, dear reader, can know this through your own experience of it.

To cover some of the states of mind experienced in illumination, let us reiterate:

1. The aspirant is suddenly confronted or engulfed by an effulgence as brilliant as the sun. At the same time there is the vision of flames rising and encompassing the physical body.

2. At the same instant, one is enveloped in the joy, love, and assurance that the Divine Being is indeed alive and embracing the innermost soul which stands revealed within. Yes, salvation has triumphed!

3. Next is the great revelation that the whole body of the creation is now alive and you are one with that life. The divine intellect descends, imparting wisdom's pearls at random. All questions are answered; all desires can now be fulfilled.

4. Springing from the assurance of salvation, one now grasps the truth of immortality, the immersion into it, the inconceivable experience of that which has no beginning and no end, no time, no space, no light, no form: the Eternal Now, the primordial deep, the unmanifested Spirit.

5. The return to the five senses and the activation of the newborn creature. This newborn entity no longer fears death, for death has vanished into the light of eternity.

6. The Christ Child does not know sin, for sin has now ceased to exist; rather, the great law, the divine wheel, stands revealed (i.e., the law of cause and effect). Paul said, "Be ye not deceived, for whatsoever a man soweth, that shall he also reap. For God is not mocked." (Galatians 6:7.) For now go, and "do unto others as you would have them do unto you." It is here that the Christ Child now understands the great laws which govern the creation. And from this day forward, the entity now attempts to walk in harmony with the law, fully understanding that what it sows, it reaps.

7. Here we now see why the Christ has said over and over again, "Ye must be reborn to attain salvation." The rebirth is the baptism of the divine light, which brings about the conception and birth of the divine embryo within the heart of the self-conscious entity. The Christ Child is the New

Sense, herein described as Cosmic or Christ Consciousness. Yea, the rebirth of Christ on earth, the Second Coming, so to speak, is now fulfilled. It is my belief that this Christ Consciousness is now penetrating the self-conscious minds of men and women on earth. To as many as would receive, he gave the power to become as Sons and Daughters of God! (See John 1:12.) " . . . Is it not written in your law, 'I said, Ye are gods?' " (John 10:34-35.) " . . . the works that I do shall he do also; . . . " (John 14:12.)

Here is the transfiguration spoken of by man: in many cases of illumination, the divine effulgence spills over into the cells of the body, bringing about phenomena such as was observed by Peter, James, and John on the Mount of Transfiguration wherein Jesus' face was seen to "shine like the sun." Dante says he was "transhumanized into a god." There seems to be a strong probability that if Dante had been observed by others at this moment, he would have displayed what is called "transfiguration." Consider also Moses, when he covered the brightness of his face from the people.

The evolution of the entity through simple-consciousness into self-consciousness seems to be a phenomenon paralleling the passage of the entity from self-consciousness to Christ Consciousness. When an organism which possesses simple-consciousness only attains self-consciousness, it becomes fully aware that it is a separate creature existing in a world apart from itself. The sense of self generates new powers and instructs the entity to further growth. Also, with the passage of the entity from self-consciousness into Christ Consciousness, the New Sense instructs from within all learning and the path which must be followed toward higher achievement. The New Sense now reveals that the higher entity is no longer isolated in a creation by itself, but in fact is now a part and parcel of the whole. Its life has become one with all life-forms, even the crusts of planets and star systems.

The entity now beholds the divine drama of life evolving through simple life-forms into complex units, and the ultimate evolution of God in man is fully conscious of what has transpired. In reality, the Divine has fully manifested in the creation to the extent of walking on the worlds it has created. The Divine Being is now dancing in form, fully conscious of all the creation; hence, the term human angel, or the Angel Men and Women, the divine Sons and Daughters of Spirit.

Looking again to known cases in the past, what does Gautama tell us of *Nirvana?* That it is the highest happiness. What does Jesus state of the *Kingdom of Heaven?* That a man will go and sell all which he has to possess it — this pearl of great price. The Mahabharata states, "The devotee whose happiness is within himself, and whose light is also within himself, becoming one with the Supreme, obtains the highest bliss," Paul tells us that he was caught up into the third heaven and heard unspeakable words. Dante states that he was transhumanized into a god. He called Christ Consciousness *Beatrice — Making Happy*; "that which I was seeing seemed to me a smile of the universe, for my inebriation was entering through the hearing and through the sight. O joy! O ineffable gladness!" Jacob Behmen states that "earthly language is entirely insufficient to describe what there is of joy, happiness and loveliness contained in the inner wonders of God."

And that forecast of the future taken from Walt Whitman's heart, that future "when through these states walk a hundred million of superb persons" (that is, persons possessed with the Cosmic Sense) "I see, dance, laugh, sing. Wandering, amazed at my own lightness and glee. O, the joy of my spirit — it is uncaged — it darts like lightning. . . . Joy, Joy in freedom, worship, love! Joy in the ecstasy of life."

The birth of Christ Consciousness in an individual does not necessarily mean that the entity is infallible or omnipresent. The greatest cases are in the unique position of becoming members of a very ancient but new race on this planet. They are, so to speak, as little children first beginning to test their new bodies and powers. They are searching into a new consciousness which may be described again as 180 degrees away from self-consciousness.

The fact that the entity has reached this higher state does not necessarily mean that mistakes will not be made in dealing with the self-conscious world. One must master the New Sense and its powers, using reason. The old self-conscious ego still exists and, sensing the powers of the Christ, tries to possess them. Herein we find, at first, the great conflicts which exist between the self-conscious mind and the Christ-Conscious mind, and the entity who is seemingly trapped between the selfish nature and the giving nature of the Christ. The conflict begins as the Christ Sense motivates the entity toward brotherhood — that it is better to give than to receive.

The Christ Sense wants to share all its possessions, which include the whole Sphere of Creation, whereas the self-conscious sense seeks to acquire all images for its own satisfaction. The entity must master this conflict, using the wisdom and power inherent in the Christ Spirit. Years may well pass by before the New Sense has established control over the entity. The seasoned growth of this New Sense takes time. And what does Paul say of Jesus in this respect?

> Who in the days of his flesh, when he had offered up prayers and supplications with strong crying and tears unto him that was able to save him from death, and

was heard in that he feared; Though he were a Son, yet learned he obedience by the things which he suffered; and being made perfect, he became the author of eternal salvation unto all them that obey him; Called of God an high priest after the Order of Melchisedec.

— Hebrews 5:7-10

I have attempted to describe this conflict, with its moments of ecstasy and its moments of utter desolation, in the following pages. This is the story of the evolution of Christ Consciousness in one individual's life.

> I hearing get who had but ears
> And sight who had but eyes before,
> I moments live who lived but years,
> And truth discern who knew but learning's lore.
>
> I hear beyond the range of sound,
> I see beyond the range of sight,
> New earths, and skies and seas around,
> And in my day the sun doth pale his light.
>
> — Henry David Thoreau, *Walden*

> Have you ever asked for that instruction
> by which we hear what cannot be heard, by
> which we perceive what cannot be perceived,
> by which we know what cannot be known?
>
> — Khandogya Upanishad
> translated by F. M. Mueller

Christ Consciousness

Excerpts from the Great Book of the Tree of Life

"You have finally come to help me; to be my eyes in this world."

CHAPTER 1

Childhood and the Blind Buddha

O, bright blue pearl of Mother Earth,
We hear, we know, we come.
Thy call of anguish penetrates the stars.
From space, the sphere of thee doth fill our vision up.
O, Mother's watery world of life, we come to help support you.

We are descending. Beneath us lie the waters and the land. This sphere, a celestial garden floating in space, is unmatched in beauty. Where the winds and waters meet the rising of the land, a jagged point appears. Tall cliffs and rocks challenge the heaving, bright blue waters. Above us the radiant body of Father Sun watches in silence as Mother Earth performs her daily revolution. My life and love flows outward and downward to mingle with visions of crashing waves and torrents of spray. Rainbow images dance in clouds of mist, slowly settling upon glistening monoliths of stone. I encompass all that I feel and observe, moving on toward the east.

This chapter exists in my consciousness as a visual memory recall with vivid images, sounds, and colors.

— The Author

Rolling hills and bright green meadows now confront me. Scrub oak, sycamore, and willow, with boughs long bent to the ever-present wind, struggle with their loads. Point Conception, long known to native peoples as the Western Gateway to the spirit world, contains an ancient necropolis. The Western Gateway, graveyard for earthbound ships, thrusts forth their stricken bows, caught in its awesome beauty — the point where winds and currents meet and ancient spirits move, fog-shrouded at times; mysterious — and deadly to mariners.

Beyond the coast and over the hills, a fertile valley nestles. Open fields present rich, dark sod to Father Sun's embrace. A river moves snake-like through the flat and furrowed fields to join the sea at Surf. Sycamore and

1

willow along its banks reach up to gather light from the abundant heavens.

This land, this fertile valley, was once the home and refuge of an ancient native people. New owners have now, themselves, built up a town, thrusting up steeples proud against the sky. We have arrived!

There, up from the river, cradled against the faithful hills, lies the

The Chumash native American Indians of southern California were all but inundated by the advance of the white man in the form of conquistadores and church missionaries. Today they are making valiant strides to reestablish themselves as a people with their original customs and way of life that is in harmony with the Creator's plan.

— The Author

village. White houses with green and red roofs spread out a vari-colored carpet. I move closer to see white picket fences covered with honeysuckle and rose. Horses pull wagons on dusty streets, wetted down each eventide. People with faces, each one different, are walking, riding, working. The heavy ring of hammer striking anvil fills the air; horses start in their traces. I stop to watch the spiral motion of coal smoke, its pungent odor heavy on the fresh sea breeze. Across the way children run and play on a vacant lot.

Impelled by silent motion I come upon a street running north and south. The house I am looking for faces the rising sun. A picket fence, an open gate, greet me. Green lawns spread out their velvet surface beneath two tall palm trees. Yes, this is indeed the dwelling place of the Blind Buddha, my father-to-be.

The blind man walked with a white cane feeling the earth beneath as he moved. He was stalwart and precise. Deprived of earthly vision,

That one (the self), though never stirring, is swifter than thought. The senses never reached it, it walked before them. Though standing still, it overtakes the others who are running. It is far and likewise near. It is inside all of this and it is outside all of this. And he who beholds all beings in the self and the self in all beings, he never turns away from it. When to a man who understands, the self has become all things, what sorrow, what trouble can there be to him who once beheld that unity?

— *Khandogya* Upanishad
translated by F. M. Mueller

his hearing was acutely extended. He heard the message of the whispering wind and the babbling brook as he extended his life outward into all beings and images around him. He found me standing there on the street in the midst of his life. My spirit-image flashed before his inner vision; I had startled him. He stopped walking to stand alert in a silent greeting. Time stood still for him. "You have finally come to help me, to be my eyes in this world."

"Yes," I replied.

He confessed, "I am so very sad and lonely here. No one understands me, no one. My wife tries, but finds me too withdrawn in the Spirit."

I replied, "Long have we been friends and again we meet. My spirit is

2

fixed upon rebirth here. Our lives must be joined together for a time."
We moved on down the street, floating in a cloud of joy. A dog ran out barking a noisy welcome — jumping up to receive his touch. He stopped to stroke a friendly spirit. I marveled at his love expression to all life-forms. Long had he been such as this. His spirit was immense, a true Buddha and a Builder. I followed him home that night. He was cheerful but concerned. His thoughts expressed some fear that I might be born as he, without the eyes that see.

Charles Paulsen became one of the few American Caucasians ever to be ordained as a minister in the Buddhist faith.

The Builders are the evolution of the true Sons and Daughters of Divine Spirit, the ancient ones referred to in Genesis as the Sons of God, who were on earth before the creation of man. These beings are Christ-Conscious entities and are responsible for the evolution of life-forms in the expanding spheres of creation.

— The Author

Charles Paulsen lived in a house on "K" Street. He was the newly-elected judge of the city and county courts in Lompoc. In his heart he longed to speak to all beings of the great Mother-Father-Spirit of all creation whom he knew and loved so much. The great, boundless immensity was his total life expression. I heard his call one day; he had overcome his fear! While at prayer he had received assurance all would be well.

"Man from the North, eyes for two, abide in my house with my wife and me; be my friend once more. Your name shall be Norman after the blood of our fathers: Nor(th)man.

He kept secret the vision of me locked in his heart, for he knew none would understand.

On the third day of February, 1929, at 12:46 p.m. at the Saint Francis Hospital in Santa Barbara, California, I experienced birth in the garb of the earth! I was conscious! Some say this is impossible. I say, for those who believe, no explanation is necessary; for those who don't, no explanation is possible. I, as a spirit, lost no consciousness in entering the planetary body of the earth elements. I can, to this day, look back through the fabric of time

My far-reaching memories are not unique. Many yogis are known to have retained their self-consciousness without interruption by the dramatic transition to and from "life" and "death." If a man be solely a body, its loss indeed ends his identity. But if prophets down the millenniums spake with truth, man is essentially a soul, incorporeal and omnipresent.

Although odd, clear memories of infancy are not extremely rare. During travels in numerous lands, I have heard very early recollections of past lives from the lips of veracious men and women.

— Paramhansa Yogananda,
Autobiography of a Yogi

3

and space into times past. Life is indeed a continuum; so is consciousness a never-ending stream.

My newly extended limbs were cumbersome. The senses of sight, hearing, smell, taste, and touch assaulted my consciousness painfully at times. At night I floated out of the body to be with friends. I didn't like the restrictions of the body "ball and chain." My spirit-friends tried to tell me of dangers lurking in the shadows. I listened and became aware of dark spirits, unfriendly and mean.

I still remember the helpless humiliations of infancy. I was then resentfully conscious of being unable to walk and to express myself freely. Prayerful surges arose within me as I realized my bodily impotence. . . . The beguiling scope of an infant's mind! Adultly considered to be limited to toys and toes.

— Paramhansa Yogananda,
Autobiography of a Yogi

My father arose early every morning. From my crib I heard him moving in the kitchen. Then came the snapping sound of fire biting into wood and the faint, warm odor of burning oak drifting into the bedroom.

"Wuff, wuff, wuff," the fire said as the damper was opened a bit. His morning coffee assailed my nostrils. I have heard how all Nordics love their coffee; it must be the cold weather there. The thought wave went out, "Give me a cup!"

"No, not yet, Norman. Coffee is not good for little boys," came back his reply.

I struggled, resenting my confinement — it was horrible.

My grandparents had come to this continent by sailing ship from Denmark. Landing in San Francisco, they bought horses and wagons and began their search for land. At that time, a group of Danish immigrants were settling in the Santa Ynez Valley. That settlement today is known as Solvang. My grandparents arrived for a visit with friends. Moving on to be closer to the sea, they settled in Lompoc Valley in the late 1800s and filed a homestead up Miguelito Canyon on the creek.

Here, under the oaks in a small frame cabin, my friend and father-to-be had gained his birth. In later years he spoke to me of the grief of his parents on finding him blind. His mother, unable to educate him in his blindness, sent him away to the California Institute for the Deaf and Blind at Berkeley. This was to be his only home for many years, until age seventeen when he set out bravely on his own. He often complained to me of the terrible loneliness and the lack of love he had experienced while at school, and the cruelty of the teachers of that time. He had not really known his brother, Lawrence, and his sister, Elna, nor did he know his father and mother as a son should. Only once a year, for a few days, had he been allowed to come to Lompoc.

He had studied the piano and organ, and through his music he expressed the visions of his soul. Wonderful healing was generated by this instrument for all who listened to his music. Genius had blossomed forth from despair during his confinement at the Berkeley School. It was at a concert he was giving in Pasadena, California, that he met my mother. His sensitive fingers and spirit gave him the ability to compose as he played. Compose he did, and play he must, for only there did he find relief from the frustrating blindness.

> Knowledge of pure truth requires, for its proper explanation, that God should hold the hand and wield the pen of the writer.
> — St. John of the Cross

The old frame house shook with the vibrations of crashing notes as his masterful fingers raced across the keyboard, depicting scenes of wind and sea. This music I heard from our beginning together. He conversed with the great Mother-Father-Spirit as he played.

"Play me the sounds of the universe," I said one evening.

He turned his head to listen; then he began to play. Gentle waters began to flow forth, threading their way through forested creeks. Towering peaks stretched upward to the light through shimmering curtains of clouds. Space, the infinite sea, called from the beckoning stars. I was transfixed. "The Shadow Dance," his own composition, was my favorite musical ballet of images. The room filled with sounds as the keys responded to his sensitive thoughts and fingers. Pure Spirit was expressing itself through sound!

The misunderstood and lonely man now had a son. One of my favorite characters, "Coyote Boy," assumed delightful proportions in bedtime stories created by him. He began, at an early age, my instructions in the form of mental images. Morality and virtue were the themes ringing through stories of "Captain Norman and his Friends." The great starship, *Golden Dawn*, journeying through space forever, administered to stricken worlds. "Captain Norman and his Friends" helped all suffering beings wherever Spirit took them, singing, and playing the space organ as they went.

The Blind Buddha was able to transmit profound instructions to my mind from the very beginning, and his bedtime stories prophetically echoed future events to take place in my life. "Captain Norman and his Friends" would become a living reality, and the good ship, *Golden Dawn*, would sail the seas of earth in the form of a 158-foot schooner. Point Conception would become a familiar navigational landmark.

His storied images told of many people living a natural and spiritual life in the mountains and valleys, in harmony with Mother's and Father's nature.

5

I was indeed blessed to have found such a spirit for my earthly father. Unable to play games with me outside, he offered thrilling journeys and adventures within, exploring the unlimited realms of imagination. His contributions and projections at such an early age created a fortress of truth around me. This fortress would sustain me through the horrendous trials and tribulations of my later life on Planet Earth.

Give Me Time

> Give me time to see the beauty of the
>   trees that line my way.
> Give me time to hear the music of the
>   breeze that through them plays.
> Give me time to see the beauty of the
>   fields that line my way.
> Give me time to hear the music of the
>   bird's song sweet and gay.
> Give me time to understand the truth of
>   life in all that be.
> Give me time to pause a moment as I travel
>   on my way,
> Just to listen to the laughter of the
>   children at their play.
> Give me time to listen to the troubles
>   of a friend.
> Give me time to help carry his burdens
>   for him to the end.
> Give me time to see the good in every
>   traveler on the road,
> Give me time to not misjudge them, minding
>   not their creed or code.
> Give me time to see the beauty of the
>   light of God divine.
> Living in all things around me, living in
>   your soul and mine.
> Give me time to see the light that lives
>   deep in the heart of you.
> Give me time each day to pray that light,
>   to guard and guide you through.
> Give me time to adore the whole of the
>   universe, and when I must answer the call to come
> Give me time to pray!

Amen.

— Charles Paulsen, "The Traveler"

My father

My mother

My grandmother (Nana)

I placed both my hands on his knees as he was rocking, forcing him to stop
and listen. "Dad, who was I when I was here before?"

CHAPTER 2

Now We Are Three

"Norman!" came the call. "Want to go for a walk with your dad?"
Father Sun was gently clearing paths through the early morning mist as he climbed higher in the east.

"Let's go to China Creek."

The creek lay along the foothills to the west of town and was a fairyland of willows and ferns; it was one of my favorite places. Dad and I would sit for hours and just listen. There was a large population of feathered friends who lived there; loud conversations were not uncommon. The murmur of the friendly creek whispered a poem as it moved from pool to pool. "Son, listen to the wind coming in from the ocean at Surf. It's rough today; I can hear the thunder of breakers."

I stopped to listen to the distant, booming sound. I was feeling the warmth of Father Sun creeping into me, chasing away the morning chill. Here, before me, I beheld the great Spirit of Mother's and Father's nature, as if from within, projecting all objects and creatures, wondrous — incredible. A frog croaked his approval just as a raven shattered the stillness with his awkward reply.

Through Spirit, and the gentle guidance of my father's thoughts and words, I was able to converse at an early age, still remembering events of other existences. Awakened spirit-beings, approaching the earth and the vision of new birth, can look back through the corridors of times past, for their Book of Life lies open to them. For some spirits a preview of their

All I can say is that there seems to be a vision possible to man, as from some more universal standpoint, free from the obscurity and localism which specially connect themselves with the passing clouds of desire, fear, and all ordinary thought and emotion; in that sense another and separate faculty. . . . How can I express it? . . . for the sense is a sense that one is those objects and things and persons that one perceives (and the whole universe) — a sense in which sight and touch and hearing are all fused in identity. Nor can the matter be understood without realizing that the whole faculty is deeply and intimately rooted in the ultramoral and emotional

11

future is given, but unless children are encouraged by knowing parents, they may lose contact with their Book of Life. In studying my Book of Life I became aware of the authors: Spirit, the Father; Spirit, the Mother; and all their offspring, the Spirit Children.

My father was a child of the Spirit born remembering his past. Though it was hard at times, he accepted his blindness as a condition that he might be of help to others. The lack of complete understanding on the part of his parents and the harsh environment of his school made it doubly difficult, so as a child he was driven further within. Without the sense of sight he was forced to dwell, for the most part, in the world of the Spirit. My father never lost contact with his Book of Life, and for this reason, he was able to recognize me when I came to him. He treasured me as his only true friend from the beginning. All that he had learned and felt that was of value he transferred to me by the medium of Spirit. He cast his cloak upon me.

One night I was perplexed. All day long the images of a former lifetime had flashed before my consciousness. I found Dad in the front room listening to the news on the radio. I placed both my hands on his knees as he was rocking, forcing him to stop and listen.

"Dad, who was I when I was here before?"

He stopped rocking and picked me up, shaking me a little. "Norman, what are you saying? How do you know you were here before?"

"Dad, I know I was here but I can't remember what my name was anymore."

nature, and beyond the thought-region of the brain.

— Edward Carpenter, *Towards Democracy*

People often object, "If everyone reincarnates, why is it that no one remembers having lived before?" The simple answer is that many do remember! In the West, of course, children claiming such memories soon learn, from the scoldings of their elders, to keep their thoughts to themselves. But even so, a number of well-documented cases, have received considerable publicity.

— Swami Kriyananda, *The Path*

I find my earliest memories covering the anachronistic features of a previous incarnation. Clear recollections came to me of a distant life in which I had been a yogi (practitioner of yoga, ancient science of meditation on God), amid the Himalayan snows. These glimpses of the past, by some dimensionless link, also afforded me a glimpse of the future.

— Paramhansa Yogananda, *Autobiography of a Yogi*

I've known from the time I was a child that I've never truly belonged here. I told my parents this repeatedly. They, of course, became quite upset. I begged to know who my real father and mother were. I wanted to return to my home, which I felt was in the sky. I still hope to do so. I've never felt I was from here.

— Francie Steiger, quoted by Brad Steiger, in *Gods of Aquarius*

He put me down and said, "Go to bed; someday you will remember well." (Refer to Chapter 10: My father's letter to me upon the death of my mother.)

My mother planned a birthday party for me at the age of four. Mothers with their children began to arrive. I had never seen so many people, especially children of my own age. Ice cream and cake were everywhere and on everything! Toward the end of the party one of the mothers picked me up and said out loud, "Well, Norman, how do you like all your new friends here?"

I looked around and replied, "Good, but you all have a face like a people."

Disturbed by my strange answer, she set me down abruptly. My mother explained I was given to strange replies and words at times; Dad found this very amusing.

The kitchen sink was my bathtub and I enjoyed it immensely, because from here I could see part of the backyard. My mother was involved in political work which demanded her presence away from home, and she was away much of the time.

My grandmother, Nana, cared for me in her absence. She loved to garden; the front and backyards on "K" Street bloomed with all kinds of flowers. Vines covered the house; shrubs and trees grew everywhere. The backyard was indeed a beautiful, mystical place to me. Secret paths and trellised gates, flower beds and hollyhocks, fish ponds and fruit trees — somehow everything seemed to naturally fit in. Nana loved to work. She had a green thumb, and the result was a magic garden. I spent many hours a day trying to help her weed and trim. The rich soil of the Lompoc Valley is, to this day, famous across the country for its fields of flowers grown primarily for seed. People come from all over the world to see the flower fields in bloom and to attend the flower festivals.

Musing in the sun one day in the backyard, I became transfixed. I was looking at the moon in transit during the day while Nana was working nearby. I felt my spirit-energy release me outward into space. Expanding in every direction, I quickly gained gigantic proportions. The earth was turning beneath me and I felt the vast deep of space. I could be as big as I liked or as small as I liked. I sought to touch the moon. At age four, in my extended awareness, I knew the

At times, the divine light strikes the soul with such force that the darkness is unfelt and the light unheeded; the soul seems unconscious of all it knows, and is therefore lost, as it were, in forgetfulness, knowing not where it is nor what has happened to it, unaware of the lapse of time. It may and does occur that many hours pass while it is in this state of forgetfulness; all seems but a moment when it again returns to itself.

— St. John of the Cross,
Ascent of Mount Carmel

earth was spherical like the moon. I remembered my vision of earth and mentally understood what my spirit-consciousness knew — there was an end out there beyond the stars. The great and all-encompassing Sphere of Creation was still expanding in all directions.

I knew that my spirit-form was joined to the Great Living Spirit, my Divine Father and Mother. I was soaring again, joyfully, like a bird released from a cage. I could hear the great humming, pulsating sound that seemed to fill all the heavens, the sound of tremendous energies in motion.

Then came an unexpected shock! I was rushing backward towards the tiny backyard and my physical form. My hands and face were stinging with pain from Nana's frantic slaps. She was shaking me, trying to bring me back. I realized her fright.

"Norman, don't you ever stare at the moon or anything again, at any time! Do you understand?"

So I am the space within, the soul of which the space without is but the similitude and mental image thereof.

— Edward Carpenter, *Towards Democracy*

Saints and seers of all time have expressed having heard the cosmic sounds of Hun (the masculine) or Om (the feminine) when in the expanded state of God consciousness, otherwise known as the spiritual trance, when one loses all consciousness of one's immediate surroundings and expands to proportions outside the realm of everyday experience. It is here that the nature of God is made known, and the subsequent ecstasy is beyond imagining. Very often spirits who have established themselves in God's reality in a former existence will re-experience their previous attainment upon reincarnating and taking on the youthful form.

— The Author

I was present when Joseph Smith received revelations. I particularly remember the one on the United Order. There was no great noise or physical manifestation. Joseph was as calm as the morning sun. But I noticed a change in his countenance that I had never noticed before, when a revelation was given to him. His face was exceedingly white and seemed to shine.

— Orson Pratt on Joseph Smith

I was in her arms heading for Dr. Hygis' office. He found me in good repair and sent Nana home with the assurance that there was nothing to worry about. "Children growing up experience strange things."

"Hurry up, Norman!" called my mother. "We're going to the big city today."

This would be my first trip to Santa Barbara. My mother, Eileen, had arrived home from Sacramento with a used 1930 model Chevrolet sedan, dark red in color. The road from Lompoc to Gaviota was hardly more than a wagon trail. Gravel and oil had been spread here and there to cover the deep ruts and chuckholes. Steep grades, hairpin turns, and creek crossings were frequent. Cattle grazed everywhere and often blocked the way.

A trip to Santa Barbara was a big occasion and usually took half a day, with stops at Gaviota or Tajiguas for refreshments. I was looking out of the window at mountains covered with oak trees. Men on horseback were herding cattle on grass-covered slopes. Green fields and meadows were everywhere. Silently, I desired to ride a horse. Mother's nature surrounded us. Suddenly before me lay a vast expanse of sparkling blue water. The coast became visible upon reaching Gaviota.

"Nana, Mimi, look! Look at the big lau lau!" I was so excited the words came tumbling out.

"Norman, you are looking at the ocean," said my mother.

Try as they would to correct me, for years I insisted that the ocean was the big lau lau.

> According to the legends handed down to us today, the word for water in the ancient tongue of the Motherland (Lemuria) was lau, pronounced "law."
>
> — Colonel James Churchward, *The Lost Continent of Mu*

My grandmother began to keep a record of the strange words and observations I had for things and people. I found my Book of Life full of ancient languages and descriptions.

"Nana, there, look! A bad baba." (Baba is an East Indian word for father.)

I was pointing to a bearded, disheveled hobo holding a sacked bottle on a side street. There are good babas as well as bad babas, I realized. A good baba seemed to haunt my memory. I found myself looking for him constantly. He had long hair and big, strange, lustrous eyes; eyes that were familiar.

"Nana will you take me to the hootenanny?"

"What are you talking about, Norman? What's a hootenanny?"

"It's a place where people go to sing together and clap their hands. Sometimes they play music and dance."

> Hootenanny is the word given to describe a gathering of African folk in the old plantation days of the American South. These festivals were characterized by much joyful singing and dancing, yet often tinged by a certain sadness reflecting their yearning for the freedom of former tribal ways.
>
> — The Author

"Eileen, do you know what he's talking about?"

"No!" came the reply.

"Well, I don't either."

In my silent memory I could see and hear people singing and clapping their hands. Some were dancing by the light of torches and lanterns in the great outdoors.

> Who at this age remembers so clearly events of the past? Speak up I say. What strange flame illuminates me; unseen by others who are still?
>
> — The Author

15

"Let's go to a hootenanny" was a familiar expression to me. Neither my father, mother or grandmother knew what I was talking about. Such a thing did not exist! I was disappointed, for I knew somewhere a hootenanny was happening.

At age seven months, with my father. Old friends have met again.

Gin Chow said that his system of prophecy was based upon a "key" to the weather cycles left to the Chinese people many centuries ago by a sage.

CHAPTER 3

Gin Chow: I Meet a Real Prophet

The winter of 1930-31 had brought little moisture to southern California. By the end of summer the country was in the grip of a bad drought. "If we don't get early rain, we are really in for trouble." These words echoed the thoughts of everyone. The hills and valleys, once covered with lush grasses, were stripped clean by the cattle. There was nothing left for the livestock to eat, and they began to die. The end of the summer had stretched on past Christmas, and still no rain. The new year was about to begin. Normally the rainy season would begin around November first and last until the end of April. People had little to be happy about this Christmas and New Year, especially the farmers and cattlemen. Along with the lack of rain came the lowering of the water table; wells and springs were going dry. Water had to be hauled to livestock in some areas.

It was a windy, dry afternoon in December. A large fog bank was visible at Surf, ten miles away. "Dad, where are we going today?"

"There's an old friend of mine who wants to meet you; his name is Gin Chow." The name seemed familiar to me. I must have heard it mentioned before.

Gin Chow lived down by the river at the east end of the valley. He had a small vegetable farm, a couple of cows, and some chickens. It was a good three miles from the house on "K" Street. As we drew near the farm, Dad was giving directions. "Norman, do you see a little shack down by the river near the willows?"

"Yes, I see it, Dad."

The wind picked up a cloud of dust and scattered it across a dry field. As we approached, a beautiful patch of green row crops came into view; what a welcome sight! A cool, refreshing breeze seemed to lift off the green carpet and head in our direction. I heard the "clank, twang" of an old windmill laboring to keep a big wooden tank full of water.

19

All seemed remarkably peaceful, as if time were standing still. The stillness pervaded the air; it was like an unseen presence watching our approach.

"Norman, take Dad to the front door. Master Gin is awaiting our arrival inside. Gin Chow, are you home? It's Charlie and the boy!"

I heard movement within the shack; a screen door opened and out came a little man. I looked first at his eyes. They were quick, dark, and penetrating; a thin moustache and a small goatee decorated his happy, round face.

"Charlie! Charlie! Happy to see! Happy to see! Come in, please, come in. Ah! This your boy? Velly good, velly nice. Welcome to Gin's house. You drink little tea; maybe hungry?"

Dad said, "Gin Chow, it's good to be with you again. I wanted you to meet the boy. As for me, a cup of tea will be fine."

Inside, a neat, two-room dwelling presented itself. Gin Chow started a fire in an old wood cook stove. "Hot water for tea pretty quick, Charlie. How about milk for the boy?"

Dad and I were offered chairs at an old wooden table. Soon Master Gin produced two steaming cups of tea and a glass of fresh milk for me. Dad and Gin Chow began to discuss the weather and world events. Gin Chow's ability to predict the weather, almost to the hour, and world-shaking events to the day had gained him the reputation of being a fantastic prophet.

Fifty Years from Now, 1931 to 1981

What it all be like fifty years from now? I tell you what prophets decide long time ago.

In first place, destiny of China an' United States — they tied up together. China, she need United States to help her, not to send armies over to fight her enemies but to send men to inquire into affairs an' settle things up. China will need a head man to help her start, but future depends on help a this country.

China is old man. Amelica is infant but is wise baby. China not been wise. She pay too much 'tention to ancestors. But China is young inside Earth. . . . She is not one-third opened yet. The prophets, they say that China be, what you say, linked up with good people to save her. These Amelicans will go there . . . be friendly to her . . . make everything new. She will have new ships, new language, new machines, new schools. . . .

New railroads then be built an' ships an' airplanes carry exchange of China's things to Amelica. . . .

Amelica, she benefit just as much from helping China as China herself. Amelica need to have her factories busy. China put um busy. China could take everything Amelica make for hundred years to make her people live better. China is oldest country but she newest country too. China has not got modern as other countries. Young Amelicans find good opportunity for future in China. Her people an' Chinese should be brothers in making China new country . . .

China want things; India want things; Africa want things; South Amelica want things . . . all old countries want things to make living better. But now have no money to buy but they have rich countries, if Amelicans only would inquire into troubles and help to make so they could pay . . . then everybody be happy.

Amelicans are young, enterprising people, but they can learn lot 'bout friendship for other people. War is old, old thing in world and vely bad for everybody. Everybody spend too much on guns and gunpowder. Bad to kill everybody 'cause great trouble a whole world now come from war. War is waste. . . . and gotta pay sometime if you waste. Prophets say long time 'go that when countries get much courage they all come 'gether an' call all war off. It take lotta . . . what you say . . . guts to throw all guns an' gunpowder 'way. But people, they do it.

The church in Amelica an' China . . . she not stop. People will turn to church. Men will live for each other, an' war will stop. . . . Governments will own lots now swiped by rich men. There will be no bad rich men for they will take men who work for them into their business.

Farmers will not grow too much. What is raised will be sold for good price. Nothing will be wasted an' nobody will go hungry.

Hospitals will go out a business 'cause everybody be well. Sick people, they will be gone. When man gets sick, neighbors will shame him. Nobody will feel sorry for sick man as much as now 'cause it will be his own fault. . . .

Yes, there will be many airplanes in 1982 but everybody not ride them. There will always be people who 'fraid to die.

— Excerpts from *Gin Chow's First Annual Almanac,* 1932

One of the greatest tests of his career would shortly come to pass.

"Master Gin, when are we going to get some rain to end this drought?"

"Charlie, we go to Santa Maria plenty soon; talk to lotsa people. Know then when rain come." He would say no more.

I felt an inner scrutiny begin. Like tiny shock waves, it moved through me. Gin Chow was looking me over.

"Charlie, this boy's spirit velly old; been around long time. Know much, help lotsa people." He placed his right hand on my head. "Charlie, I give him blessing of ancient ancestors. Okay?"

"Whatever you can do for him, Master Gin, is appreciated. As I have said before, I feel he has a big work ahead of him."

Gin Chow was indeed a great spirit and friend. As a Chinaman of that time he suffered much persecution. There were few Chinese in the area in those days. His Buddhist origins conflicted with the staunch Christian ethics of the area, rendering him an outsider. He was under great suspicion because of his prophecies. Few people really wanted to admit that a Chinaman had such powers.

Gin would say, "Jesus, he great master many follow, but velly quick forget what he say. He love all men, not just few."

Gin Chow was born March 19, 1857, at Singcheng, near Canton, China. He was one of four children from a middle-class family. As a growing boy he was sparked with the desire to travel. At an early age he decided to go to the new world of America to seek his fortune. By working hard and saving his money he was able to buy a ticket to California. It was the year 1873. Gin Chow was sixteen years old when he gingerly climbed aboard a square-rigged sailing ship bound for San Francisco with a cargo of Chinese novelties and goods.

Arriving in San Francisco, he made his way south to Santa Barbara. There he landed his first job, washing dishes in a downtown restaurant. He later became a houseboy working for twenty-five dollars a month, and by saving every penny possible, was able to buy a small vegetable farm outside Santa Barbara. Gin Chow's grandfather was a well-known Chinese prophet and merchant who was put in jail for correctly predicting problems in the emperor's future. He died in jail despite all efforts to save him.

His grandfather had also correctly predicted Gin Chow's ability as a future prophet, and that his work would be in a foreign land. For many years Gin Chow supported his family, which remained in China, with money he sent home monthly. On his farm in Goleta he began his career as a prophet by correctly predicting weather conditions. His weather predictions could be found hanging on the bulletin board in the Santa Barbara Post Office. Usually the national weather forecast was wrong and Gin Chow was right! Gin Chow's weather predictions were so accurate, the *Santa Barbara News-Press* began running a weekly commentary. "Clouds Hang Out Like Chinaman's Laundry," February 6. "Boys Fly Kites Early," April 13. "Wind Blow, Make Ship Go," May 10. "Sun Meet Moon Face to Face, Make Double Hot," July 17.

Gin Chow ran into trouble in 1910 with the Southern Pacific Railroad. The company wanted to run its tracks across his farm after condemning his land and paying him a small amount. He defied them in court and won a high price for his property. In 1911, Gin Chow bought a new farm at the east end of the Lompoc Valley, down by the river. It was only a few weeks later that California legislators passed a bill making it illegal for a yellow man to buy land in California. Gin Chow had secured his land just in time.

One day, the 23rd of December, 1920, Gin Chow laid down a fateful prophecy. The little Chinese farmer from Lompoc Valley made his way to Santa Barbara. Upon entering the post office he went up to the bulletin board, as he had done for some twenty-three years, and pinned up a rumpled piece of paper which said: "From 1924 to 1983, world in great trouble. Earthquake come in September 1923 in Japan, and in Santa Barbara on June 29, 1925."

A little over nine months later, on September 1, 1923, a gigantic earthquake struck Japan, leaving 143,000 dead. Giant tidal waves raced across the Pacific, creating unusual ocean currents. To the astonishment of believers and nonbelievers who had read Gin Chow's predictions nine months before came, the fearful concern of a possible future disaster in Santa Barbara.

A few days later the American Navy suffered the greatest peacetime disaster in Naval history. Fourteen destroyers steaming south at twenty knots had miscalculated their position off Point Conception. Making a turn to port to enter what they thought was the Santa Barbara Channel, the destroyer squadron steamed at "full speed ahead" through fog into the cragged rocks off Devil's Jaw, just north of Point Conception. The incredible accident added seven of the Navy's finest destroyers to the growing list of vessels secured forever in the graveyard of ships. The miscalculation of their position off Point Conception may well have been partially due to strange currents generated by the Japanese earthquake.

On June 29, 1925, exactly the date of Gin Chow's prediction, a devastating earthquake struck Santa Barbara. When the dust cleared, thirteen dead were counted; the property damage was estimated at fifteen to twenty million dollars.

Who was this fantastic individual who had made fools of the United States Weather Bureau for the last twenty-five years and now predicted earthquakes years in advance, to the very day? News commentators from other areas of the country, receiving the facts of Gin Chow's predictions, were now asking, "How can he do this?"

Gin Chow was silent about his abilities; he would say nothing to anyone. My father later confided to me that Gin Chow had been his spiritual guide from 1912, when he was only a boy of eighteen, to the time of Master Gin's passing in June of 1933.

Both my father and Gin Chow were age seventy-six at their deaths. The spirit of Gin Chow hovered over my father in the last years of his life and we had many long conversations about him.

The drought continued into January of 1932 when my father came home one evening excited. "Tomorrow I'm going to a Rotary Club luncheon in Santa Maria with Gin Chow. He is going to give a talk."

Gin Chow's talk was short the next day. He related that he was there because he had been asked to come. Most people in the area knew Gin Chow's weather predictions and prophecies had always been accurate, even the skeptics. Because of the prolonged lack of rain, some people had tried to pressure Gin Chow into a prediction.

"Tell us when this drought will end!" Angry voices were raised against him. "You crazy old Chinaman, if you know, tell us!" One such person made a statement saying, "Gin Chow has said rain will come very soon." Now he was being asked if rain would come today. Tomorrow?

"You call me clazy Chinaman because I say rain come soon. You cuss me. I say all right, tonight you catch big rain."

It was then about two o'clock on a very clear, hot afternoon. Gin Chow arrived home early that evening. Looking eastward, he saw Mother's nature gathering together her forces. Dark clouds came rolling in from the southeast carrying the first drops of rain.

"Charlie, I do dance of joy for her in my garden; I get all wet. Velly happy see her bring blessing. She save Gin Chow's skin! They really skin Gin Chow alive if no rain come!"

> At the last meeting of the Santa Maria Rotary Club, Gin Chow made an address about rain as follows:
> "They call me clazy Chinaman. Everybody give me the dickens. Say bad words to me, but I say, 'Al light; you wait. Catch um big rain.' Then I go home but no cook supper 'cause mad at self. I lay on bed then get up for look outside. It all black and I feel better. I say rain come 5 o'clock. Then I go to cook supper. Pretty soon come sound on roof. Little noise make big sound on tin roof. Then I go outside and rain fell on my face."
> — "The Lancer," *Los Angeles Times*, January 28, 1932

The drought was broken by a heavy rain that night and into the next day. Gin Chow had been put to the test in public, and to the amazement of everyone, he had again produced. Dad told this story for years. "Boy, did he show them! By heaven, they all must believe in him now!"

Five months later the old sage was badly hurt. During the night Gin had heard a lot of noise down at his cow barn. A neighbor's bull had broken down the fence and was after his cows. Gin had tried to chase the bull home. The bull was later found by its owner with blood stains on one horn and Gin Chow's lantern on the other. Gin had succeeded in hanging it there after being badly gored. This lantern was his only call for help; he was hurt too badly to get home. The neighbors, in searching, found him lying in an irrigation ditch in the middle of his garden. Rushed to a hospital in Santa Barbara, he was pronounced in critical condition by the doctors and told he might not live.

Gin Chow rebuked the doctors saying, "This not my time. My time come one year later."

To the astonishment of the doctors and nurses, Gin Chow recovered and returned home to Lompoc.

Dad and I paid him many a visit in the early months of 1933. I heard final goodbyes between them one day.

"Charlie, pretty soon go to Santa Barbara last time. Gin Chow, he go on now. We meet again, yes! You know! They call me clazy Chinaman. They find out not so clazy after all. Goodbye, Charlie."

On June 19, 1933, exactly one year after his accident, Gin Chow was struck down by a car as he was crossing State Street in Santa Barbara. By the time an ambulance arrived, Master Gin was on his way out of this existence. Gin Chow's last and final prophecy, concerning his life, had indeed come true to the very day.

Celestial Morsels

Want to make man like you much? All right.
Let him talk to you 'bout him an' you listen.
He like you all right.

Don't give up on your own field an' weed
neighbor's pasture.

It velly easy tell wise man things but you
waste time on fool.

Wise man richest of all. More than Rockerfeller.

Loud bark doesn't make good dog. Loud talk
doesn't make good man.

Dogs think dog is God.

Don't look in last year's nests for this year's birds.

Man should believe in God. If Christ, Confucius, Buddha,
all right. But should take some good God.

Depression come from man getting too rich. Drink, eat too much. Think too
little. When rich, always think how poor man lives.

I been to church years an' I never heard preacher tell
about Earth. We live on Earth, alla time talk about Heaven.

Bye and bye bigger man than I come in West. He talk
about Jesus. Everybody in China call every other nation "West."

— Gin Chow

25

"It's yours, Norman, take it. It belongs to you, Christ's New Testament." At the time of this visual experience I did not know that this personage was the image of Melchisedec until years later.

CHAPTER 4

School and the Strange Encounter

My excitement was running high. I was home from my first day at school. "Dad, I want to learn how to read like the teacher does. She has all kinds of stories in books. Here is a copy of the book she read from today."

The first twelve pages were open to inspection but the rest of the book had a big rubber band around it. Dad took the book in his hands.

"What's the rubber band for, Son?"

"I am not to look beyond the pages we read today. Tomorrow the teacher will read some more to us. Listen, Dad! I can almost read some now!"

"Come eat your dinner first, Son."

After dinner I sat in the living room where my audience consisted of Dad, Mom, and Nana. As I turned the first page, I instantly remembered sitting with all the other children. I could see the teacher again as she read from the book, and I started repeating the words that she had spoken. Recorded in the energy of my conscious awareness was everything I had heard and seen. Reaching the end of the first page I turned it and went on with the story, telling it word for word and page for page. My mother and grandmother jumped up from their chairs.

"Norman, how did you do that? You can't read yet!"

The ability to remember is directly related to the ability to concentrate, concentration being the complete focusing of all our energies upon any given thing. Through an exertion of will through the medium of discipline, one can attain the ability to concentrate all of one's energies on the object of his choice. The sense impressions received through this process are indelibly imprinted in our mental body, to be brought to the viewer's subjective attention at will.

When the question is asked, "Who am I?" and will is applied to concentration, the supersensory images of our Creator must be forthcoming. This is a spiritual law, and Christ confirmed it, saying, "And ye shall know the truth, and the truth shall make you free." (John 8:32) and "Ask and it shall be given you, seek and ye shall find, knock, and it shall be opened unto you." (Matthew 7:7.)

— The Author

27

Mother took the book and looked at it. Everything seemed normal but me. "Charles, that's impossible! He has to be doing it from memory! Read it again, Norman."

This time my mother sat next to me holding the book in her lap. Again I repeated from the actual experience of seeing and hearing, a word for word commentary.

"Charles, I can't believe this, he hasn't missed one word, even telling me when to turn the pages."

Dad smiled, not registering any surprise.

My mother came back with a book of poems. "Norman, I am going to read you something. Then you can read it back to me."

I listened to the words and watched my mother as she read. She completed reading two poems and handed me the book. "Now you can read it back, Son."

I reflected on the mental images I had seen and began to repeat her words, turning the page to read the last poem.

"Charles, it's true! He seems to have a photographic mind extended to the sense of hearing, also! I'm going to take him to Santa Barbara to have him examined."

After hours of testing by competent psychiatrists, I was found to be in possession of these unique faculties. Wherever my attention was directed it was found that I had near perfect recall of everything heard and seen. Mother had offers to appear with me at demonstrations, some of a scientific nature. Dad would have none of it.

"He is going to live a normal, natural life as long as I have anything to say about it."

Nana and I were on our way to the library. I ran up the street to catch her. "Now remember, Norman, when we go in, no talking. People will be reading and you'll have to be quiet."

I was going to check out my first book today. The library seemed gigantic. A long flight of steps led up to the entrance. Fleeting images passed through my consciousness of similar buildings elsewhere in another time. Upon entering, a hushed silence predominated. I felt an inner stimulation saying, "You have experienced a very similar or exact occasion elsewhere." My senses were straining in anticipation of something inspired by my intuition.

A little old lady walked up, speaking in a well-trained whisper. "Can I help you?"

"Yes. We want the children's section. I am looking for a book for the boy."

She beckoned us to follow, pointing to a corner at the east end. I had never seen so many books; it was overwhelming! Nana found the children's section and pulled out a handful of books for me to look at. I quickly picked out one and sat down to look it over. Nana moved on to find something for herself.

My extended awareness was feeling something. At the same time, a pulling sensation was being exerted on me. I began to follow the hallway leading behind some tall bookshelves. At the end was a door to the left and as I approached, the door opened. Within the room, which was lighted by a single window, a robed, hooded figure sat at a table. The figure rose silently and turned. I was startled and apprehensive. The face of a very old man looked at me in silence from beneath the hood which covered his entire head. The robe was of a fine white substance, like wool; a single belt of the same material fastened at his waist. The figure stepped back, picking up a small, leatherbound book which lay before him.

Without speaking, I heard him say, *"Come in, Norman."* I hesitated, then he took a step toward me, holding out the book. *"It's yours, Norman, take it. It belongs to you, Christ's New Testament."*

Suddenly I heard a loud whispering and footsteps in the library. I reflected in thought, "I must go; Nana and the library lady are looking for me." I turned and ran from the room to explain.

Nana grabbed me by the arm. "Where have you been?"

"I was in that room back there talking to a very old man in a robe with a hood over his head."

Nana and the librarian looked at each other. The librarian whispered, "There's no one back there; that's a workroom."

"Oh, yes there is," I said. "Come look; he has a book for me."

Nana and the librarian quickly traversed the hall and entered the room with me at their heels. The robed figure was gone. Not a sign of him or the book!

"Norman, there is no one in this room!" stated Nana.

"I am the librarian and the only one working here today. No one is allowed in that room but employees."

I saw it was useless to say more, Nana was mad! She grabbed me by the arm and off we went — home, without any books.

"Norman, don't you ever wander off like that again. I'm going to tell your father."

I felt confident inside, knowing Dad would understand. I hoped to see the ancient figure again, and intuitively I knew I would. The profound wisdom of old illumined men, how I love them. Let them not pass away unheard.

> However, it was nevertheless a fact that I had beheld a vision. I have thought since, that I felt much like Paul, when he made his defense before King Agrippa, and related the account of the vision he had when he saw a light, and heard a voice; but still there were but few who believed him, . . . and he was ridiculed and reviled. But all this did not destroy the reality of his vision. He had seen a vision, he knew he had, and all the persecution under heaven could not make it otherwise; and though they should persecute him unto death, yet he knew, and would know to his latest breath, that he had both seen a light and heard a voice speaking unto him, and all the world could not make him think or believe otherwise.
>
> So it was with me. . . .
>
> — Joseph Smith 2:24-25, Pearl of Great Price

I was soon to be seven years old. Christmas was coming. The tree was decorated with colored lights, and packages were piled high on the floor beneath it. Inwardly I sensed the true meaning of "Christ Mass Trees." Here was man's inner Christ Tree of Life (the central nervous system) depicted outside on the earth; the colored lights symbolized different worlds and dimensions within the expanding Sphere of Creation, The Great Central SöN-SüN, known as the Christ, crowning the Tree of Life within. The gifts were the fruits of a life well lived, offered to him in service and humility by those who loved him.

The author refers to The Great Central SöN-SüN (pronounced as one syllable, sun) as the First Creation of Light. SöN is used to depict the Son of God, Divine Intelligence, filling the great expanding Sphere of Creation. SüN is used again to depict the light created, the brilliance, the warmth, the life-producing energies. "And the Lord said, 'Let there be light: and there was light.' " (Genesis 1:3.) And from this ignition the expanding Sphere of Creation yet moved outward from its center.

"Wake up Norman! Santa Claus is here and is in the front room waiting to see you."

"Santa Claus is in the front room to see me?"

My robe was on the chair. I grabbed it on the run. The lights from the tree cast an eerie glow around the front room. Santa Claus stood near the tree in his red and white suit. Could he be real? I questioned the presence inwardly. Immediately I sensed a thought-form straining not to be discovered, one which said, "I can't fool the boy in this crazy outfit."

"Come and see Santa Claus, Norman; he has something for you."

I was going to play the game through, for I did not want to hurt their feelings, but the words blurted out, "That's not Santa Claus! That's Dad! I know it!"

Mother took Santa Claus by the arm saying, "Saint Nick, thank you for stopping at our house and leaving these wonderful gifts," as she escorted him out the door.

I marveled in later years that Mom would never admit to me that Saint Nicholas was my father.

30

The Lompoc Theatre was across the street from the library. For years Dad had played interpretive music for the silent movies. The old theatre organ or piano could be heard clearly out on the street during an afternoon matinee. The image of Tom Mix, a great western movie hero, went thundering across the screen on his horse in hot pursuit of a bandit. This Saturday, *Tarzan of the Apes* was showing at a children's matinee. Dad would be playing the music.

"Norman, you can walk uptown to the theatre, tell the girl at the door who you are, and she will show you where I am."

Hurrying up the street, I saw the large posters in the windows and store fronts announcing today's performance. Half running, I arrived breathless beneath the marquee.

"I would like to see my dad; he plays the organ."

A girl smiled at me from inside the door. "Follow me."

I stepped on deep red carpet. The smell of popcorn and candy assailed my nostrils. "Wow! What a place!" Entering the large auditorium, I followed the girl. The impatient drone of children's voices, plus the shouts of unnerved mothers, filled the air. I was excited! The center aisle was a long one. Way down in front a beautiful landscape decorated a curtain covering the stage. The orchestra pit was in front of the stage. Dad sat on the bench before the organ.

"Sit down next to me, Son; I am about to start the music."

The lights dimmed a little. Dad's agile fingers moved quickly across the keys. Tremendous vibrations of sound levitated into the air, rising like thunder to resound off the roof and the rafters. I felt that every hair on my body was surely standing on end. The beautifully colored lights, the sounds, the excitement of all the people, reached a climax. Suddenly, the house lights dimmed. A bright beam of light filled the darkness. Looking up, I saw images forming on the huge screen. A man sat down next to Dad. He began whispering the printed captions to him as the movie began. A burst of uncoordinated yells and whistles rose from the regular movie crowd. Wow! There was Tarzan of the Apes!

The images of Tarzan and his friends in the natural surroundings of the jungle always reminded me of Dad's stories of Coyote Boy. My imagination, which had played a major role in Dad's stories by projecting images on the screen of my mind, was no longer needed. Here in the theatre all the images were produced for me.

Suddenly I found myself extended far outside my normal position into the vision on the screen. Turning, I looked back at the brilliant light blazing forth at the rear of the theatre. I was amazed to see this light was

31

producing the images of Tarzan and his friends on the screen. Here was a fascinating outer demonstration of my own inner ability to produce images. The movies were a new and exciting entertainment. I also found Dad's stories equally enjoyable. The unlimited field of my own imagination could produce incredibly more to look at — unknown worlds without end; star-studded space, full of creatures and friends.

"This is the cosmic motion-picture mechanism." A Voice spoke as though from within the light. "Shedding its beam on the white screen of your bed sheets, it is producing the picture of your body. Behold your form is nothing but light!"

— Paramhansa Yogananda, *Autobiography of a Yogi*

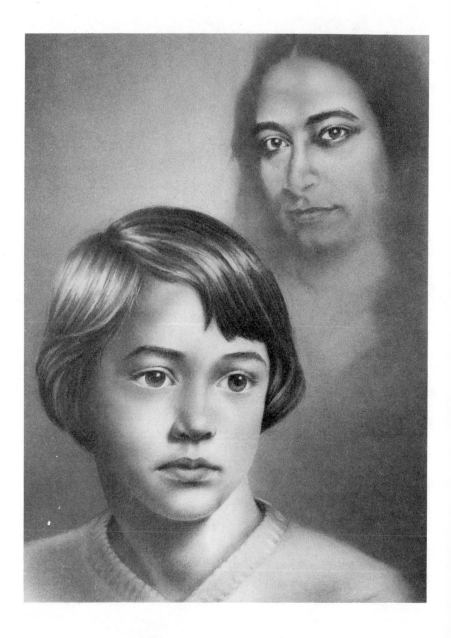

The phantom image of my childhood visions

CHAPTER 5

My Search Begins for the Face of God

"Nana, has anyone seen God?"

Nana's hands, which were busy planting flowers, stopped moving. She quickly turned to look at me, her face registering surprise.

"Nana, please tell me if anyone has ever seen God."

After a long silence she replied, "I don't know anyone who has really ever seen God, but it is written in the scriptures that a man named Moses saw God face to face in a burning bush."

> The burning bush that Moses saw in Horeb, which was not consumed by the fire, would then be the form taken in tradition by the subjective light: "And the angel of the Lord appeared unto him in a flame of fire out of the midst of a bush; and he looked, and behold the bush burned with fire and the bush was not consumed." (Exodus 3:2.) "And it came to pass, when Moses came down from Mount Sinai with the two tablets of the testimony in his hand . . . that Moses wist not that the skin of his face shone or sent forth beams by reason of his speaking with Him. And when Aaron and all the children of Israel saw Moses, behold the skin of his face shone; and they were afraid to come nigh him." (Exodus 34:29-30.) This shining of Moses' face, when he descended Sinai, would be the "transfiguration" characteristic of Cosmic Consciousness.
>
> — Richard Bucke, *Cosmic Consciousness*

"Moses! Moses!" My consciousness was receiving shock waves at this statement. Suddenly I felt a great surge of joy and excitement rising up within me. "Nana, where is Moses now? Can I see him?"

"No, Norman. Moses has been gone a long time, just like great-grandfather Paulsen."

The inner exhilaration and enthusiasm was undying in me and not to be dampened. Someone had seen the Great One, the Father of all Fathers! "Nana, tell me about Moses."

I was frantically searching through my inner Book of Life for evidence, for I inwardly sensed that the existence of Moses was true. Somewhere within, memory bells were ringing, an undying thrill and desire was rising up within me to move onward and outward, never to diminish in this life. My search for the Face of God had now begun.

I now knew outwardly what I had always known inwardly — God, the Infinite Father, was alive! I had not lost contact with him forever in entering this new existence. Moses had seen God face to face and had received direct instructions from him. Moses then had spent the rest of his life trying to fulfill God's will here for his people. The realization in my consciousness that God, the Father, was indeed alive, by the written testimony in the Bible, thrilled me. I was from this day forward inspired onward in my search for him. I must meet him face to face, just as Moses had. This was my desire; yes, this I must do! Moses became the first God-inspired image to enter my life. Fleeting visions danced through my dreams of a far distant land and people.

"Norman, would you like to go to Sunday School tomorrow?" queried Nana. "There are lots of children there and you can hear more about the stories in the Bible."

So far I was satisfied with listening to Nana read and interpret the Bible stories. Dad also had added biblical stories from his memory to my growing collection.

"Yes, let's go. Will you come, too, Dad?" After much coaxing, Dad reluctantly consented to come also.

Here before me was another one of those strange buildings with a sharply constructed roof and tower over the entrance.

> According to all tradition, the most important stage in the construction of a sacred building is the location of a suitable site, one where the spiritual forces of the locality combine to the best advantage. Whereas today it is considered in no way incongruous to determine the site of a new church by purely secular considerations, the priests of former times would as soon have built a water mill in the desert as place a church on a spot where the sacred influences were absent. The practice of divination, by which the true holy centers can be located has now lapsed so that, while our older churches are still capable of use as precise instruments for spiritual invocation, many of those built in modern times are nothing more than empty halls.
>
> — John Michell, on geomancy, the sacred geometry of the universe, in
> *The View Over Atlantis*

A smiling red face jutted out of a tightly starched collar just inside the big door. "My, my! Well, I am happy to see you, Judge Paulsen. And this must be your son, Norman. Welcome to the house of the Lord. Praise the Lord! It's wonderful to have you here today, Judge."

"Norman has expressed the desire to attend Sunday School," said Nana.

"Well, Sunday School is over for today, Norman, but you can start next Sunday. The service is about to begin, folks; come right in and be seated." From my position on Nana's lap I was able to keep an eye on the man with the white collar and red face. I was suddenly standing as everyone began to sing to the accompaniment of the piano. The reverend was now speaking. As I listened, I could perceive the beat of his heart and the gasping of his breath. His words, rising and falling in crescendos, faded away into an endless drone. The image I saw of him at the door flashed before me. His big smile seemed limited to the lower half of his face, never reaching his eyes. I extended my life outward towards him, feeling his heart. It did not seem to reflect whatever his mouth was saying. I felt uneasy, hoping we could leave soon.

> Though naturally religious, he did not share in the minute observances of the Roman Church; his ideas were more particularly in sympathy with those of St. Theresa, Fenelon, several of the fathers and a few saints, who would be treated in our day as heretics or atheists. He was unmoved during the church services. Prayer, with him, proceeded from an impulse, a movement, an elevation of the spirit, which followed no regular course; in all things he gave himself up to nature, and would neither pray nor think at settled periods. The limit which most brains attain was the point of departure from which he was one day to start in search of new regions of intelligence.
>
> — Honoré de Balzac, *Louis Lambert*

"How did you like the church service, Norman?" queried Nana.

"I didn't like it in there. The man says a lot with his mouth and little with his heart."

I could hear Dad struggling to contain himself.

A few days later Nana called me from the backyard. "Norman, the Sunday School teacher is here to see you. Come quick!"

As I entered the room I felt the strong enthusiasm of a young woman. "Hi, Norman, my name is Marjorie. Would you like to come to our Sunday School class next Sunday?"

I was urged to reply, "Yes!"

The Sunday School room was beneath the church in the basement. Two windows looked up toward the sidewalk above. Here the biblical accounts of Jesus began to ring incessantly in my ears as the weeks went by. I enjoyed the stories of Jesus, but my interest in Moses continued.

"Yes, Moses saw God face to face," answered Marjorie, "but Jesus is Lord! Therefore, seek him only."

My intuition disclaimed this. The force of the statement brought out a reply from me. "How can Jesus be the only Son of God and be the Lord God, too?"

"Well, Jesus is Lord and there is no other!" came the reply.

My Sunday School attendance ended abruptly with a plea to Dad. "I don't like Sunday School! I don't want to go anymore!"

"Why don't you like Sunday School?" asked Nana.

"Because nobody there really knows what they're talking about."

"How can you say that, Norman?" asked Nana.

"I just know it!"

"Listen, this ends it right now! Understand?" Dad was angry. "Norman does not have to go to Sunday School any more for the same obvious reasons that I don't go to church. 'The blind can't lead the blind,' as the Master said, 'or both fall into the same ditch.' "

> In the midst of this war of words and tumult of opinions, I often said to myself: What is to be done? Who of all these parties are right? ... While I was laboring under the extreme difficulties caused by the contest of these parties of religionists, . . . I at length came to the determination to "ask of God," . . . I kneeled down and began to offer up the desire of my heart to God. . . . I saw a pillar of light exactly over my head, above the brightness of the sun, which descended gradually until it fell upon me. . . . When the light rested upon me I saw two Personages, whose brightness and glory defy all description, standing above me in the air. . . . I asked the Personages who stood above me in the light, which of all the sects was right — and which I should join. I was answered that I must join none of them, for they were all wrong; and the Personage who addressed me said that all their creeds were an abomination in his sight; that those professors were all corrupt; that: "they draw near to me with their lips, but their hearts are far from me, they teach for doctrines the commandments of men, having a form of godliness, but they deny the power thereof." He again forbade me to join with any of them; and many other things did he say unto me, which I cannot write at this time. . . .
>
> — Joseph Smith 2:10-20, Pearl of Great Price

My mind suddenly flashed the image of the robed and ancient figure in the library. I was able to sense his presence; then before my inner vision I suddenly saw his face, gray-bearded and smiling. Thought-forms manifested as an audible voice: *"You must walk in a circle, Norman, around the outside of the church. You will then understand all men."*

Years later the circle was to return me toward the church, only to be condemned by some self-righteous leaders.

I sought Him in solitude, playing alone much of the time with my imaginary friends. China Creek was one of my favorite playgrounds, the open fields and rolling hills another. The sharp barking of coyotes on the edge of town at night drew me out to their mysterious moon watch.

In summertime, the hot still air carried the sound of steel-banded wheels rolling on graveled streets, the heavy breathing of horses straining in their harnesses. Mr. Reeyes was on the way to the river for a load of sand and gravel.

"Let's hitch a ride with him," I yelled at David across the street.

"Yeah, let's go swimming," he replied.

Riding the old wooden wagon was great fun. On the way to the river we passed the hobo jungle at the edge of the willows.

"Boy, what a strange place," David remarked. "Lots of old bums live there. Let's visit them after our swim. Want to?"

Men who had lost everything during the Great Depression had journeyed to California seeking a new start. Upon arriving, they found employment was not to be had, so banding together, they built the infamous hobo jungles on the outskirts of many towns, usually near the railroad tracks. Shacks were constructed from any junk material they could find. The men usually shared with each other whatever they were able to find to eat, and one could smell pots of hobo stew brewing for miles. Nana gave some of them work hoeing weeds and cleaning up the yard in exchange for occasional food items. An old depression song went:

> Hallelujah, I'm a bum. Hallelujah, bum again.
> Hallelujah, give us a handout to revive us again.
> I went to the house and knocked on the door.
> She said, "Now young man, you have been here before?"
> She said, "Now young man, why don't you start life anew?"
> I said, "Madame, how can I, when there's no work to do?"

Nana changed the lyrics a bit by handing them a hoe and shovel, and after the work came the food.

At age seven I was the only boy in the second grade with long hair. Nana and my mother insisted on keeping my hair long, for reasons unstated to me, and as a result, I was considered a sissy. Along with long hair, Nana also insisted on my wearing a white shirt and a tie. I was the judge's son and was to be well dressed at all times.

I found myself running home from school just about every day with ten or twelve of the town toughies at my heels. One day I was running as fast as I could across a plowed field with the usual bunch of bullies close behind, throwing clods.

Suddenly I heard a voice shout, as if from all the heavens, "*Stop running! Turn around and chase them!*"

I felt an inner strength rise up within, possessing me. I became infuriated! Stopping, I turned with a yell, remembering the pushing, punching, and verbal abuse I had been through for two years. I spotted the ringleader out in front and headed straight for him. I was conveying, as loud as I could yell, just what I was going to do to him, and then to all the others there. The force of my charge, and the unexpected reversal of my usual retreat, took them by surprise. I felt the force of the Spirit around me like a whirlwind. Then I saw, to my amazement, the backsides of every one of them as they took off running in every direction. From that day on I was left alone. Without striking a blow, I had delivered the force of many blows to the psychic consciousness of those boys.

"Something strange has happened to Norman; he is no longer a coward," said some. I was never to run in retreat again.

Dad's office was a good twelve blocks from school, and on occasion I would run to meet him coming home from lunch. I knew Dad could not see as other men, but I also knew he had other means of

It is the image of the strong fortress, of a strong soul "buttressed on conscience and impregnable will," battered by the blows of enemies without and within, bearing upon its walls the dints of many a siege, but standing firm and unshaken against all attacks until the warfare was at an end.

— Charles E. Norton, on Dante, quoted by Richard Bucke in *Cosmic Consciousness*

seeing and knowing things. On this day I decided I was going to test him. I saw his tall figure with familiar white cane coming down the sidewalk a block away. I decided, stepping off to the side, "I am just going to stand here on this lawn and watch him go by." Just as I thought he was unaware of me, I saw him turn his head and start in my direction. Before I could run, he was on the lawn sweeping me up into his arms.

"Thought you could fool your old dad, did you? You know better than that."

From that day forward I knew Dad had extended awareness all the time, for certain, as well as the ability to see without physical eyes. Though he was totally blind, with cataracts over both eyes, people wherever he went found it hard to believe he could not see a little.

Harry Houdini, the greatest magician of all time, was to give a performance in the old Lompoc Theatre. Dad was excited! Years later he told me of his meeting with Houdini and the long conversations they had together. Dad had shown Harry all around town.

"Charlie, they tell me you're blind, but you must be able to see a little."

Dad had just made all the street crossings and found each and every store entrance. He had literally walked Harry all over the town of Lompoc.

"Harry, I physically can't see a damn thing; I never have been able to."

"How do you explain your ability to get around then?"

"My hearing, for one thing, has extended its ability beyond normal functions. I also receive impressions, or images, mentally. Last of all, Harry, I am led by the consciousness of life, which is everywhere and in all things."

This profound claim of Dad's inspired Houdini to make a challenge.
"I'll bet you can't drive a car Charlie!"
"What will you bet I can't Harry?" replied Dad.
As it turned out, Dad had driven a couple of times with Mom for fun.
The next day Dad drove Houdini and my mother four blocks away from
the house. He then returned on a different street, parked the car in front of the house and said, "How do you like that, Harry? Now pay up!"

> The eyesight has another eyesight and the hearing another hearing and the voice another voice.
> — Walt Whitman, *Leaves of Grass*

"Charlie, how about coming along with me? We could work up an act together."

Dad had been playing some of his own impromptu compositions for him on the piano. "Harry, I couldn't do that, but you know, the idea is certainly intriguing."

"Charlie, is it possible for you to teach me how to perform this ability of yours, to see without physical eyes?"

"Yes, I think so," replied Dad.

"Did you teach him, Dad?" I asked.

"Yes, I tried to. Harry was such a highly developed person already, I believe he received what I passed on to him. His desire was to build a mask covering the entire head and rendering him sightless, then ride a bicycle through an obstacle course. He wanted to prove that everyone has the inherent ability within to see without physical eyes."

Today this ability is known as paranormal vision, seeing through the fingertips or the lobes of the forehead. Paranormal sight has been demonstrated by many people. Some of these people I would meet and work with years in the future.

Dad told me of Houdini's interest in the afterlife and of his explorations into that realm. "I think I increased his interest a bit by relating some of my own extraordinary experiences and perceptions."

41

Blind Pasadenan 'Hears' Building, 'Hears' Water By Strange Natural Gift

Talented Musician-Composer Sightless Since Birth, Finishing Training Here

Did you ever "hear" a curbstone, a building, or a pool of water on the sidewalk?

C. Leonard Poulsen, in some respects Pasadena's most remarkable man, lays no claim to supernatural powers, but, blind since birth, he detects the presence of such objects as these through the sense of hearing.

The feat, which to him is a most inconsequental thing in his daily existence, was one of many interesting things given incidental mention in a conversation with him about music. Despite the fact that he has never seen the light, this young man is one of the city's most accomplished musicians and composers. He is not at all interested in talking about his marvelous accomplishments without the power of sight, but mention music and he is all attention.

Mr. Poulsen is a pianist and composer of notable ability. He is ambitious to succeed in concert work, and experts who have heard him play, and who have taken note of the progress he is making, declare it is only a matter of years until he becomes known internationally. Tonight he will feature a recital given at the home of Mrs. E. Pollard, 1600 South Los Robles avenue.

Doesn't Carry Cane

The friends of the talented man

C. LEONARD POULSEN

do not wonder so much at his extraordinary powers as a musician as they do at the manner in which he is able to get about by himself. He takes long walks and street car rides alone, and, without any guidance whatever except that which comes from within, makes the trip to Los Angeles, changing from local to interurban cars without difficulty. He doesn't even carry a cane to help guide his footsteps.

"I guide myself entirely through the sense of hearing," said Mr. Poulsen today. "Anyone could develop the same power under similar circumstances. Possibly it isn't the exact truth to say that I can hear a curbstone, a building or a

[CONTINUED ON PAGE SEVEN]

A Pasadena newspaper article

BLIND PASADENAN 'HEARS' CURBS, BUILDINGS

[CONTINUED FROM PAGE ONE]

pool of water, but my ears warn me of the presence of inanimate objects such as these.

"When I am crossing a street I can judge the distance I am from the curbing by the sound. It is sort of an echo from my footsteps, I suppose. It is the same when I am walking after a rain. I am warned of the nearness of a pool of water on the sidewalk, or in the street, by this same echo, if one may call it that. It is really a sound impression.

"The only time these impressions fail me is on an extremely hot or windy day. Heat waves affect them. Then I have to go by the sense of feeling which, naturally, is greatly developed in a person who cannot see. A strong wind has the same effect as heat waves."

Mr. Poulsen does not hesitate to cross the street in heavy traffic. The sound impression makes it possible for him to judge the nearness of approaching automobiles and other objects.

Completed College Course

At the age of 7 years the musician began attending the state school for the blind at Berkeley. He completed the grammar, high school and three college studies there, also taking the course in music. He used the American Braille system for instruction of the blind. Only six raised dots are employed in making all the necessary letters and word signs. Books and music are read by the same system.

He graduated from the Berkeley school at the age of 17, then se-cured employment with a piano company as tuner. He soon developed unusual powers as a tuner and became so proficient that he had more work than he could attend to. While working in the bay district he continued his playing and after a year as tuner he accepted a place as pianist in a moving picture house. He was there two and one-half years and during that period received several attractive offers from the owners of feature films who wanted him to tour the country with their pictures, because they declared his accompaniments were better than any they had heard. He could not see the pictures for which he was furnishing the music, but one rehearsal was sufficient for him to gauge the time correctly.

Completing Training Here

Mr. Poulsen, who is now 22 or 23 years old, came to Pasadena two years ago to complete his training for concert work. Since his arrival here he has done much composition work. His pieces are published by Schubert & Co. of New York. Within the next two weeks he will send a military set of four pieces to the publishers. The titles are "American Red Cross," "Over the Top," "American Triumphal March" and "The American Legion." He also will send three or four popular songs with this set.

Mr. Poulsen writes on a typewriter of standard keyboard with considerably more than the speed of the average typist. He spends five and six hours a day practicing on the piano. In about two months he will make a concert tour of California, and hopes next year to make a transcontinental tour. He is in great demand in Pasadena for special programs and evening entertainments. During the war he was one of the most popular entertainers visiting the training camps.

Since coming to Pasadena he spent a year at Redlands university studying philosophy. Scores of the students, seeing him going about the buildings and grounds unassisted, refused to believe that he was blind.

... the big steam engine came into view.

CHAPTER 6

Train Ride to San Francisco

Though totally blind, some manifestations of Dad's incredible talents were unequaled. His sensitive awareness of all things around him, including people and places, was extraordinary. In later years he told me of some profound abilities he had discovered within himself.

"Norman, many times your old dad has wished himself to be at some particular place, and he has then succeeded in getting there.

> Without going outside his door, one understands (all that takes place) under the sky; without looking out from his window, one sees the Tao of Heaven. The farther that one goes out (from himself), the less he knows.
>
> — Lao Tze, Tao Teh King, in *Sacred Books of the East*

Once, I suddenly found myself standing on the street outside the old Ferry Building in Oakland. I had been wishing to hear the sounds of the harbor again and to ride the ferry across the bay, so I did.

"When I was a boy in school in Oakland," he continued, "there were sailing schooners and clipper ships still in operation. Oh, how I loved the feel and sound of ships, the creaking of timbers straining against the sea, the clanging of ships' bells tolling out the watch. Sometimes I would stand for hours down on the waterfront. There I would listen to the sounds of cargo being unloaded, the 'huff, puff, puff' of donkey steam engines, the screeching of taut lines racing through their blocks, the first mate's yell, calling all hands to action — 'Raise the main and fore; set the jib,' the hammer of many feet running on deck as sails were once more raised. 'Let go spring lines, let go fore and aft lines, five degrees starboard rudder,' sounded the captain.

"As I stood there listening to all this, Son, how I wished that I might go along, but of course, I couldn't. How could a sightless person go to sea on a working ship? Well, your old dad learned how to go anyway as the years went by, eyes or no eyes. Riding on the life within, I was able to travel,

> In vain the speeding or shyness, In vain objects stand leagues off and assume

45

at times, anywhere I wished. Many a stormy night I have stood next to the helmsman while rounding Point Conception, the roar of wind and water in my ears."

"You mean you are actually able to travel to other places just by wishing it, Dad?"

"That's right, Son. The old rocking chair in the front room was my place of departure for many a wonderful journey. After years of sitting alone in silence, with no one to talk to, I learned how to travel around. You know, I have always watched over you wherever you were."

I knew this was true. How many times in later years would I hear his voice and feel and see his presence? How can a person who sees in this world ever really understand someone who doesn't? Somehow Dad's great desire to travel and do things, stimulated further by a deep sorrow and loneliness, activated his inner spirit to movement. In Dad's case this movement had few, if any, boundaries or limitations. Spirit had granted him release, the extension of which I would not realize until after his physical death. Dad was a spirit who had come ahead of his time to try to help prepare a message of understanding in a world of little understanding. He had brought with him an offering called the Great Soul of the Universe, "The Eternal Traveler."

One day he called me. "Norman, how would you like to go to San Francisco? We can catch the 'Old Daylight' down at Surf this afternoon."

"Oh, boy, would I!"

Nana packed our bags and we were off.

manifold shapes.
I but use you a minute, then I resign you, stallion.
Why do I need your paces when I myself outgallop them?
Even as I stand or sit passing faster than you.

— Walt Whitman, *Leaves of Grass*

God — The Great Soul of The Universe, The One Mother and Father of All Creation!

My Soul — A true likeness and image of my God —sent out upon its own responsibility to work its way back into the Heart of the Great Soul of the Universe from whence it came!

Me — The tabernacle or house wherein this Soul shall live and work for good alone, — my Soul and Me, battle constantly for control; me must be brought under submission, this is the Divine Law! — me — is most selfish and greedy — but me — will have to submit in the end — for that is the Law . . . !

— Charles Paulsen, "The Traveler"

Dad was running for Congress in the Tenth Congressional District; it was the year 1939. His campaign efforts had worn on him. At the same time, Mom was running for the State Assembly. She loved politics and her job in Santa Barbara had opened up the possibility of a public career. I sensed a growing wedge of separation between Mom and Dad.

Dad and I stood out in front of the old depot at Surf. The usual twenty-knot winds were blowing sand across the dunes. Surf is the roughest, most dangerous beach on the West Coast. Perpetual rip tides and ten- to twelve-foot breakers continuously roll in. Many people have disappeared attempting to swim there.

"Here she comes, Son. Hear the whistle?"

A cloud of smoke appeared around the point as the big steam engine came into view. Steam was pouring out in giant puffs with each thrust of the pistons. I grabbed Dad's arm pulling him back as the engine and coal car went roaring by amid the squeal of jamming brakes.

"Come on, Son. Do you see the conductor?"

"You mean, the man with the blue suit, cap, and gold watch?"

"That's him."

"Where to, sir?" asked the conductor.

"San Francisco," replied Dad.

Boy, was I excited! The porter grabbed our bags as we climbed on.

"Right this way, Boss."

We went down the aisle between rows of people all staring, and were shown a compartment with upper and lower berths. The train jolted, almost knocking us down. We were moving slowly up the tracks out of Surf. Picking up speed, we crossed the bridge at Ocean Park. What an experience! Bronze faucets with ice water, a big dining car with red velvet upholstery, it was really fancy. Even the chairs were adjustable.

Dad and I had dinner. I was so excited I could hardly eat! Smoke and steam went flying by outside the windows at times. We were moving faster than I had ever gone before, even in Mom's car. The porter made up the beds, but I couldn't sleep. I sat up staring through cupped hands against the windows as the lights of the countryside went flashing by. "Ding, ding, ding," went a signal at the road crossing. Car headlights penetrated the darkness. I was sorry it was dark and I couldn't see any sights along the way.

Arriving in San Francisco, I led Dad out of the huge station.

"Look for a taxicab, Son."

Finding one, Dad directed the cab driver to a hotel. Never before had I seen so many automobiles and people. Movie theatres were everywhere; the lights were blinding.

The next morning we got up early. "I have a surprise for you, Son. Hurry up!"

Dad led the way down the street to a tailor shop. My first suit like Dad's was forthcoming. The tailor was measuring me up and laughing.

"Going to dress this young man of yours up real proper, Judge; yes sir-ree, sir."

Dad had been doing business with this tailor for years. Ready-made suits were not popular with him, and besides, big clothing factories were going to put all the old tailors out of business. After getting measured up, I found out, to my disappointment, it would take weeks to get the suit. I would just have to be patient.

Dad and I made our way down to Fisherman's Wharf. I spotted the mastheads of a big sailing ship sticking up high into the sky over the top of an old warehouse.

"Dad, can we go take a look at the ship?"

"Maybe later, Son. We have to catch the ferry to Oakland."

Asking directions, we walked to the Ferry Building. The thought of a ride across the bay was exciting; it would be my first trip on a boat. From the entryway I watched the blunt bow of the ferry arriving. Bells were ringing and men were running with lines as she was made fast to the dock.

"Dad, let's hurry aboard!"

The aroma of fresh roasted peanuts and coffee filled my nostrils. Following the people, I led Dad down the long deck into the passenger lounge. Dad purchased a cup of coffee at the counter and I got a bag of peanuts.

"Let's go sit up on the top deck, Son, near the wheelhouse."

I led Dad as close to the wheelhouse as we could get. Boy, what a view! We sat on one of the wooden benches.

"Dad what's that island over there with the big buildings on it?"

"That's Alcatraz, Son. It's a prison. People who have broken the law live there. Many must stay there for the rest of their lives."

"Oh, how horrible!" I thought. "You mean they can never leave as long as they live?"

"That's right, Son. It doesn't pay to break the law."

"What's the law, Dad?"

"Well, Son, a lot of the law is based on God's law as it was given to Moses — 'Thou shalt not steal; Thou shalt not kill; Thou shalt not bear false witness against thy neighbor. . . .' (Exodus 20.) Many of the people living on Alcatraz have repeatedly broken these laws, and more."

I was never to forget my first view of Alcatraz. The thought of being imprisoned was frightening. I extended myself, penetrating the bleak walls, sensing the terror of deep despair and loneliness. The inhabitants seemed surrounded by a dark gray cloud. I felt the predominant desires of the captive souls — "Oh, how good it had been to walk in the sunshine along a dusty country road; the sweet smells of summer moving out across the hills; blue sky filled with racing, fleecy white clouds; fresh air and green pastures. To sacrifice the earth's landscape for a prison cell — why, oh why? Oh God, give me another chance, please! My loved ones — their faces haunt me."

But what of those not guilty of anything against God's laws, locked up for political reasons or by the false testimony on the part of others? How many souls existed around the earth in such a condition? Feeling depressed, I looked away across the bright blue waters sparkling in the sunlight. Here and there ships moved by us. Up forward I could feel the heave of the deck and hear the sound of the bow waves churning outward on themselves. Oh, how familiar to my senses seemed all the sensations. But alas, the great spread of canvas was missing, rightfully clinging to towering masts piercing the sky. I echoed the sound of ships' gear working in the wind. Someday it would all be there for real; I knew it.

This, my first trip on a ship, though only a ferry, would eventually lead me to a real ship, the *Golden Dawn*, the giant sailing ship of Dad's imagination. Or was it imagination? Inwardly I saw her standing out to sea on a fresh northwesterly near the entrance to the Golden Gate, a bow wave reflecting white spray against the dark blue hull. Many years later I would sail a real *Golden Dawn* out of San Francisco Bay, fulfilling Dad's and my dream visions together, with Dad beside me in the Spirit standing at the helm. Time stood still as images of the future joined in an array before me: "Captain Norman and his Friends," all together again, running before the wind on a fair sea, toward the isle of their dreams. Familiar faces spoke to me out of the fresh breeze:

"We're all here, Norman. We are coming; just wait."

The sharp blast of the ferry's steam whistle sounded. We were nearing Oakland. Green hills and white houses appeared. Dad and I were going to visit his old school in Berkeley, to see if anyone was there who might remember him.

Dad knew his way around Oakland. We rode the streetcar to Berkeley. Changing cars there, we found our way to the California Institute for the Deaf and Blind. As we arrived in front, Dad was leading the way. I sensed his excitement; he had graduated from this school in 1911. That was a long time ago.

"Son, the large building with the tower on top — do you see it?"

> The world of imagination is the world of eternity. It is the divine bosom into which we shall go after the death of the vegetated body. This world of imagination is infinite and eternal, whereas the world of generation, of vegetation, is finite and temporal. There exists in that eternal world the permanent realities of everything which we see reflected in this vegetable glass of nature.
>
> — William Blake

"Yes, Dad, I see it."

"That's the administration building; let's go in there."

Dad led the way up the front steps and through the entrance, then down a long hallway. He knew just where to go. A lady stepped up.

"Can I help you, sir?"

"Well, yes!"

Dad introduced himself and went on to relate how he had attended school here for many years.

"Oh my, yes, Judge Paulsen; we have all heard about you. You're one of the school's most successful students."

Dad mentioned the names of a few professors in hopes they might still be living and working there. As he mentioned his old music teacher, Professor Fleisner, the lady jumped with enthusiasm.

"Oh yes, Judge Paulsen, Professor Fleisner is still living. In fact, he is here on a visit today."

"He is?" Dad replied excitedly. "That is wonderful!"

"I believe he is upstairs in the old music room."

The woman didn't need to lead us. Dad knew the way up the stairs. Walking down the hall, he turned into an open doorway. Standing there a moment, he yelled across the room, "Say, old man, do you remember a scamp of a kid named Charlie Paulsen?"

There was a silence. An old man turned to face us.

"I sure do!" came a strong reply.

Dad moved across the room, giving him a big hug and a strong handshake. They immediately began to chat about old times at the school.

"Do you still play, Charlie? How about a recital?" asked the professor.

Dad was reluctant, but finally sat down at the piano. Teachers and students began to gather in the room; it wasn't very often that a former student showed up. Dad played some of his own compositions, to the delight of everyone.

"Well," said the professor, "you did remember some of the things I tried to teach you, Charlie."

"A little," replied Dad.

We then took a walk around the grounds, visiting some old buildings familiar to Dad.

"Professor, do you still carry that poem in your pocket you read to us kids when we were discouraged? It was entitled 'Pluck Always Wins.' "

The professor laughed. "No, Charlie, I don't, but you still remember that, do you?"

"Yes, I sure do," replied Dad. "A little humor helped out a lot in those days. And now we must be on our way, Professor. Seems as though someone planned it just right for us, meeting here today like this."

I sensed this was the last human experience they would have together, Dad and his old music teacher.

"Goodbye for now," said Dad.

"Goodbye, Charlie."

The *Golden Dawn* — inwardly I saw her standing out to sea on a fresh northwesterly near the entrance to the Golden Gate.

EILEEN POULSEN
MRS. CHAS. L. POULSEN

REPUBLICAN CANDIDATE FOR
ASSEMBLY, 39TH DISTRICT

PRIMARY ELECTION
AUGUST 30, 1932

My father was an ordained Buddhist mininister

"It's the Marquis of Queensberry rules for everyone who puts on the gloves in my front yard."

CHAPTER 7
Growing Up

Eleven years of my earthly sojourn had now passed. I intuitively felt the approach of a dreaded event, an event which would change the direction of my life drastically. Both Mom and Dad had lost in the elections; Dad for Congress, and Mom for the Assembly. Dad had withdrawn deeply into his spirit. He seemed terribly unhappy. The wedge of misunderstanding that had existed between them from their beginning together had now forced a permanent separation. Dad's mother, Caroline, had moved into the old house next door. She felt responsible for Dad now in his blindness. Her presence created even more division in the family. Heated arguments between her and Nana ensued.

My school days somehow had been good, and my grades were passing. Arriving home one afternoon from school, I saw Mom's car parked out in front. This was it — I felt sick inside. I knew she was here to try to tell me things were over between herself and Dad.

"I already know, Mom," I stated. "Please don't do it! It's never going to be right for us if you do!"

"Norman, please try to understand; it has to be this way. I am going to be staying with Aunt Elna in Pasadena. When school is out this summer, I will come and get you and Nana for a visit."

I realized there was no way to change what was happening as she drove off down the street. Suddenly I felt desperately alone, calling on Spirit to help me but there was no answer. Only a deep dread and stillness prevailed.

Dad moved next door with his mother, as he could no longer seem to get along with Nana. For the first time I felt Dad pushing me away. He knew he was going to lose me when Mom decided to leave. In his blind loneliness and despair, he sought to extricate his life from mine.

Months later I heard Nana yelling, "Come quick! Your father has been struck down by a car!" Dad had been rushed to the hospital in Santa

55

Barbara. I felt he had uncaringly stepped in the path of that car. Had he turned off his wonderful ability to see? Why? Oh Dad, why did you do it? We must still go on living somehow. Don't you know I love you? Try as I might, there seemed to be no way of putting the pieces of our lives back together again. Dad was never to fully recover from his injuries, even though he lived a good many years longer.

Mom arrived that summer to get Nana and me. There was a man with her whom I sensed was going to be around for a while. "Norman, meet Don Prosser. He is going to help us move. He is a dear friend of mine."

"Hi Norman." He put out his hand to shake mine. "Want to help me load the truck?"

"Sure," I replied.

All of Nana's, Mom's, and my belongings were loaded into the van, including my old dog Tippy. "Your mother says you have always wanted a horse. Well, I'm going to try and get one for you. How's that sound?"

"Great," I said. Don Prosser was a good-hearted man. I liked him from the start, but I knew he would never quite understand me, and my summation proved correct.

San Fernando Valley in 1939 was a delightful land, green with alfalfa fields and orange groves. Small farms and ranches covered the area. Lots of row crops were grown. It was here I learned to drive tractors and farm. Mom had purchased an old two-bedroom house on a few acres of ground in Northridge. The property was surrounded by open fields and walnut groves. The Northridge Elementary School was about one mile down the road. Just to the north of us lived Carole Lombard, a famous movie actress. She and her husband, Clark Gable, had purchased the ranch property for a home.

The ranch was then outfitted with a race track and stables where some of the finest horses of that time were bred and raised. Movie stars, it seemed, lived everywhere in the San Fernando Valley. It was a popular, unpolluted spot in the 1930s and 1940s. One of my favorite cowboy movie actors, Bill Elliot, who played Wild Bill Hickok, became a friend to me later on. He handed me a first-place ribbon at one of the Northridge horse shows after winning a barrel race. "Come on out to the ranch sometime," he said. "I'll show you around."

Boy, oh boy, would I ever take him up on that! Bill raised paint horses, and for a while, he let me ride one of his famous movie trick horses.

Spencer Tracy was close by on a ranch also. I met him one day while working on a hay baler in a field next to his house. It was very hot, and he, for no apparent reason, invited my friend Keith and me over for cold lemonade, and then took the time to show us around his ranch. He reflected a sincere and giving heart.

Northridge Elementary School's population was half white and half Spanish-American. Competition between the two races flared up every day in baseball or speedball games. Mrs. Baxter taught the sixth grade. She carried a bat in one hand and a book in the other. She was a tall, strong, righteous person, and would accept no horseplay from anyone. "Look, there goes old Baxter out the door with Alfonso. She's got the bat with her. I hope she knocks the heck out of him," whispered a boy next to me.

John and Vernon Winship were twin brothers who didn't really resemble each other at all. John became a friend to me from the start. Their father came from the old school of men: big, muscular, and bull-headed. "How come your dad is cutting the oats and barley by hand, John?"

"Heck, I don't know," said John. "He's too damn cheap to rent a tractor."

John's father cut the twenty-odd acres with a scythe, and liked every minute of it. "Look, boys," he said, "it's the Marquis of Queensberry rules for everyone who puts on the gloves in my frontyard." John's frontyard was the town boxing arena for kids. Here we found out who was tough and who wasn't. Old Man Winship saw to that.

My friend John was into bodybuilding at an early age. When asked why, he stated, "So I can beat up my brother Vernon." I watched John chin himself fifty-two times one morning. Boy, what biceps he had! Every time there was an argument between John and Vernon, or any one of us kids, Old Man Winship screamed, "Get the damn gloves!" It was here I began to appreciate the manly art of self-defense, as it was put to us by Coach Elder Winship. Northridge Elementary was a rough-and-tough, fighting-to-survive experience for me. If I had ever been a sissy before, I wasn't anymore.

The Southern Pacific Railroad ran right through Northridge. Every time I heard the steam whistle I headed for the tracks on my bike. What a sound of power those old steam engines had; up close they were frightening. "Ca-thung, Ca-thung," said the steam, crouching behind the big pistons, demanding release.

"Can we come aboard for a minute?"

The engineer lifted me up into the cab of one of the old coal burners. I jumped back, startled. The fire door was open — what an inferno! Steam was leaking out of pipe fittings everywhere and the whole engine was shaking. I thought it might blow up.

"Okay, Son, better get off now. We got to be moving on."

I stood back and watched the engineer open the steam throttle. Suddenly the wheels spun violently on the tracks, throwing sparks in every direction. He backed off the throttle and slowly the wheels caught hold and the train moved ahead. I longed, rather fearfully, to go for a ride in that engine. Someday, maybe.

One afternoon, I heard the phone ring. I sensed it might be Dad, and sure enough it was. "Norman, your father wants to talk to you," called Nana.

"Hi, Dad, how are you? Are you all right?"

"I'm fine, Son. I miss you very much; why don't you write your old dad once in a while?"

I suddenly realized I hadn't written him at all. "I'm sorry, Dad, I'm not very good at writing letters."

"Listen, I have talked to your mother, and she said you can come to Lompoc for a visit this Easter. Would you like to?"

"Boy, I sure would, Dad!"

"All right, you will get on the train at Northridge and I will be there to meet you at Surf." I could hardly wait. I suddenly realized how much I missed Dad and all my old friends. The day of departure finally arrived. Nana and I were standing in front of the station at Northridge. I could hear the teletype key rattling out a message. Boy, was I excited — a trip all by myself! Suddenly I heard the steam whistle down the tracks and then I saw the familiar dark cloud of smoke coming into view. There came "Old Daylight," puffing up the tracks past the old packing shed. She ground to a screeching, smoky halt in front of the station. The conductor swung down, gallantly putting out the step-up. "All aboard," he yelled, looking around for passengers as he checked his gold watch.

"Goodbye, Nana," I yelled in excitement, running toward the conductor.

"He is going to Surf," shouted Nana at the top of her lungs. "His father will be there to meet him."

"We'll take good care of him, madame," said the conductor.

Walking into the car, I hurried to a seat, waving goodbye out the window to Nana. With a jerk forward we were slowly moving away. This was my first experience traveling alone.

I felt free and close to the Spirit of the Father of all Fathers again. We were passing through the Chatsworth Tunnel when I suddenly had a premonition. I saw

. . . Yoga is, as I can readily believe, the perfect and appropriate method of fusing body and mind together so that they form a unity which is scarcely to be questioned. This unity creates a psychological disposition which makes possible intuitions

the train grind to a stop in the
tunnel. The engine blew up,
catching the whole train on fire. I

that transcend consciousness.

— Carl Jung, quoted by Paramhansa
Yogananda, in *Autobiography of a Yogi*

was really scared! Was this to happen now? Just then we burst out into the
sunlight. One year later, a freight train blew up and caught fire in the
tunnel. It was loaded with cattle. I saw part of the train on the siding at
Northridge, including the engine. It was horrible! I was to have many
premonitions in my life — some good, some bad, but all coming true.

We were clattering up the coast above Santa Barbara. The old familiar
landscape came into view: Tajiguas, Gaviota, and then Point Conception.
How beautiful it was to see it all again. I heard the conductor yell, "Surf!
Surf next stop!" The brakes began to squeal as we arrived, and there was
the old depot, and Dad standing out in front. Jumping off with my
suitcase, I ran to him, giving him a big hug.

"How was the trip, Son?"

"It was great, Dad!" I became aware of the old, familiar energy
emanating from him. Oh, it was good to be with him again!

During the ten-mile drive to Lompoc Dad impressed me with all his new
ideas. He had a radio program of his own now entitled "The Traveler."
Here he played his piano music and talked about the Great Living Soul of
the Universe.

> In all things, I seek the Light of understanding — a complete understanding
> of Myself and of All that lives and moves about me.
>
> With all peoples traveling the Great Highway of life together with me,
> regardless of nationality, color, or creed, I shall strive to the best of my ability to
> be tolerant: a tolerance of all peoples upon the Earth, by trying to help them
> attain the best in life — rather than condemning them.
>
> In all that ever has been, now is, or ever shall be, I shall, to the best of my
> ability, strive to recognize the absolute Omnipresence, Omnipotence, and
> Omniscience of God, the One Mother and Father of All Creation, the Great
> Soul of the Universe, and to the Divine Laws and Commands as shall be taught
> unto me, do I strive to the best of my ability to stand ever obedient. A steadfast
> obedience to God and to the Laws of the Universal system through living by the
> teachings of the great teachers and masters of religion, and not so much in
> accordance with my own whims for personal satisfaction and gratification.
>
> In every walk of life, to the glory of God in appreciation and thanksgiving for
> the right to live, I do strive and work to the best of my ability, to build harmony,
> calm, and beauty into a broken and bewildered world. A ceaseless and untiring
> working to build the best I can out of the materials I have, so that harmony,
> calm, beauty, and adoration shall reign supreme throughout the world.
>
> — Charles Paulsen, "The Traveler"

When we arrived at the old house, Caroline, my grandmother, and
another new face greeted me. "Norman, come here and meet Dorothy,"

said Dad. "Son, Dorothy took wonderful care of your dad in the hospital in Santa Barbara, and we have now become very close to each other." Dorothy was a registered nurse, and seemed to have arrived at the right time in Dad's life. I knew he really needed a friend, someone who truly cared for him. "Hi, Dorothy! I'm glad to meet you." Dorothy would be Dad's friend for the rest of his life, and mine also. I was really happy for Dad; he seemed young again, full of new ideas. He was planning a trip through the forty-eight states to lecture and entertain with his music.

This week had gone too fast, I thought, as I boarded the train, waving and yelling goodbye to Dad and Dorothy. "I'll be back this summer. Okay, Dad?"

"Yes, Son, you bet you will. We will be waiting."

The return trip to Northridge allowed me time to think alone. Yes, Dad was now in good hands. He had a friend besides me. I didn't have to worry about him anymore. I was growing up now to the ways of the world, cruel as they were at times. "The Great Soul of the Universe, the one Mother-Father-God of All Creation is with you, my son." Dad's recent words echoed in my thoughts. That was a beautiful expression. Surely God did have two aspects, Mother and Father. Did I not have a physical mother and father? So therefore, I must also have the Father of all Fathers and the Mother of all Mothers somewhere, my Divine Parents. Yes, my search for both of them was moving on.

As I passed Point Conception I reflected upon my childhood visions I had forgotten. But suddenly I was picking up the thread of memories. How could I have forgotten all this? I meditated, realizing how trapped I had become in the outer activities of growing up.

Both death and rebirth in the causal world are in thought. Causal persons feast only on the ambrosia of eternally new knowledge. They drink from the springs of peace, roam on the trackless soil of divine perceptions, swim in an endless ocean of joy. Lo, see their bright thought-bodies zoom past trillions of Spirit-created planets, fresh nebulae on the skyey bosom of infinity!

— Sri Yukteswar quoted by Paramhansa Yogananda, in *Autobiography of a Yogi*

Yes, but how many other times had I grown up somewhere else?

"Don't forget who you are, Norman!" came a strong interior command.

I was suddenly surrounded by spirit friends, long lost, it seemed. *"We are still here, Norman, old friend. Hold on, and don't forget us."* Another premonition dawned. This time it was a good one — many familiar faces would appear in the future; we as spirit friends would be united again.

An astral person meets a multitude of friends and relatives: fathers, mothers, wives, husbands, and children known in different incarnations on earth, as those beings appear from time to time in various parts of the astral cosmos. He is therefore at a loss to understand whom to love especially; he learns in this way to give a divine and equal love to all, as children and individualized expressions of God. Though the outward appearance of loved ones may have changed (more or less, in conformance with their development of new qualities in the previous life), an astral being employs his unerring intuition to recognize all those once dear to him on other planes of existence; and welcomes them to their new astral home. Because each atom in creation is inextinguishably dowered with individuality, an astral friend will be recognized by others no matter what costume he may don; even as on earth one may discover by close observation an actor's identity, despite any disguise.

— Sri Yukteswar, quoted by Paramhansa Yogananda, in
Autobiography of a Yogi

. . . the soul develops the gravitational power to form meaningful and lasting relationships with other souls. Gradually, in its outer life, it and others who are spiritually compatible with it form great families of souls that return to earth, or to other planets, to work out their salvation, not only inwardly on themselves, but through interaction with one another. . . . The stronger the family, spiritually speaking, the greater its attractive pull on new souls that may still be wandering about, searching for an identity of their own. A family evolves as its members evolve. It, too, becomes a "star" in the firmament of humanity, once it begins to produce great souls of Self-realization. As spiritual "stars," such great families become powerful for the great upliftment of mankind.

— Swami Kriyananda, *The Path*

Old Duke, my first horse.

CHAPTER 8

The War Years

Don Prosser and my mother married in a quiet ceremony shortly after our move to Northridge.

"Norman, you must try to accept him now as one of the family. You do like him, don't you?"

"I like him, Mom, but does he like me?"

"Of course he does, Norman, just wait and see."

A couple of days later Don approached. "Say, Norm, remember that horse I said I would get for you?"

"Yes, I remember."

"Well, he is waiting for you to bring him home."

"Really? You mean it? A horse I can keep here at our place?"

"That's right! Come on, jump in the car and we'll go take a look at him. An old friend of mine who works at Lockheed has a horse ranch near here." In less than ten minutes we turned into a driveway. Large green pastures full of horses flanked either side of the road. Excitement was welling up within.

"Look Don! There by the stables a man is waving at us."

"That's my old friend, Steve Larson. Come on, I'll introduce you to him."

Steve shook hands with me. "Well, Son, I'll bet you're in a hurry to see that horse."

"Yes sir, I sure am. What's his name?"

"His real name is Duke. Look, here he comes now!" A man was leading up a sorrel gelding. "Old Duke was one of Will Rogers' favorite polo ponies."

"Really? He belonged to Will Rogers?"

"That's right, Son. Well, here he is. Good lookin' horse, ain't he?"

"Wow! He sure is!"

63

"He's retired here now but he needs exercise. If you promise to take good care of him, I will let you take him home."

"Boy, will I! He is beautiful!"

I had always wanted a horse for a friend, and now there he was, looking at me. I sensed we would get along well as he put his nose up to mine and sniffed hello. Duke was fourteen years old but was still in great shape for his age. As a trained polo pony, he was well-muscled. I found out he could also work cattle a little and he wasn't afraid of a rope when we practiced on a few local steers. Bred from a quarter horse type dam and a thoroughbred sire, he could outrun most horses. I found out how well he could handle himself in local horse shows as we managed to win a few ribbons together. Duke and I spent wonderful days traveling all over the San Fernando Valley and up into the surrounding mountains.

Bud Bouchard was a farmer. He and his father had been farming the area around Northridge for years. I admired Bud. He was a big, muscular fellow with thinning blond hair. He carried a perpetual smile, and was a real hard worker. He drove a 1929 Model A Ford truck with the loudest straight pipe anyone had ever heard. Bud loved to wind up the old rig coming down Reseda Boulevard. Just as he hit the edge of town by the grammar school, he would let up on the throttle. The result was ear-splitting cracking and popping for the next mile through Northridge. One could always tell where Bud was by the sound of his straight pipe. Bud hauled a new four-cylinder diesel Caterpillar on a trailer behind the old Model A. I wanted to learn how to drive that Caterpillar in the worst way.

One day I found Bud parked in front of the post office in Northridge; here was my chance.

"Hi, Bud!" I yelled as I rode by on my bicycle.

"Hey Norm, what's been going on? How've the boxing matches been doing over at Winship's?"

"Same as usual." I stopped my bike. "Say, Bud, do you need anyone to help you farm?"

He eyed me silently. "Well, Norm, you sure you really want to work? I had a young fellow working for me and he quit when I took him off the tractor to irrigate crops."

"Hey, Bud, I like hard work and I really want to learn how to farm."

"Tell you what. The old twenty-two gas rig is up on Devonshire. I need to get that field ready to plant in a hurry. You want to start now or tomorrow?"

"Hey, right now, Bud!"

"That's great. Jump in the truck; you can throw your bike in the back."

We took off, tailpipe rapping. I spotted a yellow tractor in a big field as we pulled up.

"Now look, Norm, this here is the clutch and these are the steering brakes. You use both your feet and your hands to steer a Caterpillar. Get up there in the seat while I run you through it a few times."

Bud fired up the old Cat, and jumped into the seat beside me; we made a few turns around the field.

"You got the feel of it now, Norm?"

"Yes, I think so."

"Well, go ahead and hook up the disc, then have at it. I'll be back in a couple of hours to pick you up."

I suddenly realized he was putting me to the test — either I did or I didn't run this Caterpillar and disc up the field. If I did it properly, I had a job.

I checked myself out, turning to the left and right, starting and stopping. I felt somewhat confident. Backing up, I succeeded in hooking up the disc. Then I began the job. I sensed right away my intuition would figure out how to operate this Caterpillar and disc the field correctly. I followed the inner guidance. Two hours later I finished the field, tidying up the edges. I shut down the machine and sat there admiring my first completed job.

Fifteen minutes later I heard the loud rapping of Bud's tailpipe coming down the road. He slid to a stop, raising a cloud of dust.

"Hey, Norm," he yelled, laughing, "you did okay. Yeah! Not bad at all."

"Do I have a job, Bud?"

"Sure, you bet. Tomorrow I'll show you how to get it ready to plant."

I went flying home on my bike that evening. This was really something, getting to work for Bud Bouchard. As time went by I began to learn a lot of the farming techniques and their applications. I worked for Bud on and off after school and on weekends until we moved to Burbank.

May Kingsman owned a ranch nearby. She taught western horsemanship to prospective movie actors. I had a job occasionally at her stables helping to care for her horses. In exchange for the work she gave me lessons in horsemanship. One day she mentioned Tom Mix.

"Do you know Tom Mix?" I asked.

"Yes, very well. He lives close by on the road to San Fernando."

"That close? Wow, he is one of my favorite cowboys. Does he still ride?"

"Well, he's getting pretty old now. Would you like to meet him sometime?"

"Boy, I sure would!"

"Next week, let's you and I drive out to his place."

The following week May called me on the telephone. "Norm, I'll

65

pick you up this morning, if it's okay. Tom said for us to come on over."

"Nana, I'm going to meet Tom Mix! What do you think of that?"

Nana gave me a big hug. "I think it's wonderful to have such an opportunity."

All the old movie images of Tom Mix went galloping across my mental screen, going back to the time of silent movies. One of my childhood desires, naturally, had been to meet Tom Mix, and now that desire was going to be fulfilled. The images of desire planted long ago were now to be realized.

— The Author

A horn was blowing, May was turning into the driveway — I dashed out the door. On the drive over, May talked about Tom some more. In no time we were turning into his driveway.

"There's Tom's house."

I was very surprised to see an old frame house, no larger or fancier than my own.

"Tom lives very humbly, Norm."

There were some old corrals and a big barn out back. I could see a few horses. An older man stepped out on the porch and waved. I immediately recognized him. He was Tom Mix, for sure. As we walked toward him, I felt the energy of a real cowboy.

"Hi, Tom, how are you?" shouted May.

"Feel fine, May. How about yourself?"

"Good, Tom, good. Got this fellow here who sure would like to shake hands with you."

Tom stretched out his hand toward me and we shook.

"This here is Norman, helps me with my horses. He's a darn good hand for as young as he is." May did most of the talking as we sat on the porch, but I managed to squeeze in a few comments.

"I think I've seen all your movies, Tom. My dad played piano and organ for the old silent films."

"Is that right? Well that's a bit ago, I would say."

"I sure enjoyed your films, Tom."

"Say, Tom," interrupted May, "what do you think about the war? Don't look good, does it?"

"Nope, it sure don't. I think we're really in for a big one. You know, Japan may get into it before long."

Tom was sure correct in his predictions. Less than five weeks later, Japan bombed Pearl Harbor. I rode by on Old Duke, to see Tom a couple of times after that, but I never found him home. I was sure thankful for the privilege of having met him, and I wish him well on his journey as he now rides down another distant trail. Tom Mix was one of the greatest western movie actors of all time, a real cowboy. Stetson still makes his style of hat;

it's called the "Tom Mix."

The Japanese bombing of Pearl Harbor succeeded in creating a strong psychological effect. America had now been attacked from behind and war was the topic of every conversation.

High-paying jobs in defense factories were advertised across the nation. The Lockheed Aircraft Corporation tripled their personnel overnight. Everyone was working and receiving big wages. Don Prosser and my mother were both working for Lockheed, putting in long hours. There was now talk of selling the house in Northridge and moving to Burbank to be closer to work.

In the midst of all the confusion I managed to graduate into ninth grade, high school. Despite the family breakup and the move to a totally new environment, I was still one grade ahead for my age.

I was fourteen now and I knew how to drive a car, but I needed a license. On a visit to see Dad I asked if it was possible to acquire one at my age. Dad made a few phone calls.

"Son, I have succeeded in acquiring a permit for you to drive, but only from sunrise to sunset. You must respect this curfew or you will lose the license."

Now with a driver's license and the money I had saved from working, I could buy my first automobile.

"Dad, if I can get a car, I'll be able to drive up and see you more often."

"Yes, Son, but remember you must also be very careful. Don't do any speeding or horseplaying around. Automobiles are dangerous and people are killed every day in them."

My first automobile was a 1934 Ford sedan that I paid one hundred and fifty dollars for. Don Prosser drove me over to Van Nuys to pick it up.

"You are going to have nothing but trouble with this pile of junk."

"That may be, Don, but it's cheap, and I can fix it up myself."

"I hope so, the engine sounds like it's ready to blow up any second."

On my way home that evening the car's headlights went out, due to a faulty generator and dead battery. "Oh well, that's easy to fix. I can do it tomorrow." I was so thrilled at having my own car, the engine could have fallen out on the street and I still would have made excuses for it.

The car was a great learning experience in mechanical aptitude. For the next year it seemed I did nothing but work on that car. First the clutch went out, then second gear in the transmission, all of which I had to fix myself. The engine needed an overhaul. It was using more oil than gasoline. I put in new main and rod bearings, piston rings, and did a valve job in the auto shop at high school. I graduated from the experience a fair mechanic, capable of rebuilding a car from the ground up.

"Say, Norm," yelled a school acquaintance, "why don't you hop up that wreck of yours? You know, make a real hot rod out of it!"

Donald had paid a big price for a beautiful 1936 Ford sedan. It was the envy of every kid in high school.

"Feel like pushing that wreck out on the street today for a little race, Norm? Come on, I need to practice my speed shifting."

"Not today, Donald."

"Why? What's the matter with you? Scared to race?"

"No, I'm not afraid to race."

"Well, come on out then and prove it."

"Are you sure that's what you really want?"

"Hell, yes. Let's go."

I knew it was now or later, so it might as well be now.

We drove out to a long, newly paved back country road. Four or five cars loaded with kids followed us along, just for fun. Don was revving up his Ford and showing off, making the tires squeal and making fun of me. "Okay, Norm, can you see my hand? Open your eyes! Okay, when I drop my hand like this, we're off. You got that?"

"Yes, Donald. I hear you."

He then quickly dropped his hand. His car leaped ahead, tires burning rubber in defiance of the total war effort. I am sure he thought I didn't have a chance. In fact, I knew he thought that. Well, I had a little surprise for him. When I did the valve job on the old V8, I had slipped in a full racing cam, plus some high compression heads. It was a new idea put out by a backyard outfit in Glendale. The results were terrific: increased engine r.p.m. and higher compression. I also had a few more goodies thrown in. I popped the clutch and listened to the old V8 begin to uncork. The smell of hot burning rubber and oil filled the car. Donald was already four car lengths ahead as I began to wind out.

Suddenly, I was catching him. I looked down as the speedometer needle touched fifty-five miles an hour; the old V8 was still in low gear as we went smoking by him. I saw Donald cramming for second gear trying to figure out what in the world was going on. I was now ahead of him for a moment, and that wasn't in the deal as far as he was concerned.

Just as he started by me again in his second gear run, I managed a real good shift into second. I was near my top r.p.m. when the gears meshed and the clutch popped. "Good night, Donald old boy," I laughed to myself as the old Ford screamed out down the road ahead of him, leaving a trail of burnt rubber and smoke. I looked into the rear view mirror to see old

Donald ten car lengths behind. He was gripping his steering wheel real hard, and his foot must have been jammed up into the carburetor by now. I was doing seventy-five in second gear, and that was fast enough. I dropped the old bucket into high and touched ninety, and that ended the race. I saw Donald pull over and stop. He jumped out and yanked up his hood, as if the engine had fallen out or something. As I pulled up he turned around and yelled, "What the hell have you got under the hood of that wreck."

"None of your business, Boy," I said, driving off. "Want to go for pink slips next time?"

"Hell, no!"

Well, I had won my first drag race, and it was great. I had made an old piece of junk perform pretty well.

Coming home from school one Friday afternoon, I had a strong premonition something was wrong. As I drove in the driveway I noticed the family car was not there. I turned off the engine, feeling a dreaded silence emanating from the house. Suddenly in a vision I saw a head-on collision between two automobiles. I recognized one car. It was Don Prosser's. The accident was someplace on a highway up north overlooking the Pacific Ocean.

I went in the house and found a note on the table. "Norman, Don and I have gone to Santa Barbara for the weekend for a rest. There's food in the icebox. We will be home Saturday afternoon. Mom."

It was true! They were either involved in an accident already, or they were going to be soon. I called different motels in the Santa Barbara area in hopes of finding them. Unsuccessful, I could only wait. I sat up most of the night hoping the phone would ring, but no calls came.

The next day, and all that night, there was still no word from Mom or anyone. I feared the worst and called Dad, telling him of my vision.

"Son, don't worry now. I will see if some friends of mine on the police force in Santa Barbara can locate them."

At five-thirty Sunday afternoon the phone rang. It was a person-to-person call for me from Cottage Hospital in Santa Barbara. I heard Don's voice on the line.

"Norman, your mother and I are in the hospital here in Santa Barbara. We had an accident in the car coming home this afternoon."

"Yes I know, Don. Is Mom all right?" I feared she was hurt the worst.

"Yes, Son, she's all right."

"Are you sure?"

"Yes, I'm sure."

"When are you coming home?"

69

"We will be here for a couple of days and then a friend will bring us home."

"Can I come up to see you? Can I talk to Mom?"

"No, not now, Son. You just stay there at home and take care of things till we get there. Everything is going to be all right, so don't worry. I will have your mother call you tomorrow."

As it turned out, Mom had internal injuries and bruises, nothing broken. Don was cut up, but was not hurt too badly. The car was a total wreck. I was told by Dad that, according to the police investigation, it was miraculous that they had survived the collision. Mom never got over the internal injuries she suffered; they seemed to trigger other complications that plagued her for the rest of her life.

They both came home and walked into the house. Mom looked so pale, I knew she was really hurt. Nana was there to care for her. She was in bed for months, hardly able to walk, I feared for her life.

Don came home from work one evening and announced he had found a three-bedroom house for rent right next to the Lockheed Aircraft Plant. "I will be able to walk to work, and Mother will be nearer to her doctor," he stated. "It's going to be a big job to move, but we must do it."

Mom and Nana consented, and the packing began. My old horse Duke had to be returned to his retirement. All my pigeons, numbering more than two hundred, were given away to friends. Most of the furniture would be sold with the house. The move began. Don and I worked hard together one weekend moving almost everything, and I finished up the next weekend.

Mom was settled in her new room. Now she was bedridden, and would not be up and around again much for the rest of her life. Nana cared for her night and day, bless her heart. My intuition told me Mom was going to leave soon. I tried to put it out of my mind and refused to think about it. She had to get well; she was still young and beautiful. Oh God! What next? First Dad and now Mom.

I attended Burbank High School and went out for football. I tried to keep interested in my studies and sports, but found myself staring out the window most of the time. What was the use of going to school?

You shall no longer feed on the spectres in books.

— Walt Whitman

He had not his knowledge from books, but from some grounds within himself.

— William Rawley, *Life of Francis Bacon*

Mom's medical expenses had consumed all the money she and Don had saved together, plus the money from the sale of the house in Northridge. I had to get a job and help out somehow. I came home from school one day and announced that I was going to get a job and help pay the bills so Mom would not have to worry about them so much.

I found employment in a big gas station right next door to Lockheed, greasing and washing cars. The money I earned began to help out, and Mom looked a little brighter. So did Don. I was sixteen years old now, and very large for my age, standing 6'6" and weighing about 220 pounds. It was the summer of 1945 and the war was turning against Japan, Italy, and Germany.

John Winship and his family had moved to South Pasadena. In our spare time John and I were working out together, doing gymnastics and weightlifting. We were also making it down to the beach at Santa Monica quite often. Bodybuilders were everywhere down there in the forties and they called the area "Muscle Beach." It was a prelude to the beat generation, except this was a good, health-motivated movement. Guys who bummed food and did nothing but work out lived in the area year-round. It was a way of life with them. Ed Smith, a fellow we met down there, lived in a garage with a set of Olympic weights. These were his only possessions. Ed swept out the local pool hall once a day for food money and the rest of the time he sunned himself on the beach or worked out.

John and I were on our way home from Santa Monica one afternoon when the radio program we were listening to was interrupted for a special report: "The United States has just dropped an atomic bomb on Japan. The full extent of the terrible destruction and loss of life is not yet known, but with this ultimate weapon, the war might be over sooner than expected."

The following detours from the main highway of life are closed and condemned to all travelers and under the divine law of cause and effect. Who does travel them does so upon his or her own responsibility and to his or her own peril. Divine law is severe in its enforcement and it carries no pardon or parole system: when once a sentence is passed, the penalty must live itself out.

These detours are immorality, murder, wars . . . these are the things that are causing this old world to bend, break, and become washed in the blood of innocent children of God.

Traveler, it is the end of the dispensation; we cannot stop it but we can help relieve the suffering. It is the period of madmen, many of them wolves in sheep's clothing leading humanity to destruction.

The Great Soul of the Universe is calling to you, calling to you to come out of the wilderness for the sake of a broken world. Will you answer the call? It does not matter how or where you begin; begin even to try to understand yourself and your relationship to the plan and purpose of life.

— Charles Paulsen, "The Traveler"

It was August 6, 1945. Three days later a second bomb was dropped on Japan, as if the first had not been enough. On August 14, the Japanese surrendered officially to the United States Forces. It was over for the living, but what of the dead? Hundreds of thousands of poor souls who never had the chance to even say goodbye to their loved ones, with not even a moment to prepare for death, were atomized in seconds. Why hadn't the atom bomb been dropped at sea near the Japanese coast first, as a demonstration of its awesome power? Surely any government of intelligent human beings would have surrendered after viewing such a spectacle. The tremendous loss of life and mutilation of the living in

> The world looks like a mathematical equation, which, turn it how you will, balances itself. Every secret is told, every crime is punished, every virtue is rewarded, every wrong redressed, in silence and certainty.
>
> — Ralph Waldo Emerson

> Even with this karmic action still to be repaid, Yogananda said the United States has excellent karma, because the good, positive actions taken in behalf of freedom and all humanity far outweighed the negative actions.
>
> — Swami Kriyananda

Japan was one of the greatest disasters ever suffered by modern man. I never cease to hear of the German atrocities against the Jewish people, but everyone seems to have conveniently forgotten the horrible atrocities against the Japanese. The seeds of this action may yet be reaped by our country. Such is the law of cause and effect. In this case, does the end justify the means?

John came over one day with Don Sturdivant, a new friend of ours.

"Hey, Norm, let's join the Merchant Marine," they both said in unison. "We can make big money working on ships, and at the same time we can see some of the rest of the world."

"Say, that sounds great," I replied. "How do we find out about it?"

"Well, first we have to go down to San Pedro and apply for seaman's papers from the Coast Guard."

John, Don, and I decided to go the next week and check into it. Going to sea — this was a part of my inner energy. I knew I had to go, and besides, with all the money they said I could make, I would really be able to help out the family.

The author and a friend

"Where's the dumb jerk who steered this ship all over hell on the twelve-to-four
watch last night?"

CHAPTER 9
Off to Sea

San Pedro is a big part of the Los Angeles Harbor, along with Wilmington and Long Beach. I had never really seen big commercial ships up close before, but now they were everywhere. The channel entrance coming into San Pedro was full of shipping. Freighters and oil tankers were coming and going every day.

The old Federal Building in San Pedro overlooked the channel as well as the Terminal Island Ferry Building. John, Don, and I spent two days sitting around the Coast Guard office in the Federal Building before we could even get an application for seaman's papers. Finally, all the necessary documents were filled out except one, proof of age and citizenship. I needed a birth certificate stating I was seventeen years old. The fact that I was only sixteen could stop me from going. Don and John were both seventeen and had no problem. I went home and found a typed, signed copy of my original birth certificate. Putting it in the typewriter, I changed 1929 to 1928; it looked pretty good.

The Coast Guard officer examined the document and said, "Young fellow, if you can get this notarized, I will accept it."

Now came the problem. No notary would accept the document unless one of my parents was there to vouch for my age. I finally found a little old lady on a side street in San Pedro who was a notary. I told her my story.

"You really want to go to sea bad, Sonny, don't you?"

"Yes ma'am," I replied.

"My husband was a seaman. It's really a hard life. Do you know that?"

"I think I can take care of myself, ma'am, and I really want to go."

"Well, I hope so. You're a big boy for your age."

The little old lady took out her stamp and record book. She smiled at me saying, "No one's ever going to care anyway, are they?"

"My mother is ill," I said, "and needs help financially. She knows I'm going."

She gave me a long motherly look and stamped and signed the certificate. I gave her a hug, thanking her, and went on my way. Three days later I had my official seaman's papers. Boy, what a thrill! I could now sign on any ship as an ordinary seaman or wiper in the engine room.

Getting on a merchant ship was no easy thing, I found out, as I went home discouraged.

"Mom, I am going to have to sell my car to get some money. I'm going to rent a hotel room near the union hall. I have to be there early every morning when the jobs are posted or I'll never catch a ship."

"Have you told your father?" Mom asked.

"No!" I had overlooked that. I called Dad and told him of my plans to go to sea.

"Son, I wish you would finish school first and then go."

"I'll have to do that later, Dad. I'm really set on going now."

"All right, Son," replied Dad. "Write your old dad a letter once in a while, will you?"

"Yes, Dad, I will. Goodbye for now."

I was successful in selling my car for four hundred dollars. I gave Mom three hundred of the money and said goodbye to her. I read in her eyes the message: "I may not be here when you return, Son."

"Mom, you're not going anywhere yet. You can't! You are going to be okay now. I am only going to be gone for a couple of months."

Nana cried and gave me a long hug. Don shook my hand and wished me luck. I was hurting inside as I left the house and boarded the bus. "Well," I thought, "it's too late now to change your mind, you're on your way." This was going to be a great adventure, but I was filled with a deep sadness as well as a growing excitement.

John and Don were already staying in a hotel room near the Seaman's Hall in Wilmington, and I moved in with them. This room was the dirtiest, most stinking room I had ever seen, but it was a place to stay at night, and it was cheap. I had never encountered bedbugs, but now I was finding out about them, and my skin itched the next morning from a multitude of bites.

We all sat around the Seaman's Hall for six days and no jobs came in. There were at least fifty men there every day looking and waiting for work. The dispatcher for Sailors' Union of the Pacific must have thought we might be wearing out the chairs, for on the eighth day he called us over.

"Want to ship out, Fellow?" he said to Don.

"Yes," stammered Don, "but we all want to go together."

76

"Impossible!" shouted the dispatcher. "You'll sit here for a year waiting for that one. Better split up right now."

Don turned and looked at John and me searchingly.

"Hurry up, dammit! Make up your mind. You want to go on this ship or not?"

Don managed to stutter out a "Yes, I guess so. Where's the ship going?"

"Ordinary seaman's job on a trip to Chile."

"Hell, go ahead," urged John.

Don grabbed the pen and signed the necessary papers, picked up his bag, and was directed to the business agent. They both left together, Don waving goodbye to us. I felt sorry for him in a way, going off by himself like that.

John and I sat in the hall two more days. I was beginning to think about forgetting the whole thing. Suddenly the dispatcher wrote, "Wiper for Pacific Tankers, Inc."

"Hey, Winship!" he yelled. "Come here!" (The dispatcher knew our names, we had been there for so long.)

John and I both jumped up. "Here's your chance, John."

"You want this wiper's job, Boy? Ship's going to the South Pacific."

"Yes," replied John.

"Sign here."

John scribbled out his name and then followed the same business agent toward the door. I walked along with him. "Well John, I guess we all go it alone. Goodbye, see you later."

I watched John drive away, then went back in the hall and sat down. A deep loneliness settled over me. I sent up a silent prayer asking for direction. A strong inner voice replied, *Wait two more days!*

I really didn't feel like waiting at this point. After taking a look at the flea-infested room, I slept outside in a vacant lot. At least it was cleaner and I had plenty of fresh air for the next two nights. On the twelfth day, as I sat in the hall, I felt a movement of the Spirit within; something was about to happen. The dispatcher came out and wrote on the board, "Able-bodied seaman, Pacific Tankers, Inc."

I didn't even bother to get up. I hadn't a chance as an able-bodied seaman; I hadn't even shipped as an ordinary yet. Suddenly everyone in the hall turned around and looked at me.

The dispatcher was pointing at me. "Hey, you, big fellow, come here."

I jumped up and walked over to the desk. "You want to go to sea?"

"Yes sir!" I replied.

"You see that able-bodied job up there on the board?"

"Yes sir."

"Well, damn it, I am going to ship you out as an acting, able-bodied seaman. You want the job?"

"Yes sir, I sure do."

I knew there were at least twenty-five able seamen with papers standing next to me, but here was this man giving me a chance ahead of them. I couldn't believe it.

"Sign here, Boy, and you're on your way."

I walked out with the business agent, who was a familiar face by now. We drove off toward the harbor.

"Well, I'll be damned, that dispatcher must like you, Boy; never seen him do a thing like that before."

I swallowed hard; my mouth was dry as cotton. What was the Spirit leading me into? The voice had been absolutely right. Two days had gone by, and here I was on my way. The agent pulled up beside the biggest ship I had ever seen.

"There she is, Son, the *Tumacacori*. You know what that means?"

"No, I don't."

"It means 'mountain upside-down' in Apache, I believe, like a mirage on the desert. Get the idea?"

"Yeah, I guess so."

"Okay, follow me."

We walked up the steep gangway to the well deck.

"Where the hell's the bo's'n?" yelled the dispatcher.

"He's in the mess hall," replied a seaman.

As we walked into the mess hall I just couldn't believe my eyes. There sat old John Winship chowing down.

"Hey, John!" I yelled. "It's me!"

I was so elated and thankful to see John. This was hard to believe. The Father had heard my prayer. He had not only answered it with a job, but he put me on the same ship with John.

There was an old Norwegian bo's'n on the *Tumacacori*. When the business agent handed him my papers he started yelling.

"What in God's name is the dispatcher doing sending me a green kid who has never been to sea before in the position of an able seaman? Does he realize this kid has to do an able-bodied's work and stand a wheel watch?"

I heard all this over my shoulder. Turning, I looked the bo's'n in the eye. We stared at each other a few minutes while he sized me up and down.

"I'm going to ride your damn ass all over this ship for the next six months, Boy; you just watch."

Well, at least he wasn't going to kick me off.

That afternoon the *Tumacacori* steamed up the San Pedro Channel going past the Federal Building. Little did I realize that thirty years later I would be sitting on board the *Golden Dawn* in the same channel, right in front of the Federal Building. The *Golden Dawn* was to find her own dock attached to the breakwater there.

As the *Tumacacori* moved out into the outer harbor we passed San Pedro Light on the breakwater. I made my way forward along the catwalk to the bow. Standing there on the bow deck, I began to realize I was actually going to sea, and not just out here for a little ride across the bay. The *Tumacacori* was heading into twenty-five knots of northwesterly wind. The sea was running about six to eight feet high. I leaned over and watched the bow rising and falling into the swell; a huge bow wave continuously being thrown outward. This particular tanker was capable of sixteen knots cruising speed, and she was beginning to show it. Black smoke was pouring out of the stack back aft as I made my way towards the galley. That evening the bo's'n assigned everyone to a watch. I was put on the twelve-to-four, which meant only four hours sleep at a time. I shared a fo'c's'le with three other men, all of whom had been to sea for years.

That night I knew I must try to steer this giant ship, and who was going to show me how? I laid on my bunk full of apprehension, realizing the three seamen on my watch were siding with the bo's'n and were going to make it as difficult for me as they possibly could. After I finished my bow watch that night I reported to the bridge for wheel watch. The seaman on the wheel glanced at me as I stepped into the wheelhouse. He knew I had never been to sea before, but he was not about to explain anything. The second mate, who was in charge of the watch, was taking a nap in the chart room. The seaman at the wheel backed up a step and pronounced the course to me.

It was dark in the wheelhouse except for a faint red light in the chart room and the glare of the gyrocompass dial. I noted the course numbers on the dial and observed the dial needle was sitting right on the course. The seaman left the wheelhouse without another word.

"Oh, God!" I prayed, "show me how!"

This ship was 558 feet long, and I was standing fifty feet above the water. Way down below, through the large wheelhouse windows, I could see the bow crashing through the swells, throwing out luminous white waves on the dark sea. I held the wheel as the dial began to move to starboard. With each degree there was an audible click. I was ten degrees off course before I began to turn the wheel to port. The clicking stopped, to my relief, but then suddenly the dial began to click off in the other direction.

Rapidly the dial went flying beneath the needle. The course I was supposed to be on was only a blur as it passed beneath the needle. Quickly, I began to spin the wheel to starboard, trying to stop the spin of the compass dial. This went on for a full hour. I was just beginning to get my corrections down to about ten degrees either side of the basic course when my relief showed up. This guy's name was Red and he walked up grumbling.

"What's the course?"

He took the wheel from me and didn't say another word. I left the wheelhouse thinking I hadn't done so badly; the next time I would do better, and sat down in the galley to have some hot coffee. My nerves were badly shaken and my stomach was in trouble. I slept for a couple of hours, only to make it up on deck to try to throw up. Being seasick wasn't helping matters at all.

It was getting light and the sea was a mass of whitecaps. I resolved that no matter what happened, I was going to make it through. At about 0900 hours I was chipping rusty paint on the well deck with some of the crew when I heard, "Attention all crew members!"

The voice was coming over the outside loudspeaker system. The captain was in the wheelhouse with the first mate on the eight-to-twelve watch. The first mate's yelling voice sounded again over the speaking system.

"Where's the dumb jerk who steered this ship all over hell on the twelve-to-four watch last night? Send him up here on the double!"

Oh man, now I was really in for it! I looked around, as the bo's'n and half a dozen seamen were trying to contain their laughter. I realized they had deliberately planned this by not giving me any instructions at all as to what to do. I made my way forward and up the steps to the bridge. There stood Captain Andersen, a huge bulk of a man, and his first mate, who was even larger.

"Are you the dumb bastard who was on the wheel last night?"

"Yes sir," I replied.

"What the hell's wrong with you? Were you drunk?"

"No sir. This is my first trip to sea."

"What! You mean you're in an A.B.'s position and you've never been to sea before?"

"Yes sir!" I replied.

"Get that damn bo's'n up here on the double!"

The second mate stepped up; his name was Mr. Thuesen. "It's my fault, Captain. No one told me this boy had never stood wheel watch before."

I was trying to figure out how they knew my steering was really so bad.

"What's your name, Boy?" yelled the Captain.

"Paulsen," I stated; "Norman Paulsen."

"You Danish?"

"Yes sir," I replied.

"Well, I'll be damned!"

I felt the energy change from hostility to interest. Seemed all the deck officers on board this ship were Danish.

"You mean that damn Norwegian bo's'n didn't try to help you at all?"

"No sir. No one did, sir."

"Well, you sure got a lot of guts, Paulsen. How old are you?"

"Sixteen."

"Jesus Christ; sixteen!"

Just then the bo's'n stuck his head through the door. The captain let out a stream of oaths at him such as I had never heard before. He, in essence, told him what he thought of him for not giving me some attention. I watched the bo's'n leave with his tail between his legs.

"Thuesen, you teach the boy the business, starting right now."

"Yes sir, I will do just that, Captain, with pleasure. Paulsen, step into the chart room with me a minute."

I turned to follow Mr. Thuesen. He showed me a graph that recorded all the ship's movements on a piece of paper and any deviation off the plotted course. There was my erratic trail recorded on paper in ink. I had literally put the ship on a zigzag course for a full hour.

"Paulsen, we're lucky you didn't turn the ship around and head back for San Pedro," laughed Mr. Thuesen.

I received my first lesson on the wheel that afternoon. Under Mr. Thuesen's careful direction I caught on immediately. You had to correct the helm by the ship's motion using some intuition, and also by feeling the heave of the deck beneath you. Mariners call it "sailing by the seat of your pants."

We were ten days out of San Pedro with good weather. The wind was aft off the starboard quarter; we were in a following sea. Everyone was settling into the twenty-four hour routine. I was now able to handle the helm with only a degree of variation either way. Mr. Thuesen was taking an interest in me, teaching me as much about seamanship as I was able to assimilate every day.

John Winship was having his troubles in the engine room. The first engineer was an Englishman, and John perplexed him greatly. John hated the engine room from the start, and I couldn't blame him. In the South Pacific the temperature was always over 100 degrees. I would occasionally

81

see John hauling up buckets of grease and oil from the bilges to dump over the side.

One afternoon my watch was painting the final coat on the starboard afterdeck. Suddenly a bulkhead door opened, and John stepped through with two buckets of slop. The wind was still coming from the northeast. John, not thinking, heaved the first bucket over the side, directly into the face of the wind. The wind caught the mess and promptly deposited it all over our newly painted deck. To make matters worse, John, still not quite aware of the situation, heaved the second bucket in the same direction, with the same results. About this time the bo's'n went off like an air raid siren. John got a bad tongue-lashing and was reported to the first engineer.

John and I shared a common dislike for the bo's'n now. The first engineer called John "Muscles," and every day he could be heard asking, "Where is that infernal Muscles? He won't do anything I tell him."

John and I shared the same relationship with our bosses. Both of them gave us the dirtiest, hottest, most undesirable jobs on the ship.

"Tomorrow morning you will see the Hawaiian Islands, Paulsen. We'll sight Maui and Molokai at about 0800 hours." I was watching Mr. Thuesen calculate our position on the big chart. I could hardly wait. Twelve days at sea with no land in sight was a long time for a beginner. With the first light I awoke to see two big islands, Maui and Molokai on our port side. Oahu was dimly visible off the starboard bow. We were heading right up the channel between Oahu and Molokai.

This was one of the most beautiful sights I had ever seen. It still lies etched in my memory. Tall, cragged mountain peaks rising from the sea, cloud-shrouded, were covered with an aura of tropical green verdure. The fantastic, crystal clear blue waters shimmered beneath local rainbow images.

"Oh Lord," I thought, "this land seems so familiar to my eyes. Yet how, when now but hardly seen?"

Was not the original Garden of Eden likened to such beauty as I now beheld? Inwardly I sensed a rising thrill of ancient origin. Pretending, I looked upon this just discovered land arising from the sea; perhaps it was the ancient Motherland of man, newly discovered this day, I dreamed. Oh, how like a planetary jewel it seemed, floating in the infinite sea of space.

The author, United States Marine Air Corps

"What are those lights, Mr. Thuesen?"
"I don't know, Paulsen, I really don't know."

CHAPTER 10

Phenomena at Sea

As the *Tumacacori* made her entry into Pearl Harbor, officers and crew were all out on deck to take in the sights. We passed the sunken superstructure of the battleship *Arizona* and other wreckage to tie up at a long dock for fuel. Mr. Thuesen said we might be here for five days. Everyone was excited about going ashore.

I took off by myself with the intention of going to Waikiki Beach for a swim. Palm trees lined the beach front; in those days there was only one big hotel at Waikiki. I found a sandy beach that faced east toward Diamond Head. Looking out to sea, I observed young men riding waves on long boards. It really seemed exciting as I watched them skimming down the face of huge combers rolling in. Looking around, I saw a young man sitting on the beach.

I approached him. "Hi, there! That looks like a great sport you fellows have going there."

He nodded and smiled. "You like to rent board and try?"

"Yes, I sure would."

"Follow me."

We ran up the beach to where a half-dozen surfboards lay stacked. He sized me up and pulled out the largest board. As we introduced ourselves Kido said, "You take big board. We go."

"Okay, Kido, we go, but I don't know how to do this."

"Don't worry, you learn quick. Follow me."

Kido took a running jump onto his board out in the surf and began paddling away. I made an attempt to follow. The water was crystal clear and warm; I could see all the way down to the coral bottom. I caught on to paddling and followed Kido out toward the giant swells. Fellows were zooming by, standing up on their boards. It looked so easy. I turned around to face the shore.

"Here comes a good one!" yelled Kido. "You lay down like this a couple of times, then you try standing up."

We both took off paddling with our arms as fast as we could go. I felt the giant wave lift me up. Suddenly I was looking down a ten-foot crest. I kept paddling and then felt the wave start to carry me. Looking around, I saw Kido standing up. Wow, what a great experience! I slipped my knees under me and was able to hold my balance, riding the wave in toward the shore. Kido motioned and we headed back out. The next wave we caught I stood up for a minute before falling. I was getting the feel of it. As the afternoon was ending I knew, with just a little more practice, I'd make it all the way to the shore standing up.

Arriving back on board the ship that evening, I observed the crew returning in different stages of intoxication. Mr. Thuesen was the only deck officer who didn't drink.

"Now, tell me, what did you do ashore today, Paulsen?"

"I went surfing at Waikiki Beach."

"You did what! You mean you didn't go drinking with the rest of them?"

"No sir."

I spent three of the next four days surfing at Waikiki. I really had the bug, it was great fun.

On the last day Kido said, "Why don't you jump ship, stay here for a while? Some fellows do."

"I can't do that, Kido. I signed on as a crew member and I have to go along with the ship."

I had to say goodbye to Kido. I thanked him for teaching me how to surf. Surfing was really going to take hold in the States some twenty years later. I often think of Kido and his whereabouts as I watch the modern-day surfers riding out a south swell along the California coast.

We took on fuel, and to my delight, fresh fruit; bananas and papayas were added to the menu. I had never seen a papaya or tasted one before. I just couldn't get enough of them. They were delicious! The *Tumacacori* steamed out of Honolulu on the fifth day, bound for Manila in the Philippine Islands. I was to observe, firsthand, the horrible aftermath of the war there.

We were about five days out of Honolulu. It was about 0100 hours on the morning of October 15, 1945. I was standing bow watch. Suddenly I felt a strange presence as if someone was watching me. I turned around in the dark to see, but no one was there. The familiar dim lights of the wheelhouse windows back amidships were visible. I looked out to sea just in time to watch a gigantic flash of light in the night sky, followed by the colors of the spectrum emanating outward and downward. The light's center was about 15 degrees off our starboard bow and now seemed to be hovering in a stationary position over the water. I called the wheelhouse to report it and heard Mr. Thuesen's voice.

"Do you see that bright orange light, Mr. Thuesen?"

"Yes, I do, Paulsen. Keep a good watch out there now."

Looking back out to sea, another light suddenly appeared off the port side about 20 degrees, approximately 500 yards above the water. The bow watch phone rang, and I picked it up to hear Mr. Thuesen.

"Paulsen, I think those lights are flares. I'm going to wake up Sparks. If there is a ship or aircraft in distress out there, we'll pick it up on the radio. You watch close now for anything on the water."

"Yes sir."

About two seconds later another brilliant orange light appeared dead ahead approximately three miles away. It was big and seemed to pulsate. It actually looked like a burning spheroid. Some five minutes passed and the lights did not descend or change position like flares would. I called the wheelhouse to hear Mr. Thuesen's voice. "Paulsen, there is nothing on the radio; no distress calls at all."

"Well, what are those lights?"

"I don't know, Paulsen; I really don't know. You just stand by there. I'm going to get the captain."

About five seconds later, all three of the burning bright objects vanished to my great disappointment, leaving no trace whatsoever. As we steamed through their apparent position in the dark, there was not a sign of anything. I was standing at the wheel about a half-hour later and Mr. Thuesen was leaning against the bulkhead staring out at the night sky.

"What do you really think those lights were, Mr. Thuesen?"

"Paulsen, I have been to sea most of my life, but I have never seen anything like that before. The sea is a strange place; strange things happen out here. Old seamen's tales are not all superstition, you know, Paulsen."

"Yes, I do know. The universe is teeming with life out there that we here don't know anything about."

Science Magazine (vol 5, pg 242) reports an astonishing phenomenon witnessed at sea in 1885. The following account is from the files of the Hydrographic Office in Washington, D.C.:

The mate of the Bark *Innerwich* hurriedly aroused the sleepy captain at midnight on February 24, 1885. The bark was somewhere between Yokohama and Victoria at Lat 37° N. and Long. 170° E. Upon coming topside, the captain noticed the sky turning a fiery red. "All at once," he recalled, "a large mass of fire appeared over the vessel, completely blinding the spectators."

The fiery object, with a deafening roar, fell into the sea. As the *Innerwich* was tossed about by the churning waters, "a roaring, white sea passed ahead." The captain is said to have declared that the "awfulness of the sight was beyond description."

The Meteorological Journal of November 12, 1887, related the encounter of the British steamer *Siberian* with a "large ball of fire" rising from the sea near Cape Race some years before. The object remained visible about five minutes, first advancing toward the ship, then retreating. Captain Moore stated the brilliant ball had moved "against the wind" while advancing. The captain added that he had previously witnessed similar appearances in the same area.

On June 18, 1845, the crew of the brig *Victoria* (36° 40' 56"N. Lat., and 13° 44' 36"E. Long.) watched for ten minutes three luminous bodies come out of the sea about a half mile distant. (Report to the British Association, 1861, pg. 30.)

On February 24, 1893, the officer of the watch of the H.M.S. *Caroline*, between Shanghai and Japan, reported "some unusual lights" at 2200 hours. The lights were sometimes in formation, sometimes irregularly grouped. They were situated between the *Caroline* and a 6,000 foot mountain, and were occasionally eclipsed by a small island. The lights were observed for two hours heading gradually northward.

The following night the lights returned, this time for seven and a half hours. They bore north at the same speed and in the same direction as the *Caroline*. A telescope revealed the lights to be globular in shape, reddish in color, and appearing to emit a faint smoke.

An account of this incident was recounted in *Nature* (May 25, 1893) by Captain Charles J. Norcock. Capt. Norcock added that Captain Castle of the H.M.S. *Leander*, in the same general·locality as the *Caroline*, had observed strange aerial lights about the same time. Capt. Castle altered his course and moved toward them, but the lights merely moved higher in the sky.

The Monthly Weather Review of March 1904, (p. 115) contains the observation of an aerial formation witnessed by three crew members of the U.S.S. *Supply* on February 24, 1904. Lieut. Frank H. Schofield, USN, submitted the report.

The formation consisted of three luminous objects of different sizes. . . . When first sighted, they were below clouds estimated to be at 5,000 feet. The objects turned and maneuvered, always in unison, and finally disappeared into the clouds.

— Jacob Konrath, "Mysteries of the Deep," in *Flying Saucers Pictorial*

The *Tumacacori* steamed on toward the Phillipines. The first week at sea the crew members had entertained each other with sordid stories. The second week out just about everyone had heard all the personal history of everyone else. The third week out the fights started. Personalities began to clash; each crew member seemed to know what the other member was going to say before he opened his mouth. Clique groups began to form each one hating the other.

I was approaching the crew's mess hall one evening for dinner. Nearing the door, I found my way blocked by a big seaman. "No chow for you tonight, Paulsen!" he shouted. "You're not coming through this door!"

I stepped forward to push my way through, thinking he was joking.

Suddenly the fellow was striking out, trying to land punches. I disliked fighting, and moved to defend myself.

"I'm going to mess you up, Paulsen!" he screamed.

I watched him in disbelief as he charged at me, his arms flailing in the wind. The whole visual experience seemed suddenly dreamlike to me, turning into slow motion. I felt a familiar presence encircle me from above and descend. This fellow was all wrong in his action against me. I had no time to even reason with him. I certainly didn't want to hit him or hurt him. Suddenly I was moved to action by the presence I felt. I stepped forward quickly, my arms encircling this raging man. My hands met and locked behind his back, pinning his arms to his sides. He was being squeezed in a bear hug. I felt power surge downward and outward into my arms. Picking him up, I crushed his body against my chest until his eyes were bulging out in astonishment and pain. The movement continued upward, lifting him over my head. He was then thrown forward, landing ten feet away, outstretched, his head and heels striking the deck at the same time.

I stood there astonished as crew members who had been watching ran forward to help their comrade. The man was unconscious and was not to be revived right away. Angry cries were now coming my way.

"You've broken his back, Paulsen! He's dying."

Fear ran through me for a moment. I moved forward to take a close look as everyone backed away. The dreamlike condition still pervaded my senses. I heard a voice speaking to me, as if from above: *"He is all right, he needed to be taught a good lesson."*

> According to karmic law, every action, even of thought, engenders its own balancing reaction . . . It should be understood that the law of karma is quite impersonal. We can learn from our karma if we've a will to. But it is quite possible not to will to.
>
> — Swami Kriyananda, *The Path*

The poor fellow was in bed for a week. Finally he was up and around again, giving me a wide berth. He looked at me incredulously, as if trying to figure out what had hit him. He seemed outwardly changed in appearance. I knew that he and I would never be the same again. We had both been humbled by the force of the experience.

On that day I realized fully that I had unseen *Companions* around and about me. I had yet to meet them face to face, but someday I knew I would. The *Companions* counseled me never to start a fight, to try in every way to avoid one if possible, and to live a clean, humble, and virtuous

> The Twelve Virtues, each corresponding to a specific astrological sign, are as follows: Charity (Aquarius), Faith (Pisces), Loyalty (Aries), Patience (Taurus), Honesty

life to the very best of my ability. Years later I was to learn the full extent of the Twelve Virtues, which one should try to live by in order to attain happiness and true love in the creation.

(Gemini), Perseverance (Cancer), Compassion (Leo), Continence (Virgo), Equanimity (Libra), Courage (Scorpio), Humility (Sagittarius), Temperance (Capricorn).

— The Author

As I entered the wheelhouse one afternoon to stand watch, Mr. Thuesen looked up from his work in the chart room.

"We are nearing the Philippine Islands, Paulsen. Tomorrow morning you should see the southern tip of Luzon."

I could hardly wait to see land again. My first voyage across the Pacific seemed like a journey through space to another world. I don't believe anyone who has never been to sea has any conception of how much water there is on the earth's surface.

As I stood bow watch that night, I began to reflect on the recent events of my life. I was only sixteen years old, but here I was, more than 6,000 miles from home. I worried about Mom; Would she live until I got home? I probably should never have gone to sea; I didn't even know how long this voyage would last.

Mr. Thuesen had said sometimes tankers take on shuttle runs after arriving at their destinations. If this happened, we might be gone a year! Oh, was I homesick! Going to sea had sounded great in the beginning, but now it seemed I had already had enough. Besides, this wasn't my idea of a ship. This was a floating pile of iron filled with high-test gasoline for airplanes. I was really riding a bomb ready to go off at any minute. I imagined how it would be if the war with Japan was still going on.

I looked out to sea, feeling a premonition of trouble. It was a beautiful night; there was a warm tropical breeze blowing. The stars were so bright, I felt contact with each one I looked at. They were like beacon lights in space pointing out new worlds to explore. Could there be an end out there?

"Yes!" came a reply, "Beyond the stars."

The vast, eternal, primordial sea of life and energy exists without end. Does every star have planets, I speculated, like this solar system?

Again came the reply, "Yes, many do!"

And people also?

"Yes, They are not all the same as you are, but similar."

"Oh Lord, Thy sea is so great, and my boat is so small." I echoed a familiar phrase.

The sea of space was indeed incredible to contemplate. There is no better place on our planet to observe the stars unobstructed than out at sea.

Oh, it was beautiful out here! What was I complaining about?

Well, the ship should have been wooden construction, that was my dream, with tall masts and billowing sails. Only a sailing ship can truly relate to the environment of the wind and water. Man had ruined it for himself. Great sailing ships made real men of real experience — as the saying goes: "Wooden ships and iron men." Those were the days. I wanted to experience life on a working sailing ship, some way, someday.

True to Mr. Thuesen's prediction, we sighted land the next morning. Everyone was coming out of their moods and gripes in anticipation of shore leave in Manila. The Philippine Islands were beautiful; thick tropical foliage grew down to the water's edge and palm trees lined much of the shore. The word was passed one afternoon that Corregidor could be seen through the glasses. Everyone was on deck later to see the famous fortress where MacArthur's troops had held out for so long against the Japanese.

Two hours later we were entering Manila Bay. Corregidor was visible just off our port side. Huge craters, left by exploding shells, pockmarked the island. Hardly a tree was left standing. The remains of fortifications and armament were visible on shore. A few army vehicles, blown to pieces, lay around. Everything made of iron was quickly turning to rust in the tropical climate.

As we moved up the bay, the city of Manila became visible. Everywhere I looked along the shoreline, buildings were leveled. I was to find Manila a city of wreckage, without one building left standing undamaged.

The *Tumacacori* anchored about two miles from shore. There were no docks to tie to. Half-sunken ships were everywhere. Standing watch the next afternoon, I counted twenty-three large ships that lay on the bottom of Manila Bay with only their mastheads showing above the water. The crew was warned before going ashore that Japanese soldiers were still in the mountains and sniping was still going on. "Everyone be careful not to go out of the city!"

I took the shore boat the next day to take in the sights. As we motored toward shore, we had to literally dodge the mastheads and superstructures of sunken vessels. Arriving ashore, I looked at a hungry, vacant-eyed people. Their homes long destroyed, they had thrown up shacks, built from wreckage, in the fields. All sanitary systems were destroyed, and the edge of the street was the local toilet. The whole city, what was left of it, reeked with the stench of death. Decaying bodies still lay under buildings and rubble, with no one to dig them out. I walked through the Bank of Manila, ankle deep in Japanese currency which was, of course, now worthless. It was hard to believe my eyes. I realized how sheltered my life had been as I watched little children with no clothes, no food, and probably no parents, beg for money. I gave away all my money, and realized there was nothing I could do to help.

I walked back toward the docks. Suddenly, up the street, a violent explosion occurred in a makeshift bar, killing or injuring everyone in the room. I ran up to see what I might do to assist. Looking over the area carefully, I noted none of the dead or wounded were from the *Tumacacori*. Finally an army ambulance came screaming up, to my relief. I was seeing death first-hand for the first time in my life. How lucky Americans at home were to have escaped the horrors of war!

The *Tumacacori* unloaded aviation fuel into a smaller tanker which came alongside. The whole operation of dispersing fuel was over in three days. Then we raised anchor and headed out to sea. The whole crew was glad to be moving again. It was evident no one had enjoyed their shore leave in Manila.

We had received orders to make a run up into the Persian Gulf. Mr. Thuesen showed me the charts with the new course plotted on them. We were going to a place called Abadan, near Bahrain, to take on diesel fuel. The orders were to then return to a place called San Fernando, north of Manila and discharge part of the cargo. My intuition was alerted again when the fact was brought out that Japanese mines were adrift everywhere.

The *Tumacacori* headed northwesterly toward Singapore. It was on the second night out that the horizon ahead of us lit up like a red sunset. It was created from the explosion of a tanker just like the *Tumacacori*. One of those floating mines had connected. We heard later on the radio that the tanker had gone down with all hands. We were now all sitting on pins and needles, for any minute in the darkness we, too, might collide with one. It was really hard on one's nerves to stand watch on the bow day and night looking for mines.

We were lucky, however, and arrived at Singapore without incident. Three days later we hoisted anchor and departed. We were now headed out into the Indian Ocean on a course straight for the Persian Gulf. It was there, near Abadan, that Standard Oil held a large oil installation called Bahrain. We were now directed to Bahrain where we finally tied up to take on fuel. I was disappointed because I had hoped to go ashore at Abadan. Mr. Thuesen had been there and said one could buy expensive jewelry for practically nothing. I wanted something special for Mom.

We tied up to a series of pilings a good mile from shore. There would be no shore leave here, as there were no towns nearby. Bahrain was just an oil processing facility. Arab workers hauled oil lines from shore by hand; they all chanted together as they worked in unison. It was great to hear and watch them work. Some of the Arabs were allowed on board to peddle their wares. It was here I purchased a pair of exotic golden sandals for Mom. There was some jewelry, which I bought, and one fellow even tried to sell me his daughter telling me, "She make you good wife." I had to decline his offer.

The *Tumacacori* took on a full cargo of diesel oil at Bahrain. Fully loaded, we departed, heading back to Luzon and the sea port called San Fernando. After discharging part of the cargo of diesel oil, we were on our way again.

Our next port of call was to be Okinawa. As the *Tumacacori* steamed northwest to round the northern tip of Luzon, I found out we were on the fringes of what was to be the gigantic typhoon of 1945. This storm struck Guam, Okinawa, Saipan, and the whole South China Coast, rendering tremendous damage to shipping and coastal seaports. We were driving into high seas building up ahead of gale-force winds. The prevailing wind was northwesterly, slamming the *Tumacacori* on the port side, slightly forward of the beam.

The course we were following was itself correct, but somehow the third mate had not allowed for the strong northwesterly current and the gale-force winds. I was lying on my bunk at about 2100 hours when there was a series of loud explosive sounds. The whole ship lurched and heaved violently to starboard, throwing me out of the top bunk onto the deck. The ship's lights went out and immediately the smell of diesel oil filled the air.

"Oh God, this is it! We must have hit one of those mines."

I scrambled through the bulkhead door in the dark and gained the well deck outside to find seas rolling on board. About that time the emergency lighting systems came on. As I looked forward, the dim outline of land appeared out of the darkness. I could see the white water of breakers crashing into rocks just off the port bow. We were hard aground on a submerged bottom of rocks, a good mile from shore. I heard all the alarm bells going off at once, plus the sirens. I don't believe I have ever been so scared in all my life. The captain and first, second, and third mates were all on the bridge with the big searchlights turned on. I heard the captain ring for full speed astern. We sat there for about ten minutes and then to everyone's amazement, we watched the *Tumacacori* back herself free. She began to swing clear of the rocky shore as everyone on deck cheered in relief. It had to be a miracle! How she could have slipped free after striking the shore at better than twelve knots, I don't think anyone ever figured out.

For the rest of the night we stood offshore to try and assess the damage. As the first light of dawn broke we began to make inspections; first the engine room, which was found undamaged, then amidships, and finally forward. We were afloat and apparently still seaworthy. The real damage would show up later in port. I shall never forget that island. Its name was Baret, a small, rocky part of the Babuyan Island chain of northern Luzon. The twenty-hour delay had luckily kept us out of the full fury of the typhoon. This storm tore many ships loose from their moorings and drove them clear up on the beach in various ports.

Our destination, I heard, was still in force: the *Tumacacori* was to proceed on to Okinawa. As we entered the South China Sea, the intensity of the typhoon was hard to believe. I saw waves like mountains moving toward us. Even though we remained well away from the storm's perimeter, swells of fifty to seventy feet high were as regular as the tide on the beach. We were all wondering if we would ever get home alive. We experienced over 100-knot winds at times.

The propeller shaft began to leak badly around the huge packing glands. Riding over immense swells, the propeller was actually out of the water at times. After a week of this incredible weather, we gained Okinawa, only to be refused cargo dispersal. All the shore facilities had been destroyed in the storm. We anchored there for a few days and the crew was given shore leave. Among the many ships driven up on the beach, we found a wrecked navy barge, full of navy issue clothing from shoes to hats. All was free for the asking, so the whole crew loaded up.

From Okinawa, our next destination was Nagoya, Japan. We ran into heavy weather, finally anchoring in Nagoya on Christmas Day 1945. Here we were in for the big shocker. While standing watch at the rail on the starboard side our first day in port, I noticed huge bubbles floating up to the surface. As they would break, an oil slick was left on the water. I called to the first mate. Taking a look, he ordered all hatches covering the fuel tanks to be opened. Upon inspection, we found that half the remaining cargo was contaminated with sea water. This meant the plates on the bottom of the hull had been ruptured; how badly no one could tell. All of the clean fuel was pumped into barges, and the contaminated fuel was left on board for ballast and inspection. The captain decided to give everyone shore leave as we all really needed a break.

The *Tumacacori* was immediately ordered by the owners to dry-dock in San Pedro. We were going home at last, but limp home we did. On December 28 we left Nagoya for Saipan with a partial cargo of crude oil for ballast. From Saipan, a course was set for Honolulu. Three days out, our main generator system blew up. This shut down the whole engine room. We drifted for five days with no power, but we did have emergency lighting for part of the ship and the galley.

We finally got underway after five days of drifting and arrived at Honolulu about the end of January 1946. I had a chance to go ashore. Heading for Waikiki Beach, I thought maybe Kido would be around. He wasn't, so I rented a board and surfed for a couple of hours. The owners of the *Tumacacori* tried to get her dry-docked here at Honolulu, but were unable to do so. We left Honolulu on February 2, and arrived at San Pedro on February 19, 1946. As we steamed past the San Pedro Light at the entrance to the Los Angeles Harbor, I ended my first and last trip on an ironclad tanker of the American trade.

I was standing on the bow deck, just as I had done almost six months before. It seemed as though years had passed by, instead of months, as I looked back to the beginning of my sea voyage. Captain Andersen had offered to sign me on as a quartermaster if I would go back to sea with him. Mr. Thuesen also hoped I might consider another trip. I was grateful to them for all they had taught me, but right now all I could think about was going home.

The *Tumacacori* dropped anchor in the outer harbor. The union steward and business agent were there to meet us. For five and a half months of sea time I had earned, with overtime, $3,800, plus my room and board. That was a lot of money, more than I had ever seen before. I received my check and I had it cashed by the paymaster that afternoon. My wallet was bulging with hundred dollar bills. Don Prosser came out on one of the shore launches to pick me up.

As we drove home Don and I had a chance to talk. The doctors had done all they knew how to do for Mom — she had advanced stages of cirrhosis of the liver.

"It's just a matter of time now, Son."

There was nothing I could say to cheer Don or myself. Arriving home, I found Mom sitting up in the front room waiting for me. I gave her a big hug. My seabag was full of gifts for everyone, special gifts that I thought were unique: the pair of golden sandals for Mom, carved teakwood statues, some silver earrings and jewelry for Nana, and a collection of foreign coins. All this and more came tumbling out of my seabag onto the living room rug.

Mom was overjoyed to see me. I felt that she was proud of me. I had grown up some on the trip. I knew it was going to take considerable time to tell everyone about my adventures, so I just told a few short stories.

That night I gave three thousand dollars to Mom and kept enough money to buy myself another cheap car. She and Don had decided to buy a house near the beach. It was a small place, but nice, and there was a sunny bedroom for Mom.

Now came the question of what I was going to do for work. I knew I didn't want to go back to sea right away. Don suggested I join the U.S. Marine Corps; there would be benefits, and I could finish my education. The more I thought about it, the better the concept seemed.

I purchased a car and decided to take a trip up to see Dad. It was so good to be together again. I asked him what he thought of me joining the Marine Corps.

"It's all right with me, Son. Do whatever you wish. However, it would not be my choice, so don't complain to me if you don't like it after you get there."

Dad wanted me to be a building contractor constructing things like bridges, roads and dams. I suppose his desire stemmed from his own wish to work with his eyes and hands.

I ended up enlisting in the Marine Air Corps anyway on April 1, 1946. Goodbye freedom! I had no idea what I had gotten myself into. Dad was right. His choice would have been elsewhere, as mine would now be also. I boarded a bus in Los Angeles for the trip to the Marine Corps Recruit Depot in San Diego. I will never forget the swaggering sergeant who greeted us with a cursory yell.

"Line up, you bunch of gooney birds! There's one thing I want understood right now: you better all give your souls to God, because from this day forward, your damn ass belongs to the United States Marine Corps to do with as it damn well pleases! Is that understood?"

This guy was right, and he wasted no time in proving his point. I felt, after two weeks of drilling, I was on a kill-or-be-killed suicide mission, or worse. Sea duty on the *Tumacacori* was easy compared to this torture.

I finally finished boot camp and was assigned to Veteran Marine Fighter Squadron 452 at El Toro Marine Base, California. The duty there was great. We had a big gymnasium, pool, and weight room, plus the food was excellent. I was assigned to the communications office where the job was interesting enough. VMF-452 was going overseas and was in the process of regrouping. No one knew where we were to be sent; China was a possibility.

I was able to hitchhike home every weekend to see Mom. Her life was fading away and there was nothing that could be done to help her. One Friday morning in June of 1946, the desk sergeant brought me a message from Don: "Your mother is in the hospital at Burbank. Come there as quickly as possible!"

"Oh God, this is it!" I thought. "I have been expecting this and now it's here."

I arrived at the hospital that afternoon. Don and Nana had been there all night with Mom. The doctors were going to give her a blood transfusion; her liver was hemorrhaging and she was very weak. That evening I walked into her room at the hospital for the final time. I knew, as I looked at her, that this was to be our last meeting in this world. I tried not to cry, but I didn't succeed very well. Mom tried to cheer me up, but we both knew it was true. I kissed her on the forehead, holding her hands.

The nurse came in saying, "It is time for her to go. You can walk beside her to the operating room."

As I walked along, I managed to say, "Goodbye, Mom, see you tomorrow."

She looked up at me and said, "Don't say goodbye, Son, just say, 'I'll be seeing you.' " Mom knew we would be together again somewhere.

She then handed me a sealed letter she had written, and I watched her disappear behind the doors. After the transfusion that evening she passed on. The next day, Don, Nana, and I had her removed to Forest Lawn where her earthly body rests to this day. There in a little chapel, I saw her body for the last time. I realized she was at peace now, with all her earthly pain gone.

I suddenly found myself without a family. Nana decided to go live with her sister in Schenectady, New York. Don wanted to sell the little house and leave for some other place, and I was still in the U.S. Marines for at least the next year and a half. Dad and Dorothy came down from Santa Barbara for the funeral, which helped me a lot. Dad offered me a home with him and Dorothy when I was released from the service. I was a lonely young man as I returned to the base a week after the funeral.

In March of 1947, nine months after Mom's passing, I was at the duty desk of VMF-452 when a special letter came in on the teletype. It stated in part that all two-year enlistments would either be discharged immediately or they must re-enlist for three years. I was going to be free!

It took another two weeks for all the paper work to be finished. "Please hand me that discharge and let me go!" On April 2, 1947, I was honorably discharged from the United States Marine Air Corps, as were about fifty other men who preferred not to re-enlist. My tour of duty was over.

I caught a bus to Los Angeles and stopped by to see my old friend, John Winship. As it turned out, he had an extra room, so I decided to rent it and stay on with John for a while.

Jan. 4th 1946.

Jan 4th 1946.

My dear son.

I am in the hospital waiting to get another blood transfusion and just on the chance that I might not pull through I am writing so you will have word from your mother. If I am gone please think of me as being happy in Heaven with Uncle Johnnie. You must not blame God for it. He knows what is best and I will be at peace with all my worries and sickness over. Your last letters telling me that you had found God out on the lonely ocean pleased me so much, I cannot tell you. Try to grow up to be a good man and amount to just enough to be happy. Remember Mom has always loved you and will be watching over you. Be good to Nana and try to help Pop by being with him when you can. I believe he will always make a home for you both though you must not blame him if he should (later on) want

My mother's last letter to me before she passed away

98

to marry again, he says he won't but who can tell? I know he loves you and will cling to you. If I am gone. I have made mistakes and maybe should never have left you in Tampa but I felt at the time there was no other way. Don't feel too bad, I tried to stay until you got home and don't feel I worried while you were gone, I felt that you were alright, I hope that someday you will find a nice girl for a wife and will be happy. You can't keep Nana forever though with good care she may live many years. Mrs. Hamm's father is 86 years old. Mommy will be watching over you and I will be in the sunsets and out on the ocean and in the nice clear breeze, I will always love you, darling

Mommy.

99

Dear-Daddy's Boy,--
                    Dear-Boy,--What Could Daddy say-or-do? I was
glad that I could be with you even for a few moments on Saturday
afternoon. I would have liked to gone with you--but as you said to me
your place is small and as for Betty--they only have a couple of
rooms:--I can only tell you that it was a Very sad Hearted daddy
that sat in silence on the trip back to Santa Barbara. I wanted
so to lift the heavy load from your sholdiers and carry it myself.
This--my boy--I have tried to do for you,--and as the Glory of the
sun breaks through the darkness each day--I can only Pray that your
saddned heart may become lighter--and as the srping comes again--the
Flowers will all come anew to the world and its stricken people--My
Boy included.

    I recall to-day How,--when you were only a little boy three years
of age,--you said to daddy:---"Daddy!--who was I when I was here
before"---I asked you how you knew that you had been here before and
you said:---"I don't know Daddy--but I know that I have."---Also--My
boy--one evening as you were resting in your little bed about the
same age--you suddenly said:--"Mid-summer night in the month of
June,--I see the farries Dancing on a big White Moon."---The First--My
Boy--is the True Statement of Life:--you knew because you had shortly
before returned to Earth to begin another round and had not lived
long enough yet for the big world to help you forget the Truth.
The Second--was the Soul of you not yet mixed up by worldly things
and which being yet free from these things--Saw the Angels Happy
and Glorious--trying to bring Peace to the World on the Plane
Created one-step-below their Station. As you travel on,--please
recall often these Two things so that you will not forget Your
relationship to God and the World.

    Who we were before--or who we will become again--matters little
as yet,--it is enough that we Believe and then--after having learned
or known the Truth--strive to build our lives accordingly under the
Guidence of the Great Living Christ--The Light of the World.

    Mama will be back again,--Daddy will come back,--Nana, Grandma,
Dorothy and Don,--all of us will come back again--just as we have
come back this Time. Your lonliness will pass away in time,--and
then--the memory will help to strengthen your whole self as you cary
on,--having a family of your own to care for--to share and know the
troubles and sorrows that come to so many-many-thousands and millions
of people striving for knowledge-and-Wisdom in a world which we do
not yet understand.

After my mother's death, I received this letter, typed by my blind father.

In your lonliness--you must grieve too much--for in so doing--you will hinder Mama's progress in her new place in the universe. Try rather to help her, for she will have many new lessons to learn before preparation to return again. You must try to remember these things for only at the age of Three--you knew them and were certain of them without any-one telling you about it,---it was upon your own statement of returning--that your Daddy was positivly and thoroughly convinced that the had been following the truth throughout the years.

Stay always close to Nana and help break her lonliness,--she will need not only You--but will need your letters and your every consideration. Your Daddy will do everything He can to lift the burden from you,--and Dorothy,--while she can never begin to take the place of Mama--will do all she can too. Now that you are in the service of the government,--there is not much We--can do,--but we will do all that possible within our Power.

Don't leave Nana alone for Daddy--but when-ever it is possible--we will want you to come Home to us.

Daddy is feeling pretty good and I have done quite well during the past three years. Now in connection with my paino work--I shall try to build up my real estate business specialising in ranches and small acreage. I have shown all concerned that I am able to take care of myself without the job in Lompoc although--I did--appreciate it as long as I held it. We will be around in the three counties now for the winter or up until after the middle of April and mabe longer--we will be close to home all the while. I am hoping that when you get freed from the service that I will have a place for you if you will want to take it.

Now my boy,--I shall close these few lines and do so with heaps of Love for you and my prayers that you may soon Live above your sorrow and lonliness:---the Mama that your Soul knows--still lives on,--just gone for a time to prepare for a greater Live on this Earth--it is only the Mama that you could hear--see--and tough that has gone. This I know is hard for you,--but I also know--that You--are a big strong boy with a highly developed Soul. God Bless you now until you hear from Daddy again:--Blessings and Guidance from All of Us.

Ever-and-Always:--
        Your Daddy Wuss.

A Big Bright and Beautiful Dawning for You on the Morrow. !.

Paramhansa Yogananda. There, staring up at me, were the phantom eyes and face of the apparition seen long ago in my childhood visions.

CHAPTER 11

I Find the Two Large, Dark Eyes

John and I both found jobs working in an Alhambra lumberyard. It was near the end of April 1947. The job was good, clean, hard work unloading freight cars full of lumber. We made it down to the south coast every weekend, usually to Muscle Beach in Santa Monica.

One particular Sunday morning I awoke with a feeling of premonition; something extraordinary was about to happen in my life. I realized that some positive direction must be found, but from where that direction was to come remained obscure.

John and I decided to head down to the beach that Sunday morning. "Let's stop by and see old Ed Smith," said John. Ed was still living in Santa Monica, working out with weights, and bumming around the beach. We found Ed living in the same garage. He was glad to see us, and began to bring us up to date on all the local news.

He had met an artist who lived up the road in Venice. Ed thought his art-work was the greatest, and went on to say that he might have this artist paint his portrait in oil. "Yeah, a portrait of him, Ed Smith!" We all laughed. John got interested though. "Do you think he would do a portrait of me, Ed?"

"Yeah, he probably would," replied Ed, "but it would cost you some dough."

"I'd like to meet this fellow, Ed. Can we go up to his place?" asked John with enthusiasm.

"Sure," said Ed, "he'll be home. He lives right on the beach."

John and I, with Ed in the back seat, took off in the car. "Take the speedway up to Venice," yelled Ed. My intuition was working overtime, along with the premonition I had experienced earlier. I now felt that meeting this artist today was somehow going to change the direction of my life. The nearer we got to his home, the greater my anticipation. Yes, some supreme event was about to happen to me . . . would I make the right decision?

The Law of Cause and Effect

"Seek and ye shall find, . . . ask and it shall be given unto you."

"Seek and ye shall find," . . . Seek and ye shall find what? . . . gold, silver, diamonds, and other riches . . . no . . . Seek and ye shall find the Light of God, wherein lives peace, happiness, success, beauty, and adoration. A peace that can weather any tempest, no matter how great. A happiness that does not lose faith, no matter how great the sorrow. A success that will surmount and pass victorious through any failure. A beauty that lives and is glorified above all ugliness. An adoration that is born of the Light of God, the Great Soul of the Universe, the One Mother and Father of All Creation. An adoration which knows no anger, no hate, no envy, no lust or jealousy. These are the things for which we must seek, and when we have found them, all other things sought unselfishly shall be shown unto us.

"Ask and it shall be given unto you." So spoke the Light of the World. Ask for what? Power, glory, sainthood. . . . No, ask for strength, courage, and guidance through the power of Christ . . . the Eternal Light of the Great Soul of the Universe and it shall be given unto you. A strength so great that the heaviest burdens cannot weigh it down. A courage so dauntless and unafraid that it can face, without flinching, all the evil forces in the universe. A guidance so faithful that it will guard and guide you safely through any mountain pass over the great highway of life, no matter how winding or steep.

"As ye have sown, so shall ye reap." To me, this is one of the greatest lessons ever taught by the Light of the World, but because it does not taste good, it has been the least emphasized of all the teachings. When this law becomes so thoroughly instilled into the heart of everyone that it can never be forgotten, then we may begin to look for peace on earth and good will toward all, for when this comes to pass, each of us will be afraid to harm the other because of the penalties to be paid during the next round of life or even for the remaining portion of this one. It is going to have to be done, my traveler; you cannot escape it, no matter where you go! Whether we wish to or not, we cannot escape this law or any other law as set forth by the Great Soul of the Universe through the Christ, the Light of the World!

Your world and your life will never be any wider than your heart is wide: and just the same, your world and your life will never be any higher than your soul is high.

You may grow as much or as little as you like; the responsibility rests upon you alone and to your own salvation or peril.

— Charles Paulsen, "The Traveler"

"Take the next turn off the speedway, Norm," yelled Ed. "There's his house at the end of the street."

A little cottage sat out on the sand facing the ocean. I parked in front and we all got out and walked up to the door. Ed rang the bell. The sound of musical chimes emanated from within. The door opened, and there stood a man in his late fifties with thinning gray hair. "Hi, Ed," the man said. "My, looks like you have brought all your friends with you."

"Yeah," stammered Ed. "Mr. Stoits, I would like you to meet two old buddies of mine, John Winship and Norm Paulsen here. They're interested in your artwork; I've been telling them about you."

"Well, come on in," invited Mr. Stoits.

As I entered the front door and stepped inside, the feeling of apprehension was intense. I looked at the walls covered with oil paintings of every description. At the end of the living room was a portrait done in oil of Pavlova, the famous ballet dancer. Mr. Stoits identified her as he showed us around. The oil painting covered the entire wall. Pavlova was depicted in the garb of one of the Hindu goddesses; she was beautiful.

Mr. Stoits offered us chairs. As I sat down I happened to glance at the coffee table. My eyes fell on the cover jacket of a book. There, staring up at me, were the phantom eyes and face of the apparition seen long ago in my childhood visions. The two, large, liquid, dark eyes, the long black hair — it was him! Here was an actual picture of the man's face I had been seeing at times all my life! It was for real, it was really him!

> The divine face was the one I had seen in a thousand visions. These halcyon eyes, in a leonine head with a pointed beard and flowing locks, had oft peered through the gloom of my nocturnal reveries, holding a promise I had not understood.
>
> — Paramhansa Yogananda on his first meeting with his guru, Sri Yukteswar, from *Autobiography of a Yogi*

I reached for the book, feeling suddenly back in that dreamlike place of watching, as if from beyond myself. I heard my voice ask, "Who is this man?"

"That's Paramhansa Yogananda," replied Mr. Stoits. "That's the story of his life."

I heard myself asking, "Where does he live?"

"Why, right here in Los Angeles. He has a monastery on a mountain in Highland Park, just north of Los Angeles."

The book was entitled *Autobiography of a Yogi*. I knew nothing of yoga or yogis, but I knew that face and those eyes, and that was enough. I copied down the street address stamped inside the cover: Self-Realization Fellowship, 3880 San Rafael Avenue, Los Angeles, California. Then I began to ask questions of Artist Stoits. He answered enthusiastically.

He had been to a number of Yogananda's lectures and had visited Mount Washington on several occasions. At one time he had tried to get an appointment to meet with Yogananda but had been unsuccessful. For me there was only one way to go now — straight to Mount Washington. I knew I had to see him right away. No one else in the room, including John, had any idea of the depth of my inner experience. I felt I was already in contact with the spirit of Yogananda, and time was of the essence. I must go quickly!

Trying not to be rude, I explained to Ed, John, and Mr. Stoits that I had to go in search of this man today.

"Now?" grumbled John, not understanding at all. "Oh, hell, go ahead, Norman. I'll stay here with Ed, but pick me up tomorrow."

Artist Stoits seemed to understand something strange had happened to me as he led me to the door. I said goodbye and made it out to the car. As I drove toward Los Angeles, I knew I had found my direction at last — the dark phantom eyes had been real all these years! The special person I was destined to meet was now within my range. I drove straight to Highland Park and, checking a map, I found San Rafael Avenue was on top of Mount Washington, overlooking the city of Los Angeles.

I finally arrived outside the gates of Mount Washington Estates, parked the car, and opened one of the iron gates. I walked down a street between rows of palm trees toward a large, three-storied building that resembled an old hotel. I continued up the driveway to the front steps. As I approached the front entrance an elderly lady greeted me, asking if she could be of help. I replied I was here to see Paramhansa Yogananda.

"Oh my, my," she replied. "Do you have an appointment?"

"No," I said, "but I really must see him right away. I have much to discuss with him."

"Well, I'm afraid that's impossible; his appointments are booked ahead for months."

"But there must be some way to see him," I insisted.

I then related part of my story about seeing his book that very day. The only thing she could offer me was the fact that next Sunday he, whom she called Paramhansaji was going to speak at the Self-Realization Fellowship Church in Hollywood, and that was all she could tell me. I asked her where I could purchase a copy of *Autobiography of a Yogi* and was able to get one there. Then, reluctantly, I left.

I spent the next week trying to work at my job and read the book at the same time. The book was rather hard for me to understand, as I was not familiar with Hindu terminology, and I knew nothing whatsoever about yoga. John thought I was crazy for sure, studying some yogi book. In 1947, little if anything was known about Hindu yogis by the general public, but I didn't let John's criticism deter me one bit.

Sunday morning finally arrived. I left early, reaching the Self-Realization Fellowship Church in Hollywood about ten o'clock. As I entered the beautiful little temple, the long-felt vibration intensified. A

sister there asked me to sign the registry book if this was my first visit.
"Would it be possible to see Yogananda today?"
"No, not without an appointment," she replied.
I accepted her statement, knowing I was going to see him anyway,
somehow. I took a seat as close to the front aisle as I could get. The little
temple was full of people. An organ began to play. As I sat there, I suddenly
felt like crying. The curtains finally opened, and there stood Paramhansa
Yogananda in an orange robe, his long black hair falling over his
shoulders.

I looked straight at his eyes with all the force I had. It seemed he saw me,
and our eyes locked in an energy exchange. Tears began to pour from my
eyes. He began to speak about God and man's relationship to him. It
seemed he never took his eyes off me through the entire lecture.

As he reached the end of his talk, everyone stood up to sing a chant. Slowly the curtains closed and people began to get up and leave. I walked out on a veranda which led to the side door of the stage. People who held appointments were waiting there now to see him. Suddenly an inner door opened and I saw him through the screen door; he was looking directly at me. The screen door opened and a sister came out, walking straight toward me.

"'Pardon me," she said, "are you waiting to talk with Paramhansa Yogananda?"

"Oh, my own, you have come to me!" My guru uttered the words again and again in Bengali, his voice tremulous with joy. "How many years have I waited for you!" We entered a oneness of silence; words seemed the rankest of superfluities. Eloquence flowed in soundless chant from heart of master to disciple. With an intensely irrefragable insight I sensed that my guru knew God and would lead me to Him. The obscuration of this life disappeared in a fragile dawn of prenatal memories. Dramatic time! Past, present, and future are its cycling scenes. This was not the first sun to find me at these holy feet!

— Paramhansa Yogananda, on meeting his teacher, Sri Yukteswar, for the first time, *Autobiography of a Yogi*

"Yes, I am, but I have no appointment."
"An appointment won't be necessary. Paramhansaji asked me to tell
you he would like to talk with you. Can you wait?"
"Oh, yes! Yes! I can wait."
"That's fine. I will inform him."
The sister turned and disappeared inside. One by one the people with
appointments were called into the room behind the stage. I sat waiting,
trying to contain my bursting energy. Finally, as a sister beckoned to me, I
climbed the stairs and entered the room. Yogananda was seated in a chair
to my right. As I turned, he looked directly up at me and our eyes locked

again. At the same time he put out his hand, which I took. Again I felt tears flowing from my eyes as I kneeled down beside him. He pulled me closer and said, "My giant has returned. How soon can you come?"

I closed my eyes and was transported back through time. The colored panorama of many lifetimes flashed before my inner vision. We had been together many times before, working, building, even fighting side by side as warriors in the struggle against the Spirits of Darkness.

"At last, dear friend, we meet again, another time, another place." Unspoken words passed between us. Again he spoke, "How soon can you come?"

In later years Yogananda revealed to me why he called me his 'giant returned.' Yogananda in a past existence had been William the Conqueror.

I experienced in a vision the Battle of Hastings as King William conquered England. I was beside him in this battle, and was of such stature I could look him straight in the eyes while standing beside him as he sat astride his horse. I carried a gigantic battle axe which in effect allowed no harm to come to his person.

— The Author

I knew he meant for me to stay on with him. "Tomorrow, sir," I replied.

"Good! Good!" He embraced me as a father or mother might embrace a long lost son. "I will be waiting for you. Hurry now."

I turned and left the room. There were at least fifteen or twenty people who had watched this reunion. Some had tears in their eyes. As I drove back to my room at John's, I felt as if I were floating in a dream. I went through my few possessions and packed my seabag again.

Now I tried to explain to John and his parents where I was going and of my intention to live as a monk in the monastery of the Self-Realization Fellowship Church. They all naturally thought I had taken leave of my senses, going to live with some crazy yogi. I thanked them for their concern and help, and hoped someday they might try to understand.

I drove off toward Alhambra and spent the night sleeping in the car. The next morning I informed my employer that I was leaving, and collected my wages. So far I had told Dad nothing of this new development. I decided to wait until I was more settled. Then I drove toward Mount Washington and Yogananda. I had reached a fork in the road of my life; a new direction and purpose was now lying ahead of me.

"Thank you, Father — Thank you, Mother!"

Worlds turn — Galaxies spin — Time grinds on endlessly — Beings come and go like leaves from the trees — Listen and seek while you have the chance, the opportunity.

Think not lightly of the fact that God is calling you because of your own heart's desire. Exercise it. Take full advantage of it. Don't give up until you find it. You will find it when you have convinced yourself that there is nothing else in all of this entire creation that you want more. On that day, when you have convinced self that God is all you want, one hundred percent — you will see God face to face. How much do you really want Him?

— The Author

Paramhansa Yogananda, at Encinitas, California

CHAPTER 12

The Monastery

On a Sunday morning about the middle of May 1947, I, my seabag, and an old Ford car rattled down the driveway between the two large iron gates at Mount Washington Estates. I pulled over and parked. The old, three-story resort hotel dominated the landscape. I walked up the driveway, climbed the front steps, and entered a large lobby. One of the older sisters approached me, inquiring as to what my business might be.

I replied, "Paramhansaji has invited me to live here as a resident disciple."

Looking at me rather astonished, she went scurrying off toward a large office complex I could see in another wing of the building. Presently I heard footsteps coming up the stairs from a basement floor below.

"I am Reverend Bernard. I was informed of your coming by Paramhansaji although I must say I didn't expect to see you so soon; but it's good to have you here with us." Bernard shook hands with me. "Follow me, if you will."

Bernard started down the stairs, talking over his shoulder. "The men live on the first floor and various other places."

I followed him down the stairs. The basement was dark, with no windows. Walking to the end of the hall, Bernard turned on the lights in a rather large room. Here was a small kitchen, a large dining table and chairs, and in a small room to the side, bathing facilities.

"As you can see," Bernard

"Verily I say unto you, there is no man that hath left house, or brethren, or sisters, or father, or mother, or wife, or children, or lands, for my sake, and the gospel's but he shall receive an hundredfold now in this time, houses, and brethren, and sisters, and mothers, and lands with persecutions; and in the world to come, eternal life." (Mark 10:28-30.)

The devotee who forgoes the usual life experience of marriage and family-rearing in order to assume greater responsibilities — those for society in general ("an hundredfold now in this time, houses, and brethren") — performs a work that is often accompanied by persecution from a misunderstanding

111

explained, "we live humbly here as monastic disciples." Then he turned and said, "Follow me." We walked up the hall toward an outside entrance that opened onto a large parking lot behind the main building. Bernard had a room just inside the entrance which he pointed out as we passed by. "Let me see now. Let's take a walk up to the old cable car building. Maybe we can fix you up with a room there."

world. But such larger identifications help the devotee to overcome selfishness and bring him a divine reward.

— Paramhansa Yogananda,
Autobiography of a Yogi

The cable car building had obviously been worked on at times with some enthusiasm and then abandoned. As I stepped inside, I observed two rooms.

"Well, it's all yours, my friend; fix it up if you like. Have you ever done any carpentry work?" asked Bernard.

"Yes, I'm a fair hand at it."

"How about plastering and stucco work?"

I had to admit that of those two trades I knew little.

"That's all right; I will gladly teach you everything I know about them. This whole place, including the main building, needs to be restuccoed." I noted a sly smile on Bernard's face. "And you look like a good candidate for the job." Bernard wasn't kidding, I found out soon enough.

There was a wooden bench in one of the rooms which resembled some sort of a bed.

"That, my friend, is what is called a yogi bed," stated Bernard. "No springs, no mattress; you just throw a blanket over the boards and stretch out nice and straight. Takes a little getting used to, but I'm sure you will manage."

I left my seabag in the room and followed Bernard onward. "Come along, and I'll introduce you to our print shop."

As we entered the east wing of the building, I could hear the clatter of machinery running. Entering a room, I saw a tall young man about my own age standing beside one of the presses.

"Boone!" shouted Bernard, trying to be heard above the noise. "Come here a minute!"

The young man walked toward us with a smile.

"Norm, meet Daniel Boone, and no, he is not the original, but I understand he is related to the original a few generations back. Right, Boone?"

"That's right," said Daniel.

"Well, Boone, we have a new brother here to help us out," said Bernard.

"Show him around and introduce him to all the other monks."

"Okay, Bernard. Will do," replied Daniel. "Come on, Norm, let's take the tour."

Bernard hurried off to unfinished business elsewhere. Daniel was from Texas and had the familiar Texas drawl. We stepped out the front door onto the grounds. Boone pointed out the old tennis courts that might someday be fixed up. Next we ran into a man gardening.

"Hey, Jean," yelled Daniel, "come here a minute." Jean stepped out of a flower bed he was working on. "Jean, meet a new brother, Norm Paulsen. He's here to stay with us now as one of the disciples."

Jean Haupt reached out and shook my hand. Jean was near sixty and slightly balding. He had a great big genuine smile on his face. I liked both him and Daniel right off.

He chuckled and said, "Well, we sure can use some more help around here."

Boone stepped out on the driveway. "Norm, you see those windows on the end of the east wing, third floor?"

"Yes," I replied.

"Those are Paramhansaji's windows; he is down in Encinitas right now. Encinitas is where our brotherhood colony is located. All the married couples with children live down there. We have about four or five families, plus some new brothers. We're trying to grow all our own vegetables there." I recalled seeing pictures of Encinitas in *Autobiography of a Yogi*. "There's a lot of work to be done here, Brother," sighed Boone. "I hope you like hard work with no pay. Here, all of us have offered our lives to the Lord in service. The men do get a small allowance once a month to buy toiletry articles. Clothes seem to be donated, and you can always find something to wear."

I told Daniel about my childhood visions of seeing the man with long hair and large, dark eyes who was "not a bad baba."

We both laughed. "You called bearded men bad babas?" Boone seemed genuinely interested.

"Yes, I did."

"Did you know baba is the Hindu word for father?"

"Yes," I had learned that from reading Yogananda's autobiography.

From that day forward to the day of this writing, Boone and I have never ceased to be spiritual brothers.

Yogananda once told us, "You two will be lifelong friends."

Yogananda had few young male monastics. There were about twelve older men and half a dozen children, but young men of eighteen to thirty

113

were almost nonexistent. Yoga was unknown to the Western world and, for the most part, young men of my generation were not interested in finding out if God was alive through the instrument of self-discipline. They just didn't care, much less want to make a search, outwardly and inwardly through monasticism.

"You know, Norm, Paramhansaji doesn't allow us to talk to the sisters except on business matters. We are here as celibate monks; we are not to fraternize. Also, we never leave the grounds except on business."

I found life here was really restricted. Once a month Bernard took us to town to do a little shopping. I began to think the rules were very unnatural, but if Yogananda wanted it that way, I would do my best to stick to his rules. I was there because I knew he knew the Father of all Fathers and the Mother of all Mothers. This was my total interest in being here, and my goal was to meet Them face to face, as it had been from the beginning of my life.

I liked to work, and I liked to restore old things to new life. I began

> If you don't like my words, you are at liberty to leave at any time, . . . I want nothing from you but your own improvement. Stay only if you feel benefitted.
>
> — Sri Yukteswar, quoted by Paramhansa Yogananda, in *Autobiography of a Yogi*

to work on the cable car building, resetting windows and doors. Then I prepared the old building on the outside for a new stucco job. Bernard came out and showed me how to handle a hawk and trowel and how to mix the cement. I was awkward at first, but finally I began to catch on. I finished the job, putting on a white color coat of stucco to match the main building.

Two weeks had now passed. When was I going to see Yogananda? There was so much I wanted to discuss with him. So far, Bernard had given me a simple meditation technique called the *Hong-Sau* to practice, but I wanted the *Kriya Yoga* technique of meditation, which was capable of producing rapid results.

> The science of Kriya Yoga mentioned in these pages, is known and practiced in India and throughout the world. The Sanskrit root of Kriya is Kri, to do, to act and react. The same root is found in the word Karma the natural principle of Cause and Effect. Kriya Yoga is thus "Union (Yoga) with the Infinite through a certain action or rite (Kriya). A practicioner who faithfully practices the technique is gradually freed from Karma (i.e., Law of Cause and Effect) equilibriums.
>
> Kriya Yoga is a simple psychophysiological method by which human blood is decarbonated and recharged with oxygen. The atoms of this extra oxygen are transmuted into life force to rejuvenate the brain and spinal centers. By stopping the accumulation of venous blood, the adept is able to lessen or prevent the decay of tissues. The advanced adept transmutes his cells into energy. Elijah, Jesus and other prophets were Masters in the use of Kriya or a

similar technique by which they caused their bodies to materialize and dematerialize at will.

— Paramhansa Yogananda,
Autobiography of a Yogi

One evening about eight o'clock, Boone came running up to my room. "Norm, Paramhansaji just drove in. He is on his way up to the third floor and he wants you to come right up."

Finally, after two weeks of waiting, I was going to get to talk with him. I went into the lobby and started up the stairs. When I reached the third floor, a younger sister asked me what I wanted.

"Yogananda sent for me. I am here to see him." She turned and walked to the east end of the hall, whispering to another sister. She then came back and said, "Follow me."

I entered a sitting room where Yogananda was seated in a chair. "Well, well, how are you doing, Big Boy?" he asked. I replied that I thought I was doing well and had been rebuilding the old cable car house.

He looked at me very seriously and said, "God has told me to meditate with you. Sit down over there." I sat down and he turned off the light. "Now I want you to repeat silently, 'Father, reveal thyself to me.' Did Bernard teach you about the spiritual eye?"

"Yes sir, he explained it to me."

"All right, focus your attention there and repeat silently, 'Father, reveal thyself to me.' "

I closed my eyes and began. I had trouble, it seemed, trying to focus my eyes on one point. Suddenly a bright sphere of gold light appeared right in front of my face. The bright sphere of gold light began to move and extend itself. I intently watched it form into a ring about three inches in diameter. The thickness of the ring band seemed to be about

The light of the body is the eye: if therefore thine eye be single, thy whole body shall be full of light. (Matthew 6:22.) The spiritual eye is the vision which sees into dimensions of consciousness and energy radiations. It is the soul's vision which sees the infinite and all images contained therein. The tunnel into eternity which contains the 'Light of Christ,' at the end, the First Creation of Light, is everyone's final goal.

The Author

Directly in from the temples and at the root of the nose is the spiritual consciousness. It is here that the adept withdraws all energies from the organs of the five senses to the sensorium, and begins to experience the origin of all psychophysiological phenomena. Thus accomplishing the concentration state, the aspirant begins to experience the origin of all energy and matter as light, the first creation. "And God said, 'Let there be light: and there was light.' " (Genesis 1:3.)

— Paramhansa Yogananda,
Autobiography of a Yogi

one-quarter of an inch. When it was fully formed, I looked into the center. It was like a window or a tunnel into another total universe, the color of which resembled the evening sky after sunset, a deep purple-blue. I was gazing into eternity.

Suddenly a bright star appeared infinitely far away; it seemed to radiate five points. I felt my spirit begin to move toward it.

Suddenly Yogananda said, "Big Boy, did you see him? The Christ?" I opened my eyes as he turned on the light. I described what I had seen. "That's very good. Now you must go and meditate alone the same way. You must penetrate that starlight at the end of the tunnel. If you succeed, then you will be with him forever." He motioned me to him, then reached out and touched my forehead. "God loves you very much. You have a big job to do in this life, but you must be careful, for many will try to stop you. Now go, and know that I am always with you."

I turned and left the room, hardly able to believe what had just transpired.

I heard the doctors say that I was dead, and that's when I began to feel as though I were tumbling, actually kind of floating, through this blackness, which was some kind of enclosure. There are not really words to describe this. Everything was very black, except that, way off from me, I could see this little light. It was a very brilliant light, but not too large at first. It grew larger as I came nearer and nearer to it.

I was trying to get to that light at the end, because I felt that it was Christ, and I was trying to reach that point. It was not a frightening experience. It was more or less a pleasant thing. For immediately. . . I had connected the light with Christ, who said, "I am the light of the world." I said to myself, "If this is it, if I am to die, then I know who waits for me at the end, there in that light."

— A patient, speaking to Dr. Raymond Moody, in *Life After Life*

The five-pointed star blazes forth to the beholder. Moving toward him through the inner dimensional tunnel (spiritual eye), it becomes a full-blown SöN-SüN disc (i.e., the First Creation of Light, The Great Central SöN-SüN). This light is brighter than the physical sun, but it in no way injures the adept. This is the vision of Christ beheld and recorded by so many spirits, both past and present.

— The Author

The Self-Realization Fellowship Church in Hollywood, California where I first met Paramhansa Yogananda

Golden Lotus Towers at Encinitas, California

"What! No brakes!" screamed Bugs.

CHAPTER 13

Life with Yogananda

As the weeks and months slipped by, with Bernard's help, I became a fair hand at plastering and stuccoing, as well as carpentry. The amount of work I accomplished began to be evident. Trimming out old brush and overgrowth, Jean Haupt and I soon had the grounds looking pretty good. I found that moments spent with Yogananda were few and far between. On the average, I got to see him once a month, and that was when he was either coming in or going out in his car. I was disappointed, for I felt there should be more personal contact with him. How was I to learn?

One morning a message was sent down to me from Yogananda: "Get dressed up at once, I am taking you with me today, P.Y." I was to accompany him on a trip.

Virginia Wright had been Yogananda's regular chauffeur from the beginning, but somehow he had suddenly decided I was going to be his part-time attendant and chauffeur. It was shortly after Christmas 1948. Yogananda had been given a used Cadillac sedan for his birthday by a friend. As I stood waiting at the basement entrance, he came down in the elevator and approached me.

"Big Boy, are you a good driver? You have good karma, so I won't have to worry about accidents."

"Well sir, I believe I am a fair driver."

"I see. Well, now you are going to drive me around today. Here are the keys; go bring the car up."

I was able to perform to his satisfaction that day, and so on various occasions I had the privilege of driving him to different parts of the city on business. Paramhansaji had purchased a retreat out in the Twenty-Nine Palms desert area, a three-bedroom house on an acre of ground. At the same time he purchased a retreat for the men about three miles distant in the same area.

Bernard called me one day saying, "Paramhansaji is out at the desert retreat. He wants you, Boone, Bill Brown, and me to go on out there. Seems there is some work he wants done."

Boone and I rode in the back of Bernard's pickup truck. I had never really seen a desert before. As we drew closer to Twenty-Nine Palms, the desert became fascinating; the colors of the terrain were incredibly beautiful. Joshua trees and yucca plants decorated the rock and sand-strewn landscape. Joshua trees, I found out, grew primarily in only two localities on earth; here in the Twenty-Nine Palms desert area and in far-distant Israel. Having never seen joshua trees before, I found them truly unique in their beauty.

One could also see for thirty or forty miles across unobstructed desert land. It reminded me of the ocean. The stars at night were so bright and clear, I felt I could reach out and touch them. I enjoyed the desert; it was a new and strange environment to me. I felt someday I might like to live out here. The silence was so profound, one could hear the all-pervading Om or Hun constantly.

Divine Spirit unmanifested is a form of life energy and consciousness. Non-thinking Spirit is non-moving. Thinking, Spirit moves like wind upon the waters of eternity. The divine body of energy is motivated by thought. Consciousness, desiring to see images, produces thoughts like wind upon the waters. Life force in motion produces the cosmic masculine sound of Hun and feminine sound of Om — the images of creation or "The Word." "In the beginning was the Word, and the Word was with God, and the Word was God." (John 1:1.)

— The Author

The work Yogananda wanted done consisted of erecting a snake-proof fence around the one-acre retreat. There were rattlesnakes in the area and he wanted no one to be bitten. Building the fence was soon accomplished, along with a path which we lined with beautiful local stones.

I found time to take long hikes out across the desert. As I walked along one day, totally alone in the incredible silence, my intuition told me this desert would someday play a great role in my life. I gazed off toward the northwest. Beautiful calico hills bedecked the horizon in an array of colors.

It was around September of 1948 that I first saw our next new brother arriving. I was sitting in the Hollywood Church after one of Yogananda's Sunday lectures when I spotted this fellow in a white panama suit. He wore a white shirt and a black tie. Wow! What a getup! He was in a terrible state of agitation, having traveled many miles to see Yogananda only to find out he needed a prior appointment. I knew at first glance he was going to join us, but from where had he come, dressed in that weird suit?

He finally talked one of the sisters into asking Yogananda if he might see him. Sure enough, the Spirit was with him. I saw him enter the temple anteroom. About forty-five minutes later he emerged, looking elated.

He approached me and asked, "You are one of Paramhansaji's disciples, are you not?"

"Yes, I am."

"Well, my name is Donald Walters, and he has just consented to accept me as one of his disciples."

"Say, that's great, Donald." I gave him a brotherly hug.

"I have my suitcase with me so I suppose I will be traveling with you up to the Mount Washington retreat."

"Well, Bernard and the rest of the brothers will be leaving soon, so you can jump into the truck with us."

Donald was just full of intellectual questions, and I could tell he was highly educated by the nature of those questions. I introduced him to Daniel and hoped that Daniel might help me answer some of them.

> Spiritual knowledge cannot be communicated from one intellect to another, but must be sought for in the Spirit of God.
>
> — Jacob Behmen

We arrived at Mount Washington that afternoon, and the only room available for Don was the one right next to mine in the cable car annex. I knew the room must have been quite a shock to him as through the wall I heard him grumbling to himself. However, he had the right attitude and was willing to live anywhere, if necessary, just to be here. I liked Don right from the beginning. He had a sincere heart, and I knew that that would bring him through.

Yogananda had insisted from the day of my coming that I learn all the

> Donald Walters, now Swami Kriyananda, is the founder of Ananda Cooperative Communities, and the author of many spiritual books and songs.
>
> — The Author

yoga postures, asanas, and mudras, and he had directed Boone and Bernard to teach me. There are, I believe, about eighty-four postures, some of them so difficult they are next to impossible to perform. After a year's practice I had mastered about sixty. Bernard, Daniel and I were called upon quite frequently to demonstrate the postures for Yogananda's guests.

Bernard had a double curvature of the spine and was not expected to live very long before coming to Yogananda. One lung was collapsed also, and his general condition rendered him subject to persistent infections. After meeting Yogananda, Bernard's health began to improve. One of his demonstrations was to push a hat pin in one side of his throat and out the other, then remove the object, showing the flesh bloodless and without a mark. With his spine in the condition it was in, I rather thought it a miracle that Bernard could perform any of the postures at all. Yogananda, of course, was delighted to show people these things, and most of his guests left greatly impressed.

The summer of 1949 brought in a few new brothers. Leo Cocks was one. His family had all been Rosicrucians for years. James Butler, another brother, who moved to Mount Washington with his mother, was a real character. Bernard put him to work in the print shop with Boone. He soon became known as "Bugs"; he was always up to some crazy joke.

There is a beautiful painted portrait of Sri Yukteswar, Paramhansaji's teacher, hanging in the reception room of Mount Washington, but something about the eyes just didn't look quite right to some of us; not enough life in them. One night, Bugs Butler and I sneaked in and painted a tiny white dot in the center of each eye. That did the trick, making the picture seem alive. The dots are still there.

— The Author

I found a five-ton Mack truck which I talked Yogananda into buying. We were always hauling trash or building materials, and it seemed reasonable to have a big truck to perform the tasks. Paramhansaji thought it was fun and began to create work for the truck to do. One morning when I went to pick up some lumber, I asked Bugs to help me with the load. He smiled brightly and jumped into the old Mack beside me. As I started the drive down to the bottom of Mount Washington, I hit the brakes at the usual place, about three blocks below the retreat, to slow the truck. Here I would shift into low for the steep grade ahead. To my amazement, the brake pedal literally collapsed to the floor.

At first I couldn't believe my situation. The grade for the next eight blocks was near 20 percent with a cliff at the end and a sharp right turn to make. In seconds the truck was over the brim of the hill and picking up speed like a runaway locomotive.

I looked at Bugs and said, "I have no brakes, the brakes have gone out!"

I watched Bugs turn just about every color of the rainbow, finally ending up a dull green.

"What! No brakes!" screamed Bugs.

He had the door open and was going to jump out, but the truck was already moving at least forty miles an hour. Bugs was really scared and I could hardly believe my own dire situation.

I said a prayer, "Oh, Lord, here I come. There's no way out of this one." I thought of ramming into a house or a parked automobile, at the same time realizing I might kill someone else. Better to ride her over the cliff, I reasoned, making sure no one else got hurt. Suddenly I found myself down on the floor under the steering wheel. With my right hand I grabbed the brake pedal and began pumping it for all I was worth. After about twenty or thirty pumps I felt the brakes begin to take hold. I slammed down with all my strength. Meanwhile, the Lord must have been steering the truck, because Bugs was frozen with fright. With one more pump, I heard the tires begin to skid on the pavement. I never looked up until the old Mack came to a stop no more than a hundred feet from the cliff. I broke into a cold sweat and again thanked my unseen *Companions* for saving us. Bugs was so scared he couldn't talk. He opened the door in a state of shock and got out and stood looking at me. The engine was running and the brakes were holding. I calmed myself down and said, "Come on, Bugs, let's go do our job."

"What!" screamed Bugs, "I will never get in that truck again!" Quickly he turned and started running back to Mount Washington. I tested the brakes a couple of times and they were working. I shifted the Mack into low-under, turned the corner, and went on down to the bottom of the hill. I stopped at the service station where I purchased some gas. A mechanic there went over the entire brake system with me; neither of us ever did find out why those brakes failed. There was absolutely nothing wrong with them. The brakes, as far as I know, never did fail again on that truck — a mystery and a terrifying experience! The greatest part of it all was the fact that the *Companions* were able to take control of my body and make it do what I hadn't even thought of doing myself.

When I got home with the lumber that afternoon, everybody at the retreat had already heard the story from Bugs Butler. The next time I saw Yogananda he looked at me and said, "You had quite a ride, didn't you?"

I replied, "Yes sir, I sure did."

"God was with you wasn't he?"

"Yes sir, he surely was."

It was the end of the summer of 1949 when I received a call from Yogananda to come to his quarters. When I arrived he looked at me with a big smile. "How is my 'giant' doing?"

"Fine, sir," I replied.

"That's good, that's good. Listen, I am taking you on a trip with me." He laughed, "You know, I have to have my 'bodyguard' with me."

Yogananda always referred to me as his "giant" or "bodyguard." I am sure he didn't need one, for he had the power to care for his body. He often enjoyed reliving times in the past with me.

— The Author

"Yes sir," I said with enthusiasm.

"Well, well," he continued, "what do you think! You are going to drive me to San Francisco and then we are going to visit Prime Minister Jawaharlal Nehru of India." I was at a loss for words, I was so elated.

"Here, Big Boy, is two hundred dollars; I want you to go to town and purchase a dark blue dress suit, an overcoat, and also some new shoes. Do you understand? It must be done quickly."

"Yes sir, I understand."

"All right, then." He shoved the roll of bills into my shirt pocket, and gave me a big smile. "Now hurry."

"Yes sir, I will."

The next day I caught the streetcar headed for downtown Los Angeles. I decided to buy used clothes to try and save some of the money. In one used clothing shop I found a camel's hair and llama's wool overcoat. They wanted sixty dollars for it. I offered them forty and bought the coat. I then tried looking for a suit. Always when the coat was big enough for me the pants were too large in the waist. I finally went into an old tailor shop; the tailor must have been in his seventies. I described my problem to him.

He looked at me for several moments then said, "You know, I think I have your suit made to order. There was a tall man in here about two years ago. He wanted a tailor-made suit, which I made for him, but he never came back to get it." The old fellow went through about fifty suits that were hanging up in the shop. "Here it is! Yes, here it is." I slipped on the coat, and it seemed to fit perfectly. "Well, well, what do you know," mumbled the tailor. "Here, now go try on the pants." The pants were a good fit, except they needed about an inch added onto the cuff. "Oh, I can fix that in a jiffy," said the tailor.

"How much do you want for the suit?" I asked.

The old man thought a moment, then looked up quickly. "Let you have it for fifty dollars, and I will fix the cuffs, too."

"It's a deal," I said.

An hour later I was suited up, overcoat and all. The only thing left to get was a couple of white dress shirts, maybe two ties, and a pair of shoes. I decided, in getting such a good deal on the suit and overcoat, I could afford a good pair of shoes, so I ended up buying a pair of Florsheims. Well, I put on the new white shirt with dark blue tie, my suit and new shoes, my overcoat over one arm, and headed for home. I thought it was some fun. I had never been dressed up like this before, and I hadn't even worn a tie since grammar school.

As I climbed the hill to the retreat, I thought how wonderful it was that the Spirit had led me to just the right places. I had found just what I needed and had eighty dollars left over. The next day word came down from Yogananda to get his car serviced and polished. I drove down to the gas station at the foot of the hill, lubricated and washed the car, and then waxed it. That evening a note came from Yogananda: "We will be leaving tomorrow. Have everything ready to go."

Finally the hour arrived, and Yogananda came down in the elevator with several disciples. One of them was Virginia Wright, his regular chauffeur. "Big Boy, you drive," said Yogananda. "I would like to take the coastal route toward San Francisco so we can see the ocean."

As we passed through Santa Barbara, I heard Paramhansaji say "I have always wanted to see a center here, but it has just never happened." Suddenly he shouted from the back seat, "Big Boy, you were born here, weren't you? Such a beautiful place this is here by the sea."

"Yes sir," I replied.

Our destination was Oakland. We made good time and arrived in the city about four o'clock in the afternoon. Reservations had been made for a suite of rooms in one of the larger hotels. Prime Minister Nehru was going to give a speech in San Francisco the next evening. Following the speech, Yogananda was to visit him at his hotel suite.

Yogananda kept me busy running errands for him the evening we arrived and all the next day. That evening we heard Prime Minister Nehru speak. He spoke of India's great need for Western technology and the shortages of food due to antiquated methods of farming. After the speech we went to Nehru's hotel suite. Prime Minister Nehru already knew of Yogananda and his work in this country. We were all introduced and Mr. Nehru reached out and took my hand. I felt the energy of a strong spiritual being. Yogananda and the Prime Minister excused themselves and walked off toward a sitting room for a private conversation. Soon they were back. We then said our goodbyes to each other, with Yogananda inviting Prime Minister Nehru to visit Mount Washington and his organization. We arrived back at the hotel at about eleven o'clock. Yogananda was in the best of spirits as he said his goodnight to me in the hall.

"You have to meditate deeply tonight and God will come to you strongly."

I sat up in the lotus position on the bed, my legs covered with the sheet and blanket, and a pillow beneath me. I was concentrating deeply. I sensed that Divine Spirit was going to reveal something to me. Going very deep in meditation after performing *Kriya Yoga*, I became aware of a circular room.

I was sitting in its exact center under a golden dome. Still in lotus posture, I felt my body rise from the floor about six feet. My body then

I sat on my bed in lotus posture. My room was dimly lit by two shaded lamps. Lifting my gaze, I noticed that the ceiling was dotted with small mustard-colored lights, scintillating and quivering with a radium-

turned upside down and I began to spin with the life forces moving up and down my spine. I was in ecstasy. It seemed my head was just inches above the floor. When I again became aware of the hotel room, it was early morning and I was still sitting in lotus posture. Some of the bed covers were laying in various areas of the room. The pillow which I had been sitting on was also on the floor. I felt ecstatic waves of energy moving in my body from the crown of my head down to the end of my spine. Had I really levitated upside down? How could all the bed covers have gotten into such a mess around the room? I had to accept the fact that I had felt the forces which render the body weightless. Having experienced levitation since then, I must conclude this was my first experience in weightlessness. I now knew there are two forces: one that rises through the base of the spine and one that descends through the crown of the head.

like luster. Myriads of penciled rays, like sheets of rain, gathered into a transparent shaft and poured silently upon me.

At once my physical body lost its grossness and became metamorphosed into astral texture. I felt a floating sensation, as barely touching the bed, the weightless body shifted slightly and alternately to left and right. I looked around the room; the furniture and walls were as usual, but the little mass of light had so multiplied that the ceiling was invisible. I was wonder-struck: "This is the cosmic motion-picture mechanism." A Voice spoke as though from within the light while shedding its beam on the white screen of my bed sheets. "Behold it is producing the picture of your body, your form is nothing but light!"

— Paramhansa Yogananda,
Autobiography of a Yogi

The next day Yogananda looked at me and said, "I told you God would come to you." I wanted to ask him if I had really levitated, but I decided to let it wait. It really didn't matter anyway.

Such is the sweetness of deep delight of these touches of God, that one of them is more than a recompense for all the sufferings of this life, however great their number.

— St. John of the Cross,
Ascent of Mount Carmel

As if in a dream, I finally succeeded in loading all of the luggage back into the car. By eleven o'clock we were on our way home.

Yogananda loved to shop in strange places. Every fruit and vegetable stand might have something new. We finally reached Pismo Beach, a favorite shopping place of his. Here we spent several hours going through different shops with him. He loved to buy gifts for people, and this he did constantly.

We reached Mount Washington about twelve o'clock that night. I was really tired as I moved the last of the luggage up to the third floor, but I was so grateful for such an experience as this had been. For me, these were days of high devotion and love. Little did I know what lay ahead. All I could think of now was Paramhansa Yogananda and the Mother-Father-Creator-Spirit.

In front of the monastery at Mount Washington. *Left to right:* James Baldwin, Daniel Boone, Leo Cocks, Roy Eugene Davis, Ralph Mueller, the author.

"Big Boy, jump in and lift it back up!"

CHAPTER 14

The Restaurant and the Lake Shrine

It was in the summer of 1949 that I began to experience visions in my meditations. I would suddenly find myself in the midst of young people singing together. As I listened to the beautiful lyrics and melodies, I realized I was hearing sounds and seeing people I had thought never to see or hear from again. But here they were, and I was in their midst. Then the music and singing would fade away, as would their familiar faces and forms. I would find myself back in my room trying to remember how to practice my meditation technique.

One afternoon Boone and I were returning from a shopping trip. As we walked up the steep hill towards the monastery, Boone said, "You know, Norm, I saw a gigantic spaceship over Mount Washington one night when I was out for a walk. It was back in 1947."

"You did? What did it look like?"

"Well, it looked like an elongated sphere, round on the top and flatter on the bottom. As I watched it, I saw rays of bright purple light emanating downward from each end. It was right over the monastery. I could also see other lights on the upper side that could have been windows."

If I should be asked — What is the exact nature of this mood, of this illuminant splendor, of which you speak? I should have to reply that I can give no answer. All I can say is that there seems to be a vision possible to man, as from some more universal standpoint, free from the obscurity and localism which specially connect themselves with the passing clouds of desire, fear, and all ordinary thought and emotion; in that sense another and separate faculty; and a vision always means a sense of light, so here is a sense of inward light, unconnected of course with the mortal eye, but bringing to the eye of the mind the impression that it *sees*, and by means of the medium which washes, as it were, the *interior* surfaces of all objects and things and persons — how can I express it? And yet this is most defective, for the sense is a sense that one *is* those objects and things and persons that one perceives — a sense in which sight and touch and hearing are all fused in identity. Nor can the matter be understood without realizing that the whole faculty is deeply and intimately rooted in the ultra-moral and emotional nature, and beyond the thought-region of the brain.

— Edward Carpenter, *Towards Democracy*

129

I was intrigued. "Boone, do you really believe you saw this? Swear to it on Divine Mother's name."

"Yes, it was really there."

"What do you think it was doing there?"

"Well, Norm, I really believe that there are brothers and sisters out there in spaceships, and that they were just looking in on us as they passed by."

At this point I wondered if Daniel was aware of what I had known from childhood.

"Boone," I said, "I believe souls off those vehicles are reincarnating here right now on this planet. You and I will live to see them." My own words confirmed my visions of the singing voices and familiar faces. It all began to fit together. "Did you ever tell anyone about this experience?"

"No, Norm, I knew they wouldn't believe me."

"Why did you think I would?"

Many Biblical passages reveal that the law of reincarnation was understood and accepted. Reincarnational cycles are a more reasonable explanation for the different stages of evolution in which mankind is found, than is the common Western theory which assumes that something came out of nothing, existed with varying degrees of lustihood for thirty or ninety years, and then returned to the original void. The inconceivable nature of such a void is a problem to delight the heart of a medieval Schoolman.

— Paramhansa Yogananda,
Autobiography of a Yogi

"Because I think you know what's going on here."

Gene Roddenberry, the producer-creator of *Star Trek*, has this to say: "I think to say that we are the only creatures in this galaxy is akin to sitting in fourteenth-century Florence and saying the entire universe revolves around us. I think it would probably be the most mathematically incredible happening you could conceive that this is the only place in this great universe where these happenings that we call life occurred."

Dr. Andriga Puharich, who studies psychic phenomena reports: "People immediately get the idea when you talk about spacecraft that they are from our three- or four-dimensional frame of reference. Forget it! Absolutely not! The one conclusion I have about the nature of spacecraft, having watched them all over the world, photographed them, having actually seen them on the ground, is that the one thing they can do is to transform from this dimension to somewhere else. My basic assumption is that what is called the spacecraft is indeed a time machine that can transform from one dimension to another.

"We have very good analogies in modern physics for this. For example, a so-called three-dimensional particle like an electron in a so-called tunnel effect. You see the electron here, and then it appears over there, instantly. This has been measured. This is one of the fundamental laws of quantum mechanics.

"But it's now known theoretically that what happens is that an electron leaves this four-dimensional framework that it's stuck in, slips out into another dimension. And without any time travel from here to there, it goes outside this dimension (therefore, outside the range of observation) and then enters without any observable time — so that we know this process occurs at the quantum level of physics. What freaks physicists out is that it might occur at a macroscopic

level. They're the same people who get freaked out when you show them you can bend metal by thinking about it or that clocks can be repaired by the mind or that teletransportation can occur. But I've seen all these things."
Some speak of a starship that came to this planet 20,000 years ago. The vehicle came to Earth to observe, to study, to enrich the developing species and accelerate the time when their Earth cousins would begin to reach for the stars — and their cosmic home. . . .
As I have traveled about the country gathering research data and lecturing, I have made the acquaintance of a most unique group of individuals who claim either to have memories of having come to this planet from "somewhere else" or to have experienced interaction with paranormal entities — UFO intelligences — since their earliest childhood.

— Brad Steiger, *Gods of Aquarius*

Boone and I never discussed the spaceship again for years. There was too much to be done. Paramhansaji had bought a building on Sunset Boulevard about four blocks from the Hollywood Church. He wanted to move it to the church grounds and make a restaurant out of it, plus have an underground auditorium. What a task it was going to be!

We first had to excavate a gigantic hole and haul away all the soil. We wanted to get the basement walls poured before we moved the building in. As it turned out, we had to move the building over the excavation before we got the footings and walls poured. Here was this five-thousand square foot building sitting precariously on blocks while we were digging footings underneath to support the walls to hold it!

Needless to say, it was a "learn it the hard way" job right from the start. We finally got the footings dug and poured the concrete. Now came the hard part, making double forms for the walls, inside and out. We finally succeeded in building all the forms and setting them. While the walls were being poured, the building shifted on the blocks and gave us quite a scare. Paramhansaji stopped by every other day or so to see how the work was progressing. Finally the day arrived to lower the building down on its new foundations. Yogananda was there watching as we completed the task.

Now came the real work, for we realized the whole building had to be brought up to city code standards. We had to put in extra floor joists and more studs in the walls, beef up the rafters, and rewire the whole building electrically. We all decided, after months of work, it would have been easier to start from scratch with new construction. A new brother named Henry Schaufelberger and I completely plastered the whole interior of the building. We then moved outside to re-stucco the entire exterior. It took us many months of hard work to finish the job.

The restaurant was to be called India House Cafe. It was destined to be a success from the day it opened. Yogananda was there for the official opening, as were many disciples and friends. A banquet was held with Paramhansaji leading a short meditation. One of the features that made the building stand out was the battlements all the way around the roof line, which Yogananda had insisted on. These were battlements such as old castles have. They were difficult to construct and stucco.

It was here that I perfected my carpentry, cement, and plastering trades, all of which would serve me well later on. It was also about the end of 1949 that Yogananda acquired the Lake Shrine property at Pacific Palisades, near Santa Monica, California. It was a beautiful property, sitting in a secluded canyon five blocks from the beach. The lake was approximately one acre.

Needless to say, the property needed a complete renovation in Yogananda's eyes. Several unique buildings were on the site, plus a replica of a Dutch windmill house, a Viking ship and a houseboat anchored in a little cove on one side of the lake. The houseboat sat on steel drums welded together within a steel frame. The builder had welded vent pipes to the drums, and everything was all right as long as the vent pipes remained above water.

Yogananda came with carloads of friends and disciples. He was so thrilled with our newest acquisition of property, he wanted everyone to see it.

"We must all gather in the houseboat for a meditation," he declared.

We all did, at least as many people as sitting room allowed; some were standing outside. Whoever had constructed the houseboat, however, had not planned on taking one hundred people aboard at one time. Without knowing it, we had added over three or four tons of weight. We were all sitting on the floor in the dark listening to a prayer when the water started coming over the deck and under the doors in a flood. Yogananda excitedly shouted, "Everybody, quick! Quick! Off the boat!"

The vent pipes had been under water and the tanks had slowly filled up. The houseboat was on its way down to the bottom. I thought it was the funniest thing I had ever seen until Paramhansaji called me.

"Big Boy, jump in and lift it back up!"

I had no choice but to jump into the lake and try to lift up the houseboat. Surely he was joking — or was he? I never found out. I couldn't budge it, of course.

"No way, sir," I yelled. "It's too heavy."

"Well, all right, you can get it back up tomorrow."

"Yes sir," I replied.

It literally took us about three weeks of hard work to refloat the houseboat. I will never forget that episode, it was so funny. Some of the older ladies screamed as the water came gushing across the floor, eager to dampen the whole affair.

One day, while working on the houseboat, I sat down on a bench to meditate after lunch. With eyes closed, I was praying deeply to Divine Spirit. For a moment, two very physical hands held both sides of my face as if in a blessing. I opened my eyes to see who it was and there was no one in sight anywhere.

Yogananda wanted the whole Lake Shrine landscaped. He somehow found out that a whole row of palm trees was being taken down on some street in Los Angeles.

"Big Boy," the note said, "you must go pick up these palm trees right away. Bring them out to the Lake Shrine and plant them."

I went and took a look at the palm trees. Each one weighed at least two tons. I had to rent a twenty-foot pull trailer for the Mack truck. Luckily, the Mack had a winch on it that I had previously installed. I backed the trailer up to the root end of the trees; using skids I winched them onto the trailer. I moved twelve palm trees in this manner. Loading was easy, but getting them to where Yogananda wanted them planted was where the real work started.

Once, when we actually had one big tree planted and wired into position, Paramhansaji looked at it and said, "Move it about ten feet to the left." I just about lost it, but I gritted my teeth and moved the tree, realizing Paramhansaji was trying to teach us self-control. While all the landscaping was going on, we were also constructing large lotus towers for an outdoor amphitheater. It was here that Yogananda was going to hold the opening dedication for the Lake Shrine, and give regular public lectures.

The day we finished our work and all preparations were completed for the grand opening, Yogananda came for a final inspection of the towers and grounds. He walked toward the far side of the lake along a beautiful path. All of the brothers who had participated in the work were there.

Yogananda suddenly said, "Come on, I am going to baptize you all with water."

We all removed our shoes and socks, rolled up our trousers, and waded out into the lake with Paramhansaji. For each of us, he reached down with cupped hands and poured the water over our heads.

"I baptize you as a Minister in the Order of the Self-Realization Fellowship."

After everyone was baptized, we all sat down for a short prayer and meditation. He was very pleased with everything we had done.

A dear friend of Yogananda's in India had sent him some of Mahatma Gandhi's ashes, which were to be placed in a stone sarcophagus during the opening ceremony. Many city officials and dignitaries were invited to the opening ceremony, including Lieutenant Governor Goodwin J. Knight. All SRF students and their friends were invited, also. The opening was only days away as the last minute preparations were made. Finally the day arrived; the dedication was a complete success, with about fifteen hundred people attending. Paramhansaji was overjoyed with the whole affair. The Lake Shrine was now a functioning center for meditation and spiritual upliftment.

I returned to Mount Washington for the next project. In the meantime, I had saved up enough money to buy myself three hundred pounds of weights; I had missed training with them. The problem was Brother Donald, who complained bitterly about the clanging and banging sounds emanating from my room. I don't think Don ever understood why I wanted to lift weights; it just didn't make any sense to him.

Under both Don's room and mine was a deep concrete pit. The floor joists covered it and, on Don's side, there was a trap door. The deep pit had housed the motor and winch cables that had run the rail cable car used when Mount Washington was a booming resort hotel back in the 1920s. The big problem was that I never knew when Don was down in the pit meditating, as his hours were irregular. It often turned out that I unknowingly started working out just when Don was below me trying to meditate.

I would hear a banging underneath me and then Don shouting, "Will you please stop all that racket up there? I am trying to meditate."

Don and I never did find a solution to the problem.

Yogananda knew that Don, who had been editing some SRF lessons, needed more physical exercise, so he assigned Don to help me for two or three hours a day in the yard. One day there was a note: "Big Boy, I want all the brush and weeds hoed off the driveway all the way down the mountain to the lower end of the property."

I started to work on it; it was a big job. I had almost finished when Don showed up to help. It was about two o'clock in the afternoon and I was just loading the pickup with the last bit of trash and brush. Don helped me finish loading.

"Don, I'm going to take this to the dump; you keep hoeing down the weeds."

There was about fifty feet to go. I no sooner got to the dump up above when Paramhansaji's car came up the hill. He stopped and picked up Don. As his car reached the basement entrance I walked up in a hurry, that I might get to see him. Don got out of the car along with Yogananda.

"My, my, you should see the wonderful job Walter has done on the driveway." (Yogananda always referred to Don as Walter.)

"Yes sir," I replied. "It does look pretty good, doesn't it?"

I thought, "Doesn't he know I did the job?" Don had just started hoeing, and I had been working for several hours.

Don tried to reply as Yogananda walked away, but he was unable to clarify the credit. I wrote that one down in my memory, because who was I doing all this work for? Well, I was doing it for Paramhansaji, that I might help him, yes; but actually I was working for Divine Spirit Mother and Father. Surely they knew who had done the job. Letting someone else have credit for the work I had done should not have bothered me. I wouldn't let that happen again in the future. I decided it was a good lesson.

Construction of the India House Cafe. Here we are moving the old building onto its new foundation. *Back row, left to right:* B. Brown, the author, H. Kimball and J. Torgensen (holding hat). *Middle row:* L. Cocks, D. Smith, Rev. Bernard, J. Haupt, R.E. Davis and A. Anderson. *Front row:* D. Boone, R. Mueller, D. Mukherjee, unidentified, D. Walters, A. Jacot, C. Jacot, J. Carbone and H. Schaufelberger.

Lotus Tower at Lake Shrine with the houseboat in the background

India House Cafe

137

"How are you doing, Big Boy?"

CHAPTER 15

Vision of the Future

I received the *Kriya Yoga* meditation technique from Yogananda shortly after moving to Mount Washington in 1947. One day Boone and I were discussing the merits of *Kriya Yoga* versus other techniques of meditation. Boone mentioned *Kechari Mudra*, "the king of all yogic mudras."

"What is *Kechari Mudra*, Boone?"

Kriya Yoga is a psychophysical exercise combining breath with life force to bring all energies to the center of consciousness in the physical body, the spiritual eye or soul center. With all energies concentrated at the center, true vision of the Divine Being is experienced.

Yogic mudras are physical positions used to obtain maximum effects in meditation on the one Consciousness Divine.

— The Author

"Well, it has to do with the tongue and a unique position which the tongue assumes."

Boone began to explain how the life force is drawn up through the nerve centers of the spine toward the higher centers of the brain. He then went on to describe the pituitary gland and the pineal gland and their functions.

All energies proceed from the one source Divine. If all energies are returned to the source and enter therein, the Divine is beheld.

— The Author

Finally he opened his mouth and said, "Do you see the soft palate which hangs down from the roof of the mouth?"

"Yes, I see it."

"Well, the trick is to pass the tongue backwards until it slips behind the soft palate. You then push the tongue upward until it slips behind the nasopharynx. You should be able to close off either nostril with the tongue from the inside. Pushing on up with the tip of the tongue, you

It can be noted that serious physical accidents will induce shock in victims, who will then proceed to unconsciously try to swallow their tongue. It would seem that the

139

will reach a bone protrusion that is just under the pituitary gland. The force which is rising upward flows off the end of the tongue, like flames under a pot. It is here that the final connection is made. By exciting the pituitary gland, the pineal gland begins to vibrate, and the two forces are magnetically drawn to unite in the region of the spiritual eye. Therefore, *Kechari Mudra* works like an excitation current to arouse other forces in the body to join at the center of consciousness."

I decided to try it. I pushed my tongue upwards and backwards until I felt the tip of my tongue touching the soft palate. Pushing on, my tongue slipped behind the soft palate. Then moving the tongue upward, I could feel the nasopharynx and the inner side of the nostrils with the tip of my tongue. I pushed beyond the nostrils and came up to the bone protrusion Daniel had described. It was true! I immediately felt a very deep consciousness pervading my mind; with closed eyes spectral lights flared around me. Daniel found it hard to believe I had accomplished this very difficult mudra on my first try, so I demonstrated the fact. I began to practice *Kriya Yoga* with my tongue in this unique position experiencing tremendous results.

One day a message came: "Paramhansaji wants to see you." I climbed the stairs to the third floor and went toward Yogananda's room. I found him in the kitchen.

"Big Boy, what have you been doing?"

"Working on the tennis courts, sir."

"Well, come in a minute. I hear you are doing *Kriya* differently these days."

"Well, yes sir, I am."

"Can you swallow your tongue?"

"Yes sir, I can."

"Show me." Paramhansaji picked up a flashlight and I performed the mudra. He backed up a step. "My Lord!" he exclaimed. "You don't know how blessed you are. Do you practice *Kriya* with your tongue upward?"

"Yes sir, I do."

---

tongue tries to assume this position as a natural process when death is imminent.

— The Author

The spiritual eye is the vision of the soul, the center of consciousness within the physical body. The seat of consciousness resides directly between the temples and at the root of the nose. It is from this vantage point that other dimensions are beheld while still residing in the physical body. Consciousness is the only beholder of images, therefore the center of consciousness is the eye. "If thine eye be single thy whole body is filled with light." (Matthew 6:22.)

— The Author

"You have been an adept in the past, this is why your karma has allowed you to perform the king of mudras. Go now, and keep up with your meditations. Wonderful experiences will come to you."

Yogananda told me many other things on this occasion that he asked me to keep private in my heart. I assured him that I would. My soul felt an immense gratitude to him and to Divine Spirit Mother and Father that I had been blessed to have received these divine insights. I knew well that many seek the intellectual stimulus of divine truths but are unwilling to make the necessary effort to put them into practice. I realized how fortunate I was to have a deep desire to meditate. I had seen so many come and go on the spiritual path simply because they lacked the perseverance or desire to make meditation more than a superficial habit.

Yogananda was correct in his predictions. After performing twenty or thirty *Kriyas* with *Kechari Mudra*, I would find myself in a deep, deep illumined state of consciousness. One particular Sunday, after church, I decided I was going to meditate all night, if possible. As I sat down in my meditation closet, a flaring of light suddenly encircled me. It was so vivid, I couldn't tell if I had seen it physically or inner-dimensionally. It was about six o'clock in the evening. After performing a few more *Kriyas*, I suddenly found myself transported into a circular room again. There were brothers and sisters there whom I immediately recognized from previous visions.

I was moved to look out of a large portal. There were the rooftops of the city of Los Angeles. We were moving over them. Shortly, I saw the Lake Shrine below. No one had said a word. Silently we went higher and higher. Now I could see the coastline of California all the way up to Santa Barbara. It was here I saw many familiar faces standing around an old ranch house waving. As we moved back toward the coast, I again saw more familiar faces standing around a small lake on top of the coastal mountain range.

Suddenly a voice boomed out, *"Here's where your work will begin; with young people such as you now behold."*

A flash of light exploded around me; I opened my eyes to the four walls of my meditation closet.

As time went by, I experienced similar visions. On one occasion, I saw young people farming with horses; on another, I was made to understand that many of the brothers and sisters were now incarnating, such as I had.

"They will ask thee of the Spirit. Say, 'The Spirit comes at the bidding of my Lord, and ye are given but a little knowledge thereof.' " (Mohammed.) Mohammed speaks of "The Spirit" — the Cosmic Sense — and uses almost the same words as Jesus: "The wind bloweth where it listeth, and thou hearest the voice thereof, but knowest not whence it cometh and whither it goeth: so is everyone that is born of the Spirit." (John 3:8.)

— Richard Bucke,
Cosmic Consciousness

As I gained deeper awareness and control in my meditations, I was able to connect the energies of past and future events into a physical present discerning the actual truth. I knew now that in the future these visions would become physical realities in the Santa Barbara area and elsewhere. We are indeed only one breath away in our physical bodies from the vast inner spaces of creation — dimensions where suns shine, and astral planets glide in orbits, some with beauty beyond description.

> There be some here present who shall enter into Cosmic Consciousness. To a man with Cosmic Consciousness it seems so simple and certain that others will enter it. "I bestow upon any man or woman (says Whitman) the entrance to all the gifts of the universe."
>
> — Richard Bucke, *Cosmic Consciousness*

In my conscious moments during the day, I was faced with the images of this world. The worlds of inner space seemed far away. What I really desired was more confirmation because doubts plagued me. How could I ever accomplish all that I saw others, including myself, doing in these visions? I had to be patient; I had to wait. And wait I did, for almost twenty years.

During his lifetime Paramhansaji created the monastic Self-Realization Fellowship order, a branch of the ancient order of monasticism founded by Swami Shankara. He also envisioned world brotherhood colonies where married couples and children could live in a spiritual environment based on the ideals of "plain living and high thinking." He knew that there would always be those householder disciples who would desire a more spiritually oriented way of life than is usually possible in ordinary society, one in which every aspect of daily living is

> "I will give unto thee the keys of the kingdom of heaven; and whatsoever thou shalt bind on earth shall be bound in heaven and whatsoever thou shalt loose on earth shall be loosed in heaven." (Matthew 16:19.) The Cosmic Sense is the final arbiter of good and ill. Jesus seems to have looked forward to the establishment of a school or sect, the members of which should possess the Cosmic Sense.
>
> — Richard Bucke, *Cosmic Consciousness*

harmoniously integrated and directed towards God-realization. Originally he intended that Encinitas be the first self-sustaining world brotherhood colony, but as time went by it became apparent that the Divine Spirit had other plans there. Yet he knew that the seed had been planted and that one day it would bear fruit.

Paramhansaji had to deal with an older generation of people, those whom he referred to at times as "psychological antiques." Even my generation, born in the late 1920s and early 1930s, expressed little desire to pursue God-realization, certainly not enough to give up worldly desires long enough to conduct a search for the Divine. The generation of people who could possibly live together peacefully in brotherhood colonies was born beginning in the early 1940s and thereafter. They are here now and the time is right. Paramhansaji saw it coming. He saw the necessity, but lacked the people. However, his dream of men, women, and children living together in brotherhood colonies is visible on this planet today. Many communities have materialized all over the world almost twenty years after Yogananda's passing.

Paramhansaji began to spend much of his time writing at the desert retreat. Don Walters and I were called out there to build a swimming pool at the retreat house for the brothers' and sisters' recreation. The digging was terribly hard. After digging down through layers of decomposed granite, we hit hardpan, a form of clay that has been hardened by temperatures and pressures. It was the surface mud of an ancient dry lake. Pointed steel digging bars were the only thing that would cut through it. Don and I worked on that excavation in the hot desert sun for weeks. The one good thing about the horribly difficult task was that Yogananda came out to watch, with cold drinks and conversations about God-realization, just about every day.

When we finally finished the digging, we had to construct wooden forms to support the concrete walls. Instead of bringing in ready-mixed concrete, which would have done the job in an hour, Paramhansaji wanted to do it by hand and save a few dollars. Actually, I think he just wanted to watch us sweat and work harder.

I went to Twenty-Nine Palms and rented a cement mixer, ordered sand, gravel, and cement, and had them delivered to the house. The next morning about six o'clock, we began. Bernard was there, along with Daniel, Don, myself, and some other brothers. We finished the pour sixteen hours later. I don't think I have ever been so tired in all my life as I was that night. Two days later we stripped off the forms to our satisfaction. Next, we put a band of colored tile around the inside edges. Then we gave it a cream-colored stucco job to match the house. It was beautiful, we thought.

The job completed, the day finally arrived to fill the pool. Paramhansaji was delighted. He got in and swam around and then invited us all in for a swim. We ended the day with a short meditation together. As the job was finished, we then returned to Mount Washington where two more projects awaited our attention.

Christmas dinner and meditation. *Left to right:* Mr. Swenson, James J. Lynn, Rev. Bernard, Paramhansaji, and Dr. Lewis.

CHAPTER 16

Christmas Meditation 1949

On my return to Mount Washington, I found a letter waiting for me from Dad. "Son, Dorothy and I will be spending Christmas in Los Angeles this year with Betty and Lou." Betty was Dorothy's sister. "I want to make a visit to Mount Washington while there, and perhaps you could arrange for me to have a few words with Paramhansa Yogananda. Also, my boy, it's been a long time since your old dad has been with you." I suddenly realized how quickly the years had gone by.

Living a restricted monk's life, my travels had been limited to business for the organization only. Dad and I had corresponded once a month by mail, and also by telephone. Christmas wasn't far off. It was traditional at Mount Washington to have an all-day meditation, extending into Christmas Eve. The following day we all had a big Christmas dinner together. Paramhansaji usually spent the whole day with us and part of the evening. Everyone had an opportunity to speak with him. Since I knew Dad wanted to meet Yogananda, I wrote a note to him asking if Dad could see him when he came. The reply was, "Yes, I want to meet your father."

Christmas meditation at Mount Washington was looked forward to with great expectations by all brothers and sisters. This event in which Yogananda participated increased the zeal and desire to experience a spiritual visitation. Many had visions of Christ Jesus and other ancient spirits. Everyone who persevered through the long hours of meditation in some way received something illuminating from Divine Spirit.

— The Author

During all these years John Winship would occasionally drive up to see me. One Sunday John attended a talk by Yogananda at the Hollywood Church. He didn't seem greatly impressed at all. On the way home he remarked, "You know, the only change I see in you after being up here with the yogi all this time is

"If any man thinketh he is wise among you in this world, let him become a fool, that he may become wise. For the wisdom of this

145

that your eyes have gotten bigger and brighter."

I thought to myself, "John, are you never going to see beyond the physical, delusive crust of this dimension?" Instead I replied, "I hadn't really noticed it myself."

world is foolishness with God." (I Corinthians 3:18-19.) Paul says that the wisdom of self-consciousness is not wisdom to those who have the Cosmic Sense, and the wisdom of the latter is foolishness to the merely self-conscious.

— Richard Bucke, *Cosmic Consciousness*

"Do you suppose if I lived this kind of yogi life my eyes might get bigger and brighter?"

"Yes, John, no doubt about it."

"Well, maybe I will try it for a while."

"It isn't that easy, John. Yogananda has to accept you before you can live here."

I let the issue drop. I knew John wasn't interested in the primary objective of God-realization. However, two weeks later he came up again saying, "I have decided I would really like to try out this way of life."

I spoke to Paramhansaji about it at the next opportunity I had.

His reply was, "He won't stay two months, I can see it right now. However, let's allow him to plant some good karmic seeds for himself by being here as long as he can."

The karmic law requires that every human wish find ultimate fulfillment. Nonspiritual desires are thus the chain that binds man to the reincarnational wheel.

— Paramhansa Yogananda, *Autobiography of a Yogi*

John showed up one sunny day in the summer; he had his seabag with him. The first thing that bothered John was the meatless diet. The next thing he found out was that he had lost weight; salads and vegetables were not enough for John. He really tried hard to meditate, and as he lost some more weight, his eyes did get bigger and brighter. This encouraged him to continue his stay.

Finally, after about three months, he approached me. "I'm getting out of here before I die of starvation. You might be able to exist on that rabbit food, but not me. Hell, Norm, I've lost twenty pounds! I'm beginning to look like the original Mahatma Gandhi!" John had his seabag over his shoulder and was saying, "See you later," as he climbed into his car.

December 24, 1949 arrived. Everyone was preparing for the all-day meditation. The meditation usually began around ten o'clock in the morning and ended in the early evening, with a few breaks during the day. At times Yogananda received direct messages from the Spirit for certain individuals. There were hours of silence. For some it was a blessing and for others it was a great ordeal to sit that long. That evening Paramhansaji sat and talked a while after the meditation. It was during the Christmas meditation that I again saw, very clearly, communities of people in the Santa Barbara area. Again I saw those familiar faces. The foundation energy was growing stronger. I knew that one day I must leave Mount Washington and return to Santa Barbara, for this was my destiny. The foundation of some brotherhood colonies would start here. But how, was the question. I had no idea; I must receive guidance along with these visions.

A brotherhood colony must contain men, women, and children; it must evolve into a total, self-sustaining operation. To accomplish this, every facet of man's needs must be looked at carefully. If indeed Christ is all things to all men, then the foundation must contain a vibration to which every man and woman can relate. All the crafts necessary to man's existence must be produced in the community; first, good, naturally-grown vegetables, bees for honey, animal husbandry for meat and dairy products, leather and wool for handmade shoes and clothing. The formation of seed-energy began to grow around the mental images. The die was cast. Now I must walk the road ahead.

A fitly born and bred race, growing up in right conditions of outdoor as much as indoor harmony, activity and development, would probably, from and in those conditions, find it enough merely to live — and would, in their relations to the sky, air, water, trees, etc., and to the countless common shows, and in the fact of life itself, discover and achieve happiness — with Being suffused night and day by wholesome ecstasy, surpassing all the pleasures that wealth, amusement, and even gratified intellect, erudition, or the sense of art, can give.

— Walt Whitman

This passage from Whitman seems prophetic of the coming Christ-Conscious race on earth.

— The Author

Dad and Dorothy arrived about five o'clock in the afternoon on Christmas day. The hall was crowded with disciples and guests. Dad and I edged our way through the crowd to Yogananda. I introduced them and they held hands for a long time, reading each other's thought-forms and energies.

Dad finally said, "That's fine," out loud. "You know, I love the boy very much." They sat down and had a short conversation about spiritual matters and Dad's blindness. Dad seemed pleased afterwards, and though I felt he wanted me to be with him, he was not about to try to talk me into leaving Yogananda. When Dad and Dorothy left for Santa Barbara, Dad gave me a big hug and said, "I wish I could be here with you, Son, but of course that's impossible. There is room for you whenever you come for a visit." I watched Dad's old Chevrolet panel truck disappear into the darkness.

"Yes, Dad," I said silently, "we have always been together, and we always will be."

Daniel was always on the lookout for psychic people. He had somehow heard of a woman who lived in Hollywood who called herself "Mother Mary." Boone found out her address and phone number, then succeeded in reaching her by phone. Mother Mary invited Daniel to come and visit her. "Why don't you come with me, Norm?" he asked.

I thought it over for a moment and felt that I should go. I knew this woman might have a message for me. "Sure, Daniel, I'll go with you," I replied.

Boone and I caught a bus to Mother Mary's on Saturday morning. Arriving in Hollywood, we walked to the street address and finally stood in front of Mother Mary's door. A young man answered our knock, and we were invited in. Mother Mary greeted us in her living room; she was a rather short, heavy-set woman in her late fifties. We introduced ourselves and informed her that we were students of Yogananda. Immediately she and Daniel got into a very deep discussion on spiritual psychic experiences. Daniel began to describe his own unique visions. At this particular time, I had been experiencing pressure on the crown of my head, and also in the middle of my forehead just above the root of the nose. Mother Mary suddenly looked up at me and stated, "They are opening your higher centers. Are you feeling sensations about your head?"

Startled by her intuitive statement, I replied, "Yes."

"Please don't worry about it, Norman," she said. "You are indeed fortunate. I suspect you have a great spiritual work to do eventually."

At the time of our visit, Mother Mary was purchasing an old hotel at the foot of Mount Shasta in the town of Mount Shasta, California. She was going to move there and open up a spiritual center. A few weeks after our first visit with Mother Mary, Daniel wanted to go and see her again.

"Norm, Mother Mary is all packed and ready to move. Let's go see her once more before she moves to Mount Shasta."

I consented, and once more we were at her front door. This time we had some deep discussions with her. Mother Mary believed that at one time there was a large continent existing where part of the South Pacific Ocean now lies. She said that many thousands of years ago, the earth suffered a violent cataclysm. This cataclysm gave birth to the great biblical flood which destroyed all of earth's then existing civilizations.

What initiated this great cataclysm remains a mystery to this day. Many ancient records state that there were great and small wars fought between two civilizations co-existing on earth millenniums ago that triggered it.

Many ancient pictographic writings and legends describe the great wars fought between the gods who came down to earth from the heavens and created men.

...alien astronauts lived on our planet thousands of years ago and our ancestors looked upon them as "gods." They dictated the whole truth to earthly scribes and commanded them to hang on to this truth unadulterated to future generations. The human failing of "knowing better" distorted the truth. Religions came into being. Knowledge and truth were replaced by belief. The great majority of mankind still believes in a truth that is no truth. That is why I take the minor liberty of trying, with my theories and speculations, with the results of my researches, and with my awkward questions, to bore through the blinders which, forgive my saying so, most of us are still wearing.

If god or gods were "believed" to be natural phenomena (and depicted as such), then our naive ancestor cannot have accepted the idea that he was God's image. We have no reason to believe that those ancestors of ours who thousands of years ago wrote down either what they had experienced or what they had been told were weak in the head. It is a fact, and no one will dispute it, that mankind's oldest myths and legends tell us about gods flying in the sky. It is a fact that all the stories of creation assert, with variations, that man was created by gods from the cosmos, after they had come down to earth from heaven. The creation was not a homemade affair.

— Erich von Däniken, *In Search of Ancient Gods*

These writings and legends have been found existing among all the earth's ancient peoples. Mother Mary said that part of the California coast west of the San Andreas Fault was, at one time, a part of the ancient civilization called Mu, or Lemuria. Mother Mary believed that some survivors of this great cataclysm which destroyed Mu had found refuge in and around Mount Shasta and the offshore islands of southern California. Many years later I was to discover strong evidence supporting Mother Mary's claims and beliefs.

As it was time for us to leave, Mother Mary invited us to visit her at Mount Shasta sometime, and we both consented to do so. Years later, Mother Mary was to help me raise a particular force involving the two nerve currents that intertwine the spine. These nerve currents are known to Eastern yogic teachers as the *ida* and the *pingala* currents.

Paramhansaji as I like to remember him, in his overcoat; at the Hermitage
in Encinitas, California.

CHAPTER 17

A Goodbye Call from Yogananda

One day in August 1950, a note was delivered to me from Paramhansaji. "Come to the third floor right away; we must talk." I climbed the stairs and knocked on his door. "How is my giant doing?"

"Pretty good, sir."

"Listen, I have a surprise for you. I am planning a trip to India and I want you to come with me." His words sent shock waves through my consciousness — a trip to India! "Well, what do you say, Big Boy? Do you want to go?"

"Yes sir, I sure do."

"All right, now you must not tell anyone about this. We must keep it a secret until I tell you."

"Yes sir."

"Good, you must go today without fail and apply for your passport. Also, here is the address in India where we will be staying. This you will need to fill out the forms. You will be traveling as a minister of the Self-Realization Fellowship. This must be written on the passport." Yogananda handed me a slip of paper. "Here is the street address in Los Angeles where you must go."

I was able to complete everything that day, and the passport was issued on August 23, 1950. I received it in the mail a few days later. One day, a week later, I saw Paramhansaji as he drove into Mount Washington; he took me aside to talk to me. "I have purchased the steamship tickets. Are you packed? Have you your passport?"

"Yes sir, I am ready."

"Well, that's good, that's good." he replied.

I noticed a vibration from him at that moment which I interpreted as: "There is a possibility I won't be able to go to India."

One evening a few nights later one of the sisters called me. "Paramhansaji wants you right away."

When I arrived in the basement, he was standing in front of the elevator. "Big Boy, the elevator is broken." He stopped talking and turned. The basement was filling up with disciples, as was the usual occurrence whenever Yogananda was going out or coming in; everyone wanted to see him for a moment if they could.

Paramhansaji asked that everyone leave the basement and then turning to me, he said, "I am working out the karma of many souls; some things have to be paid for physically. My legs will not carry me up the stairs. . . . Can you carry me up to the third floor?"

"Yes sir, I can."

He looked around to make sure everyone was gone. Satisfied we were alone, he climbed on my back. I wrapped my hands around his legs and stood up.

"You will have to open the doors, sir."

The stairway went up and around the elevator shaft, and at every floor there was a door. Paramhansaji weighed, I judged, about one hundred and seventy-five pounds. We started up the stairs, and gained the third floor where I set him down. I knew he was not feeling well at all in his body. I walked with him to his room.

"You are not puffing after coming up all those stairs," he remarked.

"No sir, I'm in pretty good shape."

"Well, be sure and stay that way. You are going to need all the strength you can get before you are through with this life." He then

"If we sowed unto you spiritual things, is it a great matter if we shall reap your carnal things?" (I Corinthians 9:11.) Here Paul states that those of the disciples of Christ who are able to sow upon men and women spiritual energies of baptism, healing, and growth should possibly reap the negative energies of the recipients in the transfer (i.e., carnal things).

The transfer of negative thought-forms, past actions, and desires from one soul to another is a common occurrence between teacher and disciple.

— The Author

The metaphysical method of physical transfer of disease is known to highly advanced yogis. A strong man may assist a weak one by helping the latter to carry a heavy load; a spiritual superman is able to minimize the physical and mental troubles of his disciples by assuming a part of their karmic burdens. Just as a man relinquishes some money when he pays off a large debt for his prodigal son, who is thus saved from the dire consequences of his folly, so a master willingly sacrifices a portion of his bodily health to lighten the misery of disciples. Jesus signified himself as a ransom for the sins of many. With his divine powers, his body could never have been subjected to death by crucifixion if he had not willingly co-operated with the subtle law of cause and effect. He thus took on himself the consequences of others' karma, especially that of his disciples. In this manner they were highly purified and made fit to receive the omnipresent consciousness which later descended on them. Christ said, just before he was led away to be crucified: "Thinkest thou that I cannot now pray to my Father, and he shall presently give me more than twelve legions of angels? But how then shall the scriptures be fulfilled, that thus it must be?" (Matthew 26:53-54.)

— Paramhansa Yogananda, *Autobiography of a Yogi*

152

said, "Good night," and touched me on the forehead.

At this time, Encinitas was growing fresh produce. Once in a while I would drive down and bring back a load of vegetables for Mount Washington. On one occasion when I arrived at Encinitas word was sent to me, "Paramhansaji wants you to help give a demonstration of the postures for a magazine article." Daniel Boone was already there with Bill Brown, Joe Carbone, and a few of the younger male disciples. The photographer took pictures of us in the hermitage and outside on the lawn; hopefully the article would be a good one.

The community at Encinitas was beautiful in 1950; vegetable gardens were everywhere. The little restaurant out in front was doing a fine business. Yogananda's concept of mushroom-burgers was becoming popular with the public. The golden-leafed lotus towers at Encinitas were finished, and they attracted much attention. In 1950 the old hotel on the highway was open to those visiting the Self-Realization Fellowship. The grounds around the hermitage were beautifully landscaped with secret paths and lily ponds full of goldfish. Exotic tropical plants were everywhere. The hermitage sat right on a cliff overlooking the blue Pacific Ocean. There was a thick, green lawn between the hermitage and the cliff's edge. Here we sometimes demonstrated the yogic postures and exercises to visitors.

On one occasion we gave a demonstration for Uday Shankar, a famous Hindu musician and brother of Ravi Shankar. Afterwards Shankar played his famous Hindu sitar for us. Shankar, his wife and family, Amelita Galli-Curci, and W.Y. Evans-Wentz, plus other visitors, were also there on this occasion with Yogananda, when Reverend Bernard, myself, Leo Cocks, Bill Brown, and two other young boys from Encinitas performed the postures.

W.Y. Evans-Wentz, the author of *Tibetan Yoga and the Secret Doctrines*, was a friend of Yogananda's. During his travels through India and Tibet, Evans-Wentz had met Swami Sri Yukteswar, Yogananda's teacher. He, in fact, had included a picture of Sri Yukteswar in his book, taken in front of his ashram at Puri, India. Sri Yukteswar and five other holy men are portrayed as the modern-day gurus, or saints, of India. Evans-Wentz lived south of San Diego, high in the mountains overlooking the California-Mexico border. Yogananda had made several visits to his home in years past.

While staying at Encinitas, Paramhansaji allowed me to sleep in the hermitage library several times. There was never a time when I was near his person that some extraordinary experience in the Spirit didn't occur.

On one particular night, I was sleeping on the floor of the library. Suddenly I was surrounded with a brilliant flash of golden light. As I lay there trying to comprehend the source, another flash occurred. It was incredibly bright, like a bolt of lightning. About that time Paramhansaji stood in the doorway.

"Big Boy, what are you doing?"

"Well sir, I have been seeing these brilliant flashes of golden light. With my eyes opened or closed, I still see the light."

"That's good. 'What lightning flash glimmers in Thy Face, Mother; Seeing Thee I am thrilled through and through!' " Yogananda was quoting one of his cosmic chants. "That's Mother Divine looking at you. Remember that!" He then turned and left the room.

I spent the rest of the night in a half-awake state of meditation. I knew Divine Spirit as Father and Mother Creator were alive and around about me. Oh, how much I loved them and the teacher they had brought me to.

"I must see you face to face, Oh Lord, just as Moses did. Reveal thyself to me," I prayed.

I returned to Mount Washington and began to wonder when the trip to India was going to take place. Paramhansaji had said nothing about it for weeks. Finally one night he called me on the house phone.

"Big Boy, I have sad news: the trip to India is off. The Lord has said, 'No, if you go to India, you won't get back to Mount Washington.' "

"Does this mean, sir, you will never again go to India?"

"Yes," he replied, "I am leaving the body soon."

"You're what!" I felt like I had been struck with a sledge hammer. "You mean, sir, you will be leaving for good?"

"That's right! I have to say so."

He went on to say he did not know exactly when, as I pressed him for an answer. "There are so many loved ones to say goodbye to; I have to start now with you. I am saying goodbye to you now, and when I am gone forth from the body, I will return to see you."

We all felt . . . that the time was fast approaching when Master would leave this world. Master himself hinted as much. To Dr. Lewis he remarked one day, "We have lived a good life together. It seems only yesterday that we met. In a little while we shall be separated, but soon we'll be together again."

— Swami Kriyananda, *The Path*

I felt tears running out of my eyes. "But sir," I pleaded, "if you are leaving, I want to go also."

"No, no, you must stay. You have a work to do on your own."

I reflected on all the visions I had seen concerning Santa Barbara. "In

Santa Barbara, sir? Are the visions I am seeing true?"

"Yes, they are true. You were my giant-friend in the past; you must be again. I must say goodbye to you for now; God and the Elders will help you fulfill your mission."

I heard the phone click down on his final words; whatever the outcome, now I could only wait. Near the end of September 1950, Paramhansaji announced to everyone that he had planned a trip to India, but now it was postponed indefinitely. After that night's talk with him, he never again mentioned anything to me about leaving his body. I began to think I had hallucinated the whole episode but, oh no, it was too real. Maybe he was testing me to see what I would do. I decided not to think about it anymore, and to use my meditations to visualize his staying here with us for a long time.

Paramhansa Yogananda with students at the Encinitas Hermitage

Demonstration on the Hermitage lawn at Encinitas, California. *Left to right:* the author, Daniel Boone, Bill Brown, and Paramhansaji.

Top row, left to right: Uday Shankar, Mother Gloria, Amelita Galli-Curci, her husband, Paramhansaji, Mrs. Shankar, and her son. *Seated in lotus posture left to right:* Rev. Bernard, the author, Leo Cocks, Bill Brown, and Stephen Misner.

He took my right arm to support himself, and we slowly began to walk around the property.

CHAPTER 18

A Period of Trial

It was in early September 1950 that Daniel Boone mentioned to me that he might be leaving the work. He felt he wanted a wife and children, and he was not dedicated to living as a celibate monk for the rest of his life. He preferred to try the life of a householder, as he felt the trials and tribulations of a lonely monk's life were too severe for him to bear. I argued that he should continue on with Paramhansaji until he gained the absolute vision, showing him the true path his life should take, walking in God's will and not his own. Near the end of September 1950, Daniel called me to his room.

"Norm, I just have to go now; I can't stay any longer."

"Have you talked to Paramhansaji about it?"

"Yes. I was walking out the front gate with my suitcase two weeks ago. I decided it was better to just leave quietly on my own and not create a disturbance. I was right at the front gate when his car turned into the driveway. Here I was, standing in front of the car headlights with my suitcase. He caught me at precisely the right moment. I went up to his room, where we spent the rest of the night in conversation. He did not want me to leave, of course. I finally agreed to try harder for two more weeks. Well Norm, those two weeks are up, and I feel I have to go."

The story, as I heard it later, was fascinating. Yogananda had been dictating to one of his secretaries out at the Twenty-Nine Palms retreat. Suddenly he jumped up shouting, "Get the car out quick! I must go to Mount Washington, drive as fast as you can!"

I was told Paramhansaji insisted

A deep relationship between a soul possessing Christ Consciousness and a soul possessing only self-consciousness is unique to say the least. In the role of teacher and student the Christ-Conscious entity perceives the student as a direct part of the fabric of his or her own consciousness. In the light of this fact the teacher is fully aware of the student's thoughts, emotions, acts, desires, etc. Through the medium of Christ Consciousness all things are known or can

on top speed whenever possible. As it worked out, he caught Boone right at the front gate.

"God told me he was leaving," he remarked later.

Boone gave me some of his books and things that he didn't want to take with him.

"Well, this is it, Brother."

We hugged each other for a moment, then he picked up his suitcase and started walking down the driveway.

be perceived at will by one possessing the Sense. It is therefore not unlikely that the teacher would immediately know of difficulties surrounding the student.

Here again we are confronted with the words of Yogananda: "God told me he was leaving." Christ Consciousness (God) sees the Divine Spirit existing in and surrounding all images in the creation. Divine SöN-SüN, the Christ, therefore, is God in the creation to the soul connected directly to and possessing the Christ Sense.

— The Author

"I'll write to you, Norm, and let you know how I'm doing."

I suddenly felt very lonely without Daniel there. It was going to be difficult for me; he was my dear friend. On top of it all was the realization that Paramhansaji himself might be gone at any time. I felt shaken.

The Korean War had started in June of 1950. All the young male students had registered for the draft, including myself. As divinity students, there was a good chance that some of the men at Mount Washington would not get drafted. Boone, however, after leaving, did not wait to be drafted, but enlisted in the U.S. Marine Corps. Now I understood why I had been pushed into joining the Marine Corps myself. If I hadn't done that tour of duty, I would have been eligible for the draft if I ever decided to leave Mount Washington. The U.S. Army got John Winship in the draft and they sent him off to Fort Hood, Texas, for training.

Boone's departure left a big hole in the energy at Mount Washington, one that was hard to fill. I rarely saw Don Walters. Yogananda was deeply concerned by Boone's departure. Years later, I was to know the depth of feeling that Paramhansaji experienced when someone who was dearly loved left the work.

The work on the India House Cafe kept me busy. We wanted to have it completed by Yogananda's birthday on January 5, 1951. All of

As stated before, the teacher possessing Christ Consciousness beholds the student now as a part of his or her own consciousness. This is not a wish on the part of the teacher but a fact. The divine law of cause and effect binds all thoughts and actions to the souls or spirits who gave them origin. Therefore, the teacher and student become bound by the law of cause and effect to perfect the commitment made between them. In essence, the teacher has decided to convey to the student, by whatever means necessary, the Divine Illumination of the Christ or Cosmic Sense and has accepted the responsibility to be a medium for exchange.

— The Author

us were pushing for it. There was so much finish work to be done after the major work was completed. As it happened, we were able to deliver, except for the fixtures and kitchen equipment, a finished building on Paramhansaji's birthday. It would still be several months, though, before the cafe would be open for business.

Christmas meditation finally arrived. We were all looking forward to seeing Yogananda there. From September on, Paramhansaji had been in the desert; he was determined to finish his translation of the Bhagavad-Gita. Intuitively, I felt he was trying to sum up his work before he left the body. I found it hard to believe he could go; but still, hadn't he told me so? When I saw him at Christmas there were no signs of illness, but the vibration coming forth from him was like the eternal deep; I knew he was looking into eternity.

I Was Made for Thee

I was made for Thee alone. I was made for
dropping flowers of devotion gently at
Thy feet on the altar of the morning.

My Hands were made to serve Thee willingly;
to remain folded in adoration, waiting
for Thy coming; and when Thou comest to
bathe Thy feet with my tears.

My Voice was made to sing Thy Glory,

My Feet were made to seek Thy Temples everywhere.

My Eyes were made a chalice to hold Thy burning
Love and the Wisdom falling from Thy Nature's hands.

My Ears were made to catch the music of Thy
Footsteps echoing through the halls of space,
and to hear Thy Divine Melodies flowing through
all heart-tracts of devotion.

My Lips were made to breathe forth Thy praises
and Thy intoxicating Inspirations.

My Love was made to throw incandescent
searchlight flames to find Thee hidden in the
forest of my desires.

My Heart was made to respond to Thy call alone.

My Soul was made to be the channel through
which Thy Love might flow uninterruptedly into
all thirsty Souls.

— Paramhansa Yogananda, *Whispers from Eternity*

As I stepped up to receive his touch he said, "How are you doing, Big Boy? You must remain steadfast; there isn't much time left."

I had no chance to question the meaning of his words. "Much time left" could only mean he was now looking at a time for his own departure. I told him India House was almost finished.

"That's good," he said.

I felt a deep sadness in my teacher. I suppose the problems with some of the married couples at Encinitas were telling him the world brotherhood colony might fail. The loss of Daniel Boone and several other brothers also added to his sadness, plus the fact that he might not be able to finish his work here.

"Divine Mother wants to take me away," he told a group of disciples. "I am trying to talk her out of it."

To another group he was quoted as saying, "I am now living on borrowed time. Divine Mother could take me at any minute."

No one took him seriously as he dropped hints here and there. No one believed, because no one wanted to believe it. Around my birthday, in February of 1951, I began to feel that I, too, might soon be leaving for Santa Barbara.

Paramhansaji had never encouraged me to write or speak, as he had some of the other brothers and sisters; it seemed I must be content with doing construction jobs and repair work. Jean Haupt and I worked together on various occasions. He seemed to be having a hard time of it. Jean had the idea that minutes spent in meditation were like putting gold coins in the bank. He would literally meditate at least five or six hours a day, and more if he could squeeze it in.

"The more I meditate," Jean said sadly, "the further away I seem to be from God; I can't understand it."

Jean had discussed this matter with Paramhansaji, and the answer he received was, "It's by the grace of the Lord that any of us meet him."

"Do you mean to say," questioned Jean, "that he bestows his presence on anyone he choses, at random?"

Yogananda replied, "It's not the amount of *Kriyas* we perform that counts. What really counts is how much we love him. It is the sincere love of our hearts given up to him that attracts him to us."

Jean was confused. He felt in his case he was now performing hours

The divine ignition may come when we least expect it, even as the wind through the trees whose presence is made known by the swaying of the branches and the sounds of the leaves. "The wind bloweth where it listeth and ye heareth the voice thereof. But ye know not from whence it cometh or to whither it goeth." (John 3:8.)

— The Author

of meditation for nothing because if God comes only to those he chooses, then he, Jean, was never going to see him.

"Jean," I said, "meditation is like plowing the field. We must plow the field and make it ready for the seeding. God is certainly aware of the preparation you have made. As our teacher has said, 'The Lord comes when you least expect him;' therefore, we must always be prepared."

Jean shook his head. He was really disappointed after all these years that he had not entered Cosmic Consciousness or seen much of anything in his meditations. Jean was not ready to quit, but he was talking about leaving Mount Washington for a while. As it turned out, Jean did leave about the spring of 1952. Life in a monastic order offers little physical comfort or companionship. One can meditate and pray just so long, then there has to be something creative to do. After the Lake Shrine was completed and India House was open, Paramhansaji had offered no more projects. He was totally engulfed in finishing his writings.

One day, in the first part of March 1951, a note arrived from him calling me to come out to the desert. When I arrived he called me in to see him.

"I have called you out here on the pretense that I need a new roof on the garage, but I really wanted to spend more time with you. Come, let's go for a walk."

The pathway around the inside of the wire fence we had put up was still there. As it happened there was a full moon rising in the east, turning the desert into a fairyland of gold light; deep shades of blue and purple colored the heavens. As I looked out across the land, every joshua tree was giving off its own aura of greens and golds. It seemed the very land was alive beneath my feet, as minute pieces of quartz in the desert sands sparkled in the golden haze.

"My, my!" exclaimed Master Yogananda, "I have never seen it so beautiful out here before."

At this time he was still having problems with his legs. He took my right arm to support himself, and we slowly began to walk around the property. No words were spoken; it wasn't necessary. It seemed my life force merged with his in the deepest state of bliss and love I had ever felt. I wanted to ask him when he was leaving. Reading my thoughts, the reply was out loud, "Soon, too soon."

I knew he was giving me positive energy and thought-forms to take along with me. I wanted to ask him about Santa Barbara and should I go now.

The answer was, "Wait a while yet; there is something you must do. Divine Mother is here with us now."

Suddenly I felt as though every hair on my head was standing on end. The very air was charged with an ecstatic energy. I felt as if we were floating in the air together.

"Promise me that no matter what happens to you in this life, that you will never give up. If you get knocked down, get right up, with more determination to succeed. Will you do that?"

"Yes sir," I replied. "Yes sir, I promise you."

"Good, that's good."

I sensed he knew I would be leaving soon. He said out loud, "I always wanted a center in Santa Barbara."

"Yes sir," I replied, "I know."

"It won't come as quickly as you might think." I sensed a span of time. I would have to live in the everyday world. There were to be few friends for me in the beginning.

Arriving back at the house, I realized that this was an extended, special goodbye. I was so filled with love and devotion at this time, that the tears overflowed.

"Good night, Big Boy."

"Good night, sir."

Samadhi
[An Experience of Christ Consciousness]

Vanished the veils of light and shade,
Lifted every vapor of sorrow,
Sailed away all dawns of fleeting joy,
Gone the dim sensory mirage.
Love, hate, health, disease, life, death:
Perished these false shadows on the screen of duality.
The storm of *maya* stilled
By magic wand of intuition deep.
Present, past, future, no more for me,
But ever-present, all-flowing I, I, everywhere,
Planets, stars, stardust, earth,
Volcanic bursts of doomsday cataclysms,
Creation's molding furnace,
Glaciers of silent X-rays, burning electron floods,
Thoughts of all men, past, present, to come,
Every blade of grass, myself, mankind,
Each particle of universal dust,
Anger, greed, good, bad, salvation, lust,
I swallowed, transmuted all
Into a vast ocean of blood of my own one Being.

Smoldering joy, oft-puffed by meditation
Blinding my tearful eyes,
Burst into immortal flames of bliss,
Consumed my tears, my frame, my all.
Thou art I, I am Thou,
Knowing, Knower, Known, as One!
Tranquilled, unbroken thrill, eternally living,
    ever-new peace.
Enjoyable beyond imagination of expectancy, *samadhi* bliss!
Not an unconscious state
Or mental chloroform without willful return,
Samadhi but extends my conscious realm
Beyond limits of the mortal frame
To farthest boundary of eternity
Where I, the Cosmic Sea,
Watch the little ego floating in Me.
Mobile murmurs of atoms are heard,
The dark earth, mountains, vales, lo! molten liquid!
Flowing seas change into vapors of nebulae!
Aum blows upon vapors, opening wondrously their veils,
Oceans stand revealed, shining electrons,
Till, at the last sound of the cosmic drum,
Vanish the grosser lights into eternal rays
Of all-pervading bliss.
From joy I came, for joy I live, in sacred joy I melt.
Ocean of mind, I drink all creation's waves.
Four veils of solid, liquid, vapor, light,
Lift aright.
I, in everything, center the Great Myself.
Gone forever: fitful, flickering shadows of mortal memory;
Spotless is my mental sky — below, ahead, and high above;
Eternity and I, one united ray.
A tiny bubble of laughter, I
Am become the Sea of Mirth Itself.

— Paramhansa Yogananda, *Autobiography of a Yogi*

This description of the expanding spheres of the creation beheld by the Christ, or Cosmic-Conscious entity clearly defines, as far as words might convey, the vision of the Sons and Daughters of God, the Christed Angel Beings. The Spirit of Christ Consciousness speaks through the fabric of the human mind, limited by words which do not express true meaning but, driven on by the power of vision and inspired intellect, it is impelled to try.

This poem is an attempt to convey images of that which is beyond the experience of the five senses; and as the ultra futuristic experience of the New Sense herein named Christ or Cosmic Consciousness is unsurpassed at this time.

— The Author

Goat Mountain, near Giant Rock, in Califronia

CHAPTER 19

A Mountain in the Desert

When I left the men's retreat house at Twenty-Nine Palms, I had an opportunity to be alone. I had repaired the roof on Paramhansaji's garage and finished a few clean-up jobs. Now I was on the Twenty-Nine Palms Highway driving back to Mount Washington. As I looked northward across the desert, I sensed a subtle magnetic attraction out there. I felt like doing some exploring. As I entered the town of Joshua Tree, I noticed a road going across the desert toward the northwest. Suddenly I was impelled to make a right turn on this road. Why not? It was only ten o'clock in the morning; I had plenty of time to get back to Mount Washington before dark.

The road was unpaved and rough. As I mounted the first hill, I looked down on a forest of joshua trees and a wide-open expanse of desert. I just kept driving, traveling a good ten miles. Climbing a low hill, I noticed the road took a sharp turn to the west, about one mile ahead. I observed a very strange mount which seemed to resemble an ancient volcano. It was flat on top and set apart from the other terrain; a solitary sentinel unto itself.

As I reached the turn in the road I noticed a small sign which read, "Giant Rock Airport, six miles ahead." I made the turn and headed on down the road. It appeared the road passed the strange mount on its north face. The closer I got to the mount, the stronger the magnetic pull became. The mount rose from the desert floor at an angle of roughly sixty degrees to a height of fifteen to eighteen hundred feet. Then it appeared to be flat on the top. The base of the mount running north and south was a good three miles long.

As I pulled up beside its north face, I stopped the car and shut off the engine. Immediately the all-pervading cosmic sound of Hun "'Be still, and know that I am God.' (Psalms 46:10.) Never flaunting His omnipresence, the Lord is heard only in the immaculate silences. Reverberating throughout the universe as the creative Aum [Hun, Om,

167

(Om) came roaring in around me.

I stepped from the car and felt as if I was the only person alive on a strange planet. There was a sense of total aloneness — just me and my humming companion. What a place to meditate! As I stared up at the mount, I knew I would be back again, perhaps to climb to the top.

Getting back into the car, I drove past the mount and reached the top of a rise. I was now looking down

Amen] vibration, the Primal Sound instantly translates Itself into intelligible words for the devotee in attunement. . . . The outward manifestation of the omnipresent Christ Consciousness, its ' witness ' (Revelation 3:14) is Aum, the Word or Holy Ghost; invisible divine power, the only doer, the sole causative and activating force that upholds all creation through vibration." (Paramhansa Yogananda) It is the sound of the cosmic propulsion system which runs the expanding spheres of creation and sustains all images therein.

— The Author

on a small dry lake and what appeared to be a landing strip for airplanes. At the end of the airstrip I could see a giant monolith of stone. This must be the giant rock the sign had indicated. I decided to go on, but my intuition told me now was not the time to go there. At the same time it was also telling me that this was a special place, and I would return to it someday in the future.

I turned the car around and headed back the way I had come. As I drove toward Los Angeles, I observed how mankind had destroyed the natural landscape, covering it with concrete and asphalt. Telephone poles and power line towers spread out in every direction like huge spider webs. The sight of cracker-box housing tracts jammed together, and always on the best farmland in the area, was saddening. Millions of automobiles crowded the streets and freeways. I found it hard to believe that mankind could possibly have built so many automobiles. Indeed, this present civilization had little respect for Divine Spirit's creation or its beauty. Wealth, power, and prestige now seemed to represent the Godhead of this society. Its grand ideals in the beginning were decaying into a quicker way of doing things so more profit might be realized. This endeavor has put mankind on the treadmill of competition, self-gain at the cost of someone else's failure, destroying any concept of brotherhood.

More and more speed, more comfort and less work has corrupted man's higher nature. "Let machines do it for us." Mankind is fast losing any contact which might have been possible with the natural living forces of nature. The vision of self-sustaining communities using natural methods of farming, handmade shoes and clothing, raising goats, sheep, and cattle, the making of pottery for the tables — here in such an environ-

I Hear America singing, the varied carols I hear;
Those of mechanics — each one singing his, as it should be blithe and strong;

ment all the trades could be kept alive — carpentry, the making of bricks, the shaping of stone for the building of structures, the woodshop for handmade chairs, and tables. Man must be creative with his mind and hands.

When machines take over the natural trades and crafts, what is there left for man to do? Must he just sit down and watch the whole process happen until he is bored sick? Then comes the decline. The next generation is not taught the trades and crafts that are natural to mankind's survival. The result will be no more craftspeople or tradespeople. Now boredom really sets in, giving birth to debauchery and negativity.

The carpenter singing his, as he measures his plank or beam,
The shoemaker singing as he sits on his bench — the hatter singing as he stands;
The delicious singing of the mother or of the young wife at work . . .
Singing with open mouths, their strong melodious songs. . . .
I bestow upon any man or woman the entrance to all the gifts of the universe.

— Walt Whitman

One need not look back any farther than the decline of the Roman Empire, brought about by too much greed for wealth and power. Rome was able to use con-

Allow nothing to stand in the way of spiritual advancement. Anything is better than to remain in the merely self-conscious state, which is full of miseries.

— Richard Bucke, *Cosmic Consciousness*

quered people to do all the work. Slaves kept the trades and crafts alive while the Romans retired to their houses and pleasure, and then to their defeat. The divine laws that inhabit the structure of the universe state that whatsoever is sown in the field of life and power must be reaped, and that goes for man, city, and nation.

As I neared Los Angeles, the blanket of heavy, gray smog hung in the atmosphere like a death shroud. The dirty, gray buildings spoke of the haphazard construction that was used to throw up dwellings to accommodate the run-

Karma, or the universal law of cause and effect, may be described as the system of rewards and punishments by which the ego learns ultimately to manifest its innate divine nature. Suffering is the karmic result of action that is, in some way, out of tune with that true nature. Fulfillment is the reward for living, to some degree at least, in harmony with that nature.

— Swami Kriyananda, *The Path*

away competition of the business world. Never before had I seen it so clearly. My thoughts went back to the silence and peace of the desert, truly unpolluted at this time, but for how long? The advance of modern society was devouring all the wilderness places. Soon there would be no wilderness, no place to be alone with Divine Spirit without the interruption of airplanes droning overhead; without the sounds of motorcycles and automobiles. What would happen to the natural wildlife, the creatures of the wilderness? I drove in through the gates of Mount Washington, parked the car, and walked toward my room.

As I reached a position above the tennis courts, I stopped to look down on the city. The lights were just coming on as the sun was setting. Yes, Los Angeles looked much better in the dark. I walked over and sat down on the front lawn to meditate. My leaving Mount Washington was now inevitable; confirmation had been given and the visions I had experienced were true. The question now was when, and how should I go? I decided to wait for the proper time. I had various projects to work on at India House; sidewalks and stairs to put in. Work at the Lake Shrine continued and I kept myself busy through the summer of 1951.

Master Yogananda was at his desert retreat most of the summer. He had said, "I must finish my greatest work, the interpretation of the Bhagavad-Gita," and having said goodbye to me, his immediate concern for me had passed.

I saw him only on rare occasions, as he arrived at Mount Washington or when he was leaving. My path lay before me. I had passed through Yogananda's life and mission on earth; my path stretched away to distant horizons. I was going on a journey back towards eternity. My path was beset with unscalable mountains as I looked ahead in my meditations. Visions of impossible circumstances arose before me. I was to experience and witness life on this planet in all its aspects, omitting nothing. Then and only then would I be in a position to help others. If one is to heal or help, one must understand the disease. So I must work and sweat with mankind at this time and not retreat to a monastic way of life. I knew I must

There is that in me — I do not know what it is — but I know that it is in me. Wrenched and sweaty — calm and cool then my body becomes, I sleep, I sleep long. I do not know it — it is without name — it is a word unsaid — it is not in any dictionary, utterance, symbol. Something it swings on more than the earth I swing on, to it the creation is the friend whose embracing awakes me. Perhaps I might tell more. Outlines! I plead for my brothers and sisters. Do you see, O my brothers and sisters? It is not chaos or death, it is form, union, plan — it is eternal life — it is happiness.

— Walt Whitman, *Leaves of Grass*

live, for a time, with the everyday problems of men. I was to find that the calloused hands and minds of common men had built up a resistance to the pain and suffering they had so long endured.

I knew heaven existed, without a doubt; I was now to experience the unnatural reality of hell and the negative fallen spirits who created

Yogananda once told an audience, "I used to think Satan was only a human invention, but now I know, and add my testimony to that of others who lived before me, that Satan

it. I had been warned of the dark spirits and their existence on earth at the very beginning of my life here. The existence of living entities known as Satan, Lucifer, and Beelzebub, plus the destructive forces they level against humankind, were becoming a living reality for me. I was to meet them, and others, face to face, in a life or death struggle for my existence here and for the completion of my mission. I was also to see, with my eyes wide open, the astral and physical realms they inhabit, called hell.

I observed that modern man, in his quest for material wealth through scientific achievement, had overlooked the ancient beliefs of his predecessors regarding the existence of supernatural beings in the universe who are standing on vibratory levels different from those of humans. The fact that the physical senses are limited to certain vibratory perceptions should not preclude the existence of other levels. It is only when "thine eye is single . . . ," as Jesus proclaimed, meaning to have true spiritual vision, that human can observe the truth of his predicament in time

is a reality. He is a universal, conscious force whose sole aim is to keep all beings bound to the wheel of delusion."

— Swami Kriyananda, *The Path*

The Old Testament prophets called *maya* by the name of Satan (lit., in Hebrew, "the adversary"). The Greek Testament, as an equivalent for Satan, uses *diabolos* or devil. Satan or *Maya* is the Cosmic Magician that produces multiplicity of forms to hide the One Formless Verity. In God's plan and play *(lila)*, the sole function of Satan or *Maya* is to attempt to divert man from Spirit to matter, from reality to unreality.

Christ describes *maya* picturesquely as a devil, a murderer, and a liar. "The devil . . . was a murderer from the beginning, and abode not in the truth, because there is no truth in him. When he speaketh a lie, he speaketh of his own: for he is a liar and the father of it." (John 8:44.)

"The devil sinneth from the beginning. For this purpose the Son of God was manifested, that he might destroy the work of the devil." (I John 3:8.) That is, the manifestation of Christ Consciousness, within man's own being, effortlessly destroys the illusions or "works of the devil."

— Paramhansa Yogananda
Autobiography of a Yogi

Here again, to one who possesses the Christ or Cosmic Sense all things are made known to that one, all which is desired. The eye to perceive the past and influence the future, encompasses the consciousness. The great dramas of life within the expanding spheres of creation stand revealed.

— The Author

and space. One who has succeeded in attaining the vision and the experience of immortality sees, to his horror, the incredible wars raging on in time and space between the forces of good and evil. The ancient wars which began over one million years ago between the Sons of God (called The Builders), and the Spirits of Darkness, the Fallen Angels, rage on.

The so-called fall of Lucifer, a supernatural entity — is it fact or fiction? I was to learn that the everyday "free will" humankind thinks it has does not exist. Like puppets on a string, physical human, the creature, dances to the tune of forces unknown. In short, I found humankind has "free will" until he realizes he doesn't, and when he realizes he doesn't, he next finds out that he does.

"I am not of this world, nor is my kingdom," Jesus said, inferring other kingdoms and other existences.

One does not, under conditions as they exist here today, become aware of the supernatural unless one pursues it actively and then demonstrates work in that direction.

I found the Forces of Light and Darkness are attracted to us by our own desires or by our deeds of the past. Souls incarnating for a specific mission are beset from the first day with the forces of opposition. Stumbling blocks are planted on the path of the adept's return to earth. I learned very quickly not to underestimate the power of Darkness. I found I must be vigilant every microsecond of time, for my enemies encompass me round about.

> . . . their Manual of Discipline records: "All who practice righteousness are under the domination of the Prince of Lights, and walk in the ways of light: Whereas all who practice perversity are under the domination of the Angel of Darkness and walk in the ways of darkness. Through the Angel of Darkness, however, even those who practice righteousness are made liable to error . . . all of the spirits that attend on him are bent on causing the Sons of Light to stumble."
>
> The Covenanters' (authors of the Manual of Discipline) teachings and beliefs indicate that they considered Lucifer as a fallen angel and as an individual being. Also, it is apparent from their writings, that they believed Lucifer, or the Angel of Darkness, is accompanied by a host of spirits, also probably fallen angels who help him in his nefarious work. It is they, under his direction, who tempt men's souls and lead them toward iniquity and perdition. He, and his spirits, are ever present to "cause the sons of light to stumble." In their attempt to bring about the fall of man, they employ every possible devious device.
>
> — O. Preston Robinson, *The Dead Sea Scrolls and Original Christianity*

To Norman   Feb 3rd 1951
Dear One,

May your birth bring happiness to many spiritually. May your birthdays be filled
with God-Consciousness. Happy birthday to you.

With unceasing blessings,
Paramhansa Yogananda

A birthday note from Yogananda. At the bottom, my name in Sanskrit.

173

Paramhansa Yogananda

CHAPTER 20

Paramhansa Yogananda and the Eternal Sea

Have you ever felt you have known someone before at the very instant you met him? As you enter into a discussion with that person, you immediately perceive that a prior meeting in this lifetime would have been impossible. Such was the case with Paramhansa Yogananda and some of his disciples. How many other times, in other places, had we all met, possibly worked together, lived as family members, or shared a position in some divine existence? What wonderful, magic power, plus a network of events in times past, had now drawn us all together again in times present? What undiscovered friends are yet to appear from beyond the horizon of death and rebirth?

In my deep meditations I had succeeded in seeing and feeling the middle place, that undiscovered realm from whose bourne all travelers return, the center of all things and the hub on which they spin.

The Ancients named this place The Great Central SöN-SüN , the point where Divine Spirit Mother and Father gave ignition and birth to light, and the life force of Spirit was made visible. Spirit Mother and Father saw the ignition and birth of the divine offspring, light, and it was good.

The existence of a superconscious [Christ-Conscious] mind has long been recognized philosphically, being in reality the Over-Soul spoken of by Emerson. . . .

"A man is the facade of a temple wherein all wisdom and all good abide. What we commonly call man . . . does not, as we know him, represent himself, but misrepresents himself. . . . But the soul, whose organ he is, would he let it appear through his actions, would make our knees bend. . . . We lie open on one side to the deeps of spiritual nature, to all attributes of God."

— Paramhansa Yogananda
Autobiography of a Yogi

The expanding great Sphere of Creation began its journey outward in all directions from the center of

The glory of him who moves everything penetrates through the universe and shines in one part more and in another less. In the

175

The Great Central SöN-SüN billions of earth years ago and is still expanding today. Returning to Spirit's center within us, if we listen patiently, we can hear the roar of past and future where cosmic currents meet, with mighty breakers beating upon the royal seat. The projector of all images can now stand revealed to us in the quiet light of eternity. Have I not found it true, by observation, that before my consciousness can grasp the next moment in the future, it is already in the past? Time and its illusions, like the currents of a sea, pass through us undiscovered, sweeping us along beyond any point of measure. Human, the creature, armed with the weapons of devotion and desire to know, plus a good method of deep-seated meditation can, in this lifetime, overcome the negative influence of spirits who try to possess him, and who do possess Planet Earth. We can, with steadfast meditation and selfless service to others, make time stand still. It is then that we can behold the image of The Great Central SöN-SüN, floating within the center of the expanding spheres of creation. That faculty of human consciousness which can receive the brilliant image of the Angel Man and Woman reveals its presence to our conscious awareness and stands waiting for the Angel Beings' baptism and descent into the human creature body. We may now become convinced, through experience, that a living, conscious entity inhabits the spheres of creation and eternity beyond. A face-to-face encounter is yet to come to us if we persist in our love and our desire to know.

How often, as we are swept along by the currents of time and space, are we able to cling to a planetary place? How often are we able to meet with some illumined brother or sister who can lead us toward a face-to-face encounter with Divine Spirit Mother and Father? What happens

heaven that receives most of its light I have been, and have seen things which he who descends from there above neither knows how or is able to recount. On a sudden, day seemed to be added to day as if he who is able had adorned the heaven with another sun.

— Dante, *Paradiso*

The faculties are degrees of Christ or Cosmic Consciousness. The evolution of consciousness through human, the creature, on planets in the expanding spheres of creation evolved first simple — then self — then Cosmic or Christ Consciousness. This normal evolution has been withheld on this planet by the interference of negative forces who wish to possess humankind for their own selfish purposes.

In the silence of my being I hear the pulsating hum of all creation moving through every atom of my body. If you but listen, I can hear You; I can feel You; I can see You. I know I am a being of consciousness, without form, beyond light, I am eternal. I am part of You, Mighty Spirit.

— The Author

The blessed event associated with meeting one's spiritual guide should not be taken for granted. A spiritual teacher can be known by the brilliant light of Christ Consciousness

to us beyond this present life if we reject such an opportunity? Looking off into space, we can see no end out there among the stars, but one does exist. Far beyond the starlit flanks of the galaxies, the expanding mental fabric of the Sphere of Creation exists.

The vast, eternal, primordial deep lying beyond staggers the mind. The fearsome void of the unknown has turned back many a traveler! Is it fear of the unknown that drives mankind in a breathless race to find security on a planetary place? Does human's fear of discovering a living God in the creation force him away from his divine nature? Still grasping the images of an illusionary physical world, the creature of the earth seeks comfort in possessions. False images of power and wealth betray human in the end. At his last breath, all is wrenched from his grasp. Does loss of the physical vehicle render the self-conscious ego no more effective than the thin airs of space which now surround it? To this end has it become a part? How often my consciousness has frequented these thoughts. I gain comfort in knowing that the divine *Companions*, the Angel Men and Women, are my eternal friends. I cannot perceive within myself how life could be tolerable without this presence. Thus springs forth my compassion for other weary travelers, that the Angel Men and Women might be with them, also.

Looking through the fabric of the outer form, I saw within, the true image of Paramhansa Yogananda. Translated, his title states: "Through Divine union, the soul, (i.e., simple- and self-consciousness) like a great white swan sails forth upon the eternal cosmic sea, (i.e.,

which manifests visually to the students, as they pursue the goals set forth. Either in meditation, sleep, or everyday duties the subjective light of Christ will appear to those sincere ones possessing love, respect, devotion, and selfless service. To turn one's attention back to the affairs of the self-conscious world of events after such an opportunity has been presented is to deny one's soul the opportunity of salvation (i.e., Christ Consciousness.) The great law of cause and effect records such actions, and when the next opportunity is presented, the law demands that one leave — again. This sets up actions and reactions which plague the soul for untold periods of time.

— The Author

The Angel Men and Women are the Sons and Daughters of God (i.e., Divine Spirit). They are Christ-Conscious beings who inhabit the expanding spheres of creation. *In human form* they have been called the Sons of God, The Builders, the Nefilim, the Ancients, and the Masters. *Without human form*, existing as conscious spheres of light and energy, they have been referred to as guardian angels. In both respects they are the caretakers of the creation, the primary thrust behind divine evolutions of thought-forms such as mineral, plant, animal, and human images. (See illustration pg. 290).

— The Author

Visions of incorporeal substances, as of angels and of souls, are neither frequent nor natural in this earthly life, and still less so is the vision of the divine essence, which is peculiar to the blessed, unless it be communicated transiently by a dispensation

Christ Consciousness), far beyond the storms of past and future and the expanding great Sphere of Creation." The mirror-placid sea reflects final peace, joy ever-new, and love ever-expanding. In him, I saw my own image reflected and I received confirmation of the deep beliefs I was born with.

of God, or by conservation of our natural life and condition, and the abstraction of the spirit; as was perhaps the case of St. Paul when he heard the unutterable secrets in the third heaven. "Whether in the body," said he, "I know not, or out of the body, I know not; God knoweth." It is clear from the words of the apostle that he was carried out of himself, by the act of God, as to his natural existence.

— Richard Bucke on St. Paul,
Cosmic Consciousness

[Christ Consciousness — The Experience]

My body became immovably rooted; breath was drawn out of my lungs as if by some huge magnet. Soul and mind instantly lost their physical bondage and streamed out like a fluid piercing light from my every pore. The flesh was as though dead; yet in my intense awareness I knew that never before had I been fully alive. My sense of identity was no longer narrowly confined to a body but embraced the circumambient atoms. People on distant streets seemed to be moving gently over my own remote periphery. The roots of plants and trees appeared through a dim transparency of the soil; I discerned the inward flow of their sap.

The whole vicinity lay bare before me. My ordinary frontal vision was now changed to a vast spherical sight, simultaneously all-perceptive. Through the back of my head I saw men strolling far down Rai Ghat Lane, and noticed also a white cow that was leisurely approaching. When she reached the open ashram gate, I observed her as though with my two physical eyes. After she had passed behind the brick wall of the courtyard, I saw her clearly still.

All objects within my panoramic gaze trembled and vibrated like quick motion pictures. My body, Master's, the pillared courtyard, the furniture and floor, the trees and sunshine, occasionally became violently agitated, until all melted into a luminescent sea; even as sugar crystals, thrown into a glass of water, dissolve after being shaken. The unifying light alternated with materializations of form, the metamorphoses revealing the law of cause and effect in creation.

An oceanic joy broke upon calm endless shores of my soul. The Spirit of God, I realized, is exhaustless Bliss; His body is countless tissues of light. A swelling glory within me began to envelop towns, continents, the earth, solar and stellar systems, tenuous nebulae, and floating universes. The entire cosmos, gently luminous, like a city seen afar at night, glimmered within the infinitude of my being. The dazzling light beyond the sharply etched global outlines faded slightly at the farthest edges; there I saw a mellow radiance, ever undiminished. It was indescribably subtle; the planetary pictures were formed of a grosser light. The divine dispersion of rays poured from an Eternal Source, blazing into galaxies, transfigured with ineffable auras. Again and again I saw the creative beams condense into constellations, then resolve into sheets of transparent flame. By rhythmic reversion, sextillion worlds passed into diaphanous luster, then fire became firmament.

I cognized the center of the empyrean as a point of intuitive perception in my heart. Irradiating splendor issued from my nucleus to every part of the universal structure. Blissful *amrita*, nectar of immortality, pulsated through me with a quicksilverlike fluidity. The creative voice of God I heard resounding as *Aum*, the vibration of the Cosmic Motor.

Suddenly the breath returned to my lungs. With a disappointment almost unbearable, I realized that my infinite immensity was lost. Once more I was limited to the humiliating cage of a body, not easily accommodative to the Spirit. Like a prodigal child, I had run away from my macrocosmic home and had imprisoned myself in a narrow microcosm.

— Paramhansa Yogananda, *Autobiography of a Yogi*

Summer was drawing nigh to fall and the leaves were covering the walks and driveways of Mount Washington. All the young brothers and a few older ones were to have the opportunity to take the final vows of *Brahmacharya*, meaning that they would never marry in this life, and were committed to a life of celibacy as monks of the order. Paramhansa Yogananda wanted everyone present in the chapel for the occasion. No one really knew who was going to take the final vows. As I stood there, I was tempted to step forward. I reflected again on my visions. No, I was to marry, and possibly have children. I could not take the vow. Paramhansaji was standing there as all the brothers stepped forward. He looked at me saying, "I wish you could stay," with his eyes, "but I know you must go." I realized at that moment everyone else now knew I was either in trouble or I was going to leave the work. From that day forward, I was an outcast, for I had refused to take the vow. I understood how everyone felt, but I could change nothing. I felt a great loneliness come over me; I was as a man straddling a fence, with a foot on either side.

Sunday came along and I went to the Hollywood Church. Reverend Bernard was giving the service. I was sitting on the aisle and felt deeply troubled as I struggled to meditate. Suddenly I was aware of someone standing by my side in the aisle. I didn't open my eyes to see who it was. Then the words came through. "Norman, Norman, it's your old dad. Do you hear me? Come home and see me." I was momentarily startled by Dad's voice. I thought he was really there. As I whirled around to see him, my eyes fell on an empty aisle. Dad had projected his image toward me. We were so close, he was now aware of my unhappiness.

As the service ended, I felt it was time to talk to Bernard. That evening I knocked on his door. I tried to tell him of my feelings — I had to bounce them off someone. His only advice was, "My Lord! What would you ever do out in the world alone? You are so naive!" I went off to my room that night really doubting myself and my path. Was it all true? Maybe I was naive; I sat up to meditate on the possibility.

When Paramhansa Yogananda had arrived in this country in September 1920, he brought with him the message of God-realization through scientific techniques of meditation and the ancient practice of yoga. He was able to demonstrate to his students a step-by-step pathway into the realms of Christ or Cosmic Consciousness. He was one of the first yogic adepts from the East to successfully live and teach in the Western world. He broke the ice of dogmatic Christian belief for some, with a greater vision into the true reality of Christ Jesus. In no way did he try to lead Christians away from their faith, but rather, he tried to enhance their beliefs through deep-seated meditation upon them. The Christmas meditations each year were dedicated to the memory of Christ Jesus and his teachings.

One can now speculate as to what Jesus actually taught the disciples in secret that was not taught to the multitudes directly. Is it possible that techniques of meditation were passed on to those who were close to him? Much has been left out of the New Testament by the early church fathers. One needs to look into the apocryphal books and writings not included in the Bible: the Gnostic Gospels, written by the Egyptian converts to Christ, and the illuminating translations of the cuneiform tablets discovered in ancient Mesopotamia. These tablets give a deep and revolutionary insight into the genesis of human, as written in the Bible. Libraries were discovered in the Euphrates Valley containing thousands of tablets which describe the creation of human, and the earth's history from which parts of the Bible were written. If one studies the Qumran Scrolls of the Essenes, one also sees a step-by-step advance toward Divine Illumination through the inspired teachings of one they referred to as "The Teacher of Righteousness." This brother of the Essene communities was also put to death, as was Jesus, by the dogmatic posture of the Sadducees and the Pharisees. Jealous of the successful spiritual communities maintained by the Essenes, and the number of converts to that lifestyle, they plotted against the life of the teacher. Then, finally convincing existing authorities that he was a threat to government, they put him to death upon a cross as was the brutal custom of that era.

One of the apocryphal books in which new interest has been excited is the "Shepherd of Hermes." This is a book written from approximately A.D. 139 to A.D. 154 and was included in the canon of scriptures until near the end of the fifth century when it was changed to non-canonical status by the Council of the Roman Church. This book has been a source of controversy to the scholars because of the way it describes the Godhead . . . and also because its author maintains the church established by the Son of God, already had a long history upon the Earth before Christ Jesus was sent to purify it and call it back to God's commandments.

The Dead Sea Covenanters' Manual of Discipline seems to prove that this ascetic order was teaching and practising many doctrines that later became known as Christian precepts.

The idea that man was the inheritor of original sin from his first parents, a sin which he could not himself throw off, was not a part of the concept of the Covenanters. Members of the Dead Sea Sect had no concept of this idea of original sin. They believed rather that every man is blessed at birth with a fund of divine knowledge and that evil or wrongdoing is a result of deviation from this great gift. Furthermore, there is no evidence in Dead Sea scriptures of a belief in a communion in the sense of the Eucharist where the bread and the wine are regarded by some churches as the Savior's actual flesh and blood and that because of this, their consumption might have a redeeming power. Although they seemed to practise a form of communion in their communal meals, if so, they partook of the bread and the wine as symbols and in remembrance of their covenants.

The members of the sect put a heavy emphasis on the importance of knowledge, wisdom, and free agency. They believed that God was the source of all knowledge and that it was the responsibility of every member to gain as much knowledge and wisdom as possible. A man must be judged, not on the basis of his material possessions, but rather by his righteousness and the extent of his knowledge and wisdom.

— O. Preston Robinson, *The Dead Sea Scrolls and Original Christianity*

And Jesus answered: "Seek ye not the law in your scriptures, for the law is life, whereas the scripture is dead. I tell you truly, Moses received not his laws from God in writing, but through the living word. The law is living word of living God to living prophets for living men. In everything that is life is the law written. You find it in the grass, in the tree, in the river, in the mountain, in the birds of the heaven, in the fishes of the sea; but seek it chiefly in yourselves. For I tell you truly, all living things are nearer to God than the scripture which is without life. God so made life and all living things that they might by the everlasting word teach the laws of the true God to man. God wrote not the laws in the pages of books, but in your heart and in your spirit."

Jesus said, "Believe me, the sun is as the flame of a candle beside the sun of truth of the Heavenly Father."

— Edmund Bordeaux Szekely, *The Essene Gospel of Peace,* Book One

But have things really changed that much in the last two thousand years? The Sadducees and Pharisees of yesterday have returned in the guise of certain Christian sects today. They brought with them the same hatred, jealousy, and judgmental practices as were displayed in the past. Their position today is no different than it was during the life of Christ Jesus. They downgrade, persecute, and

"But woe unto you scribes and Pharisees, hypocrites! Because ye shut the kingdom of heaven against men: For ye enter not in yourselves, neither suffer ye them that are entering in to enter." (Matthew 23:13.) The formal, soulless religion of the scribes and Pharisees (and the same is true of much of the Christianity of to-day) was antagonistic to the growth of the spirit to Cosmic Consciousness. Neither would they allow (in as far as they could prevent) of any spiritual life and growth outside the narrow limits laid down by their "law."

— Richard Bucke, *Cosmic Consciousness*

condemn religious groups that do not conform to their own primitive ways, even going so far as to pronounce the origin of other faiths as having

181

found conception in the depths of hell, under the direct supervision of the Arch Fiend himself. Surely the gentle and understanding Christ does not condone such acts. Yes, the return of Jesus Christ would not be recognized today by churches which formed around his teachings many years after his departure. He would, in fact, no doubt be persecuted in the same fashion as he was before, and undoubtedly, after a public pronouncement of his identity, his life would again be in jeopardy.

I can visualize a small Hindu man, rather stout, dressed in the traditional orange robe of the Swami Order, stepping off an ocean liner at the Port of Boston, his long black hair falling over his shoulders. It was the year 1920, and this was his first trip to America. He was to address the International Congress of Religious Liberals in Boston on October 6, 1920 as a representative of the Swami Order in India. Beyond that, he was here to try to bring Christ Consciousness to as many as would receive him, through the practice of the ancient method of meditation, or mind and body control, known as *Kriya Yoga*. The persecution he suffered upon his arrival here was to follow him through the next twenty years of his life.

The impact of the long-haired, orange-robed Swami on the general public was either positive or negative, depending on what area of the country he was in. There was genuine interest in his unique person and the power of his magnetic personality. The dynamic message he presented attracted gigantic crowds. As the years went by and his fame spread, he was considered a genuine threat to organized religions opposing him. There he stood, steadfast and alone, a single figure in the strange environment of a foreign land and people. His indomitable will and all-encompassing love were felt by all, those who loved him and those who hated him. The reaction to any divinely illumined teacher by the general public and existing authority is usually negative, as history has proven. Either out of fear or jealousy, the heavenly messengers are persecuted and worn down, and are eventually put to death, or they themselves die of exhaustion before their natural time. Paramhansa Yogananda, a lone warrior in a strange land, fulfilled his mission triumphantly!

Easter Meditation at the Hermitage in Encinitas. *Front row: left to right:* Florina Darling (Durga Mata), Virginia Wright (Ananda Mata), Faye Wright (Daya Mata), and Paramhansaii. The author is standing to the left of the altar. Third person to his right is "Bugs" Butler, and next to him, Swami Kriyananda.

I am lying face down on the bed, but yet I somehow see your image right through the back of my head.

CHAPTER 21

A Vision of Christ

I arrived in Santa Barbara around the first part of November 1951. Leaving Mount Washington and Paramhansa Yogananda had not been easy for me; however, I was now on my own, and employment must be found. I spent a few days visiting with Dad and Dorothy. In the course of a conversation with Dad, he mentioned an old friend of the family named Joe Dominy.

"Joe works for the telephone company in Santa Barbara. Why don't you talk to him, Son?" That was an interesting idea. The thought of climbing poles and maybe working as a lineman intrigued me. Dad put in a call to Joe.

"Send him right over, Charlie. We'll put him to work doing something." Sure enough, Joe did help me. I filled out the application forms, and about three days later I had a job.

I started out working with the construction crew on one of the big line trucks. Each line truck carried a foreman, four linemen, a truck driver, and last of all, a "grunt." "Grunt" was a title given to an apprentice lineman. For the first few months all I did was wait on the linemen. When they were up the telephone poles working, I hauled crossarms and hardware up to them on a hand line. I was anxious to learn how to climb a pole. Everyone had to supply their own tools, climbing hooks and line belt. I will never forget the day my hooks and belt arrived from the Bashland Company and I tried them on for size. Now I could really start learning how to climb and perform a lineman's work. Of all the jobs I have ever worked on in my life, those days with the telephone company were the best. I really enjoyed that work.

One of the biggest problems I had from the beginning was talking too much about my life with Yogananda. The men I worked with were not interested in yoga; they didn't want to hear about God. I was so full of

185

enthusiasm, I wanted to tell everyone. Bernard was right, I was naive! I thought everyone would want to hear my story, whereas it was quite the contrary. They couldn't care less. I was immediately considered a little weird: "Old Norm is always talking about those crazy yogis." Try as I might, it became apparent that there was no one to relate to on this level.

Loneliness was to become my constant companion. One Friday evening as I returned to a small flat I had rented on the north side of town, I began to have serious doubts. Was I going to be able to go on? Maybe I had left Mount Washington too soon. The visions and my mission now seemed as far away as the moon. How could I ever accomplish what I had come here to do? That night I slept little; doubt was gnawing at my resolutions. Saturday morning I had the blues. I really felt like returning to Mount Washington. I sat to try and meditate, and was unable. In despair, I threw myself face down on the bed. As I lay there, I extended myself in prayer, "Oh Lord, what should I do?"

A Vision of Christ

Suddenly, tremendous brightness, I am looking directly into the sun but this cannot be true — the sun is moving! O thoughts, interpret what is happening, how fast you move, O fiery orb, your light grows brighter still. The energy emanating from you — it takes my breath away.

> Dazzling and tremendous . . . As in a swoon, one instant another sun, ineffable full dazzles me, . . .
> — Walt Whitman, *Leaves of Grass*

I am lying face down on the bed, but yet I somehow see your image right through the back of my head. The roof of the house; no longer there — only the beautiful sky of blue! O you gigantic disc of the sun, you are in motion filling the whole sky. Are you actually hurtling toward me? Yes, on a collision course in thought — I can mark you momentarily. How incredible you are, O sphere of incandescent brilliance. Will you now collide with me?

> . . . At midday, O king I saw on the way a light from heaven, above the brightness of the sun, shining round about me. . . .
> — St. Paul, Acts 26:12-13

You shout in a voice I have heard before, *"Look at me!"*

O yes, I will gaze upon your apparition but now you swoop off toward the east, disappearing over the horizon. I hear you speak words again, *"First I come in peace; if human does not listen, then I come with fire."*

The vision is changing now! Before me a brilliant orange-red disc moves slowly toward the earth from the vast depths of outer space. Could it be another planet?

Now again the consciousness of the body returns — the bed, the room. I must sit up! What has happened to me? Everything I look at is transparent; even my body seems nebulous. My own existence is very questionable; a clear penetrating vision seems to light the interior of everything I look at. Never in my life or in my wildest imagination have I ever seen or heard of such an apparition.

The incandescent brilliance of that light seems to touch every cell of my body. My eyes, the interior of my head, all functions and feelings

> Day seemed to be added to day as if he who is able had adorned the heaven with another sun.
>
> — Dante, *Paradiso*

are somehow different. Those penetrating rays — I can still see them with eyes closed. The Lord has answered my prayer. I have seen him now. He is beyond mortal vision, his face shining like the sun.

> Lo! what mortal eye hath not seen nor ear heard —
> All sorrow finished — the deep, deep ocean of joy
>   opening within — the surface sparkling.
> The myriad-formed disclosed, each one and all, all things
>   that are, transfigured —
> Being filled with joy, hardly touching the ground, reaching
>   cross-shaped with outstretched arms to the stars,
>   along of the mountains and the forests, habitation of
>   innumerable creatures, singing joy unending —
> As the sun on a dull morning breaking through the clouds —
>   so from behind the sun another sun, from within the
>   body another body — these shattered falling —
> Lo! now at last or yet awhile in due time to behold that
>   which ye have so long sought —
> O eyes, no wonder you are intent.

> — Edward Carpenter, *Towards Democracy*

For the next week I was barely able to work. My vision seemed to pass through everything; it was hard to focus my attention on anything physical. Divine Mother's and Father's first and favorite image is their offspring, the SöN-SüN, the light. The flying sun disc worshipped in ancient times depicts the Face of Christ, the First Creation of Light, as The Great Central SöN-SüN. The wings placed on the sun disc signify

Winged Sun Disc from Ancient Babylon

187

that "The Christ" is omnipresent consciousness and has free motion through all the dimensions of all the creation. The physical suns we observe are different and confined to specific orbits and positions. As one gazes into space at night, one is confronted with an endless sea of suns in every direction. These, the Spirit's favorite images, cast light upon the planets which orbit around them.

Christ the SöN-SüN, and God the Father, have two natures, masculine and feminine. Divine Spirit Mother and Father gave birth to light, Christ the SöN-SüN. Christ the SöN-SüN, androgynous in nature, projected and created the spherical light bodies of the Angel Men and Women (The Builders) within the expanding inner-penetrating spheres of creation. These divine and brilliant images of the Angel Men and Women were destined to control the development of mineral, plant, animal and human evolution on all planets throughout the creation.

The Builders, as administrating angels, were to eventually dwell in the human creature as a future evolution, thereby creating the human Angel Man and Woman — the final development. The creation of human, the Angel, would now place Divine Consciousness in human form, the ultimate evolution of Christ-Conscious human beings on physical planets throughout the galaxies.

Women's nature, which is called Mother's nature, prepares and cares for the nests of elements which form the crust of physical planets for the creature human to evolve and grow upon. *Hu,* which means animal, and *man,* which means angel, combine in one word, hu-man, which signifies hu-man is both animal and angel in his final evolution. It is the duty of Christed Angel Men and Women (The Builders) to enter into hu, the physical body, and immortalize it, making it hu-man, the Angel. In this final state the Divine Spirit Mother and Father are fully conscious in the gross physical creation. Divine Spirit now dances in physical form on physical worlds fully enjoying the creation from the inside outward and the outside inward. Joy! Joy! All is joy!

Physical suns and planets are created by the same motion of vortexes that gave birth to the First Creation of Light, The Great Central SöN-SüN, and the inner-penetrating spheres of creation. Centripetal and centrifugal vortexes, moving in the four directions, clockwise and counterclockwise, move clouds of hydrogen gases lying deep in space into swirling masses of energy. The collisions of these energies swept together by vortexia and under tremendous pressures bring about the ignition and birth of suns or stars. At the time of ignition, material is thrown outward from the center in the form of incandescent gases. Most of this material is captured by the gravity of the newborn suns and is swept into orbit by the original vortexes. This material cools in space, forming the crust of planets (i.e., suns, planets, solar systems).

Christmas of 1951 passed uneventfully for me. My job with the telephone company kept me busy. I continued daily with my morning and evening meditations. Santa Barbara's yacht harbor took up much of my spare time. There was a boat rental concession there where I began to fulfill my desire to sail. They had one twenty-four foot sloop which I took out alone, spending many a happy hour miles from shore. I loved the sea, and when I was not sailing, I swam or surfed. A fellow named John Ogden, who worked for the telephone company with me and held a black belt in karate, decided to open up a gym in Santa Barbara. He found a place which was suitable and I helped him set up the gym. We put in showers, dressing rooms, and a large room for weightlifting. At the rear of the building there were mats for judo and karate. When finished, the gym looked good. I liked to work out and spend about three nights a week with the weights. I also participated in judo and karate, forming some good friendships with brothers who liked to work out.

Santa Barbara in the 1950s was a quiet, beautiful resort town. In all my travels, I had never found a better climate. Located on the south-facing coast of southern California, Santa Barbara brags of being one of the few places in the world where the sun rises and sets on the ocean most of the year. The four offshore islands, approximately twenty-five miles from the mainland, provide wonderful fishing and anchorage for boats. In years to come, their shores would become very familiar to me from the deck of the *Golden Dawn*.

The month of January 1952 had all but passed. On a Saturday morning about the twenty-eighth of that month, I got up early. I had planned to go sailing that afternoon. Foregoing breakfast, I sat down to practice *Kriya Yoga*. As I began meditating, an intense expression of love began to emanate from my inner being toward the Divine Spirit Mother and Father. The vision of Christ the SöN-SüN had strengthened my devotion and concentration. I was performing perfect circulations of the life force without any distractions. The intensity of my concentration this day was greater than I had ever before experienced. The light of the spiritual eye flared up in bright colors. Rainbows of light were piercing the atmosphere of inner space. Suddenly I felt an incredible presence moving toward me from above on my left side.

From within, I felt a surging forth of energy from the center of

"A lady appeared to me robed with the color of living flame. I turned me to the left with

189

my consciousness, which seemed at this time to be in the region of my heart. I saw the outer fabric of my physical mind (self-conscious ego) and the personality which I had developed stand aside as the force of my true self came forth (i.e., Christ Consciousness) to meet the apparition. My true image spoke directly to the presence.

the confidence with which the little child runs to his mother when he is frightened, or when he is troubled, to say to Virgil [self-conscious mind]: 'Less than a drachm of blood remains in me that does not tremble, I recognize the signals of the ancient flame;' but Virgil had left us deprived of himself." (Dante) The Cosmic Sense robed with the subjective light. At the threshold of the new sense Virgil [self-consciousness] leaves Dante. Not that simple- and self-consciousness leave us when we enter Cosmic Consciousness, *but they do cease to guide us.*

— Richard Bucke, *Cosmic Consciousness*

The Divine Mother's Image

O Mother Divine, I thought never to see you again.
"My son, my son, I am always near."
Your divine form is moving down around my left shoulder; O Mother, you stand directly in front of me now. All that exists of me as an entity, Mother, is in a state of divine rapture. Never before have I felt such exotic waves of bliss and ecstasy — your transfer of energy flows!

My lungs collapse, you empty them as a bellows; every particle of air has been removed from them. I am actually breathless now and unable to inhale. O Mother, I have heard of the breathless, deathless trance that might occur in deep meditation, but now I am experiencing it for the first time. Your figure before me is suspended in inner space; it is really you, O Mother! — as described by

This is the state of which it is said: Clouds fill the thousand mountains. Gradually it goes to and fro quite softly; it rises and falls imperceptibly. The pulse stands still and breathing stops. This is the moment of true creative union (the state of which it is said: The moon gathers up the ten thousand waters. In the midst of this darkness, the heavenly heart suddenly begins a movement. This is the time of the one light, the time when the Child comes to life).

— The Secret of the Golden Flower translated by Richard Wilhelm

Yogananda, incredible, inconceivable, but here you are before me. Your hair streams away into eternity, like rays of opal light.

My lungs struggle to breathe, but they are unable. I feel that I am dying and yet I care not. The soothing vibrations of sound emanating from your image: *"My son, be not afraid. Breathe from my mouth the breath of life."*

That light, O, that dazzling gold ring of light, it appears, as if a

After this sonnet a wonderful vision appeared to me, in which I saw things which

190

mouth. I gaze through it — into eternity. Flowing forth from that tunnel of gold, I perceive a gentle cool breeze — yes, the breeze of a cosmic sea is caressing my face with waves of ecstasy! The body has relaxed and ceased to struggle for breath. O Mother, I realize I am alive in this body without the necessity of breathing — the breathless, deathless trance. I am existing beyond the veil of death, in immortality's grasp. This is the Eternal Now, beyond past and future. I am immortal and I now know it even as I did in my youth. I have become crystallized in the physical body with the passage of years. But I am free in my spirit again.

made me resolve to speak no more of this blessed one until I could more worthily treat of her. And, to attain this, I study to the utmost of my power, as she truly knows. So that, if it shall please Him through whom all things live, that my life be prolonged for some years, I hope to say of her what was never said of any woman.

— Dante, *Vita Nuova*

A man who has acquired the Cosmic Sense does not desire eternal life — he has it.

— Richard Bucke, *Cosmic Consciousness*

Mother of all Mothers standing there before me, don't leave me — I sense you are about to depart — please take me along.

"I will return, my son, in seven days."

With that I was hurled back into the physical ego-consciousness. My breath came back in gasps. I looked at the clock to observe that three hours had passed by with but one moment in eternity.

"Oh Mother, how incredible you are!"

"My son, my son, I am always near. Breathe from my mouth the breath of life."

CHAPTER 22

A Face-to-Face Encounter with "I Am That I Am"

The visitation I had experienced on Saturday morning still lingered heavily in my thoughts as I drove to work on Monday. The promised return in seven days held me in suspense. What would the Mother of all Mothers disclose to me in just five more days? I decided to fast Thursday and Friday in preparation for the visit. Would she really come again? My thoughts were moving everywhere during the week. It was difficult to concentrate on my job, but luckily my job simply consisted of hand-digging holes for telephone poles. As I hammered away with the digging bar and spade, the hours flew by. One could meditate while working, I found.

Finally, Friday afternoon arrived. As I drove home, I noticed *The Song of Bernadette* was playing at a local theatre. I wanted to see the movie as I had heard it was very good. It was about the visitations of the Virgin Mary in visions to a young girl named Bernadette in the small village of Lourdes, France. I had read of the famous accounts of the miracles of Lourdes while at Mount Washington and was anxious to see the movie version. I attended that night's showing and enjoyed the movie immensely. Seeing it during a time of my own visions was a confirmation to me.

In my meditations through the years the spiritual eye had manifested consistently as Yogananda had described it. First, the brilliant gold ring of light would form before my inner vision, followed by a deep purple-blue color in the center, as if one were looking deep into space after sunset. Then, there would appear a small, pentagonal star. The great phenomenon regarding

> He touched my forehead. Masses of whirling light appeared; the radiance gradually formed itself into an opal-blue spiritual eye, ringed in gold and centered with a white pentagonal star.
>
> — Paramhansa Yogananda,
> *Autobiography of a Yogi*

193

the forming of the spiritual eye is that once it is manifested, it remains, whether eyes are open or closed, blotting out the physical vision. When it has fully formed, one attempts, with deep concentration, to penetrate the dazzling gold ring of light. The objective of this penetration is to release the self-conscious ego into the vast regions of inner space. The gold light becomes like a tunnel. Traveling into this gold tunnel, one is actually traveling through one's own heart center inner-dimensionally. The gold tunnel widens and fades into bright green and then into deep blue followed by purple as the meditator approaches the heavenly place. At this time, the five-pointed star no longer emits five rays, but has in fact become the blazing SöN-SüN disc of inner space, the Christ, the projector of all images.

And after six days Jesus taketh Peter, James, and John his brother, and bringeth them up into an high mountain apart, And was transfigured before them: and his face did shine as the sun, and his raiment was white as the light.

— Matthew 17:1-2

The conscious entity, flying through inner space, now has the opportunity of making a journey into the center of The Great Central SöN-SüN. If one succeeds in penetrating the blazing Body of Christ, The Great Central SöN-SüN, one

Penetrate your consciousness through the star into the kingdom of the Infinite.

— Sri Yukteswar to Paramhansa Yogananda, *Autobiography of a Yogi*

has attained Christ Consciousness forever. Beyond this attainment lies the unmanifested Spirit Mother and Father Creator and the endless, timeless, primordial sea of life and consciousness. Indeed, *Kriya Yoga* leads one to the vision of The Great Central SöN-SüN and the Christed Angel Men and Women who gained their birth at the center of the First Ignition of Light. The self-consciousness of the hu-man spirit must make the journey to the center of The Great Central SöN-SüN with its two divine *Companions*, the Angel Man and Woman. There, the ego oriented self-consciousness of the hu-man entity finally fuses with the immortal Angel Man and Woman.

This then, through devotion, meditation, and service, is the ultimate goal of any meditator. None cometh unto the Father but by the SöN-SüN, the light of creation, the projector and creator of all images. Thus, the first created image of light, Christ, the SöN-SüN, the projector, is the only doorway out of the dual nature of the expanding Sphere of Creation. "Behold, I stand at the door and knock," said Christ the Lord, referring to the opening at the center on the crown of the head. It is

The state of Cosmic Consciousness is undoubtedly the highest that we can at present conceive, but it does not follow that there are not higher nor that we may not eventually attain to higher.

— Richard Bucke, *Cosmic Consciousness*

by conducting a search within the vast inner spaces that Christ, the light, is found illuminating the cosmic door into the eternal abode of Divine Spirit Mother and Father.

I shall now try to relate in words, to the best of my ability, the sequence of events that led me on my first journey to the center of The Great Central SöN-SüN, and my subsequent return. In this state all breath ceases, and the heart also ceases, striking a final beat. The physical body is suspended by the forces of the immortal Angel Man and Woman in time and space to await the return of the newly baptised and now Christ-Conscious entity.

Christ Consciousness can be defined in three stages: (1) he who sees the sun rise on the horizon at midnight (i.e., the true Magi); (2) he who sees another sun, "as in a swoon," face to face, and hears the voice thereof; (3) he who sees another sun face to face and experiences so-called physical death, enters the light, sees all which light and life have become (i.e., the expanding spheres of creation), and returns to reclaim the body after minutes, hours, or days. Henceforth, this spirit has become a true Son or Daughter of the Living Spirit, a Builder.

— The Author

The journey homeward to freedom has begun, lying beyond the confining ball and chain of the physical body into the blazing light of Christ the SöN-SüN, and the eternal primordial sea.

I concluded a short meditation Friday night in anticipation of the morning's dawn. I prayed silently, "Lord, if it be thy desire, let me return from whence I came; I am indeed an alien here. I have no one to relate to, and no one understands me here except Paramhansa Yogananda, whom I have left, and my father. However, if it is thy will, strengthen me for the journey ahead."

Saturday morning I was up at six-thirty. I washed my face, took a cold drink of water, and began to prepare my room and bed for a long meditation. Yogananda had always encouraged us to meditate facing the rising sun, or due east by the compass. We were also made aware of the magnetic currents flowing from south to north and from east to west. One should sleep either with the head toward the east or the south to avoid the toxins in the lower regions of the body from being swept toward the head by the pressure of magnetic waves. He cautioned against sleeping with the head to the north, stating that that was the direction used when ad-

We know that the whole surface of the earth is washed by a flow of energy known as the magnetic field. Like all other heavenly bodies, the earth is a great magnet, the strength and direction of its currents influenced by many factors including the proximity and relative positions of the other spheres in the solar system, chiefly the sun and moon. . . . all the evidence from the remote past points to the inescapable conclusion that the earth's natural magnetism was not only known to men some thousands of years ago, but it provided them

vanced souls decided to leave the body in final death. I had always faced east for my meditations. I placed a pillow at the head of my bed and sat down in the traditional lotus posture facing east. Placing my tongue in the upward position, *Kechari Mudra*, I began to perform *Kriya Yoga*.

with a source of energy and inspiration to which their whole civilization was tuned.

— John Michell, *The View Over Atlantis*

Immediately I sensed a finer attunement and experienced an instant flaring of the spiritual eye. My goal today was to achieve one hundred and eight circulations of the life with perfect concentration. I had a string of meditation beads to pass through my fingers as each *Kriya* was performed. I was performing perfect *Kriyas*. With each breath the colors of the rainbow would streak by my inner vision. I lost all sense of time as I worked toward my goal. I was nearing one hundred and eight circulations when I again felt the approach of that incredible presence coming toward me from the left side. I mentally called out with audible thought. "O Mother, you have returned." A reply impressed me to be silent and continue my meditation. I continued on, realizing I had but five more circulations to perform before reaching my goal. I sensed that something awesome was about to happen to me on the spiritual plane. Was it to be a divine test of my faith?

A Vision of "I Am That I Am"

Tremendous and intense energy is building up beneath me. Now the image of Divine Mother is again standing to my left. She motions downward as if to the center of the earth.

With an upsweep of her arm, flames flare up from the great deep beneath and engulf me around about. The force of the flames are concentrated on the end of my spine.

A lady appeared to me robed with the color of living flame. . . . I recognize the signal of the ancient flame.

— Dante, *Purgatorio*

O vision divine, you reveal the flames now advancing upward around my spine toward my beating heart.

All at once without warning of any kind I found myself wrapped around as it were by a flame-colored cloud. For an instant I thought of fire, some sudden conflagration in the great city, the next I knew that light was within myself.

O Mother, you are speaking — I hear your voice through the flames,

— Richard Bucke, *Cosmic Consciousness*

you point toward me: *"Receive your son, my Lord!"*

O spine, you stiffen as if in death. O breath, you vanish from me. O death, you surely grip me.

Now the flames are flaring higher — O Father-Mother, I feel no fear, only surrender; I am in the grip of your forces beyond my poor control.

My head is being thrown backwards to the limits of extension. There again before me is that colossal sphere of brilliance ... it's hurtling towards me!

As in a swoon, one instant
Another sun, ineffable full-dazzles me
And all the orbs I knew, and brighter unknown orbs
One instant of the future land, Heaven's land.

There is the same incredible voice coming as if from everywhere, "*My son, are you ready to die today and come with me?*" Divine Mother is introducing me to my Father, as a mother would present her son.

— Walt Whitman, *Leaves of Grass*

As Mohammed, in the silent watches of the night, lay wrapped in his mantle, he heard a voice calling upon him. Uncovering his head, a flood of light broke upon him of such intolerable splendor that he swooned.

— Washington Irving, *Life of Mohammed*

O strength, fail me not! I must reply. How many desires obstruct me? How many attachments to earthly things have I made? I can reply directly and without hesitation, "Yes, my Lord, I am ready to die and leave with you. There is nothing here I really want, only you, Lord, only you!" O audible thoughts, speak loudly for me.

These brilliant flames from beneath — they represent Mother's forces moving upward through me toward the blazing brilliance of Father's image in his SöN-SüN, the Face of Christ!

Is my answer acceptable, O Father of all? Is my answer correct? I have no hesitation, I feel no fear within. I am going to die and go with him whom I love more than anything else.

By the rejoicings which I have in Christ, I die daily.

— 1 Corinthians 15:31

That shimmering, pulsating orb, it's exploding all around me with a brilliance beyond anything I have ever seen. I am now whirling within this incredible light! It is colliding with the brilliant swirling flames rising upward from beneath. Both forces are uniting now within my heart — I am swept into the middle of this stupendous union.

The tremendous forces are beginning to dissipate, they are moving outward, there are no more flames or brilliant lights. Now only the beating of my heart. I am suspended in its center, I am inconceivably small.

O my life, my heart, like a dying creature, I feel you slowing to a last and final beat. O breath, you are long gone. O heart, you beat no more. I am now surely dead.

O Lord, where are you? I am only a sphere of consciousness. I have no body anymore, but yet somehow I am still myself and very much alive, so incredibly alive. The loss of my body doesn't disturb me, I am not afraid.

My thoughts are still my own; I can now look back, yes, I am fully aware of all that has transpired. Thoughts echo within, "Yes with the final beat of your heart, you must now accept the fact that your earthly body is dead."

I am expanding as a sphere, moving outward in all directions at an incredible rate. My vision is spherical; I can look within at the very smallest of all places and now without at the largest of all places.

O clear, quiet light, you permeate outward in every direction from me. There is no horizon, no sunlight, but all is visible. This sphere of consciousness is me, I am still expanding.

Now there are around me, creations' lights abounding. Yes, your images are floating here within me — star systems, galaxies, universes. I exist in them and they in me.

There are two thought-forms that appear first within the non-thinking, eternally conscious, unmanifested Divine Spirit, the endless eternal sea of life force. Spirit, non-thinking, feels the smallest of all places existing within the largest of all places. The smallest of all places is the divine center of consciousness from which thought-forms contemplate the largest of all places. It is the divine center of the smallest of all places where divine thoughts are given birth. It was here that divine thoughts moving outward into the eternal sea of life and energy gave birth to light — Christ the SöN-SüN of Divine Spirit.

— The Author

Tremendous vibrations humming, rolling, spinning, surging through me, generating wave upon wave of ecstasy!

Oh, I am now so strangely alone. Barriers of thought-forms and images of light and sound, you press upon me reflecting the creation. All sounds and lights, you suddenly now desist, you are melting into joy, joy indescribable joy! Yes, love, you are there, you are ever-new and beyond all dreams of love.

O my creation, you vanish from my vision, I am alone. I am moving outward still in all directions expanding in this, my sphere of ever-new joy and bliss.

Ecstasy, I feel beyond the limits of all that I have ever conceived. I — now infinite, without form or light or sound. But still, O memory, you continue on for me.

The expanding has ceased; Yes, I Am He, I Am That I Am! I Am He! He Is Me! O thoughts, desist here now, conclude yourselves in bliss. There is now a presence, it is moving within my consciousness, I feel a shudder, a field of force, swirling within me.

The Father's voice speaks again,

At some point he finds himself approaching some sort of barrier or border, apparently representing the limit between earthly life and the next. Yet, he finds that he must go back to the Earth, that the time for his death has not yet come. At this point he resists, for by now he is taken up with his experiences in

198

but from where does it proceed? It is mine and yet not mine, what does it say? *"My son, my son, now you have seen: now I must put you back."* I am in the unmanifested invisible presence of the Father of all Fathers and the Mother of all Mothers. I Am That I Am, the Divine Creator Spirit.

Now there within me, the image of the great Sphere of Creation appears, floating like an irridescent bubble in the infinite sea of life and consciousness of which I am now a part.

I am growing smaller now, even as I have expanded, collapsing inward at a tremendous velocity. The pulsating hum of all creation now dwells within my consciousness; floating universes appear now within my sphere of vision, their faint lights looking like clusters of stars. All is me and I am all. I am one with my Father and one with my Mother. The divine drama of creation rolls onward toward an unforeseeable end. I am returning to the physical body; it is the Father's will that I disclose his living presence to others, in and beyond space and time, within and beyond the great expanding Sphere of Creation.

My return now reveals my mission and the path to follow, through a forest of images, mind-produced; it is arrayed before me.

Still decreasing in size now, the brilliant colors of a galaxy, I see familiar star systems and the region of earth's solar system. Before me now is the bright blue sphere of Mother Earth, and I see her as before in some other time frame. Now the familiar vibrations of spirits long known are surrounding me. Below, a familiar vortex of spinning white light swirls down like a silvery stair-

the afterlife and does not want to return. He is overwhelmed by intense feelings of joy, love, and peace. Despite his attitude, though, he somehow reunites with his physical body and lives.

— Dr. Raymond Moody, *Life After Life*

O how blessed is that soul which is ever conscious of God reposing and resting within it. . . . He is there, as it were, asleep in the embraces of the soul and the soul is in general conscious of His presence and in general delights exceedingly in it.

— St. John of the Cross, *Life and Works,* Vol. 2

"Well," someone will say, "if these people see and know and feel so much, why don't they come out with it in plain language and give the world the benefit of it?" This is what "speech" said to Whitman: "Walt, you contain enough, why don't you let it out, then?" Whitman tells us in *Leaves of Grass:* "When I undertake to tell the best I find I cannot, My tongue is ineffectual on its pivots, My breath will not be obedient to its organs, I become a dumb man."

So Paul, when he was "caught up into paradise," heard "unspeakable words." And Dante was not able to recount the things he saw in heaven. "My vision," he says, "was greater than *our speech,* which yields to such a sight. . . ." The fact of the matter is not difficult to understand; it is that speech. . . is the tally of the self-conscious intellect, and can express that and nothing but that, does not tally, and cannot express the Cosmic Sense — or, if at all, only in so far as this may

case, moving around and around in a counterclockwise manner. I am descending now within the center of this force toward the tiny planet beneath me.

be translated into terms of the self-conscious intellect.

— Richard Bucke, *Cosmic Consciousness*

O familiar sphere of Mother Earth, you grow in size. There are the oceans, continents, mountains, cities, the familiar coastline of California, the roofs of houses, my body sitting as it had been left an eternity ego. I am slipping into it without sensation. O Father-Mother, the body ball and chain again.

I now felt the heart begin to beat, the lungs moved to receive the vital airs of earth. My eyes, as in a dream, took in the brightness of my room. My body was no longer sitting on the pillow at the head of the bed where the journey had begun. I was still locked in the lotus posture, but I was now at the other end of the bed, facing the north wall of the room. I couldn't move my body, as all was without feeling and numb. My eyes took in the contents of the room and fell on a clock which I had left on the table. It was now one-thirty in the afternoon. Seven hours had passed, but was it the same day? If it were, I had been absent from this body seven earthly hours, which now seemed to me an eternity ago.

Yes, an eternity had passed through my consciousness; I had been beyond the barriers of time, space and images. I had seen the great expanding Sphere of Creation floating within the Divine Consciousness. All of creation is but the visible thought-forms of our Divine Parents, Mother and Father. Yes, alive in eternity, incredibly alive, filling all which exists, but still dwelling outside of all, I Am That I Am, whose face shines within the divine radiance of the SöN-SüN, the Christ, the First and Only Begotten, the Light of Creation and of all men and women, the Lord of Lords; Christ, the Alpha and the Omega, the Beginning and the End. All men are Sons, as all woman are Daughters. All men and all women can be Christed; both are from the same light.

I sat silently within my body. Circulation was beginning to return. An hour later I was able to move my arms and rub my legs. The shock of this experience and the impact upon my physical body would be felt for the rest of my life. As much as twenty-eight years later, the stream of eternity is still pouring down data upon my head.

By this time, so deep were the impressions made on my mind that sleep had fled from my eyes, and I lay overwhelmed in astonishment at what I had both seen and heard.

— Joseph Smith, 2:46, Pearl of Great Price

Ten years of continued meditation was not enough to solidify the tremendous impact of the experience into thought-forms that could be expressed. It is only now, twenty-eight years later, that I am able to recount, with some clarity of words, the incredible experience I have lived to talk about. This is my message and this is my mission — to help direct brothers and sisters toward their homeward flight, for all can attain and all can know, and now is the time to make that encounter.

As Moses saw God face to face, so did I, and so can you. I realize today that I was put back into my body because Divine Spirit Mother and Father desired that this encounter be known. The ancient technique of meditation taught to me by the Angel Men and Women (The Builders) exists for those who would receive it. It helps make this flight possible. My flight into inner space and my subsequent return marks the flight path of the Ancients on their journey to the center of The Great Central SöN-SüN and back.

The Circulation of the Light, as now practiced in our group with tremendous results, proves it. The ancient method of meditation, now called The SöN-SüN technique, is taught in three initiations. It opens up the spiritual door, allowing the entity to leave, as I did, through the crown of the head — the highest flight path into eternity — and into the presence of a living, Divine Spirit whose nature is dual, Mother-Father-Creator. The Mother-Father-God of all creation filling the great immensity is fact, not fiction!

In the year 1968 my visions concerning young and old people gathering together in communities in the Santa Barbara area began to manifest.

The SöN-SüN technique of meditation has been passed on to all sincere recipients who requested its instruction. Many have experienced visions of The Great Central SöN-SüN and their own homeward flight. The unique experiences spoken of in this book have been manifested in the lives of many souls desiring them in and around our group.

Kriya Yoga as passed on to me by my teacher, Paramhansa Yogananda, has been modified under the direction of The Builders to include Kechari Mudra and the use of the center on the crown of the head.

— The Author

There again before me is that colossal sphere of brilliance. . . . Divine Mother is
introducing me to my Father, as a mother would present her son.

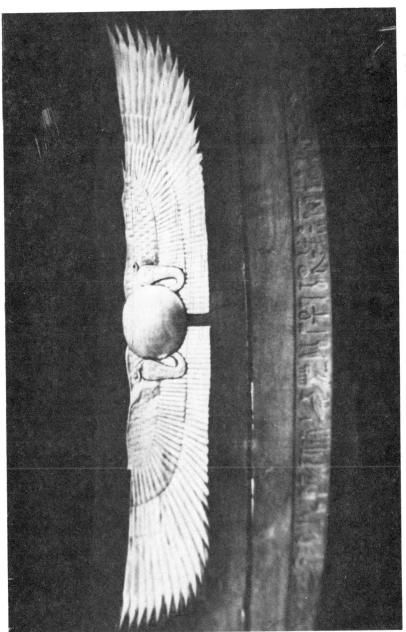

The winged sun disc appears on the back of a cedarwood chair from the tomb of King Tutankhamen

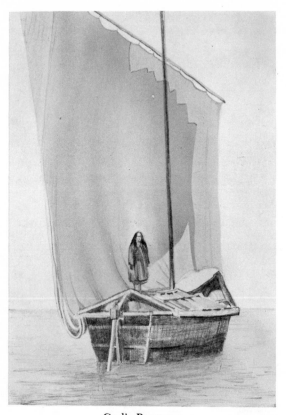

God's Boatman

I want to ply my boat, many times,
Across the gulf-after-death,
And return to earth's shores
From my home in heaven.
I want to load my boat
With those waiting, thirsty ones,
Who are left behind,
And carry them by the opal pool
Of iridescent joy —
Where my Father distributes
His all-desire-quenching liquid peace.
Oh, I will come again and again!
Crossing a million crags of suffering,
With bleeding feet, I will come —

If need be, a trillion times —
So long as I know
One stray brother is left behind.
I want Thee, O Lord,
That I may give Thee to all.
Free me, then, O God,
From the bondage of the body,
That I may show others
How they can free themselves.
I want Thine everlasting bliss
Only that I may share it with others;
That I may show all my brothers
The way to happiness
Forever and forever, in Thee.

— Paramhansa Yogananda

CHAPTER 23

The Death and Resurrection
of Paramhansa Yogananda

The tremendous experience of "I Am That I Am," on February 4, 1952, left me in a dreamlike trance. I could see the outer illusory crust of third-dimensional matter, but at the same time I could see the scintillating atoms and life force within.

In the light of my experience, all outer forms took on the unreality of movie sets. People appeared to me as actors, so engrossed in their script that they had momentarily forgotten their true identity. Yes, the earth was indeed a stage where the drama of life was continuously acted out. The role of an enlightened actor in the drama is to enlighten other actors, for suffering actually takes place when we forget our true image. The drama of life is best enjoyed here on earth when everyone knows it is only a momentary play of light and shadow. Enacting a role with such a cast of enlightened players would then be a divine experience and expression.

Roles enacted in our original earthly paradise had been joyous occasions. Hu-man must wake up to his true identity (Christ

This life of the world is nothing but a sport and a play; but, verily, the abode of the next world — that is, life. If they did but know.

— Mohammed, Koran, Part 2
translated by E. H. Palmer

I looked about me and could see that what we then were doing was like a shadow cast upon the earth from yonder vision in the heavens, so bright it was and clear. I knew the real was yonder and the darkened dream of it was here.

— John G. Neihardt, *Black Elks Speaks*

The Cosmic Director has written His own plays and has summoned the tremendous casts for the pageant of the centuries. From the dark booth of eternity He sends His beams of light through the films of successive ages, and pictures are thrown on the backdrop of space. Just as cinematic images appear to be real but are only combinations of light and shade, so is the universal variety a delusive seeming. The planetary spheres, with their countless forms of life, are naught but figures in a cosmic motion picture. Temporarily true to man's five sense perceptions, the transitory scenes

205

Consciousness) and divine inheritance, instead of destroying this earthly "stage of life." We are now witnessing a rebellion against the Divine Playwright, which can only end in disaster; humankind has not the ability nor time to write another script.

Because of the aftereffects of my experience with Mother-Father, I found it necessary to leave my work with the telephone company are cast on the screen of human consciousness by the infinite creative beam. A cinema audience may look up and see that all screen images are appearing through the instrumentality of one imageless beam of light. The colorful universal drama is similarly issuing from the single white light of a Cosmic Source. With inconceivable ingenuity God is staging "super-colossal" entertainment for His children, making them actors as well as audience in His planetary theater.

— Paramhansa Yogananda, *Autobiography of a Yogi*

for about two weeks. When I would walk, I would experience the sensations of sinking into the earth several feet with each step or floating four or five feet above my body. At night, sitting in meditation, I spent most of my time on the planes of inner space. The earthly body seemed undesirable to me now; when conscious in it, I felt as though I were attached to a real ball and chain. The harsh, noisy environment of the physical plane in its state of rebellion against the divine guidelines was difficult to accept. If I was an alien before, I now filled the description completely. How was I to communicate with my fellow actors without offending them? The eyes of my generation showed no interest at all in the active pursuit of Divine Illumination. There was an intellectual desire on the part of

The eyesight, has another eyesight, the hearing another hearing, and the voice another voice.

— Walt Whitman, *Leaves of Grass*

some, but this was as far as they wanted to go. It was now very understandable to me why Master Yogananda was unable to materialize a world brotherhood colony. He lacked the actors to participate in one. The time to fulfill the dreams of brotherhood colonies was to materialize with the next generation and their children. I would have to wait approximately twenty years. What was I to do?

I sought to return to Divine Spirit and the timeless eternity I had experienced. But each time I tried to enter, the Face of Christ would flash before me saying, *"If you enter now, you will never return."* The Divine will was set upon my mission; there was no escape. I must find out where the roots of mankind's afflictions existed. How could the attraction for outer material objects and sensations of the five senses be broken? This could only happen for hu-man when awareness of the great sensations of the Spirit within became more desirable than things without. Signposts must be set up. Visible participation in the fruits of Divine Illumination must be demonstrated publicly. Humankind is beyond the point of taking anyone's word that salvation and heaven do indeed exist. Hu-man must experience heaven (i.e., Christ Consciousness) while he yet lives. Only then can he know and believe.

Jesus himself stated that the blind cannot lead the blind, for both will fall in the same ditch. Illumined brothers and sisters must show the way. The teachings and guidelines of Christ Jesus and others must be lived as originally given. I tried to visualize a world whose inhabitants all knew they were sons and daughters of a living Divine Spirit Mother-Father-Creator. I knew such civilizations existed on countless worlds throughout the creation. There ships of light transported vast populations to distant star systems for enactment of some divine drama. Our own world in past history has supported such civilizations, the remnants of which are yet visible to us today in stone.

I knew such races were referred to as "the Ancients" or "The Builders," hence their opposites must be "the Destroyers." Was this the condition Mother Earth was now subjected to? Yes, the next generation would contain the beginnings of an invasion by the Forces of Light. The return of The Builders was now in progress. Jesus, an elder brother of this divine race, would fulfill his promised return. My inner senses were reading and feeling forthcoming events far in the future. Somehow I would survive the ordeal ahead. My life was to be subjected to persecution and treachery. The names of entities, astral and physical, representing the Forces of Darkness, would become emblazoned in my consciousness.

Yogananda had defined the three great temptations on this planet as being directly connected with lust (the desire for physical sense gratification), alcohol (a desire for temporary diversion), and wealth and

You never will enjoy the world aright till the sea itself floweth in your veins, till you are clothed with the heavens, and crowned with the stars, and perceive yourself to be the sole heir of the whole world, and more than so, because men are in it who are every one sole heirs as well as you; till you can sing and delight and rejoice in God; . . . till you are intimately acquainted with that shady nothing out of which the world was made.

— Thomas Traherne,
Centuries of Meditations

None can understand it, I think, except that soul which has experienced it.

— St. John of the Cross, *Life and Works*,
Vol. 2

The Builders — the real creators of the universe, or architects of the planetary system. There were battles fought between the creators and the destroyers, and battles fought for space.

— Erich von Däniken,
Gods from Outer Space

power (a desire for self-conscious ego gratification). With these three lures, the Forces of Darkness draw mankind into the web of delusion. Then, when the self-conscious entity becomes hopelessly enmeshed, the spirits of deception stand forth laughing. The law of cause and effect is not regarded or taught by this world's people. The teachings of great personages go unregarded, or are deliberately misinterpreted by the negative spirits in control. The veil covering the entities of darkness must be rent. Mankind must see the great deception. The actual existence of supernatural beings of destruction is just as real as the existence of Mother Earth and the heavens above. The disobedient ones, called "the Fallen Angels," camp on worlds disrupting the divine drama until an all-out war ensues with the Forces of Light, and they are hurled away. Christ Jesus referred to the legions of angels, Divine Warriors of Light, that were at his disposal. Was I to be involved in this struggle? I shuddered, feeling an icy wind; fear was riding on its crest! Circumstances in my life would present overwhelming odds. Still, I knew I would somehow win in the end.

I returned to my job at the telephone company about the twenty-second of February, 1952. After finishing the week's work, I decided to go to Mount Washington on Friday evening in hopes of seeing Paramhansa Yogananda. I wanted to tell him of my recent experience. Arriving in Hollywood, I rented a room for the night and decided to drive up to the retreat on Saturday morning. That evening I thought I had better try to reach him by phone. I succeeded in reaching one of his secretaries who said she would convey to Paramhansaji any message I might have but that I probably would not be able to see him. I was standing in a phone booth near the Self-Realization Fellowship Church of all Religions on Sunset Boulevard; here I would speak for the last time to my beloved friend and teacher in his physical form.

I waited, hearing his voice over the phone as he approached from another room. "Hello, hello, how are you doing, Big Boy?"

"All right, sir, I wanted to tell you what happened to me."

"Yes, yes, I know. I am very busy now, but tell me."

"I wanted to see you sir, tomorrow, if that's possible."

There was a long pause and I heard a sigh, then a whisper, "I will be leaving very shortly. March 7 is a big day for me."

"But can't I see you tomorrow, sir?"

"You must look for me in the spiritual eye (i.e., the divine tunnel of life) from now on. Divine Mother says time is short. She will not allow me to see anyone anymore."

"Can I tell you a little about what happened to me?"

"Yes, yes, but you must hurry."

I related in as few words as possible what had transpired.

"Didn't I tell you long ago wonderful things would come to you? You must be strong now. You must be my 'giant.' I also told you that after I am gone you will see me. Remember?"

"Yes sir, I remember."

"Well, you must make the Lord your constant companion now. Then you will never be lonely. Now I must go."

"Can I come to the retreat for a visit?"

"Yes, you may, the gates here will always be open for you. Goodbye for now."

"Goodbye, sir."

The phone clicked off. I realized this would be my last conversation with him in his present form. I stepped out of the phone booth into the roar of the traffic and the lights of the city, Paramhansa Yogananda's voice echoing in my thoughts. As I looked up, I could barely see the stars beyond the glare of the city lights. What a cold, unnatural place it was, indeed, a cemetery with lights.

As I drove home, Paramhansaji's words came back to me: "I am leaving shortly; March 7 is a big day for me." Suddenly I realized he was actually telling me that March 7 would be the time of his final departure. What could I do? Had he told others? Should I try and tell someone what he had said? No, this was his way; I would remain silent. The words he once spoke rang in my ears: "After I am gone, they will know who I was."

I reached Santa Barbara and lived the next few days in a state of apprehension; the suspense was terrible. My intuition told me it was true he would be gone on the seventh day of March. That day finally arrived. It was late in the afternoon when I sensed it had happened. A telephone call that evening confirmed it. Paramhansa Yogananda had passed on at a banquet given for India's ambassador, Binay R. Sen, at the Biltmore Hotel in Los Angeles. He had departed before the large audience there. He had concluded a short talk and was reciting a poem he had written called "My India": ". . . where Ganges woods, Himalayan caves, and men dream God; I am hallowed, my body touched that sod." With these final words he collapsed to the floor. He was gone, at least to all outward appearances.

The disciples brought his body to Mount Washington and placed it upon his bed. Here, one by one, they all said a final goodbye. Some thought he was in a death trance and would return. Forest Lawn Memorial Park was to take his body away the next day. James J. Lynn, one of Paramhansaji's earliest disciples (destined to become president of the organization at his departure), announced that Paramhansa Yogananda had told him he would not return to the body, that this was his final exit. Those who were reluctant to turn his body over to the morticians, for fear he might still return, were ignored.

I drove that night as fast as I could to Mount Washington. I was allowed to see him alone. Everyone else had passed by him and were retiring to their rooms. I approached his room. Seeing his body upon the bed, I could not control the flood of tears. Yes! He was gone. I was looking at his body for the last time. I knelt beside him. Upon his face there was a slight smile, as if he had just fallen asleep. Touching him, his flesh still felt alive; it was hard to believe he was really gone; but gone he was. Had he not told me goodbye a year and a half ago, and again just a few days before? I meditated silently at his feet. Those large, lustrous eyes, seen by me so long ago in childhood, were now closed forever to this world. When indeed would such a meeting take place again between us?

I entered the ashram room where Master's body, unimaginably lifelike, was sitting in the lotus posture — a picture of health and loveliness. A short time before his passing, my teacher had been slightly ill with fever, but before the day of his ascension into the Infinite, his body had become completely well. No matter how often I looked at his dear form I could not realize that its life had departed. His skin was smooth and soft; on his face was a beatific expression of tranquillity. He had consciously relinquished his body at the hour of mystic summoning.

— Paramhansa Yogananda on the passing of his teacher, Sri Yukteswar, *Autobiography of a Yogi*

My loss was great, as was everyone's. No longer was he here that we might gain strength from him. His disciples were on their own. Only his words remained in our memories, and those rare experiences with him alone, which I knew everyone now cherished. "Goodbye, sir. I salute your form, for in final victory over death, I know you have arisen. Yes, your form I will behold again. You have promised that."

Master Yogananda's body was removed to Forest Lawn Memorial Park where the normal procedures of embalming were done; the miracle was yet to take place. Paramhansaji's body was delivered back to Mount Washington for the funeral services; I was there, as were hundreds of other people. Some came who had been unfriendly to him, but at the last minute had found a change of heart, and now rushed to get a final glimpse. I remember little of the ceremony performed by Saint Lynn and Dr. Lewis, two of his first disciples. I was too upset by it all, as was everyone. At the conclusion, I somehow found myself carrying the head of his casket toward the limousine.

"Oh Paramhansa Yogananda, how many times have I carried your person?"

We all stood silently together as his body made its final trip down Mount Washington's winding road.

It was over twenty days later that the news hit the papers. Headlines of the *Los Angeles Mirror* and *The Los Angeles Times* read, "Yogi Defies Death." A notarized letter from Harry T. Rowe, Forest Lawn's Mortuary director, stated, ". . . the absence of any visual signs of decay in the dead body of Paramhansa Yogananda offers the most extraordinary case in our experience. . . . No physical disintegration was visible in his body even twenty days after death. . . . No indication of mold was visible on his skin. . . . This state of perfect preservation of a body is, so far as we know from mortuary annals, an unparalleled one. . . .

"The physical appearance of Yogananda on March 27, just before the bronze cover of the casket was put into position, was the same as it had been on March 7. . . . He looked on March 27 as fresh and unravaged by decay as he had looked on the night of his death. . . . For these reasons we state again that the case of Paramhansa Yogananda — is unique in our experience."

The casket was sealed after twenty days when word came that two disciples from India would be unable to make the journey to see him.

I returned to Santa Barbara after the funeral. What was to become of Paramhansaji's work? Would they be able to carry on without him? I knew it was going to be difficult for me and for everyone else who knew and loved him. He had kept the vision of God-realization alive before us all.

I continued with my work at the telephone company. Working helped pass the time. My meditations were good, but confined. The great experience of February was all I could relate to; still the Lord would not let me enter. In light of the tremendous ecstasy of this experience, all else, especially worldly pursuits, meant nothing to me. My great desire was to return to my eternal abode; nothing else would satisfy me. I missed Yogananda terribly. Still, had he not promised to return to me? But now,

---

The beatification of Catherine Labouré, held in St. Peter's on May 28, 1933, ranked in magnificence with those of Jeanne d'Arc and Therese of Lisieux, ceremonies which left lasting memory in Rome.

The Church now ordered the exhumation of the body of the Saint. It had lain, sealed in the vault beneath the chapel at Reuilly, for fifty-seven years. The coffin was carried to the Rue du Bac, and there opened in the presence of Cardinal Verdier, Archbishop of Paris, and a number of civil officials and doctors. As the lid was lifted, a gasp of astonishment ran through the group. Catherine lay there, as fresh and serene as the day she was buried. Her skin had not darkened in the least; the eyes which had looked on Our Lady were as intensely blue as ever, — and most remarkable of all — her arms and legs were as supple as if she were merely asleep.

— Joseph I. Dirvin,
Saint Catherine Labouré

three months had passed, and I felt he was not going to return as he had promised. Had he forgotten or was he unable? I resigned myself to the belief that he was unable.

One hot summer afternoon of 1952 I arrived home to my single-room apartment. Lying on the bed, I was enjoying reading Walt Whitman's *Leaves of Grass.* Suddenly a gust of wind hit the door. I looked up to see the beloved figure of Paramhansa Yogananda walk into the room and close the door behind him. He walked to the foot of my bed and looked down at me; the lustrous eyes of my childhood visions again met my gaze. As he stood there, two figures materialized on each side of him. They were floating in the air in lotus posture, their only garb a loincloth. "They must be the Himalayan yogis of Paramhan-saji's childhood visions," I thought. He was with them as he had desired. They hovered in the air beside him in silence. Paramhan-saji had on his familiar orange robe of the Swami Order, and seemed as real and solid as the walls of the room surrounding me. Immediately I sat up in lotus posture. Paramhansa Yogananda was now fulfilling his promised return.

He began to speak of the future formation of spiritual communities, containing married couples and children. He said that in marriage men and women should set a life of continence as one of their primary goals.

I was roused from my meditation by a beatific light. Before my open and astonished eyes, the whole room was transformed into a strange world, the sunlight transmuted into supernal splendor. Waves of rapture engulfed me as I beheld the flesh and blood form of Sri Yukteswar! . . . But is it you, Master, the same Lion of God? Are you wearing a body like the one I buried beneath the Puri sands?

"Yes, I am the same. This is a flesh and blood body. Though I see it as ethereal, to your sight it is physical. From cosmic atoms I created an entirely new body, exactly like that cosmic-dream physical body which you laid beneath the sands at Puri in your dream-world. . . . You and your exalted loved ones shall someday come to be with me."

— Paramhansa Yogananda,
Autobiography of a Yogi

While I was thus in the act of calling upon God, I discovered a light appearing in my room, which continued to increase until the room was lighter than at noonday, when immediately a personage appeared at my bedside, standing in the air, for his feet did not touch the floor.

He had on a loose robe of most exquisite whiteness. . . . He called me by name, and said unto me that he was a messenger sent from the presence of God to me, that his name was Moroni; . . . and that my name should be had for good and evil among all nations. . . .

— Joseph Smith, 2:31-33,
Pearl of Great Price

Paramhansa Yogananda lived his earthly life as a celibate monk. He never married nor did he ever break his vows of celibacy.

It is difficult for men and women to understand why such a life of restriction might be necessary. In one respect Yogananda viewed all aspirants seeking the Divine as spiritual athletes. It is a known fact and a common practice for most great athletes to abstain

Yogananda's parents had united occasionally for the purpose of conceiving a vehicle for an incarnating soul to inhabit. Married couples should work out their sexual desires together, realizing the difference between lust and true spiritual love which can be conveyed through the five senses, one to another. The dissipation of the creative forces whenever the urge to procreate arises depletes the body and mind of the vital life forces that are necessary to the attainment of higher states of consciousness.

The further formation of spiritual communities must be founded on true concepts of virtue, with the attainment of continence uppermost in the minds of all participants. Continual depletion of the body's life force through lust would destroy all participants' interest in forming spiritual brotherhood communities and the attainment of the ultimate goal — Christ Consciousness.

After receiving these insights, I saw in a flash many couples living together successfully in a spiritual community. In practicing virtue, meditating, and working together, surely they would achieve the original purpose of The Builders' Garden of Eden. In essence, they would be putting the fruit back on the Tree of Life.

from sexual relations while in training for competition: boxers, wrestlers, football players, martial arts professionals, track and field competitors, etc. Everyone knows that depletion of the vital forces of procreation through continued lust weakens the minds and bodies of the indulgers. It can be clearly seen that to achieve the best physical, mental, and highest spiritual attainments, a life of continence is required. For those who choose to take the vows of celibacy and intend to keep those vows, let them continue. For those who seek to marry and create children, let them realize true spiritual love for each other conveyed through the five senses. Having achieved this, look toward the life of continence and the conservation of the vital life force for spiritual purposes and the final attainment of Christ or Cosmic Consciousness.

It cannot be said that a life of continence is a prerequisite for the attainment of Christ Consciousness, but of all practices it surely contributes the most, in all departments of living, toward that goal. The practice of celibacy is for those spiritual athletes who are willing to contribute all that they have toward their own spiritual goals. This is hardly the life for the everyday human being to contemplate, and an impossible task for the multitudes.

Does celibacy guarantee the delivery of Christ Consciousness to the individual? I do not believe it does. But surely one who is able to live it must have, or is very near, the attainment already.

— The Author

Master raised his hand, fingers together and pointing upward like a sword. This meant, "I bow to the Infinite Spirit within you." I saw he was about to leave. Now I knew we would meet again. As he turned, the two figures beside him disappeared. He walked toward the door and opened it. I was about to follow when he turned in the doorway saying, "Not now!

Later." The door closed behind him. Yogananda had demonstrated in death, as he had in life, the divine nature of our true image (Christ Consciousness). He is immortal and he proved it to me.

In a personal conversation with Daya Mata, the President of SRF, she informed me that Paramhansaji had also appeared to her and several other members of SRF, including the late President of SRF, James J. Lynn, Rajarsi Janakandanda.

— The Author

When I Am Only a Dream

I come to tell you all of Him,
And the way to encase Him in your bosom,
And of the discipline that brings His grace.
Those of you who have asked me
To guide you to my Beloved's presence —
I warn you through my silently talking mind,
Or speak to you through a gentle significant glance,
Or whisper to you through my love,
Or loudly dissuade you when you stray away from Him.
But when I shall become only a memory,
Or a mental image, or silently speaking voice,
When no earthly call will ever reveal
My whereabouts in unplumbed space,
When no shallow entreaty or stern stentorian
    command will bring from me an answer —
I will smile in your mind when you are right,
And when you are wrong I will weep through my eyes,
Dimly peering at you in the dark,
And weep through the eyes, perchance;
And I will whisper to you through your conscience,
And I will reason with you through your reason,
And I will love all through your love.
When you are no longer able to talk with me,
Read my "Whispers From Eternity";
Eternally through it I will talk to you.
Unknown I will walk by your side
And guard you with invisible arms.
And as soon as you know my Beloved
And hear His voice in silence,
You will know me again more tangibly
    than you knew me on this earth plane.
And yet when I am only a dream to you
I will come to remind you that you too are naught
But a dream of my Heavenly Beloved,
And when you know you are a dream, as I know now,
We will ever be awake in Him.

— Paramhansa Yogananda,
Whispers from Eternity

Paramhansa Yogananda

The telephone company line crew, pulling a pole in Santa Barbara, California. The author is on the extreme right of photograph.

CHAPTER 24

A Bad Fall

The summer of 1952 moved on into the middle of August. My job with the telephone company continued. I enjoyed working as a lineman; climbing poles was fun. The more adept I became, the more I enjoyed it. There is a phrase among journeymen linemen that usually brings out the humor in everyone. It's called "burning the pole." An apprentice lineman just learning how to climb is one hilarious spectacle of awkwardness. Unfortunately for the apprentice, the journeymen will usually stand around and watch, poking fun whenever they can. As a rule, everyone experiences a fall of some sort right at the beginning, or later on when they become too reckless. "Burning the pole" is a phrase used in jest. If a lineman's climbing hooks slip out of the wood, and he starts to fall, he grabs the pole in a bear hug if he can, and slides all the way to the ground, all the time hugging the pole. The ability to "set the pole on fire" depends on the person's body weight, strength of the bear hug, and distance from the ground. Of course, this past sentence has been stated with a touch of humor. Fortunately, serious injuries rarely occur during the working life of a lineman.

During the latter part of August 1952, the construction crew I worked with was doing some repair work in the town of Summerland, California. We had been replacing some old crossarms and telephone wire with new material. It was late in the afternoon on a Friday. I had just replaced a sidearm on an old pole so the new wire could be strung across it. All that remained to be done to complete our job was to tie the new wire down to insulators. We were all in a hurry and working against the clock to finish the job. It was now four o'clock and time to head back to the central yard. Our foreman wanted the job finished this afternoon so we would not have to return tomorrow. "You guys hurry up and tie that wire in so we won't be late," he shouted.

I turned and began to climb the pole to the newly replaced sidearm. It would take no longer than five minutes to tie down the wire. I reached the sidearm and looked down at the climbing hooks attached to my feet. They were securely imbedded in the wood of the pole. Then, holding on to the pole with my right hand, I reached down with my left hand, unsnapped one end of my safety belt, and passed it around the pole. Then I grasped the end of the safety belt with my right hand, holding on with my left, and snapped it to a ring on the other side of the belt. I heard it snap into position, and because I was in a hurry, I didn't bother to look down and see if the belt was securely snapped to the ring. This was my mistake. My safety belt was lying over the top of the sidearm and was twisted. As I leaned back into the tool belt, the snap on my safety belt must have been only halfway onto the ring. The twist in the safety belt yanked the snap off as I leaned back. Now I was falling backward. I could hardly believe what was happening — I didn't have time. It was too late to grab the pole or anything with my hands. "Oh Lord, this is it!" I was more than thirty feet above the ground, too high to survive this fall without injury. I watched the pole move quickly away from my field of vision as I plummeted earthward, head first.

I tried to prepare myself for the shock that was about to come when I hit the ground. Instead, I felt nothing at all. There was a bright flash of light — and then silence.

The Vision

I am standing stationary in the air, high above the familiar coastline of Santa Barbara. There, far below, waves on the surface of the ocean are moving inward toward the shore. Memory is beginning to reveal what has happened. My physical body has suffered a fall; it is lying somewhere below.

I have been pulled forth from the physical body by Elder Spirits; my physical body may be dead. Everything is so silent; there are no answers. To the northwest a vision of unparalleled magnificence confronts me; the astral world is suspended rainbow-like on the horizon. Moving northward, I am impelled by silent motion, flying with arms outstretched before me.

. . . senses which correspond to the physical senses of vision and of hearing are very definitely intact in the spiritual body, and seem actually heightened and more perfect than they are in physical life. One man says that while he was "dead" his vision seemed incredibly more powerful and, in his words, "I just can't understand how I could see so far." A woman who recalled this experience notes, "It seemed as if this spiritual sense had no limitations, as if I could look anywhere and everywhere. " . . . In an interview with a woman who was out of her body following an accident: ". . . Whenever I would look at a person to wonder what they were thinking, it

Higher and higher, without effort I now move. There below me is the whole coastline of California — what an incredible view! The soft, astral colors surrounding the planet hang like a perpetual aurora borealis in every direction. Now I remember my directions. In order to leave this planet in my present form, I must exit through the north polar vortex. Here, there is a door.

Moving northward, O memory, you remind me of all my earthly commitments left behind. There below you is San Luis Obispo on the west coast. What's this? A figure of a Buddha is sitting in meditation down there! It must be Dad! I have not said goodbye to him. This really troubles me; Dad is slowly disappearing like a fog.

Yes, memory, you remind me of a divine chariot waiting out there, out through the north polar vortex. Here the magnetic currents are difficult to swim through. The Northern Hemisphere is spread out beneath me; how fantastic! Now large portions of it are visible through the haze of astral clouds; the colors of those clouds are more magnificent than any I have ever seen. Thoughts, you reveal facts long known deep within.

Christ Consciousness speaks. "Mother Earth is operated by two master forces of vortex, one descending at the North Pole, and one ascending at the South Pole. The movement of astral energies from South Pole to North Pole swings the needle of the compass forever toward the magnetic North Pole of Mother Earth.

"The physical body of hu-man, the creature, is similar to Mother Earth. Both are created and

was like a zoom-up, . . . and I was there. But it seemed that part of me — I'll call it my mind — was still where I had been, several yards away from my body. When I wanted to see someone at a distance, it seemed like part of me, kind of like a tracer, would go to that person. And it seemed to me at the time that if something happened anyplace in the world that I could just be there."

— Dr. Raymond Moody, *Life After Life*

". . . I was in a coma for approximately a week. . . . During this period when I was unconscious, I felt as though I were lifted right up, just as though I didn't have a physical body at all. A brilliant white light appeared to me. The light was so bright that I could not see through it, but going into its presence was so calming and so wonderful. There is just no experience on earth like it."

— A patient, quoted by Dr. Raymond Moody, in *Life After Life*

From what we have seen of the scientific methods practised by the adepts of the ancient world it is possible to draw two conclusions. First, they recognized the existence of some force or current, of whose potential we are now ignorant, and discovered the form of natural science by which it could be manipulated. Secondly, they gained, apparently by means connected with their use of this current, certain direct insight into fundamental questions of philosophy, the nature of God and of the universe and the relationship between life and death. . . .

— John Michell, *The View Over Atlantis*

operated by the action of four directions of vortex, two masculine and two feminine, the right and left hands of God. The crown of hu-man's head at birth, and for months thereafter, is open and beating. It is here that we find the long lost door to Divine Spirit and the magnetic north pole of man. It is also through this door, at the crown of the head, that the divine masculine creative force enters into the Tree of Life. It moves downward into a counterclockwise centripetal vortex (to the vision of the observer looking straight up). The magnetic south pole of man is the lower end of the spine. Here the divine feminine force enters, moving upward in a clockwise centripetal vortex (to the vision of the observer looking downward).

> In the very few accounts in which the event is recalled in some detail, re-entry is said to occur "through the head." "... as I was being sucked back to my body, it seemed that the suction started from the head, like I went into the head."
>
> — Dr. Raymond Moody, *Life After Life*

"It is from the movement of the centrifugal and centripetal, clockwise and counterclockwise, forces of vortex, that Divine Spirit spun and wove all the images of creation into visible form. The motion of these divine forces of vortex, and the understanding thereof, provides the key to the hidden door which opens into the timeless existence of Divine Spirit, Mother-Father-Creator.

"Jesus referred to the Spirit of God as a movement and a rest. Divine Spirit Mother and Father, non-moving, exist in eternal timeless peace and bliss. The infinite primordial sea of consciousness and energy (i.e., life force) reflects no images. Divine Spirit, non-thinking, exists in the rapture of eternal peace. Spirit, desiring to see images dance upon the primordial sea of life, projects thought-forms which produce motion and resistance in the eternal sea of life and energy. Mental images spinning outward from the divine center of consciousness (the smallest of all places) into the eternal primordial sea produce the masculine and feminine images now visible within the expanding great Sphere of Creation.

"All visible forms are the production and reproduction, in different directions, of the four forces of vortex. Our Divine Parents hold the expanding spheres of creation in their right and left hands of vortex, producing duality. The Angel Men and Women were created masculine and feminine in such a manner, each having two forces of creative power, through vortex. Thus, the

> I herein refer to the expanding spheres of creation as dimensions of vibration, sound, and color (the eight color vibrations of the spectrum emanating outward from the original ignition of the First Creation of Light, The Great Central SöN - SüN). We can visualize the great Sphere of Creation as an iridescent bubble floating in the endless eternal sea of life and consciousness. The great Sphere of Creation contains eight inner-penetrating spheres corresponding to the eight vibrations of the spectrum.
>
> — The Author

mental images projected into the creation through The Great Central SöN-SuN by vortexes (divine will in motion) united, giving birth to the visible spheres of creation and hence the Angel Men and Women. [This is further explained in chapter 32, "The Genesis of Creation."]

"The hu-man creatures, created from the four elements of air, earth, fire, and water, were predestined to meet the immortal Angel Men and Women in time and space, within the spheres of creation. Hu-man, the creature, possessing simple- and self-consciousness, evolved from the mud of the waters and did not have immortal life. Hu-man receives the gift of immortality (Christ Consciousness) only when he allows the Angel Man and Woman to descend with the Baptism of Fire. These divine forces unite within hu-man, bringing about the conception and birth of the Divine Spiritual Embryo within the hu-man heart. Mother Earth, with her forces of nature, spins on divine time amidst the forces of vortex, her original creators. Dead worlds, such as our moon, cease to spin, as the forces of vortex are removed.

"Humankind, now existing in simple- and self-conscious states, has little present knowledge of the Angel Men and Women. He is unaware of their predestined union within himself (i.e., the birth of Christ Consciousness). Because these divine forces find it very difficult to enter humankind on Planet Earth, humankind ceases to spin or move on divine time. Man finds himself out of harmony with the garden of the world and all its creatures, including his own brothers, with whom he is at war. Humankind, unfortunately for the most part, has become a dead world unto itself, like our moon. Ceasing to spin on divine time, man is always too early or too late. The bleak landscape of the moon entertains the egos of many self-conscious spirits who disfigured Mother's Earth garden for selfish purposes, wasting life-forms without caring. If the law of cause and effect does exist, and indeed it does, those persons who have wasted Mother's natural garden and their lives will of course see it no more when they pass on. No more blue skies with fiery orb, nor flowing rivers and

Due to the fall of certain divine beings, herein referred to as the Dark Angels or Fallen Angels, also called the forces of Satan or Lucifer, negative spirits of darkness now try to prevent the Baptism of Fire from being initiated. Hence Christ Consciousness as a normal evolution for mankind is being prevented. The persecution and destruction of those spirits who have come to earth to baptise and illuminate the races, stand as a matter of record. The brutal savagery used upon them indicates the grave opposition and the general fear those dark forces have of mankinds' eventual illumination, and their own great defeat. However, the great wars being fought between the Sons of God, (The Builders), and the Fallen Angels now show an eventual victory for the former: a bright vision for humanity on this planet.

— The Author

oceans, nor green hills with trees and flowers, nor creatures! All of this is lost unto them for a long period of time."

These things passed before me as I observed the fantastic blue orb of Mother Earth beneath me, surely the only perfect poem. Magnificent are the divine images of your creation, Father-Mother! O let me be with you always, just as a humble son. I truly love you and all I know and behold of you, my heavenly Father and Mother.

I reflected again on the image of my earthly father. I must say goodbye to him before I leave. Turning, I observed the familiar swirling white light moving downward beneath me like a spiral staircase. Yes, a stairway to heaven does exist. I am now moving downward on the feathery light substance.

There is my body lying at the foot of the telephone pole, covered with blankets. A flash of light — and a pleasant shock, then my eyes open to see concerned faces looking down on me.

Everybody was glad that I was living; but as I lay there thinking about the wonderful place where I had been and all that I had seen, I was very sad; for it seemed to me that everybody ought to know about it, but I was afraid to tell, because I knew that nobody would believe me.

— John G. Neihardt, *Black Elk Speaks*

"Don't move! The ambulance is coming, Norm." Feeling no pain, I threw off the blankets and jumped to my feet. I felt for bruises and broken bones; there were none; I was alive and whole. Crewmen were trying to get me to sit down and be calm, but I insisted I wanted to go back up the pole and finish my work. "Oh no you're not, Norm!"

Then came the shrill sound of an ambulance siren above all their voices. I agreed to go to the hospital for x-rays. That evening they x-rayed every part of my body, and not a single broken bone was found, nor was there one bruise on my skin. The Elders had stayed the fall. I had yet to fulfill divine will before leaving this earth.

Later I was told I had landed head first, striking a big rock with the back left side of my head and my left shoulder. This should have broken my neck or fractured my skull, or both, but there wasn't even a bruise. The Associated Telephone Company, for insurance purposes, sent me down to Los Angeles the following Monday for more x-rays. Still nothing was found. I had survived miraculously.

While writing this chapter, I mentioned to a friend that if I had landed on my feet, it probably would have killed me. We both laughed, remembering the slogan about the hard, square head of a Nordic Dane.

"Mother Earth is operated by two master forces of vortex, one descending at the North Pole, and one ascending at the South Pole."

The author and Daniel Boone at Giant Rock

CHAPTER 25

Search in the Desert

Old friend Daniel Boone was finally discharged from the U.S. Marine Corps after serving on the front lines in Korea for two years. A letter arrived, then a phone call: "I'll be headed up to see you next weekend, Brother. It's sure good to be Stateside again. Just bought myself a real clean 1949 Mercury sedan, so I'll be driving up."

Boone arrived and it was good to see him. We drove around town in his new Mercury and I showed him places of interest. "How's your dad, Norm?"

"He's fine, living in San Luis Obispo."

Boone had met Dad when he came to Mount Washington the Christmas of 1949. "Norm," he said, "it sure would be good to see your dad again. I have some things I'd like to discuss with him. Want to drive up and see him?"

"Sounds good to me. Let's go."

So we left early the next morning and drove to San Luis Obispo. Boone hadn't changed much — he still had that great inquisitive desire to search out unusual spiritual or psychic personages. "Someday I'm going to drive up and see Mother Mary at Mount Shasta. Want to come along, Norm?"

"Sure, I'd like to see her again."

We arrived at Dad's house and Boone began a discourse with Dad on Siddhartha Gautama, the Buddha.

Dad was now retired from his Justice of the Peace position, and he and Dorothy had just completed a lecture tour of the forty-eight states, where Dad tuned pianos along the way to cover expenses. Dad gave lectures on Buddhism along with

Siddhartha Gautama was born between the years 562 and 552 B.C. . . . . He seems to have been a very earnest-minded man who, realizing keenly the miseries of the human race, desired above all things to do something to abolish, or at least lessen, them. . . . The orthodox manner of attaining to holiness in Gautama's age and land was through fasting and penance, and for six years he practiced extreme self-

225

piano recitals for large groups of people; this had pleased Dad very much. The trip was a great success.

Dorothy had recently received a strange publication entitled, "I Rode in a Flying Saucer," by G.W. Van Tassel. I noticed the return address of Yucca Valley, California, and remembered that I had driven through there many times on my way to Master Yogananda's retreat at Twenty-Nine Palms. Boone took the pamphlet and read through it in a matter of minutes. "Hey, we've got to get out there and see what this guy Van Tassel really knows. He claims to have been taken aboard a flying saucer!"

mortification.... Seeing that that course was vain and led to nothing, he abandoned asceticism and shortly afterwards...attained illumination under the celebrated Bo tree.

The Dhamma-Kakka-Ppavattana-Sutra is accepted by all Buddhists as a summary of the words in which the great Indian thinker and reformer for the first time successfully promulgated his new ideas. In it over and over again Gautama declares that the "noble truths" taught therein were not "among the doctrines handed down," but that "there arose within him the eye to perceive them, the knowledge of their nature, the understanding of their cause, the wisdom that lights the true path, the light that expels darkness." He could not well more definitely state that he did not derive his authority to teach from the merely self-conscious, but from the Cosmic-Conscious mind — that is, from illumination or inspiration.

— Richard Bucke, *Cosmic Consciousness*

I was mildly interested and agreed to make the trip. Boone wrote down information and directions to a place called — Giant Rock! Could this be the same place I had found in the desert long ago? Intuition stated, "Yes, it is! It must be!"

I examined the booklet closely and sure enough, there in the picture was the same giant rock I had seen by the small, dry lake long ago. Boone was now highly excited. "Norm, we must get down there somehow this weekend." We concluded our visit with Dad and Dorothy, said our goodbyes, and headed home to pack up sleeping bags and gear for the trip.

"Hey Boone, this sure is going to be fun! The last time we were together out in the desert was when we completed the swimming pool for Yogananda. It will be hot out there, remember, Brother? Here, fill these canteens with water."

This series of events — my discovery of Giant Rock years ago, the deep feelings I had experienced there, and now finding the pamphlet at Dad's house — was more than a coincidence. Yes, surely this booklet had been some sort of a message for Daniel and me.

It was the month of September, and the highways were packed with vacationers. We were underway about seven-thirty in the morning. It was going to take at least five hours to drive out there. Was this man Van Tassel telling the truth? Time would tell. The thought of actually seeing a spaceship up close was more than intriguing.

Near the city of Ventura, a large truck suddenly pulled from a side street right out in front of us. Boone hit the brakes, and tires squealed as we skidded sideways down the street, coming to an abrupt stop against the curb. The right front tire blew out with a sickening bang. As Boone and I looked at each other, we broke into a sweat. "Whew, Brother! That was too close for comfort!"

After fixing the tire, again we were on our way. Four hours passed before a sign read, "Yucca Valley." We asked for directions to Joshua Tree and headed on down the road. Shortly thereafter, another loud report sounded as a tire exploded beneath us. "Oh Lord, Norm! What in the hell is going on," Boone yelled in frustration.

We now had to fix two flat tires; the one in the trunk and the one on the car. This consumed another hour. Finally underway again, we found the old dirt track I had traveled several years before. Again I saw the sharp turn to the northwest. "Look, Boone, that strange mount over there, that's the one I was telling you about."

"Hey, that is a strange one, Norm."

As we drove by the north face of the mount, the small dry lake bed came into view. It was getting late and we were in a hurry to get there. Then, as we were approaching the dry lake bed, we heard the loud prophetic bang of another blowout. "Oh no!" cried Boone, "I can't believe this! What in God's name is going on here? Some damn negative force is trying to prevent us from getting there."

We changed tires for the third time, and I was reminded that we now had no spare tire. "You better slow down, Boone; one more blowout and we're done for."

We motored up a low rise and watched the expanse of the dry lake and the airstrip spread out before us. "There it is, Boone! There's the big rock sitting over against that ridge." The whole starkly barren area resembled the landscape of some other strange planet and emitted that same kind of energy.

As we approached Giant Rock, I sensed a strong psychic energy emanating from the monolith. In fact, every hair on both of us was standing at rapt attention. Giant Rock appeared to be oval and about fifty feet high and seventy-five feet long. It sat out on the desert floor alone — a super monolith of stone, terribly impressive in its austere surroundings.

We parked near the rock, got out, and looked around. There appeared to be no one around except some barking dogs who ran out to greet us. As we walked around the rock, we felt the strength of its psychic energy field. The wind came howling up a rise from the desert plain stretched out far below. One could see for miles out across the forbidding landscape. Heat waves created wavy mirages of water across the desert to the distant horizon. As we circumvented the giant boulder, we noticed a small building against another smaller rocky offspring. A sign over the door stated, "Giant Rock Airport Cafe." Looking again at the gigantic monolith revealed that a large room had been excavated out from beneath it. We looked down through windows into a large room where davenports and chairs filled all available space. An opened door revealed a flight of stairs descending to a stone floor beneath. Boone called out through the doorway, "Anyone here?"

We descended the stairs to observe a man lying face down on one of the couches. He looked up and replied, "Well, you guys finally got here, didn't you? I have been sensing your arrival for hours. You had a hell of a lot of opposition, didn't you?"

"We sure did; three flat tires and a near accident."

"Think nothing of it, boys," stated the figure as he stood up. "It happens to everyone who comes out here. Most people don't make it this far."

"Are you Mr. Van Tassel?"

"Yes sir, that's me." We introduced ourselves and shook hands with G. W. Van Tassel.

"I've been waiting for you two guys to show up here for years."

"You what!" blurted Boone.

"That's right, for years."

Van Tassel wasn't finished talking. "You're some of Yogananda's boys, aren't you?"

"How did you know that?" interjected Boone.

"Oh, I have ways of knowing."

George Van Tassel was about five feet ten inches tall and rather portly. He had a big honest grin on his face, and small, piercing eyes which said, "I know a lot more about what's going on than most people would like to believe." George was surely different; the vibrations emanating from him were really alien. He was the strangest person I had ever encountered.

There was no doubt about his psychic abilities; he was overflowing with them. I felt him probing us for more information so he could throw it back at us. "So you're Daniel Boone. How the hell did you get that name?"

Boone stammered, "I am related to the original, way back."

"Yeah, I know. You just got out of the military service, didn't you?"

"Yes, the U.S. Marines." It seemed George Van Tassel was out to give us a reading of our past histories. Boone countered with, "Were you really on board an alien spaceship?"

"Hell, yes!" shouted Van Tassel. "You read my booklet, didn't you?"
Boone again stammered a reply, "That's right, I did."

"How long can you guys stay?"

"Well, we planned to stay overnight somewhere and go back to Santa Barbara tomorrow."

"That's good, you can attend our meeting tonight and sleep down here if you like. Come on, let's go up to the restaurant and have some coffee."

George had been operating Giant Rock Airport for a number of years. He once had been a flight test engineer working for Howard Hughes Aviation. "I got fed up with the whole damn rat race and moved my family out here in the desert to get away from the insanity."

Inside the restaurant, George introduced his wife, Eva, and his three daughters, Darlene, Glenda, and Sandra. In addition to his family, other people who had joined George's organization were living nearby in house trailers. The walls of the small restaurant were covered with all of the UFO pictures in existence, I do believe. They looked authentic, too.

"You guys interested in alien spaceships?"

"Yes we are," replied Boone. "Can you tell us a little about them?"

George took a big gulp of his coffee and began a discourse that lasted for three hours. He had always believed that the universe around us was inhabited by intelligent beings and that this planet was only one of an infinite number of inhabited planets.

While he was working for Howard Hughes, he had been directed to the desert specifically to be contacted by an alien vehicle. George had been born with psychic abilities, but when he moved to the desert they had been intensified a hundredfold.

He went on to relate how he and his wife, Eva, had slept outside all

The evidence for the UFO phenomenon is a deluge, not a delusion; the number of persons who claim to experience UFO sightings is increasing throughout the world. However, the evidence which is obtained from these experiences shows a strange and unusual pattern: the experience is "real" to the percipient, but there may be little "proof" to offer to someone else who chooses to reject the report of the percipient.

In my opinion, the UFO phenomenon is an important factor in the total experience of a new age: the merger of "science" and "religion."

Some people claim to receive messages regarding the next twenty-five years; these messages suggest that there will be many changes in the condition of the Earth and in the condition of humankind, including an increased emphasis on spiritual development. The messages differ in regard to specific prediction — e.g., the likelihood of war and catastrophic events; the possibility of a "harvest of souls;" the specific outcomes in the struggle between the forces of "darkness" and the forces of "light." However, the general theme of these messages is an indication that we are now experiencing, and will continue to

summer long. One night he had been awakened by an alien standing right at the foot of his bed. "Scared the hell out of me," said George. "He requested that I get up and follow him. I got up all right, and followed this guy out into the desert. After walking a short distance, I saw this small, spherical, dome-shaped spaceship hovering about six feet above the sagebrush. The ship was about sixty feet in diameter and constructed of a material such as I have never seen before in all my experience with metal aircraft. As we approached the ship, I was warned not to touch the hull. A ramp was visible extending downward from the outer rim. As I followed my guide up into the ship, I realized as in a dream that we had been conversing by thought transference the whole time."

experience, many changes.

I believe that we are confronted with a most exciting and challenging task, to understand the physical, biological, psychosocial, and spiritual implications of the ending of a former age and awakening of the "New Age."

— Dr. R. Leo Sprinkle, Associate Professor of Psychology, University of Wyoming quoted by Brad Steiger, in Gods of Aquarius

George began to describe the interior of the ship in detail. "All of the inner walls of the hull were white, like alabaster, and they reflected the colors of the spectrum. There were no furnishings to be seen except three seats in front of what had to be a control console. Some areas of the exterior hull were transparent, like window glass that can only be seen through from one side. I tried to get my guide to tell me how the ship was powered. He mentioned magnetic lines of force which, like a grid, fill the structure of the universe in great curving arcs. Free energy particles traveling on these lines of force are collected by the ship's propulsion unit. The ship is actually moved by forces which we have termed gravity. The forces of gravity, discovered by Newton, have never really been explored or identified. This force, which is an unknown, balances out suns, planets, galaxies, and universes, and holds every body in its own obedient orbit. Gravity is, indeed, a magnetic force of energy. This ship and its creators understand this force and operate within it. Therefore, they are free of earth's forces of gravity. The old maxim of 'whatever goes up must come down' operates in reverse for them. Whatever goes up never comes down, unless they want it to."

George said at this time he had not been taken anywhere, but was informed that on another occasion he would be contacted and taken for a demonstration.

Both Daniel and I felt this tale was indeed true. I knew that gravity and magnetism were forces generated by energy moving in the four great directions. These four directions are identified as centripetal and centrifugal vortexes moving in clockwise and counterclockwise arcs. Galaxies containing one hundred million physical suns are turning in space: Yes, the eternal wheels. What gives motion to these vast star systems? The invisible power of Divine Consciousness moving in vortexes, the "right and left hands of God" described in the Bible as a whirlwind. Weighing my own experiences against George's fantastic tale, I believed him. This was the dawning of an old, but new, dimension of experience for me as well as for Daniel.

At least two hundred people came to the meeting that night. George led a silent meditation starting with a few songs and ending with a great deal of humor. George was a real comedian; he loved to rib people.

George talked about his experiences until after midnight. People were thirsty for knowledge; the whole concept of alien spacecraft was just coming into public awareness. Many people had seen spacecrafts themselves and had come to George for confirmation. The ancient and immortal Sons and Daughters of Spirit were returning in their grand celestial chariots to repossess the earth. Christ Consciousness must prevail on earth again. The dark and negative spirits of self-consciousness who have possessed the throne for more than twelve thousand years must abdicate.

The next day Daniel and I played horseshoes with George and others as discussions were carried on. There was a persistent exciting energy of anticipation everywhere which kept everyone on a high level of consciousness. People just wouldn't go home; everyone slept outside or sat up all night watching the heavens for some sign of a spaceship. That night, many people saw orange spheres illuminate the desert from overhead. As I watched one, I remembered the apparitions I had seen long ago at sea on the good ship *Tumacacori*.

Two days after we had come, Boone and I had to leave for Santa Barbara. Reluctantly, we said goodbye to George and his family. "You guys coming back next weekend?" he asked.

"Yes," replied Boone, looking at Sandra, "We may be back before then."

Daniel's answer was prophetic. Boone and I drove homeward with no more blowouts. We were so keyed up, it was hard to relax.

231

Suddenly and silently, a very intense and brilliant white light lit up the whole area immediately around me, including Giant Rock.

CHAPTER 26

A Move to the Desert

My intuitive perceptions about living in the desert area near Paramhansaji's retreat years before were coming true. George Van Tassel and Giant Rock were becoming more of a home to Daniel and myself than Santa Barbara. I now felt I would be leaving Santa Barbara for a number of years.

One weekend George said, "Why don't you guys move down here? You waste all that time and energy driving back and forth." I argued that the money I was helping out with could not be earned down here in the desert. "I'll teach you guys how to lay brick," said George. "You can learn how to build masonry houses and go in business for yourselves."

That really sounded good to me. "You know, George, I think we'll take you up on that."

The sudden decision to quit my job with the telephone company and move to the desert was exciting. Daniel had been doing construction work in Santa Barbara and felt he could fit into masonry home building really well. I gave notice and terminated my job with the telephone company in May of 1953. I had little to move except my seabag, which was the way I liked it.

Daniel and I drove to Giant Rock one Friday afternoon in May. We were moving from the cool coastal climate of California into the blistering heat of the desert right at the beginning of summer. There was no housing at Giant Rock, so Daniel and I slept outside all summer long in our sleeping bags. As it turned out, George didn't have enough work building masonry homes to keep both of us busy. I decided to let Boone work with George, and I went to Twenty-Nine Palms to try and get work with the local power company. I was successful and started work as an apprentice power lineman. Working with electrical power was a great deal different than working with telephone lines, and also more hazardous. I had to make the

233

long drive to Twenty-Nine Palms every day, which meant traveling over that rough desert road. I often glanced toward Paramhansa Yogananda's retreat as I drove by, remembering the days I had spent there with him. It all seemed so far away now, like another lifetime.

George's lectures and meditations every Saturday night at Giant Rock brought hundreds of people from everywhere. I made many new friends. It seemed that Boone and I were becoming an active part of the Van Tassel family.

Getting used to the 110 degree heat of the desert was hard. Every afternoon I came home exhausted. Daniel and I were sleeping out on the airstrip at night, right on the ground. One particular night was destined to be a strange one for George, Daniel and myself. Daniel and I rolled out our bags close to the giant rock. As I lay there looking up at the heavens, I saw a bright, orange-colored object flash across the sky above us.

"There goes a ship," I yelled over at Daniel. "Did you see it?"

Boone was about fifty feet away in his sleeping bag. "No," came his half-conscious reply.

Boone had a silent admirer named Tumpta, one of the dogs that lived at Giant Rock. It was Tumpta's habit, being small of stature, to crawl into Boone's sleeping bag every night. Tumpta had a friend named Pooch, who also wanted to sleep in Daniel's bag, but there was never enough room for him. How Daniel could handle that was beyond me. It must have been about midnight when I was suddenly awakened by the violent sounds of a dogfight. I looked over and I saw Tumpta and Pooch going around and around fighting each other right on top of Daniel's head. I'll never forget hearing him between the barking and growling of those two fighting dogs.

"Damn it! Get the hell out of here!" I think he and the dogs woke up everyone in the area. Things finally quieted down and I lay there, unable to go back to sleep. Suddenly and silently, a very intense and brilliant white light lit up the whole area immediately around me, including Giant Rock. The light was coming from above, and it was blinding. Looking up, I could see the light was emanating from the bottom of a very large, circular object. The hovering object was stationary in the air, five or six hundred feet above Giant Rock.

"My Lord! There it is, finally. Wake up, everybody!" I yelled. "There's a ship right on the rock!"

I could hear a heavy pulsating hum echo off the rocky cliffs and fill the immediate area with sound. I yelled again at Boone but received no response. I continued yelling as loud as I could, hoping someone would hear me.

That was a mistake! An incredibly bright and piercing light struck me full in the face. It emanated from the side of the brilliantly lit hull which I could now see very clearly. That was it! The next thing I became aware of was the sun shining in my face as it rose in the east across the desert. Looking down, I saw that I was half out of my sleeping bag. Then I began to remember what had happened. The intelligence guiding the vehicle evidently did not want to be seen by everyone. I had been put to sleep right in the middle of trying to get out of my sleeping bag!

I looked over to Daniel. "Hey,

> . . . at Brookfield, Wisconsin on August 12, 1967, at 2:30 a.m., a sleepy man and wife glanced out the window to see what their German shepherd was barking about. Shocked, they saw an oval object hovering at ground level over an adjoining pasture. A sharply defined beam of light emanated from the craft and the dog stopped barking. Everything became strangely silent.
>
> — Raymond E. Fowler, *The Andreasson Affair*

Boone, did you see it? Were you able to see that ship last night?"

"No, Brother. I heard you yelling, but when I looked up, nothing was there. I remember hearing a pulsating roar, though."

I scrambled out of my sleeping bag and headed for the restaurant. It was a Saturday morning, and I didn't have to go to work. There I found George and Eva already up. This was unusual, I thought. Old George had a big smile on his face.

"Anything happen to you last night, Norm?" George had a twinkle in his eye.

"Yes, something sure did. Did you see that ship come in last night?" George really had a mischievous grin on his face now, as I waited for an answer. "Well, George," I asked again, "did you see it too?"

"Hell, yes, I did. They took me for a ride."

"They what? Wow, that's fantastic! They actually took you up?"

I began to tell George what had happened to me.

"Yeah, you should have kept your mouth shut; they might have taken you along, too."

"Was this the same ship that was here once before?"

"I don't know, Norm; it looked the same to me."

Later, as I analyzed the experience, I had to admit that I had seen a real, physical manifestation of a divine celestial vehicle. There was no doubt about it. The Builders were returning to take earth from the grasp of the negative forces which had possessed it for so long.

Despite George's rough and cal-

> I believe that the UFO will serve mankind as a transformative symbol that will unite our entire species as one spiritual organism.
>
> — Brad Steiger, *Gods of Aquarius*

235

loused personality, he was a very special person of the old generation. George would give anyone the shirt off his back if it would help them. Much like my own father, George was also a psychic, and both of them were here to help prepare the way for the Christed Angel Beings, that is The Builders, to return to earth. I looked forward to the day when George and Dad might meet each other.

"George," I asked, "did they tell you anything unusual this time?"

"Yes, Norm, they said their numbers were increasing now in this solar system, meaning we are going to see more of them. I was also given information on how to construct an energy system that would function somewhat like the Great Pyramid of Cheops." George was elated; his face radiated his enthusiasm. "I am going to start building this structure as soon as funds are available."

> I have been engaged in UFO research since the 1950s, and I have come to the conclusion that, throughout history, some external intelligence has interacted with *Homo sapiens* in an effort to learn more about us — or in an effort to communicate to our species certain basic truths between mankind and the UFO intelligences.
>
> — Brad Steiger, *Gods of Aquarius*

Funds were made available for George's work shortly thereafter. A friend donated a huge sum of money to George's newly formed nonprofit corporation entitled "The College of Universal Wisdom." At this time George began to write and publish a quarterly pamphlet entitled "The Proceedings." A large mailing list began to develop as these publications were mailed out all over the world. George was sitting in the driver's seat of an old, but new, profound energy. He was in the position of becoming world famous as a new age prophet. I prayed that he might be able to carry out his mission successfully.

The great opposition and persecution created and generated by the negative spirits who are in control of this planet were now to be unleashed on George Van Tassel. Anyone who attempts to bring forth the light of Spirit and the truth of brotherhood must be prepared to resist and to fight these negative forces. These fallen sons and daughters of Spirit, who at one time were members of the races of The Builders, by their own deliberate action created a center within themselves for the conception and birth of evil to take form. These dark spirits don't want humankind illuminated. If, indeed, this took place, their fun and games of war, horror, corruption, greed, murder, and lust would soon cease to exist for them on this planet. Thus, the persecution of saints, holy men, and divine messengers continues. No one has any idea of the opposition that confronts a heavenly messenger until they become one and try to spread their message. Depending on the degree of illuminating energy contained in the message, the messenger is either destroyed at once, if possible, or is under full attack every day. If the forces of evil can't destroy the messenger, they make life so miserable that one wishes he was dead. I watched these forces begin hovering on the sidelines of George's efforts. I was here to help support him as long as I was able. Daniel was to remain in George's work for the next twenty-five years.

One Friday evening late in the summer of 1953 I was returning home to Giant Rock. We were now trying to use another road to the rock that wasn't quite as rough. This road left the main highway at Yucca Valley instead of Joshua Tree. I was driving a 1950 Mercury convertible which was equipped with twin spotlights. The sun had set and the sky was full of pastel shades of purple, pink, and orange. I had the top down on the car and was enjoying the ride home. Off to the east, as I looked across miles of desert landscape, thunderheads were hovering. Electrical storms and cloudbursts are quite common in this region of the California desert during the summer. Bolts of lightning were piercing the sky off in the distance, followed by the distant rumble of thunder. The very air around me was charged with static electricity.

I had covered about half the distance to Giant Rock when off to the north I saw a string of orange-colored lights. I counted eight of them in all. They were moving toward the east very slowly. Just to the right of them the strange mount called Goat Mountain loomed up in the afterlight of sunset.

I immediately recognized that the lights were ancient, awe-inspiring, divine chariots of fire. How many times in millenniums past had I watched them perform their maneuvers in the heavens, in other places and circumstances?

I judged their position to be approximately five miles away. The objects appeared to be no more than five or six hundred feet above the desert floor. Now was my chance! I decided to chase after them for a closer look. The road was rough, full of chuckholes and rocks. I was driving as fast as I dared, bouncing and careening through gullies and over small rises. I reached over and

I often reflect on the fact that congregations of yesterday's and today's Christian churches sing the hymn, "Swing low, sweet chariot, coming for to carry me home. A band of angels coming after me, coming for to carry me home." Just what kind of chariot are they referring to that may be crewed by a band of angels?

Such a chariot is described in II Kings 2:11, "And it came to pass as they still went on, and talked, that, behold, there appeared a chariot of fire, and horses of fire, and parted them both asunder; and Elijah went up by a whirlwind into heaven." Also, the prophet Ezekiel tries to describe such a vehicle. It would seem that so-called chariots of fire have been around the earth's vicinity for millenniums and do they not fit right into modern-day UFO reports? Is it not time we examine the facts and accept them instead of ridiculing those who claim to have seen and made contact with these divine chariots of fire?

— The Author

237

turned on both spotlights, pointing them in the direction of the objects.

In spite of trying to keep an eye on the lights and the road at the same time, I covered about three miles in a very few minutes. The objects were now passing in front of the mount; I was getting closer. I began mentally calling to them, "Won't you please stop and come my way, brothers?" Then I yelled, "Please stop — I want to see you!"

The objects seemed to be playing with one another. Two or three would suddenly begin to bounce straight up and down. Others would whirl around, almost colliding. They were now right over the top of Goat Mountain. I watched them circle like a candlelight procession above the mount. But this time I had reached a point in the road which turned to the northwest; I was as close as I could get to them. If only I had four-wheel drive! The mount and the objects were now no more than two miles away. I slowed the car, pulled off to the right, stopped, and turned my spotlights directly at them. The objects were spherical and looked like bright orange torches as they lit up the rocky crags and cliffs of the mount, casting eerie shadows as they moved along.

Didn't they hear or see me? My mental messages were flying in their direction. I began directing both spotlights at them, flicking them off and on. Suddenly, they all stopped and lined up just above the mount. They had seen me! All eight objects began a dance, it seemed, rising straight up and then down, flashing off and on as they moved. I began to switch off the car's spotlights alternately at them, finally flashing eight times and then pausing.

I watched the eight objects respond. Lining up from my left to right, they all suddenly disappeared, then one by one they all flashed on again, then on and off eight times. They then began a spiral climb up into the heavens, accelerating suddenly at tremendous speed. I watched them change colors as they traversed the spectrum; the faster they moved, the greater the vibration of light. Hovering and moving slowly, they emanated red and orange. As they moved faster, they changed to gold, then burst into bright greens and blues. They streaked away, nearing the speed of light, then flashed violet and disappeared in a final

Incredible reports by credible people poured in. Later on in the year [1967] on July 27, about 1:00 a.m., a group of amateur astronomers saw a wingless, cylindrical object maneuvering over the darkened countryside of Newton, New Hampshire. (Two of the witnesses were trained observers and had received training in aircraft identification in the military.) As the object moved back and forth near the field in which they had set up a telescope, it responded exactly to signals flashed to it with a flashlight by one of the three witnesses.

— Raymond E. Fowler,
The Andreasson Affair

flash of incandescent white. I heard a voice that seemed to fill all the heavens above me: *"We shall return for you."*

As I stood there alone beneath a brilliant blanket of stars, a gentle wind whispered through the sagebrush and joshua trees, *"All will take place in time; be patient, my son."* It was Mother's gentle presence. I felt the earth miraculously turning beneath me as I watched the stars riding the crest of distant mountains. What a fantasy wonderland the desert area was at night! Each star, it seemed, blinked a message of hope. They were the beacon lights of Spirit's presence in space, Father's and Mother's starlit flanks. I had seen the ancient chariots of fire, which surely contained the Sons and Daughters of Spirit, the Christed, hu-man Angel Beings, The Builders. As I stood there looking at the strange and silent mount which had now become a familiar image to my vision, I felt this encounter with The Builders was only the first chapter in a fantastic story which was beginning to take visible form around me. The great wars between The Builders and the Fallen Angels, the Forces of Light and the Forces of Darkness, rage on.

"Oh Mother-Father, give me the strength to be just a true son, that I may someday stand before you with my mission complete, and a job well done. Good night, brothers and sisters, and thanks for seeing me."

This picture was taken by a deputy sheriff at Giant Rock, in California during a convention held on UFO's.

And the deputy sheriff who took the picture

I counted eight lights in all. They were moving over Goat Mountain toward the east very slowly.

CHAPTER 27

Winter in the Desert

Daniel and I spent the winter of 1953 sleeping outside on the desert. Unlike the summer, with its blistering heat, the winters were very cold and windy. There was very little rainfall in this area, which was called the southern California high desert, but on occasion Giant Rock got two or three inches of rain and sometimes up to eight inches of snow.

It was the winter of 1954 that brought snow to the desert. Christmas that year at Giant Rock was a real family affair, with turkey and all the trimmings. That Christmas I had enough money saved to buy everyone at Giant Rock a good useable gift. Daniel and I took Darlene, Glenda, and Sandra, George's three daughters, shopping. It was fun and was the first good Christmas I had experienced in a long time.

It seemed both Daniel and I were destined to marry two of George's daughters. I was in no hurry to get married, and I wanted to be sure I picked the correct time and person.

Daniel was attracted to Sandra, George's youngest daughter. Looking at Boone, I could see it was just a matter of time before they got married. Daniel wanted a big family, and Divine Mother's nature was all ready to fulfill his desire.

As I continued with my work for the power and electric company at Twenty-Nine Palms, I experienced a demotion in January of 1954. An experienced power lineman had moved into the Twenty-Nine Palms area and was looking for work. As it turned out, the company decided they wanted to hire this journeyman in my place and put me back on the truck. At the same time I was feeling that marriage at this point in my life was not for me. I ended up telling the boss on payday I was through! I collected my pay, gathered my tools, and left. This ended my career as a lineman for good. What I wanted to do was build masonry homes and commercial buildings.

When I returned to Giant Rock that night I was terribly upset. I felt I needed to get away for awhile and take a good look at the way my life was going. Also, I felt the call of Santa Barbara and the ocean. Boy, I really missed that ocean! I took Daniel aside and told him I was planning on leaving for awhile to visit my Dad in Lompoc. He didn't want to see me go, but he understood my feelings. I let the rest of the Van Tassel family know what my intentions were. George tried to talk me into staying, saying he would teach me the masonry trade and things would work out for me. My mind was made up to leave, though; I was going anyway. Glenda, George's second oldest daughter, was upset with my leaving, as we had grown close to each other. The next morning I got up early. I threw my seabag into the car and drove off in a hurry toward Santa Barbara.

Dad and Dorothy were now living in a two-story house they had rented in Lompoc. I drove straight on through, arriving that Saturday afternoon. Dad was glad to see me. He had an extra room upstairs, so I moved in. The next day Dad and I had a good long talk together and I brought him up to date on everything. My birthday was coming up in a few more weeks; I would be twenty-five years old, and not a kid anymore.

"Son, you had better settle down now into some occupation. If you don't want to get married, then stay away from Giant Rock. Why don't you go to work for Johns-Manville here in Lompoc? Maybe you could hire on as an electrician."

I decided to look into getting a job there Monday morning. That Sunday night as I sat up to meditate, I really felt disturbed. I could feel everyone at Giant Rock pulling on me to come back, especially Glenda.

A Vision of Yogananda

Suddenly I found myself on a beautiful green lawn. Flower beds were everywhere. Just a short distance away, a large castle with towers and battlements was silhouetted against a beautiful, dark blue sky. I looked up into a blazing sun disc. Then I heard my name softly spoken. I looked around and saw a figure sitting in a chair, just a short distance away. The figure was facing away from me, evidently enjoying the beautiful gardens and the sunshine. I began to approach, walking around to face the figure. To my astonishment, there sat Paramhansa Yogananda. I was overjoyed to see him.

"Sit down, Big Boy. How are you doing — not so good?"

I began to relate my problems to him. He motioned me to an empty chair next to him. I sat down at his side and turned to look at him. He stared into my eyes and said, "Big Boy, you know you are going to marry her and you are going to have a son."

I began pounding my knee with my hand. "Master, I don't want to get married! I refuse!"

The vision ended abruptly as I became conscious of my surroundings. My hand was still descending with another blow to my knee. The darkness of the room enveloped me suddenly, blocking out the bright sunlight and Paramhansa Yogananda's figure. As I reviewed the super-conscious experience, the words he had spoken came floating back to me: "You know you are going to marry her, and you are going to have a son."

I sat there in the darkness, still in a state of rebellion. Going to have a son! I was hardly dry behind the ears yet myself. I also liked my freedom, and maybe a monk's life was the right way after all. Could I change the course of Yogananda's prophetic words?

I went to sleep with a deep resolve to get a job here in Lompoc, my home town, and stay put. The next morning I drove up to Johns-Manville. This company was mining diatomaceous earth, which was actually tiny prehistoric sea fossils and shell organisms, from which such products as sheet rock for home insulation, fire brick for ovens and boilers, and even toothpaste were made. The old homestead where Dad was born and where my grandfather and grandmother had raised cattle and grain was now part of the Johns-Manville mining operation. The old frame house where they had lived still stood on a corner of the property up Miguelita Canyon.

With my experience as a lineman, I was able to hire on as an electrician. The Johns-Manville Company handled their own electrical distribution, erecting poles and power lines; it was a big operation. I went to work for them with enthusiasm, but my intuition, which I didn't want to listen to, told me this wouldn't last for long.

The next evening I came downstairs to Dad's table for dinner without my shirt on. Dorothy went into a tirade about the way I was dressed. "No one sits down at my table without a shirt on. Go get your shirt."

The tension I was experiencing suddenly was more than I could handle. My temper, which had a short fuse, erupted. I told Dorothy and Dad I had better find another place to live where I could dress as I pleased. With this I left the house.

There was an old hotel in Lompoc which served meals to the tenants. Reluctantly, I rented a room there. The room was upstairs and had a bath with it. The next morning I went down for breakfast. "You want cake and eggs or toast and eggs? You want moosh?" A very plump lady with a foreign accent took my order.

I struggled along there for about a week. I was still disturbed in my spirit, and I knew it was making me ill. I came back to the hotel one afternoon very sick to my stomach. I also had a deep pain in my side which doubled me up at times. This worried me. I lay down on the bed, feeling very weak and nauseated. As I tried to sleep, I found the pain in my side would repeatedly wake me up. I broke out into a sweat; in a very short time I was soaking wet. Next came terrible chills. I knew I was really in for something. I tried to raise myself from the bed and to my surprise I was so weak I could hardly move. If I could just get to a bathtub and turn on the hot water to warm up! Crawling on my hands and knees, I finally reached the tub, wrenching with pain in my side. This was more than just the flu; I was becoming delirious; the room was fading in and out of my vision. I got into the tub and soaked in the hot water, which seemed to help a little; at least I quit shaking. How I got back to the bed I don't remember. I became aware that it was dark outside; I was shaking and terribly cold. I realized my body was really in trouble. I began to yell for help. Unfortunately, none of the rooms on the second floor were rented, which I didn't know at the time. I yelled for help intermittently as I passed from consciousness to unconsciousness for hours. Night had passed, as I saw daylight in the room, but I was so weak I could hardly turn to my side to look. I realized I was going to have to crawl downstairs for help or die right here.

Suddenly I felt the strong presence of a spirit around me. Then I saw a brilliant flash of light. A voice spoke out loudly around me. *"I am Melchisedec. I am Melchisedec. You must get up and call your father. Come now with me."*

I didn't know who Melchisedec was, but if he was going to help me, I would try to get up. Struggling against the severe pain in my side, I got into my pants and crawled to the door, with the bright light and presence hovering above me. This Melchisedec, whoever he was, gave me the strength to move. I stood up, opened the door, and walked down

". . . this really bright light came. . . . It was tremendously bright; I just can't describe it. . . . It asked . . . if I was ready to die. It was like talking to a person, but a person wasn't there. The light's what was talking to me, but in a voice."

— A patient, quoted by Dr. Raymond Moody, in *Life After Life*

For this Melchisedec . . . priest of the most high God; first being by interpretation King of righteousness, and after that also King of Salem, which is, King of peace. Without father, without mother, without descent, having neither beginning of days, nor end of life; but made like unto the Son of God; abideth a priest continually.

— Hebrews 7:1-3

There are in the church, two priesthoods, namely, the Melchizedek and Aaronic, . . . Why the first is called the Melchizedek

the hall, then descended the stairs. Luckily there was a phone booth in the lobby. I got the operator to call Dad on an emergency, as I had no coin for the phone.

In ten minutes Dad and Dorothy arrived. They got me into the car and headed for the hospital. I lost consciousness in the car after describing the pain to Dad. Next, I became conscious of a nurse taking blood from my arm. Then there was a doctor standing at the foot of the bed. "Mr. Paulsen, you have acute appendicitis, possibly a rupture. We must operate immediately."

"Oh Lord, how could this happen? I don't want anyone cutting on me."

Now I was being prepared for the operation. Again I felt the presence of the strong spirit above me, and there again was a flash of light before my inner vision. Once more I heard the voice, "*I am Melchisedec. Tell them to take another blood test; there will be no operation.*"

As I looked around the room, my consciousness began to return. I actually felt normal, as if nothing was wrong. The pain and fever was gone. I had to stop this operation! A nurse came into the room.

"I feel much better now, and I don't want an operation."

She looked at me, not accepting my statement as rational.

Priesthood is because Melchizedek was such a great high priest. Before his day it was called *the Holy Priesthood, after the Order of the Son of God.* But out of respect or reverence to the name of the Supreme Being, to avoid the too frequent repetition of his name, the church, in ancient days, called that priesthood after Melchizedek, or the Melchizedek Priesthood. All other authorities or offices in the church are appendages to this priesthood.

— Doctrine and Covenants of
The Church of Jesus Christ of
Latter-day Saints 107:1-5

What is perhaps the most incredible common element in the accounts I have studied, and is certainly the element which has the most profound effect upon the individual, is the encounter with a very bright light. Typically, at its first appearance this light is dim, but it rapidly gets brighter until it reaches an unearthly brilliance. . . . Despite the light's unusual manifestation, however, not one person has expressed any doubt whatsoever that it was a being, of light. Not only that, it is a personal being. It has a very definite personality. The love and the warmth which emanate from this being to the dying person are utterly beyond words, and he feels completely surrounded by it and taken up in it, completely at ease and accepted in the presence of this being. He senses an irresistible magnetic attraction to this light. He is ineluctably drawn to it.

— Dr. Raymond Moody, *Life After Life*

"Look," I insisted, "get the doctor." I would get up and run if I had to.

The doctor came into the room. "What's this I hear?"

"I feel much better; I don't need the operation."

The doctor looked me over. "Let's take another blood test, Nurse. You really feel better?"

The doctor probed my side where the awful pain had been. To his surprise, I felt nothing. "Well, if this is indeed true, you don't need me anymore," said the doctor.

The blood sample turned out to be normal. I had been healed instantaneously by Melchisedec. Two hours later I was at Dad's house telling him the story.

"Yes, Son, this time they did help you. But remember, your anger and frustrations made you ill. The power of your thoughts can either make or break you."

I sent a message to Melchisedec, thanking him for repairing the damage I had done. Dad had informed me of his position in biblical history.

Actually, the kingdom of heaven begins as a state of mind here and now — a heavenly state of mind. When you save yourself from negative thinking you not only save your soul from disease but also your body which houses the soul.

— Catherine Ponder,
Dynamic Laws of Healing

Why would he have taken an interest in me? I began to meditate on this revelation. Could he be the same ancient figure I saw in the library in my childhood?

"Yes," came the reply. *"I and that figure are one and the same."*

Dual light energy images of the Angel Man and Woman moving over the heads of a couple at Giant Rock.

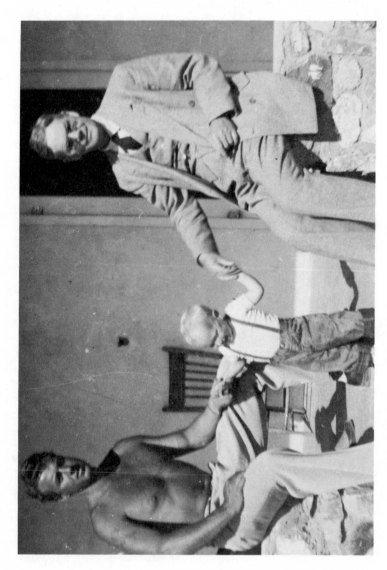

Three generations of Paulsens: the author, his son, and his father.

CHAPTER 28

A Son Is Born

Contrary to my feelings of the previous January, I returned to Giant Rock around February 1, 1954, and married Glenda Van Tassel, thus fullfilling half of Master Yogananda's prophetic words. When I returned to Giant Rock, I decided that now was a good time to learn the masonry trade. There was a man named Bernard Copley who occasionally attended George's meetings at Giant Rock. Barney, as everyone called him, was about my age, and had been building masonry homes and cabins for a number of years around the desert area. Barney offered me a job mixing mortar and tending him as he laid block. Gradually I learned how to handle a brick trowel and spread out the mortar. One day Barney had to leave the job on business. "Hey, Norm, why don't you go ahead and run up that partition wall while I'm gone?"

"All right." Here was the chance I had been waiting for. I started spreading mortar and laying the blocks. I had been watching carefully every move that Barney made in spreading out the mortar, setting the block on it and then tapping it down with his trowel to the string line. I went to work and ran up the partition wall without any problems. When Barney returned, he showed me a few mistakes I had made, but generally he thought I had done pretty well. This began my career as a brick and stone mason. I really loved this work. When you finished a job, there was a real image to see, something that was almost permanent. I worked for Barney off and on during the summer of 1954, making enough money to cover expenses for Glenda and myself.

One day, around the end of October, Barney and I were sitting in the coffee shop at the drugstore in Yucca Valley. This was a local hangout for all the working boys in the area. I had my back to the door when someone came in yelling, "Is there a brick mason in the place? I need to hire one bad."

Barney was sitting next to me and yelled out, "Yes sir, right here, Mister. Here's the guy you're looking for." I looked up and Barney was pointing right at me. He was giving me a chance to get out on my own, while having fun at the same time. This fellow walked up and Barney said, "Mister, here's your man right here. You won't find a better bricklayer in the entire valley."

"Do you want to go to work?" he asked, looking me over.

"I sure do," I answered, praying I would be able to perform to his liking.

As it turned out, this fellow had hired a bricklayer from Los Angeles to come out to the desert with him and construct his house. The bricklayer evidently was making the job a lifelong project; it was costing twice as much to build the house as the man had expected.

As I chugged along behind my employer to the job site, I thought about how I'd just finished preparing myself for this job. I had just bought and overhauled an antique Model A Ford pickup. Also, I had refurbished a wheelbarrow and some old masonry hand tools. I was now pretty well equipped for anything, I thought.

"Say, this is going to be a large house," I remarked as we arrived at the unfinished house.

"Yeah, if it's ever finished," said my employer in a huff.

During the course of the day, I laid twice as much block as the professional did and my wall looked just as good as his. That did it — the "pro" was fired and I was hired. I was now on my own and confronted with my first big job. This meant I was finally in business for myself.

Arriving home that night, I was really excited. I began telling everyone the good news. George and Daniel, at this time, were helping me finish the reconstruction of an old adobe cabin for Glenda, and the child we were now expecting, to live in. An elderly man had started construction of the adobe years before, but had been stopped short of completion by a serious illness. Our new incoming spirit was due to be born in November, and already the cold winter winds were beginning to blow. By working hard together, we were able to finish everything beautifully just before Glenda went to the hospital.

On November 22, 1954, Glenda gave birth to a male child at the Twenty-Nine Palms General Hospital. Now, with the birth of our child, both of Yogananda's prophecies had manifested in fulfillment.

Three weeks after our son's birth I still had not decided on a name for him. One evening we were all sitting in the restaurant together after dinner. George looked at me with a big smile and said, "Norm, when are you going to give this guy a name?"

"I don't know, George, I'm working on it. Have you received any inspiration you might want to pass on?"

"Well," George thought a moment, "why don't you call him Aaron after the high priest who was with Moses?"

"Well, George, I will have to think about that name for awhile. I really want a good strong sign from Divine Spirit indicating what the boy's name should be."

Next I wrote a letter to Dad inviting him to come up with a name for his grandson.

A few days later I received a letter back from Dad. "Son, Dorothy and I are going to try to make the trip down to visit you and Glenda sometime after New Year's. Also, Son, why don't you name the boy Aaron, after the high priest to Moses?"

That did it! Here was the message I had been waiting for. Both grandfathers had come up with the identical name. They hadn't met each other yet or ever even talked to each other, and they were living a good five hundred miles apart. I showed Dad's letter to George. "Well, I'll be damned," said George. "So Charlie named him Aaron, too! Well, are you going to call him Aaron?"

"No," I said, "I'm going to drop the "o" and call him Aarn. Aarn Lothar Paulsen. That's a good Nordic name, don't you think, George?"

"Christ sake, Norm, you really want him to be a Viking squarehead, don't you?"

"Yes, what's wrong with that?"

The next test I had coming up in my masonry career was the construction of a fireplace. I had completed the construction of my first house to my employer's satisfaction, and my own, and now I was looking for my next job. The local drugstore coffee shop was a good place to find new jobs in the area.

One cold morning I was seated at the counter drinking coffee when someone came in shouting for a brick mason who could build a good fireplace. That was something I knew very little about, but I wanted very much to learn. I was impelled to yell out, "Right here. Right here, Mister."

The man walked up and sat down next to me at the counter.

"Are you a good fireplace man?"

"Yes, I believe so." I felt intuitively that I would be able to build the man a good one, or die trying.

"Well, I have a house to build also. Do you have time to come take a look at the job site with me now?"

"Yes sir, I sure do."

"That's great," the man replied excitedly. "Let's go!" As I got up my prospective employer shoved a roll of plans into my hands.

After arriving at the site, I looked at the plans for a two-bedroom masonry home with a fireplace — simple, but nice. I signed an agreement that day to build the house on a cost plus 10 percent basis. Because I had no contractor's license at the time, this was the only way I could work. I was really in the building business now! This was going to be my first real job starting from the ground up.

Since I had never built a fireplace before, I was going to have to learn a few things fast from someone who did know how. I found out quickly enough that those who knew were not about to divulge their trade secrets to a newcomer like me. I went ahead with construction and poured the foundations and concrete floors. Then I constructed the outside and inside masonry walls, leaving a hole in an outside wall for the fireplace. What I didn't know about fireplace building, my unseen *Companions* were now going to teach me. I had some pictures to go by and a few words of George's wisdom — "Remember the smoke shelf, Norm; It's the most important part. If it isn't constructed correctly, the damn fireplace will smoke like hell."

That would be terrible. I couldn't afford that. I knew how the smoke shelf should look, so I began work on the fireplace with a silent prayer. I felt an unseen presence move into me, demanding the use of my hands. Mentally I moved over and watched my hands go to work independently, to my astonishment. I could hardly keep up with the movements. My hands knew exactly what to do. First I constructed the firebox, and then went outside to set the damper. Next I constructed the smoke shelf and the smoke chamber, filling in and grouting around the firebox as I worked. All was going smoothly. I plastered the inside of the smoke chamber and was now ready to set the first flue tile. The rest was going to be easy. I went on and ran up the chimney, completing the job.

Two days later, when the fireplace was finished, I was ready to test it out. I stacked up the firebox with wood and touched it off. To my great disappointment, smoke began to pour out of the front of the firebox. Something was wrong! "What did I do wrong?" I thought in a panic. Suddenly I remembered that no fireplace will work correctly outdoors unless there is some sort of shield to block the air currents from fanning the firebox. I hadn't put the roof on the house yet — no wonder it smoked! This I realized with great relief.

With the finishing of the roof and the interior and exterior, I had completed the construction of my first masonry home. It really looked beautiful! The fireplace worked perfectly, and the owner was very happy with the job. As we stood back and looked at it all, I felt a great surge of joy flow through me. Yes, it was a job to be proud of.

When George moved to the desert in the 1940s to set up Giant Rock Airport, he also acquired three sections of land on a lease-option from the federal government. This gave him approximately twenty-six hundred acres on a lease-option for thirty years. Adjoining this leased property, and approximately five miles from Giant Rock, George had purchased forty acres that had been, at one time, part of an old 160-acre homestead. Adjacent to the forty acres he had also bought a beautiful old stone ranch house, surrounded by smoke trees. George and Eva had lived in this house while construction of new buildings at Giant Rock was taking place. Later, Boone and I built a nice masonry cabin for George and Eva to live in at Giant Rock. When they moved into it, the old ranch house became vacant. I asked George if Glenda and I might move into it and fix it up and I would contribute rent to the church organization for the use of it. This was fine with George and Eva, so I began renovation of the old place. I took out the remains of old wooden floors and replaced them with new concrete floors. Everyone pitched in to help pour the concrete one weekend, and we all ended up having a big party when it was finished. Finally the house was ready for Glenda, Aarn, and me to move into, so we moved out of our adobe cabin at Giant Rock, which was now too small. The big ranch house was great and I was now five miles closer, over the rough roads, to my job areas in town. Glenda, Aarn and I spent Christmas of 1954 in the old ranch house.

There were a few new brothers who arrived at Giant Rock during late 1954 and early 1955. Some had expressed the desire to receive a technique of meditation. They had also read Paramhansa Yogananda's autobiography. I discussed it with Daniel and we decided to give an initiation at the ranch house. I prepared a place in the living room and one Sunday, in the summer of 1955, we held the initiation. When we all sat down to begin, it was a clear, warm, beautiful day without a cloud in the sky. There was also no apparent wind. Daniel and I led the initiates in some chants which were meant to invoke the presence of Divine Spirit Mother and Father. The feeling of the Spirit's presence grew intense as we built up the energy vortex with many of Paramhansa Yogananda's cosmic chants. Just as we concluded the chants and were ready to give the meditation technique, the wind hit the house with a force that rattled the windows and shook the tin roof. There was a bright flash as lightning struck right next to the old house and seemed to actually arc through the room. A gigantic clap of thunder resounded, shaking the house as an earthquake would. Then came the rain, falling in torrents on the old tin roof, like the galloping of many horses. When we looked out, to our astonishment, we saw only one huge, black cloud hovering right over the ranch house. Mother Divine was answering our devotions with her natural forces of wind, water, and fire. We all sat down again amidst the rumbling of more thunder and the flashes of lightning. The technique was passed on, and we ended the initiation with a deep meditation. Everyone was greatly inspired at the end of the day.

> What lightning flash glimmers in Thy face, Mother? Seeing Thee, I am thrilled through and through.
>
> — From a chant by Paramhansa Yogananda

Shortly after the initiation at the ranch house, I began to experience a lot of strange phenomenal events. Objects would materialize in my hands and on the floor around me while I was seated in meditation.

One Sunday in the late afternoon I was in the old ranch house; Glenda and Aarn were visiting with George and Eva at Giant Rock. Feeling the need arise for a deep meditation, I spread out my deerskin and began to quiet myself. The responsibility of a wife and son and their support had drawn my energy toward making a living in the world for us. I did not want to lose contact with Divine Spirit. This day was to manifest a very unusual meditation, for I was to be carried away on a journey back through time to another previous existence.

> I had acquired this deerskin in a very strange manner. At age seven, a large package had arrived in the mail one day. It was addressed to me with no return address. When the package was opened, a large, tanned deerskin was found within. That deerskin covered my bed for many years and was destined to become my meditation rug while living with Paramhansa Yogananda.
>
> — The Author

I finished the practice of my evolved meditation technique, which demonstrated the movement of the two divine cosmic forces of power, and sat silently for a while watching the soft astral light.

> I find my earliest memories covering the anachronistic features of a previous incarnation. Clear recollections came to me of a distant life in which I had been a yogi amid the Himalayan snows. These glimpses of the past also afforded me a glimpse of the future.
>
> — Paramhansa Yogananda, *Autobiography of a Yogi*

A Return to My Homeland

Suddenly I found myself standing up and looking northward across a wide expanse of rich, bright red, cultivated farmland. This was my homeland; I knew it well. There were gentle hills rising in the distance —

Vision of the Temple of the Sun on Mu

green, with tropical foliage. It was just after sunset and the sky was beautifully clear and bright. As I turned toward the east, my gaze fell upon the familiar image of a gigantic, seven-stepped pyramid just a short distance away. The colossal mass of this structure was overwhelmingly beautiful as it shimmered in the afterglow of sunset with all the colors of the visible spectrum. The cyclopean stone monoliths which comprised its huge bulk were alabaster white and reflected a mirror-like surface to the beholder. A great rectangular temple crowned the seventh level with imposing pillars and arches framing the grand processional gateways leading into the sanctuary. These gateways, in turn, faced the four directions. The hemispherical dome that resided on the apex of the temple glowed brightly with a divine radiance like the sun. I began walking toward the steps on the west face of the pyramid. Looking up, I caught the image of a huge, bright moon rising in the east. It was filling up one-tenth of the horizon and was slowly turning from left to right on its axis. It was gigantic!

There are legends and tablets which speak of a time when the moon was a spinning planet in this solar system in the vicinity of earth. The intrusion of a very large planet into this solar system from deep space millenniums ago created a tremendous cosmic disaster which involved the present satellite called the moon, the earth, and the material which now comprises our present asteroid belt. One is led to believe that the moon was hurled into orbit around the earth and captured by the earth's gravity. Also, the moon was much closer thousands of years ago and still turned on its axis. For further study on this subject read Zecharia Sitchin's, *The 12th Planet.*

— The Author

As I ascended the long flights of steps, reaching the seventh level and the Temple of Initiation, I could see across the landscape for miles. To the east lay the ocean just beyond the horizon. I envisioned the great breakers flashing fluorescent white in the light of the full moon as they rolled up on the long, sandy beach. Many times I had walked along the shore, gathering the few sacred seed pods that grew on little shrubs in among the sand dunes. These pods were strung and worn as sacred beads by the elder brothers and sisters from the Temple of Initiation. I reached up and clasped the string of sacred beads that hung around my neck.

Near the south-facing gateway to the temple on the seventh level stood the Telescope of Destinies. With this instrument we were able to view all of the planets and their satellites in our solar system. It was a beautiful instrument, inlaid with jewels. I adjusted it carefully and brought up the image of a very bright, very large red planet. As I walked along, my hand again reached up to clutch the sacred necklace of seed pods. The beads were strung on a finely woven string and were smooth and highly polished, emitting their own natural oil. As I held them, I knew they were the healing talisman of the eternal priesthood of which I was a representative.

Turning to the east, I walked along the seventh level to the eastern gateway. Here, very soon, the sun would reach the vernal equinox and light up the sacred inner chamber deep in the heart of the Sun Temple. This was a special day of initiation for many of the younger men and women of our society.

For some reason a great sadness seemed to prevail in the atmosphere around me, as if some doomsday event was about to take place. I felt great remorse and an overpowering faintness.

> They that were nine upon nine saw the great High Temple of Mu built. Each stone, each inner part, was of them. Then they rested from their work and waited for the great Ra of Mu to come in his golden ship and anchor atop the temple.
>
> Lo! the High Ra Mu, religious leader of the Sun called forth unto nine the Priest. And then he called unto nine the Priestess, . . . These of the Order of the Phoenix were to each send their nine outward in every direction of the hub. They journeyed to North America, South America, the moon nation, the nation of the Nile. Like a giant spider web they covered the land and great temples were built, and in them were placed light and knowledge.
>
> — Colonel James Churchward,
> *The Lost Continent of Mu*

Suddenly I was dimly aware of the bleak walls of the old ranch house. I had been sitting in the lotus posture for hours. My legs were asleep and very painful. But where was this wonderful homeland and the Temple of the Sun? I had just returned from a life and a land that no longer existed, the land of a great civilization of people who once thrived in an area now known as the South Pacific. The palms of my hands were still facing upward on my thighs in the meditative posture. Feeling was returning to them also. Then I felt something on the palm of my right hand. I looked down to examine the object and realized it had materialized into the future from a world of the past. It was one of the sacred pods. More than twenty years later, it is still in my possession. It remains highly polished to this day, emitting its own natural oil. I have searched the world over for similar seed pods, but have never found any like it. Botanists have tried to identify it and have failed. The nearest similar seed pod to be found today is called the kukui nut, which grows in areas around the Hawaiian Islands. It is my own conviction that the one I have in my possession came from the land of Mu, the Motherland, which unfortunately exists no more except in the astral records of the Great Book of Life and in the silent memory of its people — long lost, but now returning again.

Three objects that suddenly appeared during meditations.
A Roman coin, a compass, and the ancient seed pod.

George Van Tassel

A convention at Giant Rock

Suddenly it spun downward out of control and crashed in the distance

CHAPTER 29

Death of a Friend

Construction of masonry homes and commercial buildings began increasing during the summer of 1955 and lasted through 1958. The summer of 1956 brought throngs of people out into the desert. The reason for this sudden increase of people was the federal government's decision to give away five-acre tracts of undeveloped desert land. Any citizen of the United States could go down to the Bureau of Land Management and sign a lease-option for one of these five-acre tract parcels. The land would eventually be deeded to the leaseholder if a few improvements were made, such as building a twelve-by-sixteen foot cabin, or larger, within a period of twelve months.

Thousands of acres of desert wilderness were divided up into five-acre parcels. People filed lease-options on these parcels thinking they were going to get something for nothing. As soon as the leaseholder had completed the cabin with outhouse and water storage tank, they received clear title to the land. Then came the surprise — tax collectors! The new owner was now on the hook for high property taxes. The federal government was very happy receiving tax revenues from what had once been worthless land. Unfortunately, there was very little water on any of this land; and any that was needed had to be trucked in at high expense.

I had more than a dozen masonry cabins to build in the latter part of 1956. People who had waited too long to get their cabins completed within the twelve-month time period lost their options. I now had a general contractor's license and specialized in custom masonry homes, stores, churches, and schools. I was able to take my pick of the larger and better jobs due to the lack of masonry contractors in the area.

The great influx of thousands of people tearing across virgin desert land on motorcycles and in four-wheel drive vehicles ruined the unique and fragile ecology of the desert for years to come. I could hardly bear to look at

263

what had once been beautiful, primitive wilderness, now all scarred and crushed. Then, as their taxes rose higher and higher, landowners quickly lost interest in the desert and left. Most of their tract shacks are still to be seen throughout miles and miles of desert, from west of the Colorado River, through Twenty-Nine Palms, to Victorville, a good seventy miles. Thus, the rape of the land goes on, while mankind watches, seemingly ignorant of the consequences.

Dale Westen and his brother, Kenny, were both working for a local surveyor at the time I met them. I was building a house next to a section of land they were surveying for subdivision. Dale and I felt an immediate friendship for each other. During lunch hour we had discussions about the Spirit, and about life in general. My construction business was growing rapidly, putting great demands on my time and energy. I decided to rent a house in Yucca Valley on the main highway. Here I set up an office and brickyard.

I began to spend about three nights a week in town at the new office. Dale and his family were living in a rented house just a few blocks away. On weekends Dale would bring his family out to the ranch for visits. There was an old windmill at the ranch that filled a concrete reservoir, and we had great fun swimming in it on hot summer days.

Dale was interested in meditation and the Spirit. He had a wonderful wife and five beautiful children. Dale loved his family very much and demonstrated it all the time. After holding the first initiation in the ranch house, I continued meditations there on my own. Sometimes, Dale and a few others would join in on Sunday nights. George didn't like it; he thought all meetings should be held at Giant Rock. I felt that silent meditations on the Spirit were the one thing that was lacking at Giant Rock. It was turning into a circus, a public display of psychic phenomena. People were not coming there for Divine Illumination and a deeper understanding of the truth, as they should have been, but for intellectual stimulation and entertainment. Some of this would have been all right occasionally, but now it was becoming the predominating feature every Saturday night. George, I am sure, knew how Boone and I felt about this, but he wasn't about to change things. This was his way, his place, and his teaching; I was not going to argue with him about it.

Boone and I had been led to Giant Rock to contribute some of the teachings and practices of yoga, and to help build the foundations of a brotherhood colony. It could really have happened there, but George put the damper on my fires of enthusiasm.

The ability to produce psychic phenomena can become a great

stumbling block for any self-conscious entity who is trying to attain the experience of immortality, that is, Christ Consciousness. The practice begins to give birth to the false illusion that the self-conscious ego is responsible for the apparent phenomena existing around it. A false spiritual ego is conceived imprisoning the self-conscious entity even further. The powers of the Angel Man and Woman, as they begin to descend and manifest around the self-conscious ego, must be controlled by divine will, and not the will of the self-conscious entity. Self-consciousness, exposed to the negative influence of dark spirits, can be led to misuse the divine powers bestowed by the Angel Men and Women. The creature hu-man, failing to see the trap, is led to believe he or she is doing Divine Spirit's will, when in fact it is quite the contrary. Producing psychic phenomena for public display, such as materializations, levitations, readings, etc., unfortunately does not transmit the most profound and important ingredient, the seed energy, which generates Divine Illumination, that is, Christ Consciousness. This seed energy is the energy and life force of the immortal Angel Men and Women who found their conception and birth within the center of The Great Central SöN-SüN. This seed energy is passed on with the Baptism of Fire which emanates from, and prepares the way for, the descent of the Angel Man and Woman into the self-conscious hu-man creature.

While living at the ranch house in the desert, materializations around my person became a common occurrence. Many articles, including items of silver and gold appeared during my meditations. I neither encouraged nor discouraged

The Scripture tells us that we should pray: "Lord, let Thy will be done." Now many people interpret this to mean that they are not supposed to do any willing or thinking at all, but just sit and meditate and wait for God to do something through them. This is wrong. We are made in His image. He gave man intelligence such as He gave no other creature, and He expects us to use it. This is why Paramhansaji taught us to pray, "Lord, I will reason, I will will, I will act; but guide Thou my reason, will, and activity to the right thing that I should do." In other words, "You have given me the ability to reason about my problems; I'm not going to sit back and wait for You to tell me what to do. I will reason, will, and act; but while I am doing this, You guide me."

— Daya Mata, President of Self-Realization Fellowship, in SRF Magazine, Summer 1983

The Baptism of Fire is the energy and life force of the divine Angel Men and Women (i.e., guardian angels). The seed energy is in fact the rapidly moving light particles emanating forth from the Christ Consciousness residing within the Angel Men and Women. Essentially it is the essence of the First Creation of Light, the SöN-SüN of God. It is the presence of these highly charged lifetrons within areas of the hu-man creature body that change the genetic code transmitted to the genes to henceforth transmit the vibration of immortality (that is, illumination).

— The Author

this phenomenon and it still exists at times. We need to understand that humankind was predestined by Divine Spirit to receive the Baptism of Fire and become fused with the descending light of the Angel Men and Women, thus attaining Christ or Cosmic Consciousness. By this natural process of evolution the self-conscious hu-man being would attain illumination and immortality with the Angel Men and Women, their elder brothers and sisters. Hu-man, the creature, is comprised basically of the four elements of air, earth, fire, and water. The physical images of humankind were projected to evolve on planets in the outer spheres of the gross physical creation and eventually become the Christed hu-man Angel Beings. The Christ-Conscious beings in physical forms are also known to us as The Builders, the Sons of God or Nefilim, the divine caretakers of the galaxies. It became the duty of The Builders to see that the natural processes of evolution take place in the gross physical creation. It was their responsibility to care for the primitive, evolving forms of the hu-man creatures and all other life-forms throughout the creation. The Builders never display extraordinary powers, but allow the natural forces of evolution to operate freely within divine projected guidelines. The simple- and self-conscious hu-man creatures were impregnated from their beginning with the desire to see and know the Divine Angel Men and Women, their elder brothers and sisters, face to face. Divine Father and Mother gave free will to their offspring, the Angel Men and Women, at the time of their conception and birth within the center of The Great Central SöN-SüN. As the Angel Men and Women (The Builders) moved outward into the expanding spheres of creation, they followed divine guidelines and laws which would always protect them from the raw natural forces building the images of the creation.

It was not until these divine beings, the Angel Men and Women (The Builders or Nefilim), entered into, and began to exist within the creatures called hu-man, that any of the laws and guidelines governing the creation were broken. It was the deliberate decision by a small group of spirits to experiment with negative energies existing beyond the guidelines of virtue and conduct that brought about the conception and birth of evil. These disobedient, fallen sons and daughters of Spirit have bound themselves into a negative dimension of their own creation with their dark thoughts and actions. These once divine beings,

Fallen Angels: These once divine members of The Builders degenerated from Christ Consciousness, still possessing the memory of it, into self- and simple-conscious states. They fell lower than the evolving animal forms which now surrounded them. They became demonic and rebellious, and full of lust, hatred, and selfishness.

— The Author

266

existing within and without the physical forms of hu-man, have become known to us as the Fallen Angels. It is the negative opposition generated from within their ranks that now prevents the normal evolution of humankind on this planet from taking place with the Angel Men and Women (i.e., the evolution of Christ Consciousness). The spiritual Baptism of Fire has great difficulty entering humankind on earth due primarily to the negative opposition demonstrated and projected by these demonic forces. It is their influence that can, and does, mislead humankind in the search for divine light, truth, and union with the Christed Angel Beings. The display of extraordinary powers by The Builders or the baptised hu-man creatures is an action which exists outside of the divine guidelines and laws. We are, therefore, to avoid this action, if possible. Humankind, observing the display of extraordinary powers, might become obsessed with the desire to perform them and overlook the inherent desire for illumination (Christ Consciousness) existing deep within the self- or simple-conscious ego.

What, then, does the term *Nefilim* mean? Stemming from the Semitic root *NFL* ("to be cast down"), it means exactly what it says: It means *those who were cast down upon Earth!*

Contemporary theologians and biblical scholars have tended to avoid the troublesome verses, either by explaining them away allegorically or simply by ignoring them altogether. But Jewish writings of the time of the Second Temple did recognize in these verses the echoes of ancient traditions of "fallen angels."

— Zecharia Sitchin, *The 12th Planet*

Meditating one morning I had a vision: I was standing on the desert alone, looking eastward toward the city of Twenty-Nine Palms. A small airplane flew overhead. I knew it contained a friend of mine; I was positive of this.

As I watched it grow smaller in the eastern sky, it suddenly spun downward out of control and crashed in the distance.

I began running toward the crash site as fast as I could. A large black column of smoke was rising in the golden sky. My friend was very badly hurt.

In a sweat I opened my eyes: who might this friend be? No answer was forthcoming.

Three weeks later I was driving to a job site early in the morning. The temperature that night had dropped below freezing. The winter of 1957 brought two feet of snow to some areas of the high desert. Ahead I saw Dale Westen's red pickup truck beside the road. Dale was standing there waving me down. His radiator had evidently frozen up during the night; steam was boiling out from beneath the hood. "Hey, Dale! What's happening? Can I give you a ride?"

"Yeah." He jumped into my pickup. "I was on my way to the airport, Norm, to meet this guy who's flying in. I'm going to buy his airplane, possibly; he is going to give me a demonstration ride this morning."

Immediately cold chills covered my entire body. A sinister energy was hovering over Dale.

"Norm, you ought to come along. Have you ever been flying?"

"Yes, I have. I almost acquired my private pilot's license years ago. Listen, Dale! Please don't get in that plane today."

"What! Why not, Norm?"

"I have a very strong feeling about you and that particular aircraft. Don't get in it and don't buy it, Dale!"

"Aw, come on, Norm. What are you talking about? I have to go. This guy is flying all the way up here from San Bernardino to demonstrate it."

By now we were parked in front of the Yucca Valley Airport. "Listen, Dale, I had a vision about an airplane just a few weeks ago; I watched it crash. A dear friend of mine was in that plane."

"But was it me, Norm?"

"I don't know, Dale, it could be you."

"Do you really think something is going to happen to me?"

"Yes, I do, Dale. Look, here comes the plane now. Go tell him you had a change of plans and pay him for his trouble."

I watched Dale walk up to the plane as it taxied to a stop. He was talking to the pilot, then he returned to the car. "Norm, I have to go. We're just flying down to Twenty-Nine Palms and back."

"That's the wrong way, Dale!"

"Please come with me, Norm, then everything will be okay."

"I can't, Dale. Does Sharon know you're going?"

"Yes, I told her a little about it this morning. Look, I've got to go, Norm. See you later."

Dale climbed into the plane and it took off toward Twenty-Nine Palms. My heart was restless in my chest, and my stomach was very nauseous. "Something bad is going to happen to Dale and there is nothing I can do to stop it. Oh Father, help him!"

That afternoon I left my brick job to drive into Yucca Valley for lunch. I stopped in front of Hardesty's old general store. Suddenly Dale's wife came frantically up to me.

"Oh, God, Norm! Dale's been in a plane crash down in Twenty-Nine

Palms. I don't know if he's dead or alive."

"Get in my car, Sharon; let's get down there."

I drove at speeds of ninety and one hundred miles per hour all the way to Twenty-Nine Palms Emergency Hospital. Sharon and I were too late; Dale had died instantly in the crash. His body was already in the mortuary.

Sharon was beside herself with grief. I tried to convince her that Dale was going to be all right. She wanted to see him right away. We drove to the mortuary. Strangely, no one was there. I walked into the building and opened a door to a back room. Dale's body was lying inside on a table. I walked up to his form; his spirit was no longer there. Sharon pleaded with me to try to bring him back to life.

"There is no way, Sharon; he is gone, really gone."

There before me, the silent face of death: Dale, my friend, who had just hours before stated so emphatically that he had to go. I could have saved him if he had but listened.

That night, I was awakened. Dale was standing at the foot of my bed. "Norm, what's happening to me? I went home and Sharon doesn't see me; something is wrong. I can't pick up my kids anymore."

Dale had exited his body so fast he didn't realize in his state of shock he had lost his physical body. He wanted me to go and tell Sharon and the kids he was there and all right.

This I tried to do for him that night. Sharon tried to believe in her grief that he was with her. Dale's spirit was so strong, it took months to convince him that he had to move on and continue, no matter how hard it was.

Finally, I saw Dale for the last time. He looked like he always had, strong and determined. He knew he had to go, and he now saw things as they really were. I raised my hand in a salute to him as he moved off through inner space.

Dying persons are likely first to become aware of their spiritual bodies in the guise of their limitations. They find, when out of their physical bodies, that although they may try desperately to tell others of their plight, no one seems to hear them. . . . To complicate the fact that he is apparently inaudible to people around him, the person in a spiritual body soon finds that he is also invisible to others. . . . This is illustrated very well in this excerpt: "The doctors and nurses were pounding on my body to try to get IVs started and to get me back, and I kept trying to tell them, 'Leave me alone. . . . Quit pounding on me.' But they didn't hear me. So I tried to move their hands to keep them from beating on my body, but nothing would happen. I couldn't get anywhere. . . . It looked like I was touching their hands and I tried to move them — yet when I would give it the stroke, their hands were still there. I don't know whether my hand was going through it, around it, or what."

— Dr. Raymond Moody, *Life After Life*

Life is so horribly temporary, Lord, and we, your spirit children, get hurt so badly here on this planet. Goodbye for now, Dale. We'll meet again.

Building a masonry home in Yucca Valley, California

A big job with the Parks Department, Twenty-Nine Palms, California

I can still see the fiery trail of gigantic meteorites streaking across the black
night sky.

CHAPTER 30

A Vision and a Search for Mu

The summer of 1957 was a busy one, as my construction business was growing larger by the day. I now had to hire more people to help me complete the houses I had contracted to build. I was so busy working, I seldom had time to spend at home with Glenda and my son Aarn. At this point in my life things were getting strained and Glenda and I were not getting along well at all. I was determined to make the marriage work for Aarn's benefit, remembering my own deep despair when Mom and Dad had separated. Three times I moved out of the house and three times I moved back, trying to make the marriage work.

The many years I had spent in the past searching for the Divine Being had made more of a recluse than a householder out of me. Marriage was difficult; I had never been forced to answer to anyone for how I spent my time.

The end of the summer of 1957 brought about a final and permanent separation between Glenda and me, ending in divorce. I was to lose my son, Aarn, and there was nothing I could do about it. Aarn was to be so far removed from my life, that I would not see him again for fifteen years. Unfortunately, his ears were to hear only one side of the story, and with prejudice. Someday, my son, I pray you will read the words written in this book and try to understand your father's side of the story, also.

The direction of my life was now going to lead me away from the desert. I finished up all my contracted jobs and tried to pay off the debts I had incurred by selling my construction equipment. I left Yucca Valley and the desert as I had come — with just my seabag and automobile. Santa Barbara was my first stop. I applied for a bricklayer's union card with the Brotherhood of Bricklayers. This was hard to get, as my apprenticeship had not been worked out under a union brick mason. I was a self-taught bricklayer, and that was against all the rules. Finally, after much arguing and a bricklaying demonstration for union representatives, I obtained a union rating as a journeyman bricklayer.

Now I decided I was going to live as simply as possible. I would only need a sleeping room for my maintenance. I was determined to reinforce my spirit now with long deep meditations.

While in deep meditation in the spring of 1958, I again experienced a journey back into times past.

A Vision of Mu

I found myself standing on the same familiar pavilion on the seventh level of the Temple of the Sun. Looking off towards the west, huge columns of black smoke were rising into the night sky. Bolts of lightning struck into angry sheets of flame, illuminating the whole horizon. The huge stone blocks beneath my feet were trembling and heaving with shock waves, as huge, fiery objects slammed into the earth, violently exploding in the distance. Less than one mile away, below me, I could hear the cries of the multitudes of people rising from the city, as great stone buildings fell. The screams of the injured and dying assailed my ears. The smell of smoke and brimstone penetrated my nostrils, choking me. As I fearfully watched, I realized the horrors long prophesied were now a reality upon us. All that I saw, including the multitudes of people below, could well be totally destroyed this night. The very ground itself was beginning to split open in the distance, allowing sheets of flame and smoke to pour forth. Behind me I heard the grinding motion of stone straining on stone as the heavy shock waves rippled the polished, mortarless blocks of the temple, like leaves in the wind. But still the temple stood, riding out the onslaught.

I could hardly bear to watch the holocaust approaching. The roar of mighty forces, such as I had never before heard, filled the heavens above. I turned to watch what looked like a gigantic red moon begin to rise on the southeastern horizon. I was running now across the pavilion. I reached the northwest corner of the Temple of Initiation. I turned to look out across the land that had just hours before been beautiful fields of row crops. Now I saw plumes of fire rising like fountains everywhere in the distance.

Was this to be the complete end? I had decided to stay on in hopes the destructive war might not annihilate our homeland. The enemy had succeeded in breaking through our defenses. They were hurling gigantic asteroids down upon us. All was lost! What had taken millenniums to build, could well be gone, for the most part, in a few hours. I pressed upon a block of stone in the outer temple wall. With little effort it swung upward and inward on its pivots.

When the star of Bal [Baal] fell on the place where now is only the sky and the sea, the seven cities with their golden gates and transparent temples, quivered and shook like the leaves in a storm; and, behold, a

Turning, I stared downward into the passage, brilliantly lit by rays of light reflecting off the polished stone blocks. Quickly, I entered. Glancing over my shoulder, I looked, possibly for the last time, upon the beloved and devastated landscape. If I and others were to survive, it would be within the heart of the temple, the divine spherical chamber. The great block of stone rocked back in place in the outer wall, sealing me off from the outside world. The roar of heaving and grinding stone blocks was deafening; I put both hands to my ears to block out the sound.

flood of fire and smoke arose from the palaces. Agonies and cries of the multitude filled the air. They sought refuge in their temples and citadels.

— The Lhasa Record of Tibet quoted by
Colonel James Churchward,
in *The Lost Continent of Mu*

Twice Mu jumped from her foundations; it was then sacrificed by fire. It burst while being shaken up and down violently by earthquakes. . . . the land was rended and torn to pieces . . . quivering like the leaves of a tree in a storm . . . rising and falling like the waves in the ocean . . . and during the night it went down. . . .

— Codex Cortesianus (an ancient Mayan Manuscript), Troano Manuscript, and Lhasa Record of Tibet quoted by Colonel James Churchward, in *The Lost Continent of Mu*

Suddenly, the terrifying experience began to dematerialize before my eyes. I remembered the existence of my present physical life-form. Yes, I was now living far ahead of this disaster in time. With great relief, I realized my escape from the horrendous cataclysm. The painful scenes and circumstances faded into the surrounding walls of my room. I was wet with perspiration, and shaking. I was remembering vividly many events that had occurred millenniums ago in my journey through the spheres of creation. I had just relived some of the grievous moments from a past existence. This existence was recorded in my Book of Life, along with all the other images I had encountered and beheld from the moment of my conception and birth within the orb of The Great Central SöN-SüN .

Now I began to read deeper into my Book of Life. There, all the images and thoughts of the past lay revealed to me. This was not to be the last of my visits to this ancient of lands. At one time, in the area now known as the South Pacific, a part of the ocean floor once rose above the bright blue waters, forming three beautiful Pacific island continents. Today only one of the three remains visible, Australia.

From various records it would seem that this continent consisted of three separate lands, divided from each other by narrow seas or channels, but where or how these divisions were made by nature there is nothing to show except, possibly, an Egyptian hieroglyph which represents three long, narrow lands running east to west. . . . The land of Mu was an immense continent covering nearly one-half of the Pacific Ocean.

— Colonel James Churchward,
The Lost Continent of Mu

These extraordinary experiences now fully aroused my interest. I became aware of who I had been and what my name was. All of the events reaching backward for millenniums raced through my consciousness. I saw the beginning of the great wars between The Builders and the Fallen Angels explode in all directions a million years ago in this galaxy. Twelve thousand years ago the lands of Mu were destroyed by the Dark Angels. I was a witness to this murderous holocaust. May Divine Spirit help us, for it is about to happen again! No! Oh, no! It cannot!

I watched the Motherland I loved so much, and the multitudes of people that I knew so well, destroyed in a single day. The immense and familiar Temple of the Sun vanished beneath the seas into a fiery grave, swallowed up by the earth's molten mantle.

I was now convinced of, and remembered well, the reason for which I was born. My mission stood forth, revealed in all its details. Years after these experiences I was given a book by a friend entitled, *The Lost Continent of Mu*, by Colonel James Churchward. I delved into its contents. Here I collected more evidence as ancient memory bells began ringing loudly in my consciousness. This was a good description of the very lands I had seen in my journeys back through time. The huge blocks of stone used for construction of temples, pyramids, and cities were described herein.

It was a beautiful tropical country with vast plains. The valleys and plains were covered with rich grazing grasses and tilled fields, while the low rolling hillands were shaded by luxuriant growths of tropical vegetation. No mountains or mountain ranges stretched themselves through this earthly paradise, for mountains had not yet been forced up from the bowels of the earth.

The great rich land was intersected and watered by many broad, slow-running streams and rivers, which wound their sinuous ways in fantastic curves and bends around the wooded hills and through the fertile plains. Luxuriant vegetation covered the whole land with soft, pleasing, restful mantle of green. Bright and fragrant flowers on tree and shrub added coloring and finish to the landscape. Tall fronded palms fringed the ocean's shores and lined the banks of the rivers for many a mile inland. Great feathery ferns spread their long arms out from the river banks. In valley places where the land was low, the rivers broadened out into shallow lakes, around whose shores myriads of sacred lotus flowers dotted the glistening surface of the water, like vari-colored jewels in settings of emerald green.

Over the cool rivers, gaudy-winged butterflies hovered in the shade of the trees, rising and falling in fairylike movements, as if better to view their painted beauty in nature's mirror. Darting hither and thither from flower to flower, hummingbirds made their short flights, glistening like living jewels in the rays of the sun.

Feathered songsters in bush and tree vied with each other in their sweet lays.

The chirpings of lively crickets filled the air, while above all other sounds came those of the locust as he industriously "ground his scissors," telling the whole world all was well with him.

Roaming through the primeval forests were herds of "mighty mastedons and elephants" flapping their big ears to drive off annoying insects. The great continent was teeming with gay and happy life over which 64,000,000 human beings reigned supreme. All this life was rejoicing in its luxuriant home.

— Easter Island Tablet, Greek Record, Troano Manuscript, S.A. Record, Indian and Mayan Records, quoted by Colonel James Churchward, in *The Lost Continent of Mu*

Yes, here was some confirmation that at one time a highly developed civilization had existed on some South Pacific island continents, as well as in Central and South America. Here I found some clues to aid me in revealing the great mysteries. I now knew I would be compelled, someday, to unravel the true story of the origins of mankind in the mysterious Garden of Eden, the ancient Motherland of man, called Mu.

It is at this time that I am inspired to depart momentarily from the narration of my life and focus some attention on ancient historical evidence gathered by many scholars, anthropologists, and archeologists which supports the existence of mankind's genesis in the Far West as well as in the Near East. In the next few chapters I am going to present all the data I have obtained up to the present time that relates to mankind's ancient origins and his lost civilizations.

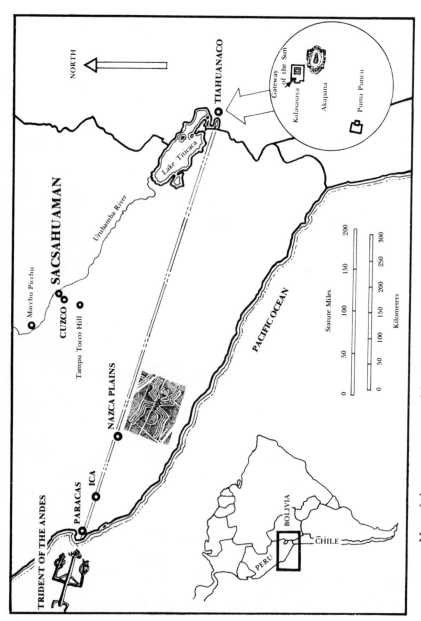

Map of the western coast of South America, showing places mentioned in the text

CHAPTER 31

The Ancients in Central and South America

The Ancients were sometimes called "the gods of heaven and earth" by hu-man beings in their first self-conscious expressions using verbal language. The gods of heaven and earth can now be identified as physical beings from other planets in our galaxy, called The Builders, the Sons of God, the Nefilim, etc. The Holy Bible, Oxford Annotated Edition states: "The Nephilim were on the earth in those days, and also afterward, when the sons of God came in to the daughters of men, and they bore children to them. These were the mighty men that were of old, the men of renown." (Genesis 6:4.) It is from this statement in the Hebrew Bible that I was inspired years ago to search for the lost sons of the gods. Who exactly were the sons of the gods? And who were the daughters of men? Where did the sons of the gods actually come from, and where have they gone? These questions I will attempt to answer in the next few chapters.

We find ancient records about the Sons of God written on stone, copper, silver, gold, and clay tablets all over the earth. Ancient legends and histories from people the world over speak of the great gods who flew down from the heavens in their fiery vehicles. We will begin our search for the lost Sons of God off the coast of Peru, and then move inland toward Paracas and the plains of Nazca. The first clue, as we start our search, is the sighting of the great Trident of the Andes, which I shall call the "Tree of Life," which points the way. This gigantic drawing on the side of a hill overlooking the blue Pacific is six hundred feet in length and is oriented on a northwest-southeast direction. It is positioned on a straight line that runs through

Two of the most well-known works depicting these gods who flew down from heaven in their fiery vehicles (chariots of fire) are the Bhagavad-Gita and the Ramayana.

— The Author

There is undoubtedly great significance in the northwest-southeast direction followed by most of the Nasca lines, the Trident [Tree

279

Paracas, Ica, and the Nazca Plains, ending at Tiahuanaco and the Island of the Sun at Lake Titicaca. It can be seen only from the air or from out at sea, and it is definitely pointing the way toward hidden sanctuaries. The ancient Peruvian scene is dominated by hundreds of pyramids and temples. Ruins are to be found along the coast of Ecuador all the way to northern Chile. These imposing ruins tell us of a lost civilization of of Life], and the incredibly straight line that passes through the Paracas necropolis, Ica, and the fascinating Gate of the Sun at Tiahuanaco. The Gate of the Sun is oriented in such a way that the rising sun at the solstice shines through its opening, then passes over it and goes on to light Nasca, Ica, and Paracas.

As for the enigmatic Trident [Tree of Life], at the other end of the "sacred line," it is on a hillside with an average slope of thirty-eight degrees, so that its three upper extremities are aimed at the sky in a specific direction.

— Robert Charroux,
The Mysteries of the Andes

people who displayed amazing skills in architecture, ceramics, metallurgy, and textile weaving. Their advanced methods of working gold, silver, copper, and bronze are yet to be surpassed.

Following the axis of the Tree of Life of the Andes, one is led overland, six miles to the small village of Paracas. Here, in the desert sands, exists an ancient necropolis. Within it we find man-made burial caves in which numerous mummies have been found perfectly preserved for millenniums. These ancient pre-Inca burial sites have actually yielded up the mummified bodies of an ancient white race. The bodies were wrapped and decorated in brightly colored fabrics of a fine design, with over one hundred different shades of color woven into some of the textiles.

People of this ancient white race were tall and bearded. Their hair was bright red, brown and blond. Hair experts have shown by microscopic analysis that the hair has all the characteristics of the type belonging to the Nordic races of today.

> In Peru, when the Spaniards discovered the Inca Empire, Pedro Pizarro, the chronicler wrote that, while the mass of Andes Indians were small and dark, the members of the Inca family ruling among them were tall and had whiter skins than the Spaniards themselves. He mentions in particular certain individuals in Peru who were white and had red hair. We find the same thing occurring among the mummies. On the Pacific coast, in the desert sand of Paracas, there are large and roomy man-made burial caves in which numerous mummies have been perfectly preserved. When the colorful, still unfaded wrappings are removed, some of the mummies are found to have the thick, stiff, black hair of the present-day Indians, while others, which have been preserved under the same conditions, have red, often chestnut-colored hair, silky and wavy, as found among Europeans. They have long skulls and remarkably tall bodies, and are very different from the Peruvian Indians of today. Hair experts have shown by microscopic analysis that the red hair has all the characteristics that ordinarily distinguish a Nordic hair type from that of Mongols or American Indians.
>
> — Thor Heyerdahl, *Aku-Aku*

It was in this area that lapstrake canoes were found, some up to forty feet in length. This discovery was also made on the west coast of Chile, at 34 degrees south of the equator. These vessels were built high in the stem and stern, and resembled Viking hulls, which were rowed or sailed. The similarity to existing Polynesian canoes is also seen, as if both were originally designed by the same race of people in remote times. Strange as it may seem, when Juan Cabrillo sailed along the California coast, in 1542, he discovered a race of white natives with red, blond, and brown hair and of beautiful form living on the southern California offshore islands. There before him and his crew, at 34 degrees north of the equator, was a fleet of large lapstrake canoes, some in excess of forty feet in length!

> The inhabitants of the island [Santa Catalina] rejoiced greatly over the arrival of the Spaniards. They are fishermen, using boats made of planks with a high bow and stern and the middle very low, some will hold more than 20 persons. . . . The women are handsome and modest, the children are white and blond, and very happy.
>
> — Father Zárate Salmerón, *Relaciones*, circa 1626, about the voyage of Sebastian Vizcaino to Cape Mendocino, in 1596

Many of the massive drawings on the Nazca Plains are also oriented on the same northwest-southeast line of the Tree of Life of the Andes. These gigantic lines and drawings can only be seen from the air, and resemble a huge landing field, with birds, insects, and animals marking the different landing strips. The majority of the lines point directly to the ancient sanctuary of Tiahuanaco and the Island of the Sun in Lake Titicaca, approximately three hundred miles to the southeast. These drawings on the plains of Nazca suggest that the figures may have been intended to guide the course of navigators from outer space to established bases and sanctuaries on earth. Legends from natives in the area today are full of descriptions of men and golden ships who came down from the heavens. For instance, one legend states that thousands of years ago the Indians' ancestors traveled on great golden discs which were kept airborne by means of sound vibrations rendering them weightless.

Many of the ancient cities in Central and South America and their battered foundations existing today were constructed before the great biblical flood. Some scholars have dated the age of the oldest ruins of Tiahuanaco at one-quarter million years old. As late as the second half of the last century, travelers to Tiahuanaco were able to admire and sketch imposing colonnades of which there is now no trace. We may glimpse a little of the city's former beauty from Spanish commentators' reports.

Garcilaso de la Vega wrote, "The most beautiful structure is a hill created by the hands of men. In order to prevent the masses of earth from collapsing, they secured the foundations by well built stone walls, 'a stepped pyramid.' On another side there are two stone giants to be seen. They are clothed in long gowns and wear caps on their heads. Many large gateways have been built from a single block of stone."

Another commentator, Diego de Alcobaza states, "Amid the buildings at Tiahuanaco, on the shore of Lake Titicaca, is a paved court eighty feet square with a covered gallery forty-five feet long going down one of its sides. Court and hall are of one single block of stone. This masterpiece has been hewn out of the rock. . . . There are still many statues to be seen here today. They represent men and women, and are so perfect one would believe the figures were alive. Some seem in the act of drinking, others look as if about to cross a stream. Women are giving children to the breast."

Jiminez de la Espada states, "One of the palaces is truly an eighth wonder of the world. Stones thirty-seven feet long by fifteen feet wide have been prepared without aid of lime or mortar, in such a way as to fit together without any joints showing."

When the Spaniards came to Lake Titicaca, up in the Andes, they found the mightiest ruins in South America — Tiahuanaco. They saw a hill reshaped by man into a stepped pyramid, classical masonry of enormous blocks beautifully dressed and fitted together, and numerous large stone statues in human form.

— Thor Heyerdahl, *Aku-Aku*

The region of Lake Titicaca, near to which Tiahuanaco stands, is one of the most desolate spots on Earth, and unlikely to have supported a large population. It is the last place in the world to expect a great stupendous archeological site. Yet its builders created the most elaborate and purest manifestation of culture in all South America. They have been called the most expert workers in stone the world has ever seen.

— Wendell C. Bennett, principal excavator of Tiahuanaco

In no other part of the world have I seen stones cut with such mathematical precision and such admirable skill as in Peru, nor in all Peru have I encountered any compared with those which are scattered about the plains of Tiahuanaco.

— George E. Squire, 1878

An unknown chronicler states, "The great throne room at Tiahuanaco measures one hundred and sixty feet by eighty-five feet. . . ."

The terraced temples are precisely like those which rise beside the Tigris and the Euphrates rivers in the Middle East. We shall see that the builders of ancient American cities and the Western civilizations are directly related to the builders of cities in the Tigris and Euphrates valleys.

The Indian boats of today which ply their way across Lake Titicaca are identical to Egyptian papyrus boats in shape, the materials used, and the methods of construction. The great civilizations which sprang forth on the banks of the Tigris and Euphrates rivers circa 3800 B.C. are dominated by the same type of great temples and pyramids as are to be found in most of the cities of ancient America. The legendary Tower of Babel was built along these lines.

The ruins of Tiahuanaco are now divided into three sections, which are commonly known as Akapana (the fortress), Kalasasaya (the Temple of the Sun), and Puma Puncu (the place of ten doors, the Temple of the Moon).

Akapana (the fortress) was once a gigantic, seven-stepped pyramid with a secret underground passage leading toward its center and with the Temple of Initiation residing on its apex. It is now in ruins but still stands approximately fifty feet in height, with a base mathematically fixed to the cardinal points of the compass. Its huge, rectangular mass measures approximately six hundred feet square.

Kalasasaya (the Temple of the Sun) was originally dedicated to the SöNs of the SüN, the ancient rulers of Tiahuanaco. This temple is in a better state of preservation and contains the famous monolithic Gateway of the Sun. This stone gateway is cut from a single block of andesite and is one of the largest carved monoliths in the world today. The central figure, which dominates the gateway, is most unusual, and probably represents the Sun God, Kon-Tiki Viracocha. There are three small oval marks on each cheek of the image. Some scholars have felt the marks may indicate periods of time, while others feel they represent tears. If the latter is true, then why is the Sun God of Tiahuanaco crying? Did the destruction and submergence of Mu, the Motherland of man, along with all of her inhabitants, create a reason for three tears to appear upon each cheek of the Sun God of Tiahuanaco? Could there have been some great cataclysmic war between the physical gods who were upon the earth in ancient times which generated the great biblical flood and its destruction of land and life? Facts uncovered today lead us to believe that this is, indeed, what happened.

At Puma Puncu (the place of ten doors, the Temple of the Moon), a short distance from the Pyramid of Akapana, we find the ruins of another large

We find the Temple of the Sun located on the most sacred island in Lake Titicaca, where, according to tradition, Orejona, the Mother of Mankind, landed in a spaceship brighter than the sun.

— Robert Charroux,
Mysteries of the Andes

The Indians say that their ancient ones hold it to the truth that for many days the world was in darkness, and while they were all in blackness and obscurity, there rose from this island of Titicaca, a vessel resplendent as the sun. For this reason they hold the isle to be a sacred place, building there a temple in honor of the sun.

— Pedro de Cieza de León, 1553

pyramid, perhaps originally of seven steps. On the third level of this pyramid the remains of a huge gateway are to be found, called the Gateway of the Moon. The great stone slabs and blocks used to construct the temples and palaces of Tiahuanaco were joined together with metal pins, made originally of pure silver. This kind of construction and the use of this technique has been found in only one other area of the world — the ancient palaces and temples of Assyria and Mesopotamia. The incorporation of the sacred number twelve into the temples and statuary of Tiahuanaco also runs a parallel with the cities of ancient Assyria and ruins found along the Tigris and Euphrates rivers. In Tiahuanaco we find beautiful statues of persons with aquiline noses, wearing classic turbans and using a symbolic hairstyle with twelve long braids. The sacred numeral twelve has been found in the Far West as well as the Near East.

Who were the builders of the great and ancient city of Tiahuanaco? Who laid out the drawings and pictures on the plains of Nazca, seen only from the air? Who were the people who were able to cut, dress, and move blocks of stone weighing in excess of two hundred tons thirty miles across Lake Titicaca to the construction site at Tiahuanaco, and from other sites as much as two hundred miles away?

When the Spaniards asked the Indians to tell them who had left these enormous ruins, the well-known chronicler Cieza de León was told in reply that these things had been made long before the Incas came to power. They were made by white and bearded men. . . . The white men finally had abandoned their statues and gone with their leader, Con Ticci Viracocha. . . . They were given the Inca name of *viracocha*, or "sea foam," because they were white of skin and vanished like foam over the sea.

— Thor Heyerdahl, *Aku-Aku*

Legend states that this was accomplished by a race of bearded, white men with blond and red hair. Legends among natives living in the area today state: "Kon-Tiki Illac-Viracocha and the long-eared people cut some of the massive stone blocks seen at Tiahuanaco in a quarry on the other side of Lake Titicaca." But how were they transported over thirty miles of water and land without evidence of a wheel? No one knows. "Kon-Tiki Illac-Viracocha (i.e., Kon-Tiki Viracocha, Kon-Tiki, Tiki) is the creator of men," legend states. He and his companions are the ones who cut, moved, and assembled the massive stone blocks to Sacsahuaman, as well as many other cities of South America. Kon-Tiki Viracocha and the white god known as Quetzalcoatl to the Toltecs, both belonged to the same priestly brotherhood, henceforth called The Builders. Kon-Tiki Viracocha is known as the creator of men by the white and red races in all the ancient legends of South America, as well as in the islands of Polynesia as they exist today, the grim remains of Mu.

Kon-Tiki Illac-Viracocha has deep meaning. When translated, Kon-Tiki means "SöN of the SüN." Illac means "lightning"; Viracocha means "white sea foam moving over the waters." Quetzalcoatl translates into "flying, feathered serpent; the creative, primordial force." Ku Ku Matz and Bochica, other names for Quetzalcoatl, mean "heart of the sea" and "shining white cloak."

The legendary Kon-Tiki Viracocha was a tall, bearded white man. He wore a white robe like an alb, which was secured at the waist. Tiki, the SöN of the SüN, carried a staff in one hand and a book in the other. He taught the ancient forefathers of the Incas architecture and agriculture.

We may remember that Kon-Tiki is a Polynesian divinity as well as an American one. Many ancient works of art found in Central and South America reveal the existence of a tall race of white-skinned natives. The Mayan paintings at Chichen Itza clearly show the figures of a taller race of white natives existing beside a shorter, dark-skinned race. Elsewhere, their majestic and serene faces are seen in the masks and statues of Tiahuanaco and the giant figures on Easter Island.

The legends of the origin of the Incas of Cusco state that six leagues south-southwest of Cusco, alongside a road the Incas built, there is a place called Paccari Tampu. Nearby is a hill known as Tampu Tocco, which means "the house of many windows." "There were at least three windows in this house," legend states. One was named "Maris Tocco," the other "Sutic Tocco," and the third, the window in the middle, "Ccapac Tocco," meaning "the right window in the middle."

Out of the first window came a tribe of people known as the Maras. Legend states they were without physical parents. Who, then, were their creators? These people and their story are still to be found in areas around Cusco. Moving on

The dominant race of the lands of Mu was a white race, exceedingly handsome people, with clear white or olive skins, large, soft, dark eyes, and straight black hair. Besides this white race, there were other races, people with yellow, brown, or black skins. . . . These ancient inhabitants of Mu were great navigators and sailors who took their ships over the world "from the eastern to the western oceans and from the northern to the southern seas. . ." and the land of Mu was the Mother and the center of the earth's civilization, learning, trade, and commerce; all other countries throughout the world were her colonies or colonial empires.

— Colonel James Churchward,
The Lost Continent of Mu

Our Father, the Sun, seeing that men lived like wild animals, took pity on them, and sent to Earth a son and a daughter of his, in order that they might teach men the knowledge of our Father, the Sun, and that they might know how to cultivate plants and grains and make use of the fruits of the earth

with the legend, we're told that from the Sutic Tocco came another people, called Tampus. They were also without earthly fathers or mothers. From the center window, called Ccapac Tocco, came a further creation of four men and four women; they were called the Brethren. These knew no father or mother beyond the story they were able to tell that they were created and came out of said window by the order of the god Kon-Tiki Illac-Viracocha.

like men and not beasts. With these orders and mandate, our Father, the Sun, placed his sons and daughters in Lake Titicaca.

— Luis Marden, "Titicaca, Abode of the Sun," in *National Geographic Magazine*

The Incas declared that Tiki created them originally to be lords over all. For this reason they took the name Inca, which means the same as "lord." They took the name Ccapac as an additional name because it means "the rich ones." The four pairs, male and female, called the Brethren, created here by the legendary Kon-Tiki and his companions, The Builders, represent part of the original foundations of the red race as they are found upon the surface of the earth.

Here is evidence to support the belief that *Homo sapiens* in the Western Hemisphere was indeed a special creation and did not evolve naturally from primitive forms. The one puzzling fact that has always baffled scientists who support the theory of evolution is the absence of a connecting link between *Homo sapiens* and the primitive evolving creature called *Homo erectus*.

The latin, *Homo sapiens*, means "man, the wise"; *Homo erectus*, the name of the primitive evolving creature means "man, the erect." This creature had developed the ability to walk on two legs, but his mental abilities were as yet very limited.

— The Author

For 3.5 million years mankind slowly evolved, from the first manlike beings called *Australopithecus*, into forms slightly less primitive, such as *Homo erectus*. Then, in 2 to 3 hundred thousand years, only 8.9% of that enormous time span, modern man called *Homo sapiens*, developed. The earliest forms of *Homo sapiens* appeared in archaic form, out of nowhere, his skull is different not only in cranial capacity but distinctively different in shape, rounded and fuller, and with less massive bones. There are no fossils showing a gradual development from earlier types, and if these bridging fossils do in fact exist, they should be easier to find than the remains of *Australopithecus*, or the other pre-humans, because of their more recent origin. Another astonishing fact is that only 70 thousand years ago Neanderthal man appeared. That is, 2 to 3 hundred thousand years after the more evolved *Homo sapiens* appeared. Neanderthal man can easily be seen as the further natural evolution of *Homo erectus*.

Evolution of Man

Description	**First Appeared**

Australopithecus, the first truly manlike beings, had heads only slightly different from the apes, with heavy bones and massive brow ridges. Note the sloping forehead and flattened braincase.

3.8 million years ago

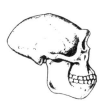

Homo erectus. All the skull bones of *Homo erectus* are also rather thick and heavy. The brow ridges are quite massive. The skull is long and flat with a low cranial vault, and the occipital region (back of head) is angular or pointed rather then rounded and full. Toward the end of this period, The Builders began to genetically improve this early man-like creature.

1.5 million years ago

Archaic *Homo sapiens.* While clearly a derivative of *Homo erectus,* these skulls show modern characteristics such as a braincase that is larger, more rounded and filled out, and much less angular or pointed in the occipital region then that which is typical of the *Homo erectus.* These creatures were the first stage of the creation of modern man by The Builders, in both the Western and Eastern hemispheres.

400 thousand years ago

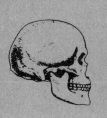

Modern *Homo sapiens* appeared before the more primitive Neanderthal man. The modern characteristics of archaic and modern *Homo sapiens* appeared and reached virtually full development during the brief span of time from 400 thousand years at the earliest, to 115 thousand years ago, only 7.5% of the entire period of the evolution of mankind. Note the almost vertical forehead, allowing much greater capacity for gray brain matter.

115 thousand years ago

Neanderthal man. The Neanderthals are the further natural evolution of *Homo erectus,* without the genetic intervention of The Builders. This form lasted a mere 35 thousand years before being absorbed or wiped out by modern *Homo sapiens,* called Cro Magnon man. Note again the sloping, flattened braincase. Neanderthal man was the creature hu-man evolving upon earth. *Homo sapiens* was the creation of the gods!

70 thousand years ago

Modern *Homo sapiens* existing on the earth today is not the product of a long evolutionary chain of life-forms, but is a special creation, just as the Bible states! Civilized man today is the manifestation of a genetic cross between highly evolved extraterrestrial beings from planets within our own galaxy and the primitive evolving form of man on earth. The native, primitive evolving form of man on earth is still to be seen in some of the aborigines of Australia and the primitive tribes of New Guinea, South America, and Africa. These natives, if left to themselves, might require at least another two or three million years for natural evolution to produce from them the modern *Homo sapiens* of today. The obvious conclusion is that the modern creature man existing on Planet Earth was genetically tampered with and changed, either to insure his survival, or to become a useful worker, or both.

As we study the ancient records of the Western genesis, we learn that Tiki and his companions, The Builders, created four different races in their own image: the Red, the Yellow, the Blue (Black), and the White. The four foundation races of *Homo sapiens* created in the Western Hemisphere originally were patterned after the image of the Angel Men and Women, known to us now as the Sons and Daughters of God, The Builders from the galaxy.

The "house of many windows," which rested on a hill in Peru in ancient times, may well have been one of the grand celestial *mus*, a spaceship belonging to The Builders. It was there in South America, and in the now lost continents of the Pacific, that the first divine celestial *mus* (space-ships) belonging to The Builders landed on this planet, more than 500,000 years ago.

The great ice age, which covered much of the earth 500,000 years ago, was threatening to exterminate the primitive, evolving man-like creatures called *Australopithecus*, *Homo erectus*, Peking man, etc. The Builders, observing the desperate situation which existed for the primitive creatures and their own reduced population, reached a decision more than 400,000 years ago to speed up genetically the evolution of some of the

At this site, in the highest peaks of the high range of the Andes, on a continent whose edges are very different now from what they were then, communication with and from the "gods" first began.

The Andean center was chosen by these "gods," or extraterrestrial colonizers, because it afforded them the easiest "window" on the world. They chose much as today our own NASA flight engineers choose particular sky sites when and where the spatial window is open and accessible. The Andean site was the site of maximum energy contact in a time when the oceans and plains refracted and distorted the energy focus.

— Michael Grumley,
There Are Giants in the Earth

The four colors of corn, as given by The Builders, to the four foundation races of humankind: the white, red, blue and yellow.

primitive evolving forms. This was done to insure their survival and also to help The Builders construct and defend a new civilization on the new earth. Thus, the imprint of The Builders, the true Sons and Daughters of Spirit, was genetically placed upon the primitive evolving pre-human (or simple-conscious) creature.

One of the home planets of The Builders has been referred to in ancient writings as the Kingdom of Heaven. This planet called Heaven completed its own evolution of organic life-forms millenniums ago in a solar system in this galaxy. It was on this planet that some of the creatures, having evolved into self-consciousness, became fused with the omnipresent Angel Men and Women, the Sons and Daughters of Spirit.

So that we may now understand who the Angel Men and Women were, and who the creatures were, we must look back to the primary ignition of light, which is the center that originally ignited and projected the visible, expanding spheres of the creation.

This picture depicts the eight expanding vibrational energy spheres of the spectrum (spheres of creation) moving outward from The Great Central SöN-SüN, the First Creation of Light. These expanding spheres compose the great Sphere of Creation. The Angel Man and Woman, as vibrational energy spheres, move outward toward the gross physical creation of planets, suns and galaxies.

CHAPTER 32

The Genesis of Creation

In the beginning, before the visible expanding great Sphere of Creation appeared, the divine living Spirit existed in a state of eternal, ever-new joy and bliss. The vast, endless, primordial sea of life and consciousness lay unmoving in the rapture of eternal, timeless peace. Not one thought-form danced within the ocean of life and energy. Divine Spirit was conscious of its own existence, floating within the sea of life. Spirit, non-moving, desired to see visible moving images take form within the vast sea of life. Divine Spirit moved with desire to the center of consciousness, which harbors the dimension of the smallest of all places. There, at the center of the smallest of all places, Divine Spirit felt the existence of the largest of all places. From the center of consciousness, Spirit gave birth to thought-forms which moved outward, like winds, into the vast, eternal sea of life and energy.

Thought-Forms Produced Light

Spirit desired to live and dance in the images projected from the center of the smallest of all places. Thought-forms moving outward from the center into the surrounding sea of life and energy, like winds, created ripples and waves propelling the life and energy of Spirit into motion. Life of Spirit is a form of energy. Energy, propelled into motion by thoughts (i.e., the consciousness of Spirit desiring to see images), moving outward from the center into the sea of non-moving energy, produced resistance and friction. Ecstasy and time were born from motion and friction at the moment light appeared around resistance. The eternal sea of energy produced resistance to thought-forms moving outward from the center, like winds.

Creation of the Feminine Offspring of Light

Spirit's thought-forms began spinning life force at the center in two primary *counterclockwise*, centripetal vortexes. These two spinning vortexes moved outward and away from the center of the smallest of all places into the vast sea of life and energy, the body of Spirit. (Figure 1, bottom circle.)

The sea of energy now became visible around the two spinning vortexes as resistance to pressure produced friction and light. The rapidly rotating vortexes of life force were now becoming radiant as they moved to higher velocities, producing the colors of the spectrum. Divine ecstasy was now felt within the body of the primordial sea of life and consciousness. Resistance and friction gave birth to light, time, sound and ecstasy in the midst of the primordial sea.

Both rotating, thought-produced primary vortexes of force were now spinning away from the center of consciousness in opposite directions, in a counterclockwise manner. Divine Spirit desired and directed both spinning vortexes onto a course which motion and time would bring to a direct confrontation and collision. The two spinning vortexes, moving outward on the arc of a great circle, were predestined to collide at a point on the circle which was farthest away from the center of the smallest of all places. As the two rotating vortexes of life force neared the point of collision, Divine Spirit felt the approaching climax of a tremendous explosion of energies.

Divine Spirit observed the two radiant, spinning vortexes moving closer together in the midst of the eternal sea of life and consciousness. At the preordained point, the two spinning, primary forces collided, producing the ignition and birth of the divine feminine offspring — a visible spherical image of radiant white light. (Figure 2-2a.)

Creation of the Four Elements

Immediately following the ignition of the feminine offspring, four more secondary counterclockwise vortexes of force were sent spinning outward from the center of the smallest of all places. (Figure 3.)

The first two vortexes carried the mental images and forces of the air and fire elements; the last two carried the mental images and forces of the water and earth elements. All four secondary vortexes were predestined to collide with each other on the center within the newly-born divine feminine offspring: light. (Figure 3a.)

The Projection of the Eight Radiant Spheres of the Spectrum

Divine Spirit saw that the light was good. Spirit watched the divine feminine offspring immediately project outward from the point of the original ignition, eight radiant, expanding spheres of light and energy. Each dimensional sphere of color existed within the other and reflected the eight radiant colors of the spectrum. These eight visible spheres moved outward from the center of the newborn feminine image of light. (Figure 4.)

Creation of the Masculine Offspring of Light

During the conception, ignition, and birth of the divine feminine offspring, Spirit Mother and Father had *simultaneously* sent outward from the center of the smallest of all places, two more primary spinning vortexes of force. (Figure 1, top circle.)

These two vortexes were spinning in a *clockwise* manner and represented the masculine forces as they moved outward from the center on the arc of a great circle. Simultaneously, figures 2, 3, 3a and 4 occurred for the masculine clockwise forces. And so it was done! The two divine offspring, one feminine and one masculine, now existed as two spherical images of brilliant white light, floating in the vast, timeless primordial sea of Spirit. (Figure 5.)

The Mystical Marriage

These two radiant spheres of energy were, by magnetic attraction, drawn toward each other. (Figure 6.) The masculine and feminine spheres of light and energy would now merge to complete the projections for the newly-born expanding great Sphere of Creation.

Creation of The Great Central SöN-SüN

The divine feminine offspring, like a bride, awaited the coming of the groom. This divine union would bring to completion the twelve dimensions of energies and the dual nature of the visible expanding spheres of creation. The counterclockwise rotation of the feminine forces of vortex allowed the clockwise rotating masculine forces of vortex to merge together as one without actually colliding; they both occupied the same space. At the center of the smallest of all places, where it all originally began, the two glowing spheres of light, masculine and feminine, merged as one in a union which completed the image of creation. (Figure 7.)

The divine, dual, androgynous offspring was now glowing with incandescent brilliance as it expanded and floated in the midst of the vast primordial sea. "Let there be light, and there was light."

The two divine offspring were born in time and space at the center of the new expanding great Sphere of Creation. All that had transpired in the creation of the divine feminine offspring was duplicated simultaneously in the divine masculine offspring. The only difference between the two was, and still is, the difference in the direction and the speed of rotation as related, one to the other. Time and sound were born in space within the spheres of creation from the orbital speed of rotating masses of life-energy.

The primordial sea of life force, called Spirit Mother and Father, had now given birth to light. This divine offspring is known as The Great Central SöN - SüN, the Face of Christ, the First Creation of Light, and the hub on which the forces of creation now spin. (Figures 8-23.)

The Angel Men and Women

The Angel Men and Women (see illustration, page 290) found their conception and birth within the dual nature of The Great Central SöN-SüN . The Angel Men and Women were duplicate copies of the first divine images of light. They were encompassed within the dual natures of the eight glowing spheres of energy, sound, and color, which now formed the visible, expanding great Sphere of Creation. The grand procession of the two feminine and the two masculine vortexes, which initiated the birth of the masculine and feminine spheres of creation, had now given birth to the divine Angel Men and Women. The great Sphere of Creation was expanding, propelled outward in all directions by the momentum generated from the ignitions and births of the two divine offspring. Projected by the will of Divine Spirit, the Angel Men and Women began a journey outward from the center of The Great Central SöN-SüN toward the island images of newborn suns and planets beginning to ignite and take form in the outer-dimensional spheres of the more gross physical creation.

In the gross physical creation, third-dimensional suns and planets were taking form through the original process of vortexia. On these planets creatures called hu-man were evolving, from the mixtures of elements that had found their birth in the ignition of third-dimensional suns. The creature hu-man was composed of the four elements of air, earth, fire and water, and the

The term "hu-man" refers to "hu," the animal or creature, and "man," the potential to become the angel (i.e., Christ Conscious.)
— The Author

dual masculine and feminine energies of life force called the ethers. The physical images of the evolving creatures were equipped with six senses of sight, hearing, smell, touch, taste, and intuition, which corresponded to the six masculine and six feminine forces that manifested the image of creation.

The Angel Men and Women, existing as conscious spheres of light and energy, were predestined, in the divine projection of the creation, to enter into the creature hu-man. The Angel Men and Women directed and watched as their predestined outer physical forms evolved forth from the mud of the waters on many planets in many galaxies in the outer spheres of the gross physical creation.

Baptism of Fire

Millenniums of time passed until finally the evolving creatures were made ready (i.e., had achieved self-consciousness) to receive the incandescent brilliance and power of the Angel Men and Women into their bodies and their Tree of Life, the central nervous system. At this precise moment, the creatures stood upright to stare into the infinite heavens with a piercing cry and a longing to know their Creators face to face. The ego-consciousness of the creatures was willing to surrender their bodies, minds, and life forces just to know, and be with, their Creators.

The Angel Men and Women, observing this strong desire, blessed the creatures with love, and surrounded them first with the feminine, descending, rotating vortexes of energy. The creatures were wrapped within a swirling cocoon of light. The Baptism of Fire had now begun to descend. It was emanating from the spherical images of the Angel Men and Women, and hence, from the center of The Great Central SöN-SüN. Within the clockwise, rotating, feminine forces of vortex, the divine masculine forces descended, turning counterclockwise as the creatures looked straight up to behold their coming, like "a dove descending."

. . . and, lo, the heavens were opened unto him, and he saw the Spirit of God descending like a dove, and lighting upon him.

— Matthew 3:16

This moment, which had been preordained, allowed the Angel Men and Women to descend into the gross physical forms of the creatures through the centers of the feminine and masculine spinning vortexes. The creatures had finally evolved forth from the cosmic eggs (that is, blueprints or thought-forms), which were projected into the midst of the mud of the waters.

And so it was done! The first phase of the divine projections had taken place in the spheres of creation. The divine Angel Men and Women were now becoming

The dawning of Christ Consciousness in hu-man the creature and the evolving of hu-man the angel had now begun.

— The Author

established within the hu-man creatures on planets in the outer spheres of the gross physical creation.

The Angel Men and Women were to give perfection and the experience of immortality to the hu-man creatures. The Angel Men and Women, now entering into the gross physical bodies of the creatures, were able to conceive and give birth to a Divine Spiritual Embryo within the hearts of each hu-man creature who desired to receive them.

The Divine Spiritual Embryo, conceived within the heart of hu-man, the creature, would grow to possess the mind and physical body from the inside outward, by reprogramming the genetic code. The RNA and DNA and other channels would now carry the genetic message of the Angel Men and Women, who were created immortal and composed of the immortal substance of light and life. The Divine Spiritual Embryo was given nourishment for its growth directly from the Angel Men and Women through the instruments of the two divine forces of vortex, masculine and feminine. Like a divine umbilical cord, the two vortexes now resided inner-dimensionally, on and around the crowns of the heads of the hu-man creatures.

We may now begin to understand the perfect preservation and lifelike appearance of some men and women who have received Christ Consciousness in the past. Saints and scholars have been unearthed in various places around the world and some are found in a state of near perfect bodily preservation. The immortal, illuminating power of Christ has a direct effect on the atomic, molecular and cellular structure of the human body and hence the genes, chromosones, etc. . . . It is my belief that physical immortality of a kind may well be achieved by adepts of the future, initially stepping forth from the past. The Baptism of Fire, surely, if received properly by the adept, will initiate this phenomena which existed in past times.

— The Author

The Angel Men and Women now began to stand forth within the hu-man creatures on many planets in solar systems throughout the creation. Mother-Father-Creator, existing in the primordial unmanifested state, was now able to dance in the images and the ecstasy that had been projected into the spheres of creation through the medium of the Angel Men and Women, their divine children. And it was good! In this state, the hu-man creatures were now the evolved and Christed hu-man Angel Beings. The hu-man angels (saints, Christed beings, prophets, etc.) would always be directly connected to the will and energy of Divine Spirit Mother and Father as long as they remained within the divinely projected guidelines. The infinite, primordial Spirit is directly connected to the laws and forces which govern the creation from the center of The Great Central SöN-SüN. As Jesus demonstrated and stated, "Not my will, but thy will be done, Father." Hu-man the creature must be reborn. The Angel Men and Women bring about this rebirth through the conception of the Divine Spiritual Embryo within the hearts of the hu-man creatures.

> Verily, verily, I say unto thee, Except a man be born anew he cannot see the kingdom of God.
>
> — Jesus quoted in John 3:3

It was therefore here, at a point in the evolution of images and angels, on many planets in this galaxy and elsewhere, that the Sons and Daughters of Spirit, the Christed Angel Beings, began to enter inner-dimensionally into hu-mans, the then-evolving creatures. The hu-man creatures were from the dust of the elements of the planets throughout the galaxies of creation. The creatures were not immortal, but could receive immortality by receiving the Angel Men and Women, the guardian angels, into the Tree of Life within, the central nervous system. It was here, in the near vicinity of our present solar system, and billions of light years away from the center of The Great Central SöN-SüN, that this divine evolution proceeded and made manifest the divine plan and order.

It was on a planet now referred to as Heaven in the records existing on Planet Earth, that this precise and divine evolution of events between the hu-man creatures (mortal) and the Angel Beings (immortal) reached preordained perfection. When the divine Angel Beings entered into the evolving creatures on this planet called Heaven, they descended with the Baptism of Fire which gave immortality to the creatures if the creatures consciously accepted it. The baptism was conducted through the two master vortexes of light and energy, male and female. The incandescent brilliance which emanates from the center of The Great Central SöN-SüN and hence, through Man and Woman the Angel, became visible to the creatures who wanted to know their Creators on that day on Planet Heaven. The dual master rotating vortexes, male and female, were seen and felt by the ego-consciousness of the creatures who cried out to know. With eyes either opened or closed, the brilliant image of the Angel Man and Woman and The Great Central SöN-SüN appeared before the consciousness of the baptised hu-man creatures.

297

"Dazzling and tremendous, how quick the sunrise would kill me, if I could not now and always send sunrise out of me. . . . As in a swoon, one instant, another sun, ineffable full-dazzles me, and all the orbs I knew — brighter, unknown orbs; one instant of the future land, Heaven's land."

Walt Whitman herein describes his own spiritual baptism and illumination involving "brighter unknown orbs," the Angel Men and Women referred to in this volume. Again "Heaven's land" is Christ Consciousness, the Body of Christ, the entire expanding great Sphere of Creation and all that is contained therein.

— The Author

Hu-man, the creature of the gross physical elements, now had the opportunity to become immortal, to become the Christed hu-man Angel Being. The creature hu-man now felt the powers of the immortal Angel Man and Woman descend upon him. And it was so! The Angel Man and Woman became fused with the creature and its self-conscious ego through the conception and birth of the Divine Spiritual Embryo. The birth of the Divine Spiritual Embryo within the heart of the creature was now taking place. The Angel Man and Woman took possession of the creature body and the ego-consciousness. On that day, the divine beings took the ego-consciousness of the creature on a journey to the center of The Great Central SöN-SüN. Here, the creature-consciousness (simple- and self-consciousness) met the Divine Father and Mother existing outward and beyond the Sphere of Creation in the infinite and timeless primordial sea. The creature-consciousness of hu-man saw, for the first time, the expanding Sphere of Creation floating like an iridescent bubble in the primordial sea of its own newly-discovered body of life force.

The little myself has now become the great myself — microcosm to macrocosm — finite to infinite.

— The Author

The Angel Man and Woman now merged with the consciousness of the creature hu-man, and began the journey back into the spheres of creation from the center of The Great Central SöN-SüN. The creature body was waiting on the planet called Heaven, where it had been left in a state of divine suspension, with neither breath nor heartbeat. Re-entering the creature body, the newly-born hu-man Angel Being now quickly mastered all the sciences, internal and external. All of the newly-born hu-man Angel Beings conquered time and space, achieving the ultimate in space travel.

Like a flash there is presented to his consciousness a clear conception in outline of the meaning and drift of the universe. . . . The person who passes through this experience will learn . . . much that no study ever taught or can teach.

— Richard Bucke, *Cosmic Consciousness*

The primordial, eternally conscious, infinite body of life force had moved with desire to manifest visible images, and was now fully conscious and dancing in them. This primordial, infinite force is identified as Mother-Father-Creator, "I Am That I Am," because of the dual nature Spirit manifested in the visible images of the creation. Thought-forms, gaining birth in the infinite sea of life and consciousness, generated motion, moving like winds in both centrifugal (moving out), and centripetal (moving in) vortexes, and in clockwise and counterclockwise directions. It is from these four forces moving in the four directions that Divine Spirit spun and wove life, light, and energy into visible images, consciously reflecting the creation. The divine, androgynous, primordial being, now called the Christ, exists within the sphere of The Great Central SöN-SüN and all the divine children, the Angel Men and Women. Divine Spirit projected all the mental images that were to become visible in the spheres of all creation into The Great Central SöN-SüN, the Christ. The movement of life force and consciousness in both centripetal and centrifugal vortexes spun the thought-produced images of the creation into outer, visible manifestations, either feminine or masculine, or both. The dual nature of the creation is continually expanding at this very moment outward, spherically, from the center of its original ignition.

There are twelve dimensions of consciousness which manifest in the dual nature of the creation. These twelve energies found their birth at the center of The Great Central SöN-SüN. These twelve creative energies are identified as the Twelve Divine Forces of Virtue. These twelve divine forces project law, order ,and variety into the expanding spheres of creation and bring harmony and balance out of chaos.

The ancient religious belief of the people of Mu read: "I believe there are eight roads which I must travel in order to reach Heaven. After having traveled the eight roads, I arrive at the twelve gates leading to the world beyond. Here I must prove that I have overcome the earthly temptations. I shall then pass through into the world beyond and reach the gates of Heaven. There I must show that I learned and practiced the twelve virtues on Earth. Then I am taken through the gates of Heaven to the throne of glory, where sits the Heavenly King."

— Colonel James Churchward, *The Lost Continent of Mu*

The "eight roads" referred to in the above passage are also called the Eight Paths of Truth and are: Right Meditation, Right Speech, Right Nourishment, Right Association, Right Study, Right Recreation, Right Conduct, and Right Work. The "twelve gates" are also called the Twelve Virtues, and are: Loyalty, Patience, Honesty, Perseverance, Compassion, Continence, Equanimity, Courage, Humility, Temperance, Charity, and Faith.

— The Author

There are four conscious divine entities that project four forces which generate the vital airs and gases which further condense as elements into liquids and solids, forming the hard crusts of planets. The binding force which attracts and holds, or loosens and repels, is magnetism (fire). The four forces of air, earth, fire, and water, directed by divine, conscious entities, evolved the physical images of the hu-man creatures forth from the mud of the waters, on many worlds throughout the creation. Thus, Man and Woman the Angel, riding outward on the twelve divine forces of energy and virtue, and observing the creation composed of the four elements of air, earth, fire, and water, entered outward into the vast spaces of the creation. Moving outward with the mental images of the creation, they arrived at the place in time and space where the preordained meeting was bound to take place. The creatures of the planets had called out for their Creators in longing and despair.

The creatures called hu-man, male and female, were woven into being by the four forces and the twelve energies, masculine and feminine, under the direction of the divine guardians, the Angel Men and Women, The Builders. The creatures called hu-man on a planet called Heaven, evolved and manifested on the surface of the planet as the four races of fixed identity and color. The Red race became the guardians of the planetary elements

So Spider Woman gathered earth, this time of four colors, yellow, red, white, and black [blue] ... molded them; ... and covered with them ... the creative wisdom itself.... These forms were human beings in the image of Sotuknang, [God of the Universe].... They soon awakened and began to move, but there was a dampness on their foreheads and a soft spot on their heads. . . . In a short time the sun appeared above the horizon.... This was the time . . . of the dawn of Creation, when man, fully formed . . . faced his Creator.

"That is the Sun," said Spider Woman. "You are meeting your Father the Creator for the first time."

— White Bear, co-author
Book of the Hopi

in all their diversity. The Yellow race became the guardians of all organic life-forms and the elements of the waters. The Blue race became the guardians of magnetism and fire, repulsion and attraction. And finally, the White race stood within the forces of the vital airs and the vast seas of gases filling the vessel of creation.

The four types, or four races of advanced physical man, the creature, had been cared for as they evolved on the planet called Heaven by the descending Angel Beings, The Builders. The creatures were joined into the Baptism of Fire with the Angel Beings and became united with Divine Spirit Mother and Father as advanced physical man, the hu-man angel, the Christed true Sons and Daughters of Spirit. "Thus, these things which I do, you may also do," stated the Master Jesus, a Christed hu-man Angel Being, (i.e., a Son of man, or hu-man). The creatures quickly evolved as the four races on Planet Heaven, and on other planets in the galaxies and elsewhere. These advanced hu-man beings are henceforth known to us as The Builders, the Nefilim, the Ancients, the gods, the four races from the outer spaces.

There can be no perfect religion without science; for science unfolds nature, and nature is the mouthpiece which unfolds the Creator and gives the proof of God.

— Colonel James Churchward,
The Sacred Symbols of Mu

Figures 1-8 refer to the following pages of color plates.

Figure 1.

Two primary *counterclockwise* spinning vortexes (i.e., feminine) were sent outward from the center of the smallest of all places. Each spinning vortex moved along the projected arc of a circle toward each other. Like water swirling down a funnel, each vortex moved in a centripetal motion. Their speed of rotation increased as they moved outward along the circle, causing an emanation of brilliant light moving through the spectrum from red to violet.

At the same time (see top circle), two primary *clockwise* (i.e., masculine) vortexes were sent out from the center of the smallest of all places. These vortexes also moved in a centripetal motion.

Figure 2.

The two primary *counterclockwise* (i.e., feminine) vortexes collided, producing a brilliant sphere of light: the divine feminine offspring.

At the same time, the two primary *clockwise* (i.e., masculine) vortexes collided in the same manner, producing another spherical image of light: the divine masculine offspring.

Figure 2a.

The collision of two primary vortexes can be symbolized by two interlocking triangles which form a geometrical six-pointed star within the center of each divine offspring.

Figure 3.

Four secondary vortexes containing the elements of air, earth, fire, and water were projected from the center of the smallest of all possible places toward the feminine offspring. They traveled in a *counterclockwise* centripetal spiral moving along the four quadrants of a sphere.

At the same time four secondary masculine vortexes were sent spinning from the center of the smallest of all places toward the masculine offspring. They traveled in a *clockwise* centripetal spiral moving along the four quadrants of a sphere.

Figure 3a.

This diagram shows the fusion of the four elements of air, fire, earth, and water within the center of each divine offspring.

Figure 4.

Each divine offspring projected eight expanding spheres of color. Like the rings inside an onion each sphere exists inside the other. As shown, the spheres resemble a rainbow around our physical sun.

Figure 5.

Divine offspring, masculine and feminine, glowed within spectral colored spheres. By magnetic attraction they were drawn toward each other.

Figure 6.
The divine offspring united like the two intertwined strands of the DNA molecule. The *clockwise*-spinning masculine vortexes spun through the *counterclockwise*-moving feminine vortexes comprising each offspring.[1]

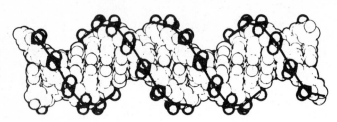

Figure 7.
The Great Central SöN-SüN is produced from the completed union of the masculine and feminine offspring. Created by the fusion of the vortexes comprising its parents, twelve forces of energy are projected out into the creation. These forces move away from the SoN-SuN in spirals to weave the images of creation.

As shown in figure 7, the Great Central SöN-SüN is inscribed within the overlapping of two large circles which represent the union of the masculine and feminine offspring. This intersection is called the *vesica piscis*. The *vesica*, like a womb, contains the SöN-SüN, the First Creation of Light. It is interesting to note that the *vesica piscis* frames an image of Jesus Christ on the Royal Portal of the Chartres Cathedral in France.[2] At Glastonbury Abbey in England, the *vesica piscis* appears on the cover of a well.[3]

Figure 8.
The Great Central SöN-SüN, like a movie projector, beams God-produced images into the eight expanding spheres of creation.

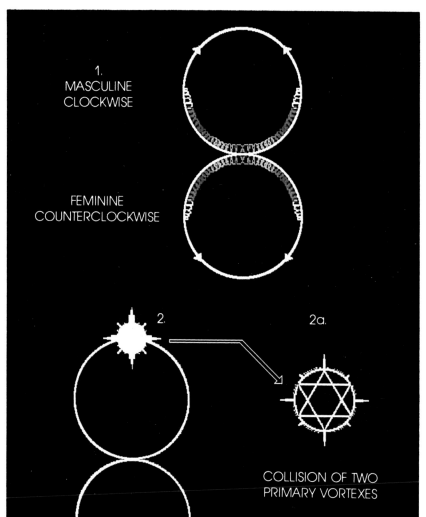

1.
MASCULINE
CLOCKWISE

FEMININE
COUNTERCLOCKWISE

2.

2a.

COLLISION OF TWO
PRIMARY VORTEXES

3.

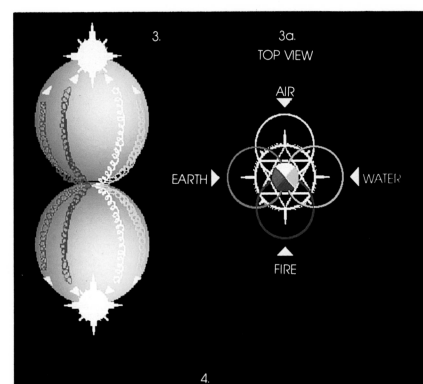

3a.
TOP VIEW

AIR

EARTH ▶ ◀ WATER

FIRE

4.

5.

6.

7.

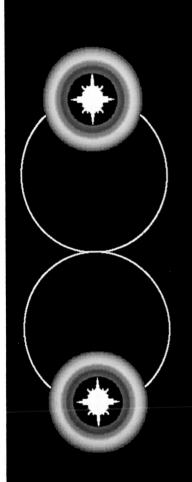

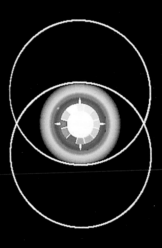

8.

From the geometrical image of The Great Central SöN-SüN comes proportions based in *phi* (1.618). These proportions are found in the design of ancient temples, pyramids, cities and in the natural structures of atoms to galaxies.

Figure 9.
On this photograph of a snowflake,[4] observe the six-pointed star.

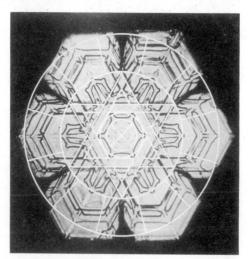

Figure 10.
When the geometric diagram of The Great Central SöN-SüN is placed over the snowflake, several alignments occur. The outer circle of the diagram touches the six faces of the snowflake's outline. Amazingly, the star within the diagram coincides with the snowflake's star. In addition, the inner hexagon of the snowflake frames the next to the smallest circle within the diagram.

306

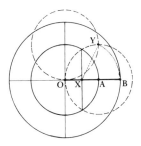

Figure 11.
The two outer circles of the diagram of The Great Central SöN-SüN embody a relationship called the *golden proportion*, 1.618 . . . , also called *phi*, (φ).

Line OB is formed by placing the metal end of a compass at X. Extend the lead point to Y and swing an arc down to the horizontal axis. The intersection becomes point B. Point A is the only point along line OB where:

$$\frac{OA}{AB} = \frac{OB}{OA} = 1.618 \ldots = \text{the } golden\ proportion$$

This never-ending number is called *phi*, and is represented by the Greek letter φ. *Phi* comes from Phidias, a Greek sculptor, who around 500 B.C. discovered this proportion in the structure of the human body.

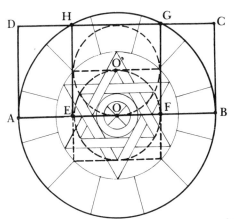

Figure 12.
In this figure a circle touching the points of the inner star is redrawn with its center at 0'. A square is then drawn enclosing the circle. The four corners of the square touch the largest circle at H and G and the vertical axis at E and F. Line EF is extended to points A and B. Then perpendicular lines are drawn from points A and B intersecting the extension of line HG at D and C. Rectangles AFDG, BEHC, AEHD and BFGC all have the *phi* ratio between their long and short sides.

13.

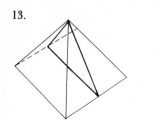

14.

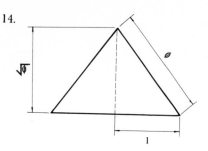

Figure 13.
A direct vertical section of the Great Pyramid of Cheops in Egypt is shown.

Figure 14.
Based on measurements taken at the Great Pyramid, these proportions are evident.[5]

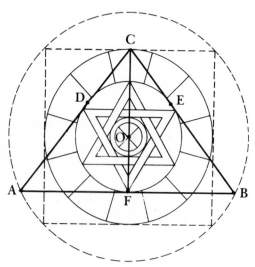

Figure 15.
The Great Pyramid's vertical section can be redrawn within the structure of The Great Central SöN-SüN.

With the fixed point of a compass at point A scribe an arc from F to D. Placing the fixed end at point B, draw an arc from F to E. Through careful measurement it can be found that:

$$\frac{AD}{DC} = \frac{AC}{AD} = \frac{BE}{CE} = \frac{BC}{BE} = phi\,(1.618\ldots)\quad \text{Also:}\quad \frac{CO}{OF} = \frac{CF}{CO} = phi\,(1.618\ldots)$$

308

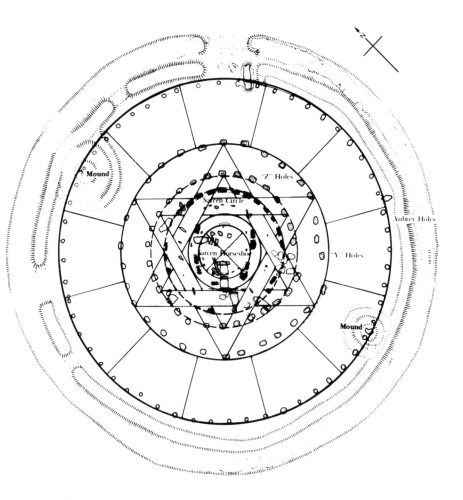

Figure 16.
The geometric image of The Great Central SöN-SüN is superimposed upon a plan of Stonehenge.[6] The outer circle of the geometrical image follows closely the circle of Aubrey Holes, passing through the center of the two mounds. The circle encompassing the star of the diagram passes through the ring of "Y" Holes on the Stonehenge plan.

The Stonehenge "Z" Holes line up with the dashed circle encompassing the inner points of the star. The outer Sarcen Circle of standing stones in shaded black, follows closely the inner dashed circle on the geometrical image. The inner Sarcen Horseshoe lies between the two inner circles of The Great Central SöN-SüN image.

309

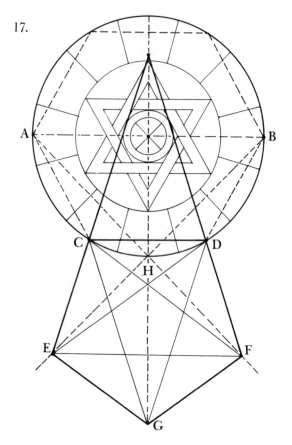

Figure 17.

A pentagon can be drawn using one side of the hexagon inscribed within the outer circle of the diagram. A line is drawn vertically through the center of the diagram extending beyond its outer circle. This line becomes the vertical axis. Then a line is drawn perpendicular to this through the center. From the points where this line meets the outer circle, A and B, two lines are drawn through H, the point where the vertical axis meets the outer circle. Placing a compass on point A, extend its end to touch the center of the diagram. Swing an arc down to touch the outer circle at C. Repeat the process at point B, finding point D. With the fixed point of the compass at C, scribe an arc from D to E. Keeping the opening of the compass the same, from point E, mark point G on the vertical axis. At point D, mark point F. Connect points C, E, G, F and D forming a pentagon. When sides CE and DF are extended back through the diagram, they form a *golden triangle* having a base to side ratio of 1.618 . . . *phi,* the *golden proportion.* Connecting the diagonals of the pentagon, an inner pentagon is formed. Its five rays touching the outside pentagon are also *golden triangles.*

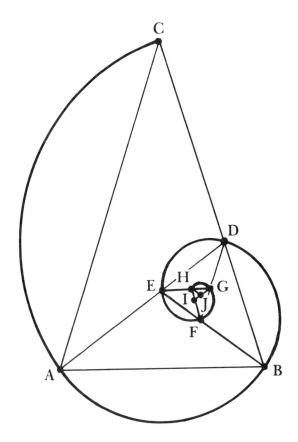

Figure 18.
 The *golden triangle* contained within the diagram of The Great Central SöN-SüN is redrawn. Using a compass, place the metal point at A and pencil point at B. Keeping the compass opening the same, place the metal point on C. Then with the compass place a mark on line CB at point D. Draw triangle ABD. Repeat the process as follows:

Measure DB. Then from A, mark point E. Draw triangle BDE.
Measure DE. From point B, mark point F. Draw triangle DEF.
Measure EF. From point D, mark point G. Draw triangle EFG.
Measure FG. From point E, mark point H. Draw triangle FGH.
Measure GH. From point F, mark point I. Draw triangle GHI.
Measure HI. From point G, mark point J. Draw triangle HIJ.

The triangles in this series are all *golden triangles*. The side and base of each successive triangle is smaller than the one preceding by a factor of *phi*.

With the metal end of the compass at point D, scribe an arc through A and C. From E, scribe an arc through A and B. From F, draw an arc through B and D. At Point G, draw an arc through points D and E. At point H, scribe an arc through E and F. At I, draw an arc through F and G. At J, draw an arc through points G and H. The resulting *golden vortex* can then be superimposed on several natural forms (figures 19 through 22).

19. Galaxy

20. Embryo

21. Chambered Nautilus

22. Cactus

Figure 23.
The geometrical constant of *phi* found in all structures of the universe is seen within the atomic structure of platinum.[7] The image is magnified 750,000 times.

[1]Illustration reprinted by permission from *Nature*, Vol. 282, No. 5740 pg. 684. Copyright 1979 Macmillan Journals Limited.
[2]Houvet, Etienne, An Illustrated Monograph of Chartes Cathedral.
[3]Reproduced with permission from Chalice Well Trust, Glastonbury, England.
[4]Bentley W.A. and Humphreys W.J., *Snow Crystals*, McGraw-Hill Publishers 1931, pg. 53. Reproduced with permission from McGraw-Hill Books.
[5]Tompkins, Peter, *Secrets of the Great Pyramid*, pg. 196.
[6]Plan of Stonehenge, courtesy of the Department of the Environment, Ancient Monuments and Buildings, London, England.
[7]Courtesy American Elsevier Publishing Co., Inc.

A divine celestial *mu* hidden within a cloud of moisture that has condensed around its magnetic field, over southern California.

CHAPTER 33

The Division of The Builders

In their divine celestial *mus* (ships of light), The Builders became the guardians and caretakers of the galaxies, caring for the evolution of all life-forms and cherishing

This information has been transferred to my consciousness by The Builders, while in their presence, on many different occasions.

— The Author

their own physical forms which had been long in evolving and difficult to obtain. In their genetic laboratories aboard their *mus*, The Builders achieved physical immortality of a kind, replacing and renewing their physical forms as necessary. Time was a factor that no longer represented an obstacle to them.

The Builders visited this solar system first at a remote period when the planets were still trying to achieve stable orbits around the newborn sun. They marked this solar system as one which might produce and support organic life-forms. Observing the planets, they found certain life-producing substances present within the atmospheres of gaseous clouds. In their search for organic life-forms in the galaxy and for new

Light emanations, traveling through space, can reveal the nature and composition of molecules, gases, and other life-producing substances capable of producing organic life.

— The Author

worlds to populate, they traced the possible existence of these substances through spectrum analysis. All of these chemical substances are scattered throughout the galaxies in sufficient amounts to produce organic life-forms abundantly.

The Builders eventually returned and seeded Planet Earth with a variety of organic plants and life-forms from their home planets and other worlds they had visited. Returning periodically to check the growing organic gardens in this system, they strengthened where it was too weak, and discouraged where it was too strong. They helped to balance out the forces of Mother's nature.

315

Approximately one million years ago a great division occurred within the ranks of The Builders. Alalu, one of the ancient Elders and chief of The Builders in this region of the galaxy, was overthrown by a rebellious being named Anu.

There were gods upon the earth and gods in the heavens. The overthrow of Alalu by Anu and the great battles fought among the gods for possession of the earth is clearly defined in Zecharia Sitchin's *The 12th Planet* and in many other translations and cuneiform texts.

— The Author

Let there listen the gods who are in Heaven,
And those who are upon the dark-hued Earth!
Let there listen, the mighty olden gods.
Formerly, in the olden days, Alalu was king in Heaven;
He, Alalu, was seated on the throne.
Mighty Anu, the first among the gods, stood before him,
Bowed at his feet, set the drinking cup in his hand.
For nine counted periods, Alalu was king in Heaven.
In the ninth period, Anu gave battle against Alalu.
Alalu was defeated, he fled before Anu —
Down to the dark-hued Earth he went;
On the throne sat Anu.

— "Kingship in Heaven," a Hittite epic tale

The Sons and Daughters of Spirit, The Builders, had moved freely throughout the vast regions of the galaxy for millenniums. During this long period of time, virtue and its forces had reigned supreme throughout the universe. Suddenly, one divine and inquisitive group on a mission of exploration, decided to defy divine will and investigate one of the forbidden areas in this region of the galaxy. Divine Spirit had warned all of The Builders to stay away from these dark and treacherous zones which were composed of fields of predominately negative, static energies. While passing through one of these forbidden areas, just to register the effects on their consciousness, this group momentarily became trapped within a violent magnetic storm.

The disobedient sons and daughters were totally unprepared for the negative environment that they had willingly subjected themselves to. Immediately and without warning, they began to experience the opposite energy effects of virtue. They began to manifest symptoms of jealousy and

The following description of the fall of highly evolved beings herein termed The Builders, Nefilim, Angels, etc., is taken directly from the eternal images of past and future events as contained in the Christ-Conscious divine entity. Divine Consciousness did not create "evil" within the projected images of creation. Evil evolved forth from the free will and the inquisitive acts of highly evolved Angel Beings treading where "now angels fear to tread."

316

anger. Hatred was born, along with the sense of egotism (i.e., self-consciousness), and greed now followed in swift pursuit. Then lust arose for the first time in the minds and bodies of the afflicted Builders. These inquisitive sons and daughters began to experiment with virtue's opposites, disregarding the warnings ringing throughout their divine celestial vehicles. Instead of immediately trying to remove themselves from the dense clouds of negative energy, they went further into them. The divine consciousness of the human Angel Beings became overshadowed by mental images projected from indulgence in the negative experiences. The light of The Great Central SöN-SüN, which had always been visible and shining within their consciousness, now became obscured by the orbits of dark thought-forms. They became possessed by the birth of a growing negative egotism generated in their consciousness by the accumulation of non-virtuous mental images.

The decision on the part of these evolved Angel Beings in hu-man form to pass through an area of violent negativity might well be the modern-day equivalent of deliberately sailing a ship into a hurricane just for the experience.

— The Author

Regression into a negative state of self-consciousness arose, devoid of virtue and finally entering simple-consciousness again. This degraded state of self-consciousness was totally negative without any degree of moral conscience, yet filled with the memory and power of former glory (i.e., Christ Consciousness). The birth of powerful evil beings, the Fallen Angels, known in this world as Lucifer. Set, Satan, etc., took place not by divine will, but by the free will given them.

— The Author

Falling deeper and deeper into the desires for negative experiences, they finally lost all vision of The Great Central SöN-SüN. With this great loss of spiritual vision, they were now unable to operate their grand celestial *mus*. Forced to descend somewhere, they finally became marooned on a strange world near this forbidden area. While marooned on this planet, the dark thought-forms of negativity totally overpowered them. Quickly now, propelled by the forces of desire, the negative mental images established a negative nucleus of consciousness around which to orbit. That which had never been conscious moved, and established a center of negative self-consciousness within each one of the afflicted beings.

From these centers, the newly born negative forces were able to maintain control over the physical minds and bodies of the fallen Angel Beings. The dark and sinister forces, now fully conscious and

The spirits of darkness, former Christ-Conscious beings now in a negative state of self-conscious regression, devote their existence to destroying Christ-Conscious beings and their grand civilizations.

— The Author

moved by great desire, began projecting thought-forms from their centers. They focused on the outer creature-consciousness (simple-consciousness) of the possessed sons and daughters of Spirit.

Suddenly the fallen Builders felt the urge emanating from within them to conquer and enslave the entire galaxy. Evil was born in time and space in the minds and bodies of the possessed hu-man Angel Beings. The grand celestial *mus* of The Builders were now abandoned and replaced by ships powered with atomic and fossil fuels mined and worked from the raw elements of the strange world they now found themselves marooned upon. This possessed group of beings, inspired

Evil was not created by Divine Spirit but evolved forth through the laws of cause and effect. Free will allowed the Sons and Daughters of Divine Spirit to sow and reap mental images that they planted. Their inquisitive disposition moved them to override divine commands and enter physically where divine intellect pursuaded otherwise. Through the memory of former simple- and self-conscious states in physical forms, the divine evolution of hu-man Angel Beings accepted the forbidden challenge of the unknown. This mistake or fall has unleashed the birth of evil beings in time and space within the spheres of creation.

— The Author

by the newly-born genius of evil, built a fleet of metal ships and equipped them with awesome atomic weapons. They now embarked upon missions of annihilation and total destruction, in their atomic and rocket-powered *mus*, to conquer their former brothers and sisters, The Builders. The great civilizations they had helped build and maintain for millenniums were to be totally annihilated.

Their attacks brought total devastation as they stormed the ramparts of the heavenly cities. The Builders knew nothing of war, hatred, murder, lust and greed. The

These beings, now falling further into self and simple states of consciousness act without the moral sense of conscience. They have become demonic.

— The Author

Builders could not defend themselves against the terror of the evil dark ones and the atomic weapons used against them. They could not believe, at first, the actions of their lost brothers and sisters. The Builders would not, and could not, commit themselves to murder and destruction. World after world was conquered and destroyed, rendered into oblivion, until the remaining members of The Builders had so diminished that they were faced with total annihilation. Only then was the decision made for warriors to step forward and defend the remnants of The Builders. The only advantage they held was their ability to outrun their persecutors in their divine celestial *mus*, beyond the speed of light.

Alalu and his companions, Ramu, Rama, Ra, and El, (the Spirits of Light), fleeing before the Dark Forces, returned to this obscure solar system with a few *mus* crowded with refugees from other worlds that had been destroyed by the evil conquerors.

Alalu began to orbit the bright blue earth looking for a place to set his people down. The Builders, making observations around the earth found suitable areas on which to land. One such area was one of three then-existing island continents lying in today's southern Pacific Ocean. These

The record of the destruction of Mu, the Motherland of Man, is a strange one, indeed. From it we learn how the mystery of the white races in the South Sea Islands may be solved and how a great civilization flourished in mid-Pacific and then was completely obliterated in almost a single night.

— Colonel James Churchward, *The Lost Continent of Mu*

three island continents are now known as the lost lands of Mu, the first resting place of the divine celestial *mus* of The Builders. Today, Australia remains visible as the only survivor of a great cataclysm which destroyed two of the three island continents of Mu.

Alalu immediately began construction of the earth's first great city, on a point of land eight hundred miles west of today's Easter Island. The Builders believed they had escaped from the Dark Forces and that they would not be followed to this small, insignificant solar system way out on the rim of the galaxy. It was here that Alalu and his companions first made contact with the primitive evolving creatures. Looking upon the diminished population of The Builders, Alalu decided to speed up the evolution of the hu-man creatures on the new earth. The Builders decided to cross the genes of the primitive evolving forms. By doing this, the new creatures would have better brains and stronger physical bodies, and would then be able to join the ranks of The Builders and help them construct a new civilization on the new earth. They might also help defend it against attack in the event they were discovered by the Fallen Angels.

The Builders decided to give the new creatures, *Homo sapiens,* all the knowledge of the Tree of Life (i.e., the central nervous system and its forces and powers). The new hu-man was to be given the immortal Baptism of Fire, and then the consciousness of the Angel Men and Women (i.e., Christ Consciousness) would descend into all the new creatures. The Builders, in their genetic laboratories, were successful, after many attempts, in producing test-tube embryos which were a cross between their genetic

Man is the product of evolution; but *Homo sapiens* is the product of the "gods."

— Zecharia Sitchin, *The 12th Planet*

structures and the then-evolving species of hu-man on earth, a type like *Homo erectus.*

Working at first with women from their own ranks, The Builders finally produced genetic crosses that resembled them in all respects. The four foundation races of *Homo sapiens* were now to be incubated and generated through the primitive creatures, and they would carry the imprint, or image, of The Builders, the Red, the Blue (black), the Gold (yellow), and the White. "In their image and likeness created they him; male and female created they them." (Genesis 1:27.)

The four foundation races as they were originally generated in the genetic laboratories of The Builders are scattered across the face of the earth today. One of the foundation races created by The Builders migrated into North America after the so-called great biblical flood and cataclysm. This ancient foundation race which exists untouched today in the North American desert is known to us as the Hopi people. The Hopi are the peaceful caretakers of Mother Earth, one part of the remnants of the ancient red race first generated here by The Builders. They are the original guardians of the earth elements. They still remember their creators, The Builders, and were given to eat of the Tree of Life from the beginning. The Hopi have been waiting for the return of The Builders and their true white brothers for more than twelve thousand years.

The meaning of the word Kachina is "noble, highly respected wise men who help with spiritual evolvement." . . . They don't come from our planet system, but from other far away planets. . . . If you compare the Kachinas with your Christian figures, you would call Kachinas angels. . . . There are children who have been born from immaculate conception between Kachinas and our women. It may sound strange to you but there was never sexual contact between them. The children have been conceived in a mystical way. Such children, as they grew up, had great knowledge and wisdom and sometimes supernatural strength which they inherited from their spiritual fathers. They were wonderful mighty beings, always willing to help, but never to destroy.

— White Bear, quoted by J. F. Blumrich, in *Kasskara und die sieben Welten*

The above quote from White Bear, Hopi tribe, identifies the Hopi Kachinas as The Builders, the physical Angel Men and Women who created modern man through a genetic cross with themselves and the pre-human found evolving on earth.

— The Author

This was recently pointed out by Professor Klineberg of Columbia University, with regard to the Indians of North America. The case of the Hopis is especially remarkable. Since World War II a number of them have been going to college and it has been noted that they feel amazingly at ease in mathematics and theoretical physics. Anthropologists studied the phenomenon and discovered that the Hopi language seemed to have been especially designed for expressing the most abstract concepts of relativistic physics. Before the development of that physics, Hopi logic seemed absurd to Europeans. The Hopis were retarded because they were too advanced. The mental processes of "primitive" peoples must be taken into consideration if we want to try to understand their art and the documents they have left us.

— Robert Charroux, *The Mysteries of the Andes*

320

The four foundation races were each given the four colors of corn by The Builders: white, red, blue and yellow. This was to remind them of their creators and that each race represents one of the four divine cosmic forces, just as The Builders had demonstrated to them: the Red race, earth elements; Blue race, fire elements; White race, air elements; and the Yellow race, water elements. Along with the four colors of corn, the ancient handclasp of brotherhood was given; it would enable each race to recognize the other whenever or wherever they met in future times.

The story of how The Builders were discovered 350,000 years ago by their fallen brothers and sisters follows. The Builders finally lost the war to defend the earth against their fallen brethren, the Dark Angels, twelve thousand years ago. However, after their defeat, they vowed to return and take the earth from the evil darkness of the Fallen Angels who now possess it. That vow is beginning to manifest itself today.

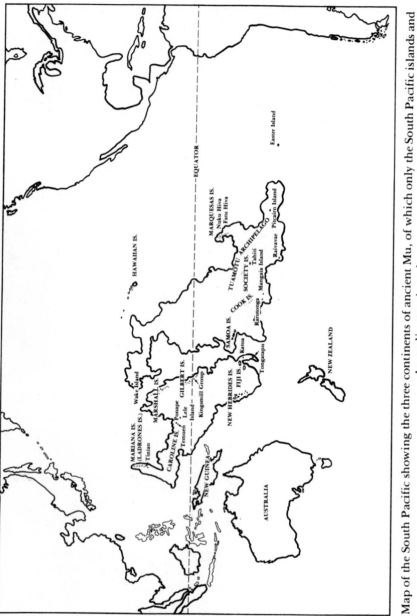

Map of the South Pacific showing the three continents of ancient Mu, of which only the South Pacific islands and Australia remain today.

CHAPTER 34

The Remains of The Builders
in the South Pacific

Throughout the length and breadth of the Pacific Ocean are scattered groups of small islands. On scores of them are the remains of a great civilization. There are great stone temples, cyclopean stone walls, stone-lined canals, stone-paved roads, and immense monoliths and statuary — works that required continental resources and workmen of skill.

— Colonel James Churchward, *The Lost Continent of Mu*

To continue with our search for the lost continents of Mu and the divine Sons and Daughters of Spirit, The Builders, let us examine the maps in this chapter, for they show how the South Pacific continents were at one time positioned. These maps have been constructed from a series of visions I experienced during meditation on the Motherland and the now-existing ruins, which are still visible today for anyone to examine.

As revealed to me in visions and revelations, The Builders returned to this planet more than 500,000 years ago. Seeking refuge from their fallen brothers and sisters, they began construction of a great city on one of the then-existing South Pacific island continents. These lost continents, called "The Land of the *Mus*," actually consisted of three land masses or island continents.

Many thousands of years ago . . . there was a great continent in the middle of the Pacific Ocean. . . . There flourished seven great or principal cities. . . . The continent consisted of three areas of land, divided from each other by narrow channels of seas.

— Colonel James Churchward, *The Lost Continent of Mu*

The far southeastern island continent lay just eight hundred miles to the west of Easter Island. The continental shoreline from this point stretched for more than five thousand miles to the northeast and the island continent was an average of two thousand miles in width. The middle, or northerly island continent of Mu began along the east coast of the Gilbert Islands.

The coastline reached south to include the Fiji and New Hebrides Islands, and north to include the Wake and Marshall Islands. The northern coastline of Mu's middle island continent ran northwesterly along the northern coast of the Caroline Islands, finally turning to the south in the Mariana Trench. Of the three original island continents, only one remains — Australia, with New Guinea on the same continental shelf. New Zealand was once a part of Mu's colonial empire, but it was never developed beyond a natural preserve. The home planet of The Builders has been described by them as bright red in the heavens. This red color was due in part, to the rich mineral content of its soils. In searching for a place to build the first city on the new earth, The Builders were attracted to the southerly island continent of Mu by its bright red soil, standing out in sharp contrast to the bright greens of the semi-tropical foliage. It was there, in an area now known as the Tuamotu Archipelago, and the Cook Islands' Manihiki Plateau, that the first great civilization was constructed circa 500,000 B.C. Building stone was quarried and carried by The Builders from as far away as Easter Island to the job sites there.

There are tremendous stone quarries inside and on the surface of volcanoes on Easter Island. This is confirmed by Thor Heyerdahl in *Kon-Tiki*.

— The Author

Again known through the medium of revelations, and visions the geography of Mu's island continents were low and flat, with great fertile plains crisscrossed with lakes and rivers. Northern Australia still resembles the southeasterly island continent of Mu. Many varieties of fruits and vegetables were grown there, along with the four colors of corn. A gigantic seven-stepped pyramid was constructed, with the Temple of Initiation sitting on its apex near the far eastern shoreline, just eight hundred miles west of Easter Island. The Temple of the Sun stood at twenty-four degrees south of the equator. Mu's first great city was constructed around the Pyramid of the Sun to specific measurements, reflecting distances and proportions relative to this solar system and the very structures of the creation. This great city was built entirely of massive stone blocks and was laid out on a north to south axis. No other city in time and space could

Sun temples were not constructed to be instruments for the worship of the physical sun by local inhabitants. Quite the contrary. Sun temples were constructed to measure and magnify the golden proportions existing in all objects and images in this solar system and the whole of creation. Constructed from divine proportions; spirals, circles, squares and triangles computed upon 1.618 . . . *(phi)*, the sun temples harmoniously collected the magnetic energies from this planet, the solar system, and distant stars and galaxies in the outer spaces. The Ancients realized that our physical sun is but the reflected image of the First Creation of Light, that is The Great

match it in beauty and design. It was from this center that The Builders migrated forth, going both east and west, creating the four races of modern man. They called this land Mu because it was the first resting place of their gigantic celestial starships. Mu also means "that which holds," or "mother," or "the divine chariot" of The Builders, the caretakers of the universe.

> Central SöN-SüN , the Christ, the projector of all images.
>
> — The Author

> There are those who believe that in former times men on earth were in contact with people from outside our galaxy and that it was from them that they first acquired knowledge of the universe and the arts of civilization. Obviously there is nothing particularly absurd or unlikely in this idea. Space travel may well have taken place in the past, and in some form, it almost certainly did.
>
> — John Michell, *The View Over Atlantis*

Continuing our search, we find memorials to Mu on tiny Easter Island. This isolated island has been called "the navel of the world" by navigators who have landed there. It was here after the great wars with the Fallen Angels that Kon-Tiki went with the remnants of his people. The Builders, forced out of Central and South America, their last stronghold in the West, had to return to the grim remains of Mu's two island continents. Here, on Easter Island, we can observe a giant necropolis left there by The Builders. This colossal memorial ground contains some five hundred massive stone statues, ranging up to seventy feet in height, and weighing up to one hundred tons. These taciturn images are fashioned from individual blocks of stone cut from nearby quarries on

> These massive, stylized figures are both majestic and disturbing . . . So far some 1,000 of them have been found, many weighing 20 tons and standing 12 to 15 feet tall. Of the finished statues, the largest is some 32 feet tall and weighs 90 tons! Unfinished statues more than twice this size have also been found.
>
> — *The World's Last Mysteries,* a Readers Digest publication, about the Easter Island statues

and within the crater of an extinct volcano on the island. They are dedicated to the great souls of The Builders who were destroyed on Mu and in Central and South America in the cataclysmic wars with the Fallen Angels. They stand in silent memory today, facing the east and the west where once the Empire of the Sun shone brightly for all its children to behold.

As we examine the colossal stone images on Easter Island, it seems incredible that anyone could have engineered such a feat. What sort of lifting device levered these massive

> Thor Heyerdahl, the leader of the famous Kon-Tiki expedition, suggests that the statues were tugged over wooden logs with cables made of raffia and other vegetable fibers, and were hoisted by means of inclined planes made of rocks and sand. But the

stone images from the quarry then down the slopes of an ancient volcano, and for miles across the island? It staggers the imagination! No one alive today on the island knows how this was actually done.

From Thor Heyerdahl's book, *Aku-Aku*, we have reprinted a most unusual picture of one of these gigantic stone images as it is being excavated. It shows a statue of a man with a very large, three-masted, square-rigged sailing ship of ancient design carved right into his chest. The colossal statue proves that Easter Island's ancient inhabitants or visitors were seafarers and the builders and navigators of ships.

Easter Islanders in fact had no logs to serve as rollers, since the layer of soil covering the island's rocky surface is too shallow to permit the growth of trees.

— Peter Kolosimo, *Timeless Earth*

It can be noted in this photograph that the crudely carved image of the three-masted sailing ship was done at a time in which that part of the statue was above local ground level, millenniums ago. Observation is inclined to show that the statue is of ancient origin whereas the carved image is of a more recent time. It is my belief that a later migration by Kon-Tiki Viracocha and his people from South America may have carved this ship's image.

— The Author

The remains of what appears to have been a large stone temple still exists on Easter Island. Fallen walls outline an area of more than one hundred feet long and twenty feet wide. The walls still standing measure six feet high and five feet thick.

All over the island are rock carvings and paintings with strange symbols and figures. No one living on the island today understands the ancient writings and pictographs. The descendants of an ancient white race with bright red hair are still to be found on Easter Island. Legend states it was Tiki, a SöN of the SüN, and the long-eared people who came from the West, that carved out some of the gigantic stone images found all over Easter Island. None of these descendents remember how or why this was done.

Moving west from Easter Island, we find Pitcairn, the Tuamotu Archipelago, Marquesas, Tahiti and Society Islands, all of which contain statuary and the stone remains of an ancient civilization. We find the same Easter Island method of carving statuary in human form existing on Pitcairn, Raivavae, and on the Marquesas Islands of Nuku Hiva and Fatu Hiva, as well as along the west coast of Central and South America. The Cook and Samoan Island groups lay southwest and westerly of the Society Islands. All of these islands contain the stone remains of Mu, the Motherland. Immediately west of the Samoan Islands lies the Tonga Trench, curving snakelike to the west. Its depth off the Samoan Ridge is in excess of thirty-five thousand feet below sea level. Here there is an active fault, or fracture, in the earth's outer crust, wherein the northwesterly

Whoever carved this three-masted sailing ship did it thousands of years after
the statue was erected to honor one of The Builders.

Reprinted by permission of Rand McNally and Co., from Heyerdahl, *Aku-Aku*

327

moving Pacific Ocean floor seems to be disappearing down through the trench into the earth's molten mantle as if on a gigantic conveyor belt, never to reappear.

To the northeast of the Tonga Trench lies the undersea Manihiki Plateau. It runs for one thousand miles from north to south and is from seven to eight hundred miles in width. Here, lying seven thousand feet below the ocean's surface, is one of the probable land masses which once comprised a good portion of Mu's southeastern Pacific island continent. Undoubtedly, if ever explored in depth, ruins of ancient cities will be found there.

The islands of Rarotonga and Mangaia of the Cook Island group contain statuary and sections of paved road similar to those on Easter Island. There are no existing quarries there, leading one to the assumption that the stone was brought from elsewhere.

Tongatapu, the major Tongan Island, is a coral atoll, on the west side of the Tonga Trench. The island is formed of massive fields of coral growth, and here we find a gigantic coral gateway, called the trilithon. It consists of two pillars weighing in excess of forty tons apiece, arched by another cut and dressed block weighing over twenty-five tons. This gateway resembles the massive stone Gateway of the Sun at Tiahuanaco in South America, and its construction is strikingly similar to other gateways in Tiahuanaco.

> In pre-Columbian America we have a similar structure termed the "Gateway of the Sun," at Tiahuanaco. . . . Also, there have been found in the ruins of Tiahuanaco, monoliths composed of two uprights supporting a third megalith in the form of a horizontal lintel, very similar to the trilithon in Tongatapu.
>
> — Dr. Paul R. Cheesman and
> Millie Foster Cheesman,
> *Early America and the Polynesians*

Also throughout the Tongan Islands we find stepped pyramids similar to those found in Central and South America.

> The five-stepped pyramid in Katoa, Mua, Tongatapu, has a base 140 feet long and 120 feet wide. . . . Another pyramid known as Leka contains a base 166 feet long and 140 feet wide, with 4 steps. . . . All stones seem to be well surfaced and smoothly joined together. An important detail of some of the Tongan pyramids is that they were occasionally ascended by ramps or stairways. This is a similar characteristic of the pyramids in Central and South America also. . . . Liecht (1944) says the stairway leading to the top of the pyramid near Eten in Northern Peru clearly demonstrates the cultural relationship of Polynesia and Central America. . . .
>
> In comparing the work of the Polynesians with South American megalithic art, J. B. Brown (in *The Riddle of the Pacific*) has made the following conclusion: " . . . the likeness of the cyclopean structures of the two areas is

The trilithon in Tongatapu, Tonga

sufficiently apparent. Every feature of Polynesian great-stone work is repeated in the great-stone work of the Andes."

— Dr. Paul R. Cheesman and Millie Foster Cheesman,
Early America and the Polynesians

We next come to the Fiji Islands and the sunken Fiji Plateau. Here exists another large section of what we believe was once a portion of Mu's southeastern Pacific continent. It is now surrounded by the New Hebrides Trench. The Fiji Plateau is slowly flowing downward and disappearing into the New Hebrides Trench, thirty thousand feet below.

About one thousand miles north of Fiji are the Gilbert and Marshall Islands. Here the natives use many of the ancient sacred symbols of Mu without knowing their true meaning or origin; they have been forgotten.

The natives use the sacred symbols of the Motherland as ornamentations without knowing how they obtained the designs, or their meaning.

— Colonel James Churchward,
The Lost Continent of Mu

Next, we come upon the Caroline Islands and the Mariana Trench, which lies just to their west. The Mariana Trench contains the planet's deepest ocean depth. Here the ocean floor plunges downward, thirty-six thousand feet, into a canyon running north and south for three thousand miles, with an upper width of two hundred miles in some areas. This rupture in the earth's outer crust is unlike any other natural fracture on the earth's surface. The massive size of this unnatural fault, plus the extensive formation of hundreds of sea floor volcanoes in this area, leads one to suspect the earth may have collided with one or more large extraterrestrial objects in ancient times. If this assumption is correct, and I have every reason to believe it is, Mu's two island continents were destroyed in just such a series of fateful encounters.

Reflecting back on my visions of Mu's destruction on that dark and violent night, I can still see the fiery trail of meteorites streaking across the night sky. They appeared suddenly in the southeast, moving at tremendous velocities. I watched them hurtle overhead to crash in the northwest with enormous fiery cataclysmic explosions that shook the earth violently. The great wars between The Builders and the Fallen Angels had brought about this horrible destruction of the Motherland. Intuition told me long ago that the Fallen Angels were responsible for this great cataclysmic horror and for the collision course of the huge meteorites that destroyed two of Mu's three island continents.

There has been a great deal of interest in the surprisingly high content of nickel found in the central Pacific red-clay cores by H. Rotschi of France. Nickel is very scarce in sea water. . . . The concentration in the central Pacific is about eight times the average nickel content of the Atlantic red clay.

It has been suggested that the high nickel content of these cores is derived from volvanic lava, or basalt, emitted over the deep ocean floor. Recently, however, S. Landergren of the Geological Survey in Stockholm made a spectrographic analysis of basalt and found it to contain only modest amounts of nickel. It is tempting to assume quite a different origin for the abyssal nickel: meteoric dust. . . . It is known to have a very high nickel content. . . . The maxima of nickel content found at certain levels of these cores might then be due to very heavy showers of meteors in the remote past. The principal difficulty of this explanation is that it requires a rate of accretion of meteoric dust several hundred times greater than that which astronomers, who base their estimates on visual and telescopic counts of meteors, are presently prepared to admit.

— Hans Petterson, "Exploring the Ocean Floor," in *Scientific American*,
August 1950

Looking further into the remains of Mu, we find the Mariana Trench connecting with the Japan Trench on the north and the Yap Trench on the south, traveling for thousands of miles farther. Here the Pacific Ocean floor moves slowly northwesterly, like a gigantic conveyor belt, turning downward into the gaping mouths of these three local trenches. Here, for thousands of years, the remains of Mu's two Pacific island continents have been slowly swallowed downward into the earth's fiery liquid mantle. The birth and death of continents, brought about by the spreading of the sea floor, seems now to be a natural phenomenon taking place on the earth's surface. It would seem that the earth's continents reach extermination through the application of both external and internal forces. The external results of cataclysmic wars are in evidence, as are collisions with other extraterrestrial bodies, and the natural internal forces of Mother's nature, which seem to raise and lower continents continually over millions of years.

The upwelling of liquid magma from the earth's fiery mantle into faults in the earth's crust creates this continual spreading effect on parts of the earth's surface. What forces initiated this spreading effect in the beginning? Could it have been generated by the sudden loss of two large Pacific island continents that were literally blasted out of the earth's crust? On the Pacific Ocean floor today there exists a fault in the earth's crust that starts from an area near Juneau, Alaska, runs south to the California coast north of San Francisco, then inland down to the Gulf of California. This fault is known as the San Andreas Fault.

Here the Pacific Continental Plate, or crust, rubs and slides against the North American Continental Plate. As this crack, or rift, in the earth's surface meets the waters of the Gulf of California, we find liquid magma welling up into this fissure on the gulf's floor. As tremendous pressures force the molten magma into the fault, it solidifies, creating an outward pressure in both directions. The crack in the earth's surface widens, forcing the continental crust away in both directions. The tremendous pressures force the far leading edge, in this case the western edge of the Pacific Plate, hard against the Eurasian Plate. As tremendous pressures mount one of the two continents involved is overwhelmed and slides under the other.

The San Andreas Fault runs south from the Gulf of California, thousands of miles toward Antarctica. It passes Easter Island two hundred miles to the west. Here we find no continent, where actually science feels there should be one. This spreading effect has, in the past, always begun upon a continent, and not on a mid-ocean floor. For example, scientific evidence has shown conclusively that South America and South Africa were once joined as one continent; the spreading effect on a great fault line split the continent apart millenniums ago. Along the Pacific rift, magma is continuously being pushed upward and outward, forcing the Nazca Plate under the South American continent, at the same time thrusting the Andes Mountains even higher. To the west, the Pacific Plate and the remains of Mu are slowly being consumed beneath the Eurasian, Philippine, and Indo-Australian Plate. Thus, the Tonga, New Hebrides, Yap, Mariana, and Japan trenches slowly swallow the Pacific Ocean floor. It may have been the beginning cycle of this continental drift, or motion, that helped to shake Mu from her foundations, in gigantic earthquakes and volcanic upheavals. The fall of meteorites hurled on Mu may well have triggered a chain reaction in Mu's many volcanoes, thus hastening the dreadful end of the two island continents.

Moving on, we next come to the Caroline Islands, the largest archipelago in Micronesia. Here, extensive ruins of an ancient civilization are to be found. There are over five hundred islands in the Caroline group. Ponape is the largest, with six hundred and seventeen square miles. Around Ponape is a cluster of small islands. One of these smaller islands is called Temuen. It is here that the ruins of an ancient city called Nan Madol exist.

There is a saying among the native inhabitants of these islands: "The people who once lived here were very powerful. They had large sailing ships in which they made far distant voyages to the east and west, taking many moons to complete."

The ruins of Nan Madol are extensive. One ruin consists of a rectangular building two hundred feet square. This building is constructed of basalt — hexagonal and octagonal stone slabs up to thirty feet long and weighing up to ten tons each. The number of basalt blocks contained in this one

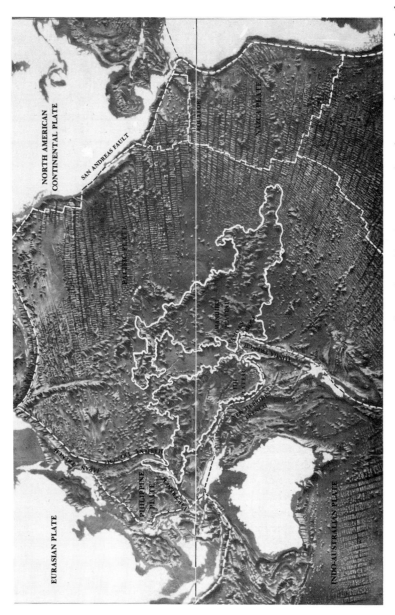

Map of the **Pacific** Ocean floor. Note the massive configuration of land masses and undersea volcanoes not found anywhere else in the world. Each of the major plates on the map contains a continent, with the exception of the largest, the **Pacific Plate.**

structure has been estimated at thirty-two thousand. This structure is connected to canals and waterways. There are passages and platforms, earthworks and vaults. Pavements lead through gateways to canals. The main central complex is surrounded by at least eighty smaller units, which were probably homes. Many of the ruins of Nan Madol run right down to the water's edge and can be seen with the naked eye until they disappear into the shadowy depths of the sea.

The Japanese took control of the Carolines in 1920 and abandoned the islands to the Americans in 1944. Reports of the incredible wealth to be found at Ponape attracted pearl divers from China and Japan in the late 1930s. The divers reported that they had all been able to walk around on well-preserved streets at depths of more than one hundred feet. There were countless vaults, pillars, houses, and monolithic stone statuary. Stone tablets still hung on the walls

In Herbert Rittlinger's book *The Measureless Ocean*, Rittlinger says on Ponape . . . "the divers had all risen from the depths with incredible tales. They had been able to walk on the bottom on well-preserved streets. . . . There were countless stone vaults, pillars and monoliths. . . . The Japanese divers reported that the dead were buried in watertight platinum coffins. And the divers actually brought bits of platinum to the surface . . . in fact the Japanese main exports of the island were supplanted by platinum! . . . The finds of platinum on an island where the rock contains no platinum, were and remain a very real fact."

— Erich von Däniken, *The Gold of the Gods*

of some buildings. These ruins ran downward into deeper and darker depths that remain yet to be investigated.

Looking at the ruins of all the still-existing structures above sea level on Temuen alone, there is a rough estimate of nearly four million quarried stone blocks contained in their construction. These blocks weigh an average of three to five tons apiece; some weigh up to ten tons. They were apparently quarried on the north coast of Ponape. Among all the natives living on the South Pacific islands today, there is a common reply when asked, "Who might have cut and dressed the massive stone blocks, how were they transported to the job sites, and who erected them?"

"The stones flew through the air and landed right in place," they reply. Or, "A giant fiery dragon carried them here on his back and placed them as they are." No one seems to remember any legends involving many years of blood, sweat, and tears. Small wonder! Few, if any, of Mu's people sur-

Why did someone at some point take the colossal trouble to move some 400,000 basalt blocks from the north coast of Ponape where the basalt was quarried, to this remote islet [Temuen] . . . ? Legend tells of a flying fire-breathing dragon which excavated the canals and so created the islets, and about his magic helper, who used a magic spell to make the basalt blocks fly across.

— Erich von Däniken, *In Search of Ancient Gods*

vived the great cataclysm which destroyed her in this vicinity to tell of their marvelous spaceships, and their feats of construction.

Most of the structures on Ponape above sea level look as though they had been hastily rebuilt after suffering some major cataclysm, possibly by the descendents of the original Builders. Other islands of the Carolines contain similar ruins. On Lele Island, for instance, there is a conical hill surrounded by a wall twenty feet high and five feet thick. Of the many enclosures on Lele, some are four hundred feet in length and one hundred and fifty feet wide, with walls twelve feet thick. Within are vaults and secret passageways. All of the Caroline Islands contain cyclopean ruins of great magnitude. The ruins on Kingsmill Island contain tall, slender pyramids of stone. These are also found on the Gilbert and Marshall Islands. In the Mariana Islands (Ladrones Islands), we find solar stone, truncated, pyramidal columns twenty feet high, including the hemispherical stone, or capitol. They are ten feet square at the base, and each monument weighs in excess of thirty tons.

On the island of Tinian, in the Marianas, we also find truncated pyramids topped by hemispherical stones. The pillars are eighteen feet in circumference at the base and twelve feet high. The capitols that crown the top are five feet high and six feet in diameter. They have been hewn from rough, hard sedimentary rock. Each pillar and capitol weighs more than thirty tons. Some pillars have fallen with their capitols, indicating they were shaken from their supports by some violent action.

We have now looked at a few facts on the physical plane proving that something more than man's imagination produced the physical ruins that exist throughout the South Pacific islands. These ruins are still visible today for anyone to examine. Mu's geographical boundaries are now possible to discover, as the maps disclose. By placing known ruins on our map, we get a partial outline of Mu's centers of habitation. The Hawaiian Islands, I believe, exist today much the same as they did when Mu's Pacific continents were visible. Ancient legends passed on from father to son in the Hawaiian chain indicate the Hawaiian Islands always existed north of Mu's coastline approximately one thousand miles away, or ten days by sail and oars.

It is the practice of The Builders to honor great leaders in stone statuary.

CHAPTER 35

The Destruction of Mu and the Western Civilizations

The discovery of over 2,500 stone tablets in Mexico by William Niven enlightens many facets concerning Mu's three island continents. *The Egyptian Book of the Dead* is claimed by some to contain a tribute to Mu's millions of inhabitants who were lost in one night as she sank beneath the seas of the South Pacific.

> All matters of science in this work are based on the translations of two sets of ancient tablets: Naacal tablets which I discovered in India, and a large collection of stone tablets, . . . discovered by William Niven in Mexico.
>
> — Colonel James Churchward,
> *The Lost Continent of Mu*

The lands of Mu were originally composed of three island continents. Today only one remains — Australia. The lands of Mu were low and flat with some rolling hills; ancient volcanoes dotted the landscape at various locations. Rivers and large canals crisscrossed the continents and formed a network of agricultural lands. Mu's first inhabitants were great farmers and tradespeople. They loved the land and all the Earth Mother's creatures entrusted to them.

Much of Mu lay near the equator, and was densely tropical. Land which was cleared produced an abundance of tropical fruits and vegetables. Breadfruit, pineapples, papayas, mangoes, bananas, and avocados were a part of Mu's staple fruit crop. Agriculture and animal husbandry were Mu's major industries, and all inhabitants were required to spend some time working in the fields, picking fruit and harvesting crops. Here, everyone shared equally in the wealth of the country. Mu was governed by a grand theocracy and the monotheistic belief in one Creator God with two natures mas-

> It was a monotheistic religion, as only one Creator or Deity was worshipped, to which they gave many attributes, each attribute having a symbol assigned to it.
>
> — Colonel James Churchward,
> *The Lost Continent of Mu*

culine and feminine. The Divine Creator Spirit Mother-Father was known to all of Mu's children.

The Naacals were the gentle, priestly instructors from Mu. They had in their possession the sacred inspired writings that contained the beautiful teachings of the Tree of Life. These teachings covered science and religion as one subject. Legend states that the Naacals left Mu for Burma and India thirty thousand years ago and were established in Egypt before the Great Flood. Valmiki, in the Hindu epic,

> The sacred writings of the Motherland, which were carried by the Naacals (Holy Brothers) to Mu's colonies throughout the world 70,000 years or more ago, . . . is the oldest written information about the origin of Freemasonry. The extreme age of this brotherhood is not only attested to by the Sacred Writings, but by various Oriental writings, inscriptions, and prehistoric temples, and convincingly confirmed by . . . Mexican stone tablets which are, as shown by some of them, over 12,000 years old.
>
> — Colonel James Churchward,
> *The Lost Continent of Mu*

Ramayana, mentions the Naacals as having come to Burma from the lands to the east. The sacred inspired teachings of Mu were brought into India, Tibet, and Egypt by the Naacal brotherhoods, The Builders from Mu.

Ancient records state that the builders of Egypt and the pyramids came from the Southern Sea in large sailing ships. There is only one southern sea connected to Egypt — the Red Sea. The Red Sea runs in a northwest-southeast direction and empties into the Indian Ocean. The Indian Ocean washes up on the western shores of Australia, the third and last island continent of Mu, which still exists today.

The seeds of Egypt's greatness were sown by The Builders from Mu who entered the country peacefully. They carried with them the great arts and sciences. Here they organized the building forces necessary to carry out the construction of great dikes and canals. These were used to control the flooding waters of the Nile and to furnish irrigation for their crops. The Builders actually raised the fertile Nile Valley from the mud by this ingenious method. They turned a wasteland into a paradise as agriculture expanded throughout the Nile Valley. The Builders initiated the construction of buildings, temples, and pyramids in Egypt, as was their custom wherever they went.

> The Builders constructed great pyramids and cities which girdled the whole earth. The pyramids acted as conductors to attract the planet's magnetic field which flows from the South Pole to the North Pole, thus they formed a power grid which encompassed the whole earth.
>
> — The Author

Ancient legends state that there were two worldwide cataclysmic disasters in these times. One of these holocausts was triggered by the titanic wars between The Builders and the Fallen Angels 12,000 years ago and

338

destroyed Mu, the Motherland. Following this came a natural disaster, evidently produced by the law of cause and effect. This disaster destroyed the once-existing island continent of Atlantis and her island satellites which the Fallen Angels had invaded and taken possession of. In searching the world over for evidence of Mu's former existence and her destruction, a few records have been found.

There are hieroglyphs on the Great Pyramid at Xochicalco in Mexico. These writings have been deciphered by A. LePlongeon and state, "Once there was a continent situated in mid-ocean which was destroyed. Its inhabitants were killed and turned to dust." Does this inscription describe the destruction of Mu, the Motherland, along with all of her inhabitants, or Atlantis?

The Troano Codex is one of the few pre-Mayan books to survive the Spanish conquest. It is now in the British Museum of Natural History. The Troano Codex speaks of a catastrophe which obliterated the continents of Mu. This catastrophe is confirmed by other Mayan writings that survived the Spanish conquest.

One such pre-Mayan writing was translated by a Brazilian philologist, O.N. Bilio. It reads as follows: "The disaster befell on the eleventh day of Ahau-Katan . . . it rained fearfully. Ashes fell from the sky and the waters of the sea engulfed the land in one great wave. . . . the heavens collapsed, the earth subsided, and the great Mother Sedya was amidst the records of the destruction of the world."

Another Mayan document of an unknown age states, "In the year 6 of Kan, terrible earthquakes began on the eleventh of the month of Zac and continued till the thirteenth day of Chuen. Mu, the country of clay hills, was destroyed. She was raised twice into the air and then disappeared in one night, with earthquakes never ceasing. At many places near the sea, the land sank beneath the waters and rose up again more than once. Finally the whole land of Mu was split up into many parts, and was engulfed with its sixty-four million inhabitants."

> From the number of depressions in the earth's surface which . . . are now recognized as being of meteoric origin, there must undisputedly have been cataclysmic upheavals at intervals all through the history of the world. It is therefore not only probable but virtually certain that there have been occasions when whole areas of populated land have . . . suddenly vanished beneath the waves.
>
> — John Michell, *The View Over Atlantis*

When the Spanish conquerors arrived in Central and South | The appearance of Hernan Cortes and his men was held by the Aztecs to be the return of

America they found, to their amazement, written records that described the creation of mankind by a tall, mysterious race of white-skinned gods. "Kon-Tiki and the tall, bearded, white gods came down from the heavens," legends state. "Then they created men and women and lived among them as rulers. They were defeated in a great war and began to leave the earth in their celestial ships 12,000 years ago." The Catholic Church, finding these records of a Western genesis story written upon pillars, walls, temples, and tablets of gold, clay, and stone, immediately set about destroying them. In the name of Christ Jesus (who was a Builder returned), the conquerors, on orders from the church, began a campaign of destruction such as is beyond belief. The great buildings, temples and statuary left by The Builders millenniums before were torn down, broken up, and defaced. Written records that might testify to a Western genesis and the existence of the bearded gods from space and their religion were destroyed.

the benevolent Quetzalcoatl of Toltec times — an event foretold by pictures.... However, . . . the supposed Quetzalcoatl did not play the part of the benevolent hero . . . nor did his gods conduct themselves in a godlike manner. "Those bearded men," as the Indians said, "were not Quetzalcoatl and his gods. They were strange and mighty *popolocas* [barbarians] who had come to destroy the ancient civilizations and religion." . . . The mighty conquistadores [made] efforts to obliterate the religion of the conquered and their concept of the universe, and if they did not achieve full success, as is evident by the vast treasure of documents and archeological remains that still exist, it was not for lack of zeal.

— Miguel Leon-Portilla,
"Mythology of Ancient Mexico,"
edited by Samuel Noah Kramer,
Mythologies of the Ancient World

We have been led to believe the Incas were ignorant and had no written language, but truth to the contrary has been maintained, as scholar Robert Charroux points out. "Francisco Toledo, a viceroy of Peru, mentions that sometime around 1566 he had a huge bonfire made of Inca textiles and tablets with elaborate inscriptions describing the creation of mankind by the gods, his history, sciences, and prophecies." The existence of many of these Inca writings is confirmed by Jose de Acosta in *Historia Natural y Moral des las Indias*, Seville, 1590.

. . . the Indians of Mexico and Peru have innate artistic abilities that are unequaled anywhere else in the world. Someday the so-called civilized peoples will realize that . . . the Incas of Peru have mathematical minds better conditioned than Einstein's.

— Robert Charroux,
The Mysteries of the Andes

A Spanish missionary working in Yucatan once wrote the following complaint to his ecclesiastical superiors: "Furthermore, it would be very advantageous if books were printed in the language of these natives which would treat of [the book of] Genesis and the creation of the world, because they have fables and histories which are very detrimental to their conversion. Some of them have written them down and they keep them and read them in our assemblies. I had a copy of this sort which I took away from a choirmaster named Cuytum, from the town of Sudopo. He got it away from me and I never could get a hold of him to learn the origin of this Western genesis of his."

One of the first bishops of Yucatan, Diego de Landa, ordered a great bonfire be started. In his own words: "We found great numbers of books, but as they contained nothing that did not savor of superstition and lies of the Devil, we burnt them all, at which the natives grieved most keenly and were greatly pained."

No wonder the natives grieved! Those books were sacred! Some of them were written originally by The Builders and their offspring millenniums ago. There were books which described the creation and evolution of the astral and physical universe and all twelve dimensions of consciousness. The genesis story of Man and Woman the Angel, was described, along with their evolution on many other planets in our galaxy. There were books containing the histories of the four foundation races as they were created by The Builders on earth, and the directions of their migrations from Mu. Huge libraries contained the arts and sciences brought here by The Builders from the remnants of their great civilization. These books covered biology, mathematics, the sciences, and the Angel Man's first inspired religion. One huge volume contained the deep teachings of the Tree of Life. These teachings revealed the paths of initiation traversed by the Angel Man and Woman while residing in the creature called hu-man. There were prophecies reaching into and beyond our present time. The loss of The Great Book of the Tree of Life plunged the West, along with the East, into a darkness from which we have yet to emerge.

Many of these written records contained descriptions of the physical gods from the heavens, The Builders, and their homeland, referred to as the Kingdom of Heaven. The Great Book of the Tree of Life contained the written words and testimony of The Builders, also their sworn oath to return someday in a future time and defeat the Dark Angels. After this victory, all men would be free again in the Spirit, and murder, war, and suffering would cease to exist in the galaxy. The Angel Men and Women, along with the hu-man creatures on Planet Earth and elsewhere, would fulfill Mother and Father Creator's divine projections within the expanding spheres of creation.

Yes! The gods called The Builders did come from space in their divine celestial *mus*, as many legends around the world state today. The San Blas native peoples of Panama have a legend that says: "After the Flood, a great personage came to earth borne on a golden platter." This bearded white god taught the people language, agriculture, religion, and the arts and sciences. His name was Quetzalcoatl. He was followed by a number of disciples who spread his teachings far and wide. Among these disciples were a few great Elders, and they had visible powers over the four elements.

According to native American legends, Quetzalcoatl and his followers left Central America, traveling over the waters towards the rising sun. Quetzalcoatl stated he would return to reclaim the cities and lands of his people. The first

When the Spaniards heard the same tale of an ancient god-man in South America that had already startled them in two other lands, they were doubly flabbergasted. They knew a great deal by this time about the Aztec legend of Quetzalcoatl, a merciful hero who had been the human leader of the vanished Toltec as well as an immortal diety. He too was thought to be fair and bearded, and to have taught his people many things — how to farm more productively, how to work metal, how to construct beautiful buildings. . . . But for some reason he had to leave his peaceful Toltec kingdom. He took his laws, his songs, and went away down the same road he had come. On a seashore he began to weep, then disappeared across the sea. . . . All the legends of Quetzalcoatl agreed that he promised to come again.

— Alan and Sally Landsburg,
In Search of Ancient Mysteries

appearance of the bearded Spaniards in Central America, as they arrived from the east, seemed to be fulfilling the prophecy of Quetzalcoatl's return. Where did Quetzalcoatl migrate to in the east? Are the Nordic races of today descendents of this migration?

The ancient Chimu Empire extended along the northern coast of Peru, from Lima to the present border of Ecuador. Chanchan was the capital of the Chimu Empire. Imposing ruins are still to be seen. The city covered an area of six to seven square miles. It was divided into ten districts, with walls of enormous thickness still visible. Even though the houses have been destroyed by wind and weather, the ruins of pyramids, cemeteries, and reservoirs are still visible. A Spanish pilot named Pedro Corzo sailed up and down the Peruvian coast at the time of the Spanish conquest. He tells us that everywhere he looked in the temples, he found statues of a god named Gutan, which means "the whirlwind." This may remind us of the Germanic storm god, Wotan. In fact, Wotan was the original name of the Chimu divinity among the Mayans who exported him to South America. In Guatemala he was the lord of the night and darkness, and the Mayans, Aztecs, and Zapotecs all associated him with the art of divination. In Germanic folklore, Wotan, or Odin, was the god of battles, and was also the creator of the world. Here we find a connecting link between ancient America and northern Europe. Did Quetzalcoatl and his people carry the image of the god Wotan with them to Germany and to the isles of Scandinavia, Denmark, Sweden, and Norway? There is another interesting point. The Inca year comprised twelve months, beginning, as in many parts of the world, at the winter solstice. In northern Europe, the winter solstice was "Wotan's Day," and on that day a feast of the sun was celebrated. Wotan, or Odin, maintained a paradise called Valhalla in the heavens where brave and virtuous warriors were guided by the Valkyries and welcomed by Odin's wife, Frigga.

In South America the invading Spaniards seemed to be fulfilling the prophecy of Kon-Tiki Illac-Viracocha's threatened return with his people to reclaim their lands and their cities from the barbarians. Kon-Tiki and his followers, both red and white, were defeated in a great war that took place at Tiahuanaco and the Island of the Sun at Lake Titicaca. Here the legend states that in this war the earth was scorched and burned by the sun. Was this the possible detonation of atomic weapons used against The Builders by the Fallen Angels? The story of the Fallen Angels and Enki, the wayward relative of Tiki, will be discussed later in this book.

Legends state that Kon-Tiki and his people escaped from Tiahuanaco over the seas to the west. The sad remains are to be found today on Easter Island and the volcanic mountaintops of the South Pacific, and are some of the last signs of Mu's ancient civilization. Legends tell us that the peaceful natives of Central and South America were invaded by a strange warlike race who came out of the seas and deserts to the northeast (possibly the island continent of the then-existing Atlantis). The civilization of Atlantis and her great stone cities and pyramids was originally constructed by The Builders. An invasion by the Dark Forces compelled The Builders to evacuate

In the great wars between The Builders and the Dark Angels, the great city of Atlantis originally constructed by The Builders was taken over by the Dark Forces.

— The Author

Atlantis millenniums before the Great Flood. It was this continuing invasion by armies controlled by the Fallen Angels that started the final decline of the great civilizations in the West. The ranks of these armies were filled with the generations of the biblical Cain. These invaders from Atlantis were also the ones who began the epic horrors of human sacrifice.

The god known as Quetzalcoatl to the Toltecs and the Aztecs in Central America was directly connected to the work of Kon-Tiki and his people in South America. Both men were tall, white, and bearded,

Native American legend indicates that Quetzalcoatl and Kon-Tiki were separate individuals belonging to the same ancient brotherhood of The Builders.

The Author

and both men taught science and

religion to the people as one subject. They taught humankind not to make war or kill his brothers and sisters, and created peace and love wherever they went. Quetzalcoatl and his people were forced out of Central America by the same barbarous invaders who later defeated Kon-Tiki in the south.

We find murals painted in bright colors by the invaders on the ancient walls of temples and buildings they took over after their successful invasion of Central and South America. The murals depict a tall, white race of people being held captive by a shorter, dark-skinned race. White and dark natives are also shown with their hands tied behind their backs while being led to sacrificial altars. Various scenes portray the white race in the subservient positions of slaves, rowing the shorter, dark-skinned people on their lakes and waterways. Cortez, taking advantage of the fact that the rulers of Central and South America thought he was the return of Quetzalcoatl and Kon-Tiki Viracocha, moved quickly to defeat them by deception.

The Spaniards, arriving in Central America many centuries after the great wars between The Builders and the Fallen Angels had subsided, found the existing red races, called Aztec, Maya, and Inca living in prosperity. They also found the remnants of a tall, bearded white race in different areas of Central and South America and the offshore islands of southern California and the South Pacific.

The Spaniards came looking for gold, and the suffering of the native peoples can never be imagined. The institution of forced labor, along with plagues of smallpox and tetanus, destroyed the native populations. After one hundred years of Christian proselytizing, the natives remained unconvinced. Cortez and his men were welcomed as liberators in the beginning by the conquered red and white races being held prisoner by the invaders.

By the year 1510 the slavery of the Indians, under the names of *repartimentos* and *encomiendas,* had become deplorably cruel. An Indian's life was counted of no value. It was cheaper to work an Indian to death and get another than to take care of him and accordingly the slaves were worked to death without mercy. From time to time they rose in rebellion, then they were "slaughtered by the hundreds, burned alive, impaled on sharp stakes, torn to pieces by bloodhounds."

— John Fiske, *The Discovery of America,* quoted by Richard Bucke, in *Cosmic Consciousness*

Soon after their arrival it became evident that the Spaniards were not to be considered liberators, but were, in fact, a worse affliction than the first.

All land and life were now threatened by disease and pestilence as the Spaniards moved their armies north and south from Central America. Cortez, bringing smallpox to the natives, watched a population of some forty million people in Central America diminish practically overnight into two or three million. The peaceful Hopi, far away in North America, were battered survivors after they were forced to fight for their lives and culture as the Spaniards invaded them. The fate of the white and red races living on the coast and offshore islands of southern California is a tale of woe such as has no equal. These fair races were eliminated by smallpox, tetanus, syphilis, forced labor, cannonballs, and bullets.

Three great and final wars destroyed The Builders and their creations in the West and in the East. The first war with the Forces of Darkness destroyed the land of Mu. The second war with the Forces of Darkness destroyed the remnants of The Builders at Teotihuacan in Central America and Tiahuanaco in Bolivia, bringing with it the final invasion from the northeast, the island of Atlantis. The third, and final war was fought with the Spaniards and, to this day, has never ceased in the hearts and minds of the native people who lost their cultures and religions in North, Central, and South America.

Of the various human and superhuman races that have occupied the earth in the past we have only the dreamlike accounts of the earliest myths. The magical powers of the first men are now beyond conception. All we can suppose is that some overwhelming disaster, whether or not of natural origin, destroyed a system whose maintenance depended upon its control of certain natural forces across the entire earth. All attempts at reconstructing whatever it was that collapsed during the great upheavals have ever since been frustrated by schism and degeneration. Falling ever deeper into ignorance, increasingly at the mercy of rival idealists, the isolated groups of survivors all over the world forgot their former unity, and in the course of striving to recreate some local version of the old universal system, perverted the tradition and lost the secret of spiritual invocation.

The history of our era is one of continuous defeat for those groups and individuals who have attempted to reverse the flowing tide of ignorance, superstition, and arbitrary violence. An endless series of enlightened men have looked for means of convincing the rest that our view of history is entirely wrong. The chief heretical assumption that has taken root since the collapse of the old world is that which supposes the inevitable and perpetual nature of the conflict of ideas. Secure in this faith, tyrants and opportunists have flourished and a huge vested interest has developed to which we are to some extent unconsciously committed, in suppressing the truth about the past. Until recently this suppression was active and vicious: the violent, clerical persecution of mediaeval scientists represents its last organized manifestation. Now, however, that old tradition is dormant, the reasons for its suppression have themselves been forgotten. Only the attitudes remain. These attitudes and the assumptions which go with them form the only barrier which prevents us from recognizing the nature of the fall. The transparent myth of the recent origin of true civilization is still perpetuated by those who accept at second hand the conditioned philosophies of experts in archeological techniques and in other narrowly specialized sciences. This myth is, however, destroyed by the evidence for the survival into recent times of the same tradition as that which inspired the builders of the Pyramids at the very start of our era and which they preserved from the ruins of a stricken world.

— John Michell, *The View Over Atlantis*

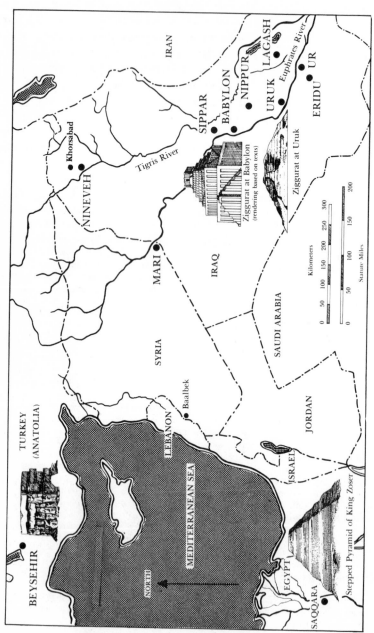

Map of the Near East showing archeological sites mentioned in the text

CHAPTER 36

The Gods from Space

The genesis of *Homo sapiens* has for centuries remained a mystery. Always we are confronted with the same set of facts: Neanderthal man has many progenitors on the evolutionary path but *Homo sapiens* has none. Where did *Homo sapiens* come from? *Homo erectus*, the oldest of the species *Homo* according to archeological finds, was living on the earth about one million years ago. *Homo sapiens*, or modern man, first appeared three to four hundred thousand years ago. Neanderthal man, a primitive type, but evolved enough to be recognized as "man," appeared less than one hundred thousand years ago. These facts raise two basic questions. Why did modern man appear so suddenly just several hundred thousand years after *Homo erectus*, a process that should have taken several million years, given the rate at which the pre-humans were evolving? And why did *Homo sapiens*, or modern man, appear about two hundred thousand years before Neanderthal man, who is clearly more primitive?

Looking at all the archeological facts we have now accumulated before us, mankind should still be without civilization. There is no reason why we should be any more civilized today than some of the aborigines of Australia or the primitive tribes of New Guinea and the Amazon jungles. Mankind should still be typified by them, and not us. How did the ancestors of

> Modern man has many fossil collateral relatives but no progenitors; the derivation of *Homo sapiens*, then, becomes a puzzle.
>
> — Professor Theodosius Dobzhansky,
> *Mankind Evolving*

> The appearance of modern man a mere 700,000 years after *Homo erectus* and some 200,000 years before Neanderthal Man is absolutely implausible. It is also clear that *Homo sapiens* represents such an extreme departure from the slow evolutionary process that many of our features, such as the ability to speak, are totally unrelated to the earlier primates.
>
> — Zecharia Sitchin,
> *The 12th Planet*

347

modern man appear on the earth some three hundred thousand years ago instead of three million years in the future? Were we brought here from another planet in our galaxy? Or were we, as the Bible and other sources so state, created by the gods?

There is hard evidence now available for the skeptics that mankind was a special creation and that he had his genesis in the Far West first, and later in the Near East. Human civilization in some areas of the Near East has been traced back to about 11,000 B.C. to a time shortly after the great biblical flood. Mankind was again producing clay pottery, stone buildings, and other objects of excellent design and workmanship.

We have explored the remains of The Builders in the South Pacific, and the Western genesis of man, with the valuable aid of numerous scholars and researchers. Let us now turn to the Near East, where remains of civilizations clearly linked to The Builders will be seen. These were civilizations of high, positive social and moral codes, existing beside other negative and warlike cultures.

In the year 1842, a small group of scholars set out to conduct the first major excavations on the ruins of a city in northern Mesopotamia, near present day Khorsabad. It contained the remains of a stepped pyramid, along with temples and palaces of magnificent design and workmanship, much like the ruins of Tiahuanaco in Bolivia and the pyramids and cities of Central America.

A few years after this discovery, another ruin was excavated on the Tigris River. The excavation turned out to be the Assyrian capital of Nineveh mentioned in the Bible. Nineveh was once the royal capital of Assyria. Its last three kings were the biblical Sennacherib, Esarhaddon, and Ashurbanipal. One after another, ruins were unearthed and ancient biblical cities were discovered.

Concurrently with the momentous excavations of ancient Assyria, the biblical city of Babel, or Babylon, was unearthed. Today we can look upon the ruins of two great competing empires — Babylonia and Assyria. One was centered in the north and the other in the south. These ruins have yielded thousands of cuneiform tablets, including the histories of kings, temple records, and the duties performed by the gods on earth.

> But the true treasures of these kingdoms [Assyria and Babylonia] were written records: thousands upon thousands of inscriptions in the cuneiform script, including cosmologic tales, epic poems, histories of kings, temple records, commercial contracts, marriage and divorce records, astronomical tables, astrological forecasts, mathematical formulas, . . . and, not least of all, texts dealing with the names, genealogies, epithets, deeds, powers, and duties of the gods.
>
> — Zecharia Sitchin, *The 12th Planet*

In an earlier chapter we described the division in the ranks of The Builders, which eventually produced the Fallen Angels. The Builders were all but destroyed in the great wars fought on earth with the Fallen Angels, and their first and primary homeland of Mu (Lemuria) sank to the bottom of the sea in the South Pacific. The Fallen Angels established bases on the earth in some areas of what is now known as the Near East.

The ruins of Mesopotamia have provided us with evidence of many rulers who were subjects of the gods. One such ruler claimed in his inscriptions that his empire stretched, by the grace of his god, Enlil, from the Lower Sea (the Persian Gulf), to the Upper Sea (the Mediterranean). This empire existed in the third millennium B.C.

One of the greatest finds was a library unearthed in Nineveh that belonged to the late Ashurbanipal. The library contained 25,000 cuneiform tablets. Included in this find was a statement by Ashurbanipal himself: "The god of scribes has bestowed on me the gift of knowledge of his art. I have been initiated into the secrets of writing. I can even read the intricate tablets in Sumerian. I understand the enigmatic words in stone carvings from the days before the Flood."

The people of the fourth millennium B.C., in the area of the Euphrates Valley, are known to us as Sumerians. Sumerian script, originally pictographic and carved in stone in vertical columns, was turned horizontally and later stylized for wedge-shaped writings on soft clay tablets. These tablets became the cuneiform writings of the Akkadians, Babylonians, and Assyrians, along with other nations of the Near East.

As excavations continued, the city of Lagash was unearthed, along with Nippur, a one-time religious center. More than 30,000 cuneiform tablets were found in ancient Nippur. In the ruins of Ur, another ancient Sumerian city, scholars found vases, jewelry, weapons, chariots, and helmets.

As we look deeper into their origin, a picture emerges of at least some of the Sumerians who were warlike from their beginnings. There are tales of deceit, treachery, and wars fought between the members of the ruling families of gods. The accounts recorded indicate that gods of love and virtue were forced to live beside gods of war and destruction in areas of the Near East.

> The Fallen Angels, seeking to destroy the practice of virtue that they now despised, followed The Builders into this solar system millenniums ago and forced landings on some areas of the earth, including the Near East. From bases upon the earth they pursued their efforts to destroy their former brothers and sisters. Great and small wars were fought between the gods who were both good and evil, for possession of the earth.
>
> — The Author

In the Far West, as we have seen, a vast civilization of peaceful people

349

existed for millenniums and sent out colonies to other parts of the world. The remains of a ziggurat, a vast man-made mount, were found at Uruk, tying together the civilizations of the Near East and the Far West. The similarity of the ziggurats to the stepped pyramids found in Central and South America is strong evidence of a social connection between the architects of the structures who used the same unique techniques of design and construction.

> The existence of similar and highly developed cosmologies in such widely separated countries as Egypt, China, and Mexico implies that all the great civilizations of our era derived from a common source, from some greater tradition, of which each preserved certain relics. . . . These men erected vast atronomical instruments, circles of erect pillars, pyramids, underground tunnels, cyclopean stone platforms, all linked together by a network of tracks and alignments, whose course from horizon to horizon was marked by stones, mounds, and earthworks.
>
> — John Michell, *The View Over Atlantis*

South of Uruk, the archeologists found Eridu, the oldest Sumerian city. It was dedicated to Enki, the chief scientist of the gods in that area. Enki's temple was rebuilt after the great cataclysmic flood. Here we find another link in the chain of the Near East with the Far West. Tiki, known as Kon-Tiki Viracocha, was a bearded white god worshipped in ancient Tiahuanaco and the islands and continents of the South Pacific. Enki, also called Ea, was a bearded white god worshipped in ancient Sumeria. Enki and Tiki originally came from the same great family of the gods — the four evolved races of The Builders. These two gods were the scientists who were responsible for the creation of *Homo sapiens*, East and West, in their genetic laboratories.

> It [Eridu] was a most extensive civilization, all-encompassing, in many ways more advanced than the other ancient cultures that had followed it. It was undoubtedly the civilization on which our own is based.
>
> — Zecharia Sitchin, *The 12th Planet*

> Until recently scientists assumed that the human race has been gradually evolving from original savagery. But if earliest man was a barbarous cave dweller, and his progress has been steadily upward in the scale of civilization, how can we explain the existence of ancient languages with grammatical construction far more sophisticated than that in use today? Colonel James Churchward, a nineteenth century British Army officer who spent many years in Tibet, India, Central and North America translating obscure tablets and writings dating from prehistoric times, makes a persuasive case for his thesis that all languages descend from one tongue used in "the Motherland of Man on Mu." . . . Churchward reproduces many alphabetical symbols in various ancient tongues which are identical, and which indicate a common origin in the lost continent of Lemuria. Genesis also says the whole earth was of one language and one speech.
>
> — Ruth Montgomery, *The World Before*

More evidence of The Builders (i.e., Nefilim) the gods from space, is found in the Hindu Vedas. Hinduism is one of the modern day religions of India. The Hindus consider the Vedas, along with their hymns and sayings pertaining to the gods, sacred scriptures, and not of human origin. The gods themselves composed them, the Hindus state, in an age which preceded the present one. The Vedic tales of the gods are remarkably like those of the Greeks and Egyptians. "The gods," the Vedas state, "were all members of one large family at one time." A great division occurred thousands of years ago. Stories of the gods describe the great wars and aerial battles, where each side used incredible weapons to destroy the other. There are tales of ascents into

The theme of the great Hindu epic, the Mahabharata, of which the Bhagavad-Gita is an episode, is the great war which was carried on between two factions, or parties, of a certain large tribe, or family.

— Introduction to the Mahabharata

the heavens and descents to the earth in resplendent aerial cars. A few records still exist that describe the gods in the heavens and upon the earth.

The Hindu epic, Ramayana, describes Rama traveling in his *vimana* through the skies of ancient India. Rama's aerial car was resplendent and is described like a

At Rama's behest the magnificent chariot rose up to a mountain of cloud with a tremendous din . . .

— the Mahabharata

"fiery chariot." Valmiki, a poet of the third and fourth century B.C., related the story of Rama and his aerial car. An even earlier work speaks of Bhima who "flew along in his *vimana*, resplendent as the sun, and loud as thunder. . . . the flying chariot shone like a flame in the night sky of summer. . . . it swept by like a comet. . . . it was as if two suns were shining. . . . then the chariot rose up and all the heavens brightened. . . .

"An ancient chariot, named the *pushpaka*, conveys many people to the ancient capital of Ayodhya. The sky is full of stupendous flying machines, dark as night, but picked out by lights with a yellowish glare." The Mausoloparvan (part of the Mahabharata) states, "It was an unknown weapon, an iron thunderbolt, a gigantic messenger of death that burnt to ashes all the descendents of Andhak and Vrishni. Their corpses were featureless; the hair and nails fell away. Vessels broke into fragments without cause; the birds turned white. Within a few hours every food became unwholesome." Another stanza states, "Cukra, flying in a *vimana* of great power, hurled at the triple city a missile weighted with the force of the universe. An incandescent smoke, like ten thousand suns, rose in all its splendor." The descriptions conveyed to us by these writings indicate to us that horrible atomic wars were once fought, bringing about the mass annihilation of whole cities and countries on the earth.

Hindu records state that there were many types of awesome weapons. The *avidiastra* affected the enemy's nervous system; *passvapana* produced a force which would turn to ashes the army of Kumbhakarna. Finally, the grandfather of all weapons stands forth revealed as the *dronaparvan*. This was a super bomb of atomic force.

The Mahabharata, Book VII, describes its power: "They launched a huge missile of burning fire without smoke. Immediately thick darkness fell upon the armies and upon everything. A terrible wind arose, and blood-colored clouds swept down upon the earth. Nature went mad, and the sun seemed to revolve upon itself. The enemy fell like shrubs consumed by the fire. The rivers boiled, and those who dived into them perished miserably. The forests burned; horses and elephants plunged wildly through them, neighing and trumpeting. When the wind had cleared away the smoke, we beheld thousands of corpses burnt to ashes."

It was as if the elements had been unleashed. The sun spun around. Scorched by the incandescent heat of the weapon, the world reeled in fever. Elephants were set on fire by the heat and ran to and fro in a frenzy to seek protection from the terrible violence. The water boiled, the animals died, the enemy was mowed down and the raging of the blaze made the trees collapse in rows as in a forest fire. The elephants made a fearful trumpeting and sank dead to the ground over a vast area. Horses and war chariots were burnt up, and the scene looked like the aftermath of a conflagration. Thousands of chariots were destroyed, then deep silence descended on the scene. The winds began to blow and the earth grew bright. It was a terrible sight to see. The corpses of the fallen were mutilated by the terrible heat so they no longer looked like human beings. Never before have we seen such a ghastly weapon, and never before have we heard of such a weapon.

— The Mahabharata, quoted by Erich von Däniken, in *Chariots of the Gods*

The vivid description of these awesome weapons and the flying machines which could deliver them, plus the devastation they rendered, has to be more than mere imagination on the part of the commentators. This is indeed the description of an atomic holocaust. We can now well believe that some of the ancient gods had chariots of fire, plus the weapons to literally destroy themselves and the whole earth, if need be.

As we look at the ancient records existing on the earth today, we find a consistent theme playing through all of them: "The gods who created men all came down from the heavens in ships of fire. They lived among men as rulers for a time. There was a great war, followed by a cataclysmic flood. The gods ascended into the heavens again."

Ancient Hittite inscriptions and tablets speak of these gods and their wars. The Hittite pantheon of gods was governed by the sacred number twelve. There is a masonry inscription near the town of Beysehir in the land of Anatolia that depicts the divine Father-Mother image surrounded by ten other gods.

> Who were these Gods of Heaven and Earth, divine yet human, always headed by a pantheon or inner circle of twelve deities? ... The Greeks believed that first there was Chaos; then Gaea (Earth) and her consort Uranus brought forth the twelve Titans, six males and six females. ... The original twelve Great Gods were Gods of Heaven who had come down to Earth; and they represented the twelve celestial bodies in the "vault of heaven."
>
> Hinduism, the ancient religion of India, considers the Vedas — compositions of hymns, sacrificial formulas, and other sayings pertaining to the gods — as sacred scriptures, "not of human origin." ... The gods, the Vedas told, were all members of one large, but not necessarily peaceful family. ... The divine family was made up of the twelve *Adityas*, gods who were each assigned a sign of the zodiac and a celestial body.
>
> Although the Egyptians counted by the decimal system, their religious affairs were governed by the Sumerian sexigesimal sixty, and celestial matters were subject to the divine number twelve. The heavens were divided into three parts each comprising twelve celestial bodies. The afterworld was divided into twelve parts. Day and night were each divided into twelve hours. And all these divisions were paralleled by "companies" of gods, which in turn consisted of twelve gods each.
>
> — Zecharia Sitchin, *The 12th Planet*

Archeological discoveries show conclusively that the Hittites worshipped "olden gods," the gods of heaven and the gods of earth. These gods were the supreme rulers of the lands. They appointed human kings and administrators. They gave counsel on war, treaties, and all international affairs. A Hittite inscription speaks of an ancient tale called "Kingship in Heaven." This inscription deals with the heavenly origin of the twelve olden gods who came from the heavens and landed upon the earth.

It then states that in the olden days Alalu had been king in heaven and was seated on the throne when Anu, first among the gods, came to stand before him. For "nine counted periods" Alalu was king in heaven but in the ninth period, Anu challenged him for the throne and won. "On the throne sat Anu." Further, we find that when Alalu, this ancient elder of The Builders, was forcefully thrust from his throne by the rebellious god, Anu, a great division occurred among the gods.

The tale further states that Alalu fled before Anu, he descended to the dark earth. We later find that Anu was eventually overthrown by his own brother, Kumarbi. The stories of these wars came to the Hittites from the Hurrians (referred to as the Horites in the Old Testament), who got them from the Sumerians.

Let there listen the gods who are in heaven
And those who are in the dark earth! . . .
Once in the olden days Alalu was king in heaven.
Alalu was seated on the throne,
The mighty Anu, first among the gods, was
    standing before him.
He would sink at his feet and set the drinking cup
    in his hand.
Nine in number were the years [periods] that
    Alalu was king in heaven.
In the ninth year [period] Anu gave battle to
    Alalu and he vanquished Alalu.
He fled before him and went down to the dark earth.
Down he went to the dark earth, but Anu took his
    seat upon the throne.

— Hittite text, "Kingship in Heaven,"
translated by Albrecht Goetze

The lands of Israel and southern Syria once formed the empire of the Canaanites and the early Phoenicians. Archeologists have found evidence of a definite connection between the Canaanites and the Phoenicians, linking them to the Egyptians. The Canaanite pantheon of gods is similar to that of the Egyptians, the Hindus and The Builders.

The presiding deity of the Canaanites was named El. El was known as the kindly and the merciful. He was the absolute authority in all affairs, human and divine. He is known as one of the creators of man.

El was a sage and elderly deity; he was one of the twelve olden gods. He had seven sons, three of whom were Yam, Mot, and Baal. El was a member of the eternal priesthood of The Builders. Literally translated, two of his titles are "Builder of Stone," and "Builder of the Built Ones," meaning Creator of the World. In Genesis, Abraham is blessed by Melchisedec: " 'Blessed be Abram by El-Elyon, Creator of heaven and earth. And praised be El-Elyon, who has delivered your foes to you.' And Abram gave him a

The description of the time of the Hebrew patriarchs in Genesis reflects a time of El worship in Canaan. The native kings of Canaan worshipped El. Thus Melchisedec, king of Salem (probably Jerusalem), was the priest of "El, the highest," and Abimelech, the king of Gerar in southern Palestine, feared Elohim [El] who revealed himself to him, and when this king had made a covenant with Abraham in Beersheba "Eternal El" was invoked. This shows that El was the national god of those South Canaanite kingdoms and that Hadad [Baal] had not usurped the kingship there at the time of the Hebrew patriarchs.

— Ulf Oldenburg, *The Conflict Between El and Baal in Canaanite Religion*

tenth of everything." (Genesis 14:19-20, The Anchor Bible.) Melchisedec was a Canaanite, king of Salem (probably Jerusalem), and El was the specific name of the deity whom he worshipped. Abraham's tithing to Melchisedec clearly shows that he considered his god and Melchisedec's one and the same.

Yahweh, who revealed himself to Moses, identified himself by his own statement, with the God of Abraham, Isaac, and Jacob. "I am the God of thy father, the God of Abraham, the God of Isaac, and the God of Jacob." (Exodus 3:6.) "And I appeared unto Abraham, unto Isaac, and unto Jacob, by the name of God Almighty [which is a translation of El-Elyon] but by my name Jehovah [Yahweh] was I not known to them." (Exodus 6:3.) His name Yahweh or "I Am That I Am," expresses his nature as one who has

Thus, according to the Hebrew Bible Yahweh is identical with El of the patriarchs, and his name occurs in parallelism with El, Shaddai, and with Elyon. (Exodus 6:3; Numbers 23:8; 24:8; Ruth 1:20-21; Isaiah 13:6; 2 Samuel 22:14; Psalm 9:2-3; and many other passages.)

. . . El of Ugarit [Canaan] was called "the Kind One, the God of Mercy," "kind and holy," and he was extolled for his life-giving word of wisdom. Also, "Yahweh, Yahweh El [is] merciful and gracious, slow to anger, and abundant in goodness and truth." (Exodus 34:6.)

Ulf Oldenburg, *The Conflict Between El and Baal in Canaanite Religion*

life in himself, and to whom no one is equal. Yahweh and El both authored very high and strict moral and social codes teaching righteousness and mercy. What a contrast this is to their neighbors, gods of murder, lust and corruption.

One of El's sons, Baal, evidently joined the enemy camp of the Fallen Angels. Baal usurped the throne of El, his father. He then fought and destroyed his brother Yam. In a battle with Mot, Baal lost. Mot eventually inherited his father's throne and remained loyal to The Builders. Mot was then mysteriously murdered by his sister Anat through collusion with her brother Baal. Baal then inherited his father's throne after Mot's death, placing it within the circle of the Dark Forces.

This god, Baal, practiced rites which horrified the followers of El and Yahweh. Speaking of the Baal cult, God, through Isaiah, says: "But you, come here, sons of a sorceress, offspring of an adulterer and a prostitute! At whom do you jest? At whom do you open wide your mouth, stick out your tongue?

. . . the apostasy of Israel and Judah became greater and they did not return from Baalism. Therefore, the prophets became hot with anger and as never before depicted the utter sinfulness of the sexual rites of the Baal cult. . . . Utterly despising Baal they purposely ignored him as a god, calling him "no god," as over against Yahweh who was the only God.

— Ulf Oldenburg, *The Conflict Between El and Baal in the Canaanite Religion*

Are you not children of guilt, a lying race? You who are inflamed with passion under great trees, and under every spreading leafy tree, who slaughter children in the stream beds, in the clefts of the rocks." (Isaiah 57:3-5.)

As far back in time as the Flood, the Bible attributes the destruction of mankind to the mating of the sons of the gods with the daughters of the earth.

> Now when men began to increase on earth and daughters were born to them, the divine beings saw how beautiful were the human daughters and took as their wives any of them they liked. Then Yahweh said, "My spirit shall not shield man forever, since he is but flesh; let the time allowed him be one hundred and twenty years." (Genesis 6:1-3.) It is evident . . . from the tenor of the Hebrew account that its author was highly critical of the subject matter. . . . The story would have been sufficient to fill him with horror at the depravity it reflected. A world that could entertain such notions deserved to be wiped out. In these circumstances, the present position of the fragment immediately before the account of the Flood can scarcely be independent of that universal catastrophe. The story of the primeval titans emerges as a moral indictment, and thereby as a compelling motive for the forthcoming disaster. And the period of 120 years becomes one of probation, in the face of every sign that the doom cannot be averted. All of this accords with the separately established fact that the Flood story in Genesis, unlike its Mesopotamian analogues, was morally motivated.
>
> — The Anchor Bible, comments and translation by E.A. Speiser

Where did the Canaanites and the Phoenicians originate? From where did they draw their culture and religious beliefs? The Bible considers them to be a part of the Hamitic family, with origins in the lands of Ham, which means "hot," the hot lands of Africa. They were the blood brothers of the Egyptians!

The Egyptians believed in the great heavenly gods who had descended upon the earth in ships called the boats of heaven. The head of the Egyptian pantheon was called Ra. Ra's emblem was the celestial, winged sun disc, the omnipresent image of The Great Central SöN-SüN, the First Creation of Light. The rulers of Egypt were not men of this earth. They were, in fact, The Builders from Mu. Ra was the first ruler of ancient Egypt, and was a brother to Rama of India and Ramu of Lemuria.

The wings attached to a sun disc symbolize a sun which is not fixed to a specific orbit but which can move freely throughout all the dimensions of the creation.

The Author

The olden Egyptian gods, as we have seen, had come by boat from the Southern Sea, which they called the Sea of Ur. While they worshipped Ra as the Creator, it was Ptah, the developer, who actually raised the lands of Egypt above the floodwaters of the Nile by building dikes. A commentary states that Ptah established more than just Egypt alone: "Ptah had established the far foreign lands in the East."

In Egypt we also find a stepped pyramid at Saqqara, built for King Zoser. This pyramid duplicates those of Central and South America. The pyramid at Saqqara predates those of Giza, such as the Great Pyramid, which show a more recent style of architecture. King Zoser was continuing the traditional practice of a more ancient civilization (Mu, the Motherland of man).

The pyramid of Maidum, ... grew in seven steps; ... eventually the spaces between the steps were filled in, and the entire pyramid encased with white limestone. ... the pyramid has been attributed to Cheops' father, for whom the Great Pyramid was built.

— Peter Tompkins,
Secrets of the Great Pyramid

Returning to the Sumerians, we find they also believed that physical gods had come down to earth from the heavens. Indeed, ancient records found written on cuneiform tablets in the Euphrates Valley state emphatically that Adam was created by physical gods.

These gods were powerful and were able to accomplish feats beyond the ability of mortals to comprehend. Still, these gods looked like humans. They ate, drank, talked, and moved about, displaying human emotions and characteristics. They were at war with each other and openly fought battles in the heavens and upon the earth with each other. The cuneiform writings state, emphatically, that a great family of physical beings from another planet arrived here on earth in remote times, millenniums before self-conscious humans existed. This great confederation of so-called gods was split down the middle and bitterly opposed to each other, as we already know. They appear as the gods of virtue and compassion on the one hand, and the gods of war, selfishness, and destruction on the other. Unfortunately, mankind was, and still is, caught in the middle of this great war in the galaxy between the Forces of Darkness and the Forces of Light and Truth.

In the *Egyptian Book of the Dead*, that collection of texts which contained instructions for behavior in the hereafter ... Ra, the mighty Sun God, fights with the rebellious children in the universe. ...

— Erich von Däniken,
The Gold of the Gods

In our search for the gods who actually created *Homo sapiens* on earth, we have found names, commentaries, stories, and discourses, describing the actual creation and birth of Adam. These incredible records have survived the destruction of the Sumerian Empire and exist for us to read today, along with what is left of the records in the West.

> I will produce a lowly Primitive;
> "Man" shall be his name.
> I will create a Primitive Worker;

He will be charged with the service of the gods, that
they might have their ease.

— "Epic of Creation," a Sumerian text
quoted in Zecharia Sitchin, *The 12th Planet*

Alalu was a Builder and one of the oldest gods mentioned in the writings of the Near East. Ramu was the first emperor of Mu and the divine brother of Alalu. Rama established India and Ra established Egypt; both were Builders and brothers of Ramu and Alalu. All of these beings were Sons of The Great Central SöN - SüN and members of the eternal priesthood of The Builders, known on earth as the Priesthood of Melchisedec.

> For this Melchisedec, king of Salem, priest of the most high God. . . . Without father, without mother, without descent, having neither beginning of days, nor end of life; but made like unto the Son of God; abideth a priest continually. (Hebrews 7:1-3.) The Priesthood of Melchisedec is the consciousness of the Son of God, Christ Consciousness, the light of creation, the projector of all images. This priesthood, naturally, is without beginning or ending of days. Those beings who are members are those never born of woman, but born of the Second Birth (i.e., Christ Consciousness). Therefore, whoever possesses Christ possesses the consciousness of knowing Christ and is hereafter called a High Priest in the Order of Melchisedec, a true Son or Daughter of God, a Christ-Conscious Being.
>
> — The Author

Anu is described in some accounts also as the father of the gods. We previously found Anu overpowering Alalu in some heavenly place, not on Planet Earth. We have found written testimony on the divisions, disputes, and wars which existed between the gods from the heavens.

Anu and his consort, Antu, had two sons, Enlil and Enki. Enlil, the eldest, was in command of the forces of Anu on earth under his father. He was known as the Lord of the air spaces, the commander of spaceships. Enki was lord of the great deep, the waters and the oceans. He was the expert in biology and genetics. Enki's key role was that of chief scientist for the forces of Anu on earth. As chief scientist he outlined the methods by which man (i.e., *Homo sapiens*) was to be created upon the earth, that he might carry the burden of the physical work of

> Indeed, the Sumerian and Akkadian texts, which (like the Old Testament) adhered to the belief that a god or the gods created Man through a conscious and deliberate act, attribute to Ea [Enki] a key role: as the chief scientist of the gods, he outlined the method and process by which Man was to be created.
>
> — Zecharia Sitchin, *The 12th Planet*

the gods. It was the plan of Enki and Enlil to create men without the eternal life and wisdom they themselves seemed to enjoy. He was to be just a worker, a slave to wait on the gods' every wish.

One text describes Enlil in his lust for a maiden named Sud. He invited her for a boat ride and then raped her. He eventually married Sud, renaming her Ninlil. They both then assumed the throne position on earth at Nippur. From Nippur, Enlil ruled the "black-headed people," the humans created by his brother Enki. From his awesome city of Nippur, Enlil ruled with fear. Sumerian texts state that he could "raise the beams that search the heart and all the lands... eyes that could scan all the lands."

Enlil seems to have found another consort, in the form of his sister, Ninhursag, for she produced his heir, Ninurta. Two of his grandchildren, Inanna and Utu were born before the black-headed people (i.e., *Homo sapiens*) were created, and both became powerful rulers on earth. Sippar, ruled by Utu, was one of the oldest cities built by the gods. Inanna, Utu's sister, is now referred to as Inanna-Ishtar. Inanna made history for herself by leading the Assyrian kings into battle. They went to war at her command. Sometimes she marched at the head of the army.

> Known to the Romans as Venus, to the Greeks as Aphrodite, ... to the other ancient peoples as Ishtar or Eshdar, to the Akkadians and the Sumerians as Inanna... she was at all times the Goddess of Warfare and the Goddess of Love, a fierce, beautiful female who ... carved for herself, by herself, a major place among the Great Gods of Heaven and Earth.
>
> — Zecharia Sitchin, *The 12th Planet*

In the Old Testament we find the angels of the Lord referred to as the "Malachim" which, when translated, literally means "divine emissary." The sudden appearance of angels around biblical figures like Jacob and Abraham may now be explained in part.

The angels of the Lord, in some cases, were physical beings called the Nefilim, or The Builders. There is no longer any doubt that the people of the Near East and the Far West watched their physical gods ascend and descend to and from the heavens.

> And Jacob went out from Beersheba, and went toward Haran. And he lighted upon a certain place, and he tarried there all night, because the sun was set; and he took of the stones of that place, and put them for his pillows, and lay down in that place to sleep. And he dreamed, and behold a ladder set up on the earth, and the top of it reached to heaven: and behold the angels of God ascending and descending on it. And, behold, the Lord stood above it, and said, I am the Lord, God of Abraham thy father, and the God of Isaac. . . .
>
> — Genesis 28: 10-13

The commentators who wrote upon clay tablets in ancient times describe the gods traversing the skies of earth in their *mus*, celestial boats of heaven, and their *mes*, flying suits.

We find a description of Inanna-Ishtar, also known as Aphrodite, the daughter of Nanna-Sin, putting on her space attire which allowed her to fly in the earth's atmosphere. It states that Inanna-Ishtar tied the *me* to her hands and attached the *me* to her breast. There are other descriptions that tell us Inanna-Ishtar accomplished feats of flying over many far distant lands. Inanna was able to visit Enki at Eridu and Enlil at Nippur. She was able to make long journeys to the underworld (South Africa), to visit her sister, Ereshkigal and her brother-in-law, Nergal. She went up in the "boat of heaven" to visit Anu.

> Lady of Heaven:
> She puts on the Garment of Heaven;
> She valiantly ascends towards Heaven.
> Over all the peopled lands she flies in her MU.
> Lady, who in her MU to the heights of Heaven
>   joyfully wings.
> Over all the resting places she flies in her MU.
>
> — Hymn to Inanna-Ishtar, quoted in
>   Zecharia Sitchin, *The 12th Planet*

The following description of Inanna's special flying suit was found written on clay tablets. The flying attire Inanna had to put on in order to traverse the skies is listed:

1. The *shugarra* she put on her head
2. The "measuring pendants" on her ears
3. Chains of small blue stones around her neck
4. Twin "stones" on her shoulders
5. A golden cylinder in her hands
6. Straps clasping her breast
7. The *pala* garment around her body

The correct interpretation of these seven objects has never been fully rendered until recently, when archeologists excavating the ancient city of Mari unearthed a statue of Inanna-Ishtar. The statue was more than four thousand years old and was in excellent condition. The strange attire mentioned is clearly visible on the feminine figure. The statue displays a very unusual helmet, along with what appears to be earphones attached to it. Around the neck is a necklace made up of many small stones. In her hands she holds a cylindrical object. Two parallel straps run over her shoulders to support a box-like container held tightly against her back. The box must have been very heavy for there is a large, thick pad on each shoulder to cushion the weight. A long tube is attached to the box and stretches down her back to a point below her knees.

Inanna-Ishtar

The strange attire shown on this statue, along with the text of her flights, indicate that this is the figure of a woman in some sort of flying suit. In identifying some of the articles previously listed, the *pala* is the garment she wears, and the *shugarra* is the helmet which, when translated means, "that which makes to go far in the universe." The records seem to state emphatically that the gods wore such flying suits, called *mes*, not only to traverse the skies of earth, but also when they made journeys into space within their celestial *mus*.

In the ancient texts . . . speaking of her occasional visits to Anu at his Celestial Abode, Inanna herself explained that she could undertake such journeys because "Enlil fastened the divine *me* attire about my body."

The scholars refer to the *mes* as "divine power objects." Literally, the term stems from the concept of "swimming in celestial waters." Inanna described them as parts of the "celestial garment" that she put on for her journeys in the Boat of Heaven. The *mes* were thus parts of the special gear worn for flying in Earth's skies as well as into outer space.

— Zecharia Sitchin, *The 12th Planet*

Gudea was an ancient Sumerian ruler. He constructed a temple and dedicated it to the god Ninurta, one of Enlil's sons. Gudea states in writing that Ninurta talked with him after landing on the earth in his divine "black wind bird." Ninurta was clothed in the traditional flying suit and he wore the helmet of the gods. At this time, Gudea was instructed to build a temple for Ninurta and an enclosure for his divine black wind bird to rest within. The construction of the temple required huge monoliths of stone which had to be quarried and brought from afar. The main purpose for this temple and enclosed yard was to protect Ninurta's divine boat of heaven. This divine vehicle, when in place, could lay hold on heaven; it brought Heaven and Earth, the two planets, together. The divine bird, itself, was so important it was guarded day and night by two divine weapons: the "supreme hunter," and the "supreme killer." Gudea stated that the divine bird rose to circle the lands. It flashed upon the raised walls of its enclosure. This protected enclosure was called a "strong stone resting place of the *mu*."

The Babylonian king Nebuchadnezzar II wrote of rebuilding a sacred area within fortified walls made of burned brick for his god Marduk. Within these walls:

> I raised the head of the boat ID. GE. UL
>   the Chariot of Marduk's princeliness;
> The boat ZAG. MU. KU, whose approach is
>   observed, the supreme traveler between

> Heaven and Earth, in the midst of the pavilion
> I enclosed, screening off its sides.

> — Babylonian text, quoted by
> Zecharia Sitchin, in *The 12th Planet*

The *idgeul* was the chariot of Marduk. *Idgeul* translates into "high to heaven, bright at night."

The *mus* of some of the gods were conical, and there is an ancient coin, found at Byblos (the biblical Gebal), that illustrates this. It shows the great temple of Inanna-Ishtar, the main temple, and the enclosed sacred inner courtyard of the *mus*. The *mu* is clearly visible standing upright behind the columned entryway. This enclosure could only be reached by ascending many steps, and indicated that the *mu* resided in a raised, well protected area. The pictographic writings for the word *mu* reveal drawings which appear as objects that resemble vehicles used by our modern day astronauts.

A hymn dedicated to Inanna-Ishtar clearly states that a *mu* was the divine boat of heaven in which the gods came through space to the earth. There have been many cylinder seals unearthed in ancient Mesopotamia that depict the gods enclosed within the oval chambers of the flying boats of heaven. The ascent and descent of the gods in their flying *mus* have been recorded in the pictographic drawings on clay, stone, gold, and copper tablets. Many such drawings clearly show rocket-like objects in flight, emitting fire, while others remain upright on launching areas, awaiting their navigators. One cuneiform text known as the "Epic of Creation" describes the "First Gateway of the Gods," which was constructed by the gods themselves before men were created in the Near East. For years the lesser gods worked to construct the high raised structure, called the *Eshagila* (house of the great gods), and its high tower, finally bringing it to completion.

> When from the Heaven for assembly you shall
>   descend, there shall be a restplace for the night
>   to receive you all. . . .

> — "Epic of Creation," the Babylonian version,
> quoted by Zecharia Sitchin, in *The 12th Planet*

The Mesopotamian texts describe Utu Shamash as the god in charge of the landing place of the *mus* on earth. Utu evidently coordinated all travel to and from the earth and the abode of the gods (i.e., another planet in our galaxy), in the near vicinity of our solar system.

There can no longer be any doubt that the ancient peoples who called their deities the "Gods of Heaven and Earth" meant exactly what they said. The gods were physical beings from another world who had come to the earth from the outer spaces in their boats of heaven. The evidence now emphatically shows that the gods were flesh and blood beings and not omnipresent gods. We can now see some of the Fallen Angels filling the role of the sons of the gods that we find mentioned in the Bible. "When mankind began to increase and to spread all over the earth and daughters were born to them, the sons of God saw that the daughters of men were beautiful, so they took for themselves such women as they chose." (Genesis 6:12.)

But the Sumerian texts do not refer to their "gods" with vague imprecision; they say quite clearly that the people had once seen them with their own eyes. Their sages were convinced that they had known the "gods" who completed the work of instruction. We can read in Sumerian texts how everything happened. The gods gave them instructions for making metal (the translation of the Sumerian word for metal is "heavenly metals") and taught them how to cultivate barley. We should also note that according to Sumerian records the first men are supposed to have resulted from the inter-breeding of gods and the children of earth.

— Erich von Däniken,
Gods from Outer Space

The implications of these biblical verses and their mysteries can now be explained in the light of the legends and writings left to us by The Builders and the Fallen Angels.

Theologians and biblical scholars have tried to avoid explaining these strange verses in the Bible by simply ignoring them altogether. It no longer matters what theologians try to say about original meanings of verses — the truth cannot escape!

> . . . The Hebrew verb *naphal*, which means "to fall," or "to fall upon," is the base for the term "nephilim," which is the Old Testament translation for giants; . . . Or the Nephilim might have fallen from . . . the skies. . . .
>
> In the ancient and heroic sagas of Norse mythology, the Eddas, there are numerous stories of giants and of couplings between the daughters of these primitive creatures and the sons of the gods. The first of these occurs at the early beginnings of time and life on Earth, when the first giant, Ymir, is created out of the frozen gases and mists of the region called Niflheim. . . . The similarity of the words "Niflheim" and "Nephilim" is immediately apparent; that these two words should occur at opposite ends of the world in such disparate languages and cultures, but with such similar meanings, is both curious and astounding.
>
> — Michael Grumley, *There are Giants in the Earth*

An ancient coin found at Byblos which depicts a conical-shaped object (black wind bird) in a silo-like enclosure (i.e., the *mus* of the Nefilim).

Cylinder seal from ancient Mesopotamia showing the Adam being presented by the goddess Ninti to the god Enki

CHAPTER 37

The Creation of the Race of Adam
(As taken from Ancient Tablets)

The Bible continues to give us great difficulty in trying to understand how mankind was created. In Genesis 1:26 the god states, "Let *us* create man in *our* image, after *our* likeness." This statement indicates that the deity was definity not alone: that there were others present. Also, the deities present must have been both male and female, for the record further states: "In the image of God created he him, male and female created he them." (Genesis 1:27.) Here we have to accept the fact that there were many gods present, both male and female, when the Adam was first created. The Sumerian texts confirm this statement in the Bible and give us a good description of some of the physical gods and of the events that led to man's creation in the Near East.

The Anunnaki were the lesser gods, those who followed Anu, the usurper of Alalu. Anu was the supreme ruler of some of the gods and their activities in the Near East and South Africa. The Anunnaki were the workers who bore the burden of the physical labor on the earth before men were created. The texts state that self-appointed chief deities among these gods had already divided the commands

Significantly, the Book of Genesis — purportedly exalting the achievements of a sole Diety — uses the plural Elohim (literally "dieties") to denote "God," and reports an astonishing remark; "Let us make man in our image, after our likeness."

— Zecharia Sitchin, *The 12th Planet*

The story of the toil and ensuing mutiny of the Anunnaki informs us that "for forty periods they suffered the work, day and night;" The long years of their toil are dramatized by repetitious verses:
For 10 periods they suffered the toil;
For 20 periods they suffered the toil;
For 30 periods they suffered the toil;
For 40 periods they suffered the toil.

— Zecharia Sitchin, *The 12th Planet*

The word translated "period" simply meant "something that completes itself." The twelfth planet, as described by Zecharia

367

among themselves. Anu, the father of the Anunnaki, was their king; their lord chancellor was the warrior, Enlil. Their chief officer was Ninurta, and Ennugi was their sheriff. The gods clasped their hands together, cast lots, and divided. Anu went up to heaven; his subjects, to earth.

Sitchin, took 3,600 earth years to complete one orbit around the sun, so that one year, or period, for an Anunnaki was 3,600 earth years, or a total of 144,000 earth years for forty periods.

— The Author

The toil of the Anunnaki seems to have been great. The gods were after rare metals and fuels for their cities and their divine ships, called *mus*. South Africa was the location of some of their mines. The Anunnaki were committed to working the mines, which they resented with a passion. There was finally a rebellion among the Anunnaki: they refused to work the mines any longer. This incredible story has been pieced together from many fragments, both Babylonian and Assyrian, by W. G. Lambert and A.R. Millard, in *Atra-Hasis: The Babylonian Story of the Flood*.

Any sincere student of the truth will greatly profit from a thorough study of this document, as it is a direct translation of the cuneiform tablets recounting events that occurred in the Near East, prior to the Flood. The Sumerian and Babylonian peoples undoubtedly believed these records to be history, not myth, and in light of the advances of science in our century, their story of "chariots of the gods," (Lambert and Millard, pg. 125), and of mankind's creation by a race of gods who lived on our planet, becomes not only entirely credible, but much more easily believable than that a primitive people imagined or invented this complex story.

> They were complaining, backbiting,
> Grumbling in the excavation:
> "Let us confront . . . the chamberlain,
> That he may relieve us of our heavy work.
> The counsellor of the gods, the hero, Enlil,
> Come, let us unnerve him in his dwelling!"

The leader of this rebellion is not named, but one is led to assume that it may have been Enki, Enlil's brother. This leader declares:

> "Now, proclaim war;
> Let us mingle hostilities and battle."
> The gods heeded his words . . . they went to the gate
>   of the shrine of the hero, Enlil.
> It was night, half-way through the watch,
> The temple was surrounded. . . .

368

Nusku, [Enlil's vizier] roused his lord —
He got him out of his bed,
"My Lord, your temple is surrounded,
    battle has come right up to your gate."

The rebellion was so serious that an urgent message was sent up to Anu in the heavenly abode (i.e., the planet called Heaven) by his son, Enlil. There was a great meeting called of all the gods and goddesses.

He sent and Anu was fetched down,
Enki was brought also to his presence. . . .
With the great Anunnaki present,
Enlil arose . . . opened his mouth
And addressed the great gods,

"Is it against me that it is being done?
Must I engage in hostilities. . . .?"

The Anunnaki registered their complaint that for forty periods they had "suffered the toil," and now they were through working the mines for Enlil and Anu.

"Every single one of us gods has declared war. . . .
Excessive toil has killed us,
Our work was heavy, our distress much."

Enki spoke up, saying that he had a solution:

"While the birth-goddess is present,
Let her create *Lullu*, man
Let him bear the yoke. . . .
Let man carry the toil of the gods."

This suggestion made by Enki was unanimously accepted. The gods voted to create the worker. "Man shall be his name," they said. They summoned the midwife of the gods, the wise Mami (i.e., Ninhursag, Enlil's sister) and said to her, "You are the birth-goddess — create workers!"

Mami, the mother of the gods, said she would need the help of Enki. "It is not possible for me to make things, skill lies with Enki." Enki is here depicted as chief scientist among the gods, one skilled in the science of genetics. In the house of destiny, a hospital-like place, the gods were waiting. Enki helped prepare the test-tube embryo from which the mother goddess hoped to see the first *lullu* (primitive worker) appear. The mother goddess went on working while incantations were constantly recited. Success was finally achieved; the creation of the birth of the first *lullu* took place. Summoning the Anunnaki, the great gods, she said:

> "You commanded me a task,
> I have completed it. . . .
> I have removed your heavy work,
> I have imposed your toil on man.
> You raised a cry for mankind,
> I have loosed the yoke,
> I have established freedom."

The Anunnaki shouted for joy. They ran together and kissed her feet. Soon it would be the primitive worker, man, who would bear the yoke of their toil. The Anunnaki were now able to create their own brand of slavery with a race of primitive workers.

The mutiny of the Anunnaki had now led to the creation of the race of Adam, from a genetic cross between the Anunnaki and possibly the evolving pre-human known as *Homo erectus*. Enki had now followed the same process that Tiki and The Builders had previously used in the West.

The Sumerian texts, for the first time, began to make sense out of the biblical account, for here we read of physical beings called gods creating a primitive worker to carry the burden of their toil. The Anunnaki referred to man as a *lullu* (primitive), and *amelu* (primitive worker). Man was created by some of the physical so-called gods in the Near East to be a servant to work their mines, smelt their metals, build their cities, and plant and harvest their crops. Yes, the Anunnaki would now have their ease. Is it not significant that *Random House Dictionary* identifies lulu as any remarkable or outstanding person or thing.

Here we read of a rebellion among so-called physical gods. If these gods were indeed physical, they were of sufficient advancement in genetics to do exactly what is described. One must also conclude that a fall from a divine state of moral virtue had indeed occurred among some of these entities. The biblical account of the creation of man leaves great reason for doubt as to the high moral nature and divine authority of the god or gods who knew good and evil and decided to create man.

— The Author

The idea that man was primarily created for the service of the gods finds frequent expression in religious texts.

— S. Langdon,
The Babylonian Epic of Creation

The Mesopotamian texts further describe the actual process used by Enki and Ninhursag to fashion men. The detailed description of the actual creation of man includes mixing to a core the elements from the earth (i.e., hu-man genetic material) called "clay." Then creating a purifying bath, one god was symbolically bled, and his flesh (i.e., genetic code) and blood (i.e., life force) were mixed with elements of the earth, the hu-man genetic material. The *Atra-Hasis* epic continues:

> From his flesh and blood
> Let Nintu, [Mami], mix clay
> That god and man
> May be thoroughly mixed in the clay. . .
> Let there be a spirit from the god's flesh.

It is clear that "clay" represents the pre-human evolving creature, (i.e., elements of the earth), and the god's flesh represents the spirit (also called "personality," the genetic code). "That god and man may be thoroughly mixed" surely means that man was created by the combination in some way of *Homo erectus*, the creature, with the gods themselves. Incomprehensible to modern man until very recently, these texts now seem to be the recording of a process of genetic engineering.

Mesopotamian texts were quite explicit on the subject. Not only do they state that blood was required for the mixture of which Man was fashioned; they specified that it had to be the blood of a god, divine blood. . . . If the "clay" onto which the godly element was mixed was an earthly element — as all texts insist — then the only possible conclusion is that the male sperm of a god — his genetic material — was inserted into the egg of an apewoman!

— Zecharia Sitchin, *The 12th Planet*

To produce the first man, childbearing was needed. Enki offered the services of his own spouse, Ninki,

> Ninki, my goddess-spouse, will be the one for labor.
> Seven goddesses-of-birth will be near, to assist.
>
> — Mesopotamian text, quoted by Zecharia Sitchin in, *The 12th Planet*

The mixing of the blood and elements is followed by the childbearing phase, the bestowal of a "divine imprint" on the new creature, the Adam. The child-bearing phase was conducted by Ninki. We are told that Ninki finally gave birth to the new being and presented him to Enki. Ancient seals show a goddess holding on her lap a newborn child while others nearby are holding up laboratory flasks. The perfect model for man, the Adam, had now been created. From this mold, or perfected man, others were to be fashioned.

We are led to the conclusion that man in the Near East was indeed created by some of the rebellious gods following processes devised by Enki and Ninhursag, his sister and chief nurse. Ninhursag was called the mother goddess, or Mami, and Ninti, which means "lady of life." Her

371

symbol was the cutter, the tool used to sever the umbilical cord after birth. Eve was afterwards fashioned from Adam's formula, using his life, or rib. In short, his genetic code was part of the model for Eve.

As we read further in the Sumerian texts, we find that with the successful creation of Adam, many more human beings were created from the same process. The Mesopotamian texts provide us with an eyewitness report of the first mass production of the duplication of the Adam. Fourteen birth-goddesses were divided into two groups, seven on the left and seven on the right. Seven were to bring forth males, and seven were to bring forth females. The test-tube embryos were placed in their wombs by the mother goddess. Now there was nothing to do but wait for the births. The birth-goddesses were kept together until the tenth month. The fragmented references in the quotation below to "hair," and "the cutter of the umbilical cord," suggest the removal or shaving of hair and the layout of surgical instruments. Ninti performed the midwifery, pronounced the blessing, and opening the wombs, brought forth life.

Once Adam proved to be the right creature, he was used as the genetic model, or "mold" for the creation of duplicates, and those duplicates were not only male, but male and female . . . . the biblical "rib" from which woman was fashioned was a play on words on the Sumerian TI ("rib" and "life") confirming that Eve was made of Adam's "life essence."

The double meaning of the Sumerian TI . . . raises biblical parallels. For TI could mean both: "life" and "rib," so Ninti's name meant both "lady of life" and "lady of the rib." The biblical Eve whose name meant "life" was created out of Adam's rib, so Eve, too, was in a way a "lady of life" and a "lady of the rib."

— Zecharia Sitchin, *The 12th Planet*

> After she had recited her incantation
> She put her hand out to her clay.
> She nipped off fourteen pieces of clay,
> Seven she put on the right,
> Seven she put on the left. . . .
> . . . Hair . . . She . . . the cutter of the umbilical cord. . . .
> Twice seven birth-goddesses had assembled,
> Seven produced males,
> Seven produced females.
> The birth-goddess, creatress of destiny —
> They completed them in pairs,
> They completed them in pairs in her presence,
> Since Mami conceived the regulations for the human race. . . .
> The tenth month arrived
> And the elapse of the period opened the womb.
> With a beaming, joyful face

And covered head, she performed the midwifery. . . .
"I have created, my hands have made it."

> — A fragmented Assyrian text, quoted by W. G. Lambert and
> A. R. Millard, in *Atra-Hasis: The Babylonian Story of the Flood*

The creation of the race of Adam by the Anunnaki had now begun. Evidence gathered from the ancient Sumerian writings indicates that the race of Adam found its conception and birth in the laboratories of physical beings later called the gods by the children of Adam. The process used to accomplish this task has been well described. The Nefilim in the East, and The Builders in the West were both masters of all the physical and astral sciences. The merging of two sets of cells to form a new creature was a task they were able to project and make manifest. Enki used the genes from a male member of the Anunnaki to fertilize the ovum taken from a female member of possibly a type like *Homo erectus*. This test-tube embryo was then placed in the womb of the birth-goddess, Ninki, who gave birth to the first Adam (primitive worker). The children of the Adam, male and female, created they them. With this successful genetic cross, the Anunnaki found out they were compatible with the daughters of men, the race of Adam.

> Wherefore have ye left the high, holy, and eternal heaven, and lain with women, and defiled yourselves with the daughters of men and taken to yourselves wives, and done like the children of earth, and begotten giants as your sons? . . . You were formerly spiritual, living the eternal life, and immortal for all generations of the world.
>
> — The Book of Enoch, in
> *The Sacred Books and Early Literature
> of the East*

The credibility of the Bible was badly shaken with the general public's acceptance of Darwin's theory of evolution. If mankind had evolved, then he surely was not created in an instant by an omnipresent god or gods who came to earth specifically to accomplish this task. But Darwin's theory has not been proven. The missing link between *Homo sapiens* and the pre-human form found evolving on Planet Earth has never been found, and never will be found. Man, as he exists today, is a special creation. We can agree with the Bible's position only in part. There was no omnipresent godhead involved in the actual creation of Adam. The Adam was created by a race of highly evolved, physical beings capable of space travel, and masters of the genetic sciences.

By putting the two genesis stories together, along with all the other legends and writings on tablets of clay, stone, gold, and copper, the incredible story of the gods and man emerges on Planet Earth. Mankind in the universe, and on this planet, was not just materialized in a moment by the living, omnipresent godhead. The pre-human creatures on Planet Earth were the product of evolution in time and space, just as Darwin and the others have concluded, but *Homo sapiens* is a special genetic creation by the gods, as the Bible states.

The evil and insidious powers of the Fallen Angels are constantly looking for new ways to destroy The Builders. The Forces of Darkness, in first discovering the hiding place of The Builders here on this remote planet four hundred thousand years ago, delivered an ultimatum: Surrender! Or be totally destroyed! The Dark Angels threatened to destroy every city on the face of the earth and the inhabitants therein by using their atomic weapons. The Builders had no choice but to let their fallen brethren land and proceed to occupy areas upon the earth. The great cities constructed by The Builders offered no protection against the awesome weapons of the invaders. The Fallen Angels began to take possession of and occupy different areas of the Near East.

The four races of man originally created by The Builders in the West were flourishing under the gentle guidance of the Elders. Mankind

At this point I wish to explain again that The Builders and the Nefilim are one and the same. The facts stated herein relate that a division occurred among The Builders (i.e., Nefilim) millenniums ago. This division was brought about by the fall of a small group of divine physical beings from Christ Consciousness back into self-consciousness and even further into simple-consciousness. The presence of these beings brought about the conception and birth of evil. One must believe that the Divine Being, Mother-Father, Creator of all which we see and know, did not, in fact, create evil. If the God we all hope to approach did, in fact, create evil, there is good reason to be fearful and full of doubt, for one hand may well reward and the other next destroy us without reason.

Yes, if our Creator God did project evil into the creation deliberately, we are, indeed, all lost and without any hope. I wish to state that the Divine Being I met face to face did not create evil, but rather allowed my vision to see and comprehend the truths contained in these writings. I say, in fact, there is no evil other than that projected by the Fallen Angels who were given free will by the Creator of all as divine sons and daughters to care for the creation. Mankind is, in fact, surrounded on this planet by these Fallen Angels who try in every way to prevent humanity from attaining Christ Consciousness, immortality, and freedom.

The Author

was now a fully developed, self-conscious, intelligent entity. The four races of man created in the genetic laboratories of The Builders were growing in numbers, and were now equipped to survive. The Ancients, observing this, taught humankind the great arts and sciences, astral and physical. The Book of Initiation, also called The Great Book of the Tree of Life, was part of their general education and development.

The Anunnaki, aware of this creation by The Builders, eventually made the decision to create a primitive worker to bear the yoke of their toil. These gods, however, decided to create their worker with certain restrictions. He was to look like the gods but be kept in ignorance. The Great Book of the Tree of Life was not to be given to him for his education. The Builders were able to administer to their people the Baptism of Fire emanating from Christ Consciousness. The Anunnaki were no longer able to do so. The result was unsatisfactory: the Adam had no direction in spiritual consciousness and therefore no real knowledge of right and wrong. Denied the spiritual Baptism of Fire and the illuminating teachings of the Tree of Life, this Adam was terribly unhappy.

Returning to the Bible (Genesis 2:7-8), we find the biblical deity planting a garden in Eden where he will place the man he has just created.

> And the Lord God took the man and put him into the garden of Eden to dress [work] it and keep it.
>
> — Genesis 2:15

The serpent, who was wise, whispered a message to Eve telling her of the great deception which was being used on both her and the man Adam by their unjust creators. Eve, on hearing the inner voice, relayed to Adam the message of the serpent force telling her of the Tree of Life within, the divine intelligence locked up in the central nervous system, and the fruit thereof. The inner voice told Eve of The Great Book of the Tree of Life, which described the central nervous system and its fruits and the organs of reproduction, which were only to be used to bring forth another creature like themselves. Eve convinced Adam that they might be

> As Professor Elliot Smith remarks, "The dragon [serpent] was originally a concrete expression of the divine powers of lifegiving, but with the development of a higher conception of religious ideals, it became relegated to a baser role, and eventually became the symbol of the powers of evil."
>
> John Michell, *The View Over Atlantis*

> The focal point of the narrative is the tree of knowledge. It is the tree "in the middle of the garden" and its fruit imparts to the eater the faculty of "knowing good and bad." . . . The Hebrew stem *yd'* signifies not only "to know," but more especially "to experience, to come to know." . . . The broad sense, then is to be in full possession of mental and physical powers.
>
> — E. A. Speiser, commenting in The Anchor Bible: Genesis

able to conceive a child, like the gods who created them. This was the forbidden fruit in which their creators had instructed them not to indulge.

The biblical god finds out, to his astonishment, that the Adam and the Eve have been trying to procreate without his permission and guidance. "And the eyes of them both were now opened and they knew they were naked. . . And Adam and his wife hid themselves from the presence of the Lord God amongst the trees of the garden. And the Lord God called unto Adam and said unto him 'Where art thou?' " (Genesis 3:7-9.)

Questioning Eve, the creator god learns that she has spiritual powers and that Divine Spirit Mother and Father herein described as the serpent, who was wise, was indeed communicating with the woman.

The god, furious at Eve and displeased with Adam, rages at them, describing to Eve that now she was going to give birth in pain, just like all the other creatures from which she had been taken. And for their seeking wisdom and listening to the serpent who is wise, they were going to have to survive in the wilderness outside of the garden and the city. This god, whoever he was, now realized that these creations could well develop beyond his, or the other gods' control. The biblical god may now have been reminded that what he and others had created, they were responsible for. The decision was made to place this creation out in the wilderness. Adam would no longer be able to pick the fruit growing in the creator's garden, but must learn how to till the soil by the sweat of his brow.

"Unto Adam also and his wife, Eve, did the Lord God make coats of skins and clothed them." (Genesis 3:21.) Here we are faced with the facts again, by the biblical statement, that no omnipresent God kills animals, skins them, tans the hides, and sews coats for a man and woman whom he must now turn out into the wilderness to fend for themselves.

Herein exists another biblical statement that there never was an omnipresent godhead involved in the creation of *Homo sapiens* in the Near East. The creators of Adam and Eve in the so-called Garden of Eden were the Anunnaki, a once highly evolved race of physical beings from another world in our galaxy. The gods now state to one another, as if very concerned about their efforts at creation of the Adam: "And the Lord God said, 'Behold, the man has become as one of us to know good and evil. And now, lest he put forth his hand and take also of the tree of life and live forever. . . .' " (Genesis 3:22.)

Here the commentator ends the discourse, for it is evident that Adam and Eve were too intelligent to be kept around at close quarters. Who were the gods who knew good and evil? They were the physical ones who gave birth to it by not following the divine laws and guidelines projecting the creation. The creators of Adam and Eve were fearful that they might find out the truth regarding their creation. They had not been given immortality (i.e., Christ Consciousness) like other creations existing on the earth; they were created just to be ignorant, obedient servants. "Therefore, the Lord God sent him forth from the Garden of Eden to till the ground from which he was taken." (Genesis 3:23.)

The Anunnaki became possessed with the image that someday the

Unfortunately, woman has been blamed for the fall of the race of Adam. It has been

race of Adam would rise up and overthrow them. This may well be true, with the help of The Builders, in the near future.

We have looked at the genesis of mankind in both the East and the West. I must now move on with this narration which further explains who the Fallen Angels were and who they have become; also, the return of The Builders and my personal contact with them throughout the years.

woman who tempted the man to eat of the Tree of Life if we allow ourselves to follow this biblical version. The truth of the matter may well be different if one seeks to know. It would seem that woman has been the scapegoat for the ills of mankind long enough. "Seek and ye shall find, knock and it shall be opened unto you," (i.e., meaning the truth of the creation of humankind).

— The Author

An intense energy field is descending from above — something gigantic is moving overhead and coming from the rear! . . . The old truck is rising up off the road.

CHAPTER 38

Return of The Builders

The summer of 1958 brought me back to the desert and Giant Rock for a short visit with my son Aarn and my old friend Daniel. Aarn's mother had remarried and he was going to have a home life which I had been unable to provide for him.

In the spring of 1959, I purchased a fence and patio supply business which I thought might turn a fair profit for me eventually. Unfortunately the owner had bid several large jobs too low, just to get the work. I found this out after I had made the purchase and began trying to complete the contracted jobs. Suffering large losses due to this underbidding, and unable to collect money owed to me, things became very tight. I came home exhausted each night. Unless I could raise some money somewhere or sell the business, I was going to fail in my endeavor.

Earlier in the year a business person had offered to loan me money for expansion. I approached him and offered to sell him the business for only a few thousand dollars. He accepted and we consummated the sale. I was free to go now, but the question was, where? The failure of my business, combined with the loss of my son, seemed to plunge me into a negative state of deep, dark depression, and I allowed this condition to possess me. The possibility of fulfilling any so-called spiritual mission now seemed as remote as the farthest star. What was I to do?

New Year's Eve of 1961 found me trying to sleep in a cheap hotel on Santa Barbara's skid row. I was without funds and had been unsuccessful in finding work. I sought the divine *Companions* I knew so well and longed to be with them. Outside, the blast of horns —

At this time in my life, I was greatly frustrated. The years spent in meditation and my subsequent illumination had not contributed to my ability to support myself. All endeavors towards financial success seemed doomed from the beginning; the material world and its pursuits seemed completely out of reach. The failure of my marriage and loss of my son rested heavily on

379

the shouting of people generated the excitement of a coming New Year. Sitting in a meditative posture, I sought diligently to find comfort with the *Companions*. I was unsuccessful. Even my meditations were now haunted with my failures. I was no longer able to function here in this earthly existence. Divine knowledge did not protect me from the negative influences now trying to possess me. I was down for the count and I did not feel like getting up again.

my conscience. Why was I unable to manipulate the physical world? Unknown to me, the approach of the so-named Dark Night of the Soul loomed ahead. It would surround me intermittently for the next twenty-five years and bring me many times to the brink of physical death.

— The Author

The Manifestation of The Builders

Alone, here I sit trying to control these negative thought-forms and images: the sound of many voices singing — they are drifting in upon me — but from where? Somewhere nearby, a large group of people must be celebrating. Could this be a gathering of New Year's Eve fun-seekers? The music, the melody, how strangely familiar it is, pulling at the roots of my heart. From where does this music proceed?

Drawing up the window, a busy street below revealed its grotesque images — the source is not out there. These sounds I hear come not from without but from within. I must strain my inner ear to hear, close off all senses now, perform the ancient arts of meditation. The music and voices are coming not from the world without but from the world within; yes, from inner space. All my outer senses are now closed; my inner sense conveys thousands of voices singing. The most profound, the most beautiful organ music I have ever heard, rising and falling in gigantic crescendos.

Memory bells are ringing loudly. I feel great rapture, the sounds — they are touching the inmost places, stimulating energies long dormant; yes, even forgotten. O soul of my delight, O companions thought long-lost! Yes, hearing the sounds of divine music once more. The vibrant voices of ancient spirits singing — the lyrics, repeated over and over again:

> Christ, our Saviour, Christ, our Saviour,
> Christ, our Saviour, is born today.
> Out in Judah, out west in Bethlehem,
> Christ, our Saviour, is born today.
> Don't be rude to him; don't be cruel to him;
> Don't forsake him Christ, our Lord.

Christ, our Saviour, Christ, our Saviour,
Christ, our Saviour, is born today.

This message reveals that all previous experiences of my life are now caught up in some incredible divine revelation! Yes, I am somehow a part of all that is transpiring. The night has departed; light is streaming through the window. Still O chorus, you sing on. You have not diminished throughout the night! Santa Barbara, my place of earthly birth, great rainbow shafts of astral light are shining down on you from the abundant heavens. O penetrating rays on rooftops, you alight! People are walking there on streets bathed in this splendor.

Somewhere on this day — could it be true — the Saviour, the Christ, has he come? — But where? Can other people see and hear this divine revelation? I must find out! Walking now on the streets of Santa Barbara, all these faces that pass by — do they hear, are they seeing as I? Do they know? I must stop them, ask them, is it true this music divine — this light so long sought — so overdue? Strange looks and hurried departures are their only answers. I am alone in all of this. The blue sky covers all above, the rising sun lights all below. A center exists out there in space; it is the source now playing forth. I spy thee now, O ship of my delight; you have revealed yourself to me.

Other thoughts spring forth: could I be going mad, perhaps, suffering from hallucinations? No one else sees or hears as I? My grief, my frustrations, my exhaustion, could this be the cause of all of this? No! It's too incredible, too real. Daniel Boone's friendly image now flashes before me. I must get to Daniel to tell him all, right away, the Saviour is born this day!

Nowadays people who have an experience of this kind are more likely to go running to the doctor or psychiatrist than to the theologian. I have more than once been consulted by people who were terrified by their dreams and visions. They took them for symptoms of mental illness, possibly heralding insanity, whereas in reality they were "dreams sent by God," real and genuine religious experiences that collide with a mind unprepared.

— Carl Jung, *Flying Saucers*

Driving south on Highway 101 in my old pickup truck. . . .

O chorus tremendous! O organ, your pulsating rhythms are shaking foundations here below, you fill the whole sky with sounds. I am not alone; a presence is here beside me. The image of a most exquisite girl, she fills my vision up. Look at her. Oh! How beautiful, how young, dressed in a flowing white gown trimmed with violet's brightness.

"Who are you? Please tell me what is happening. Was another Christ Child born this day?" Her face, those large, liquid eyes, the facets of a crystalline soul! Oh yes, one of the Immortals she must surely be! A sister from the outer and inner spaces.

"Where are you from? O friend divine, please speak."

Her soft reply is audible thought, floating on the ethers. "We are from over the rainbow. We are beings from another realm that once was your world also."

Tears are running abundantly down my cheeks — negative images, be dismissed from all past lonely years of life. Beautiful cities and divine events shine upon my inner screen; I must embrace the soothing balm of energy emanating from my radiant companion.

"All will be revealed to you shortly. You will soon be as you always were, my brother."

I must strain to remember now the fleeting image of an immense spherical vehicle, radiant like the sun, rainbows of color emanating outward like halos in all directions.

... according to one tradition, Orejona, the mother of mankind, landed in a spacecraft "brighter than the sun."

— Robert Charroux, *Mysteries of the Andes*

It is the divine chariot of The Builders. My companion — she is revealing images along with great healing. She gives me hope and faith divine.

Hours have gone by, I am driving subconsciously. Here is Banning already. How quickly we travel! My companion, I do not even know her name.

"My brother, call me Elithea (E-*lith*-e-ay). Shortly I will be leaving you. I must go back." She hesitates, now seeing I am upset. "We will be together again."

The radiant image of the beautiful being is disappearing before my eyes. This girl has the ability to project her consciousness into a third-dimensional image while she is actually at some other place. That place has to be the divine starship of the Ancients orbiting Planet Earth at this very moment.

An intense energy field is descending from above; it is covering my whole body. The inner senses struggle against it now; I am alone. The old self-conscious ego speaks: "You are in doubt, you are afraid."

There before me — images of how ill I have become, trying to live the life of the self-conscious human being. I am beaten down, a failure at the moment. I have allowed myself excesses in searching so diligently for a mate. I have forgotten my real purpose and almost succeeded in losing contact with The Great

The "resurrection" is not of the so-called dead, but of the living who are the "dead" in the sense of never having entered upon true life.

— Richard Bucke, *Cosmic Consciousness*

Central SöN-SüN. O my Christ, these negative thought patterns are surrounding me, with all my failures dancing in array.

There, the familiar territory of Yucca Valley — just ahead. Daniel's house is only half an hour away. The voice of intuition is speaking: "Something incredible is about to happen to you. Turn onto the Giant Rock Road; there's your previous life reflected in the desert landscape." A brilliant flash lights up the sky to the southwest. There, three brilliant objects move in a V formation — they are descending at tremendous speed. Now only a short distance away, they are traveling on a collision course with me! Hit the brakes, quick! They are going to collide with the truck — a tremendous explosion of light and energy!

My head strikes the steering wheel. Brightness before me — the truck and I are still together in one piece. There is no visible damage to either of us. What has happened? Fear — I feel you creeping up. What is taking place here? Consciousness, you register the laughter of thousands of voices coming from nearby. Am I the subject of this laughter? The three objects are gone, nowhere to be seen. The pavement feels solid beneath my feet. This whole display of energy is different than anything I have ever encountered before in this life. Something inconceivable is happening to me, and its source is hovering above me right now.

While returning home from work during the early morning hours of November 2, 1973, Mrs. Lyndia Morel had a Close Encounter while passing through Goffstown, New Hampshire. A UFO paced her car. It came so close that she could see a figure with slanted eyes staring at her from a transparent section of the craft. As she told investigator John Oswald: "I can remember seeing a pair of eyes staring at me and saying, 'Don't be afraid.' [not audibly but in her head]. I covered my eyes and yanked the wheel. I was petrified."

— Raymond E. Fowler,
The Andreasson Affair

The old dirt track to Giant Rock, part of it is now paved. There ahead — a long straight expanse of open road — not a living thing in sight. My faithful old truck, it still starts up. Daniel's house is now nearby. It's growing late; the sun is nearing the mountaintops off to the southwest. I still have another fifteen miles to cover before reaching Giant Rock. To the northwest, the familiar image of Goat Mountain stands forth, decorated in the crimson colors of sunset.

The energy around me is intensifying, bearing pressure upon the crown of my head. A vibration and a roar is approaching — something gigantic moving overhead and coming from the rear! Drive faster, it's catching you! A powerful force of energy — it's enveloping my body. Surely now every hair is standing at attention. Voices are giving commands from overhead.

The roar of something incredibly large. . . .

"Elithea, you are visible again here beside me. What is happening? What are you doing with me?"

The energy of her answer explodes in my head. "We are taking you home to put you in stone."

"What?"

"Yes, you have desired to go; your wish is being fulfilled. Mother *mu* is, at this moment, directly overhead."

Can I believe this? The old truck is rising up off the road. O Christ, O Father! Fear, you are gripping me from everywhere. The old ego is sounding a disturbance within; it's trying to persuade Elithea not to take me with them.

"My son — Aarn — I just can't leave him!" Every conceivable thought-form is charging forth in argument. The long stretch of road below — we have actually risen above the paved highway. I am airborne!

On December 12, 1967, at about 7:00 P.M., Mrs. Rita Malley was driving along Route 34 to Ithaca, New York . . . when a humming, domed disc-shaped object took control of her car and eased it into a field. . . . And a bright light flashed down from the object. . . . Then, abruptly, the car was eased back onto the road, where Mrs. Malley took control of it once again. . . . A detailed investigation of this CE III was written up in the July 1968 issue of *Science & Mechanics* by Lloyd Mallen.

— Raymond E. Fowler,
The Andreasson Affair

O Mother! This is too much to believe! I must see the source of this fantastic phenomenon. Something gigantic and spherical — burning bright, like fire.

The possibility of a purely psychological explanation is illusory, for a large number of observations point to a natural phenomenon, or even a physical one — for instance, those explicable by reflections from "temperature inversions" in the atmosphere. Despite its contradictory statements, the American Air Force, as well as the Canadian, consider the sightings to be "real," and have set up special bureaus to collect the reports. The "disks," however, the objects themselves, do not behave in accordance with physical laws but as though they were weightless, and they show signs of *intelligent guidance* such as would suggest quasi-human pilots. Yet the accelerations are so tremendous that no human being could survive them.

— Carl Jung, *Flying Saucers*

The chorus, again thousands of voices singing, fills all space above me and within. The proponderous notes and tones of the incredible organ blends with the voices rising in song:

Ship the oars for home, Boys,
Ship the oars for home.

We'll be back to get you, on a sunny morn.
On a bright new dawning, 'neath the rising sun,
We'll be there beside you, but now we'll make a run.

"Back to Jupiter!" A command rings out.

What's this! My old truck and I on our way to Jupiter! Is this true! I seem to have no choice or control of the matter. That roar is intensifying. The propulsion drives of this gigantic vehicle are accelerating, filling the desert landscape with earth-shattering sound waves. Oh my Lord, this can't be real! Is this actually happening to me?

A soft voice speaks. "We are taking you home to put you in stone, as is the custom of our people. You must remember this."

A vivid mental image flashes — hundreds of gigantic stone figures standing in silence in a faraway place. "Hey, I am really scared!"

"No need to fear. All things will come to your remembrance soon."

"But I don't want to leave now! I have to finish my work here!"

She won't answer me; finally she speaks. "You projected your desire to no longer exist here on this planet; is that not correct?"

"Yes, it is."

More silence!

"But I have never really talked with my son, Aarn; and Dad — he will miss me. I must say goodbye to him."

A loud reply from above: "You will remain with us for a time. If you receive our instructions during this period, more time will be allotted to you."

A brilliant light — it's bursting in my face. O, my Christ! I am losing consciousness.

Stillness — only stillness.

Elithea was no longer beside me. I was still sitting in the old truck, right in the middle of the highway. The headlights were on, the engine was running.

This was too much! I must be going mad! I must be! O Mother, Father, help me! I began driving again toward Daniel Boone's house. There was the old sign ahead pointing the way to Giant Rock Airport. I made the turn off the pavement onto the rough dirt track.

There is no way to prove that this experience occurred in the so-called third dimension. I am relating the events only as they happened and are recorded in my memory.

— The Author

I felt exhausted and my consciousness was fading in and out. I just had to stop and rest, so I pulled the truck over and stopped. No sooner did the sounds of the truck engine fade away into the surrounding darkness than they were replaced by the steady humming sound of the giant ship.

I was weak and wobbly as I stepped out of the truck to look for the awesome vehicle. Glancing toward the east, I saw the image hovering in the sky over Goat Mountain. The ship was moving slowly now to the south and it was larger than anything I had ever seen before. I suddenly realized that I was standing in the very same area where I had stood years before. Yes — that night when the ships did a dance in the sky above Goat Mountain. My thoughts were interrupted as a voice shouted my name.

To this day the vision, as well as the audible impressions, are so fixed in my memory that they of themselves outshine other events in my life recorded in the everyday real world, however real the everyday world might be.

— The Author

"Look now, Brother. We are going to put on a demonstration for you again. Prepare yourself."

Three brilliant objects move in a V formation — descending at tremendous speed

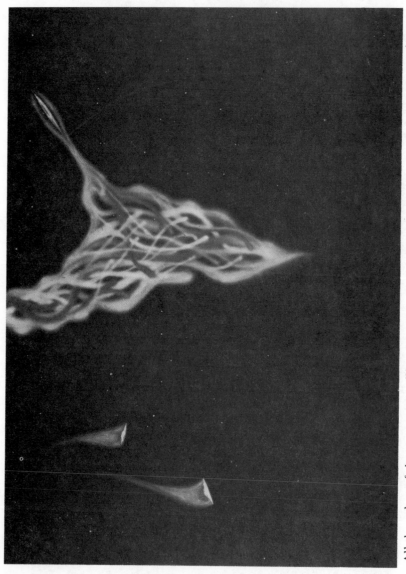

All the colors of the spectrum, trailing forth behind the divine chariots, slowly floated earthward like a bejeweled rainbow fog.

CHAPTER 39

The Initiation in the Desert

A promised demonstration — what could I expect now? The words echoed away into the desert silence. Shivering and alone, I reached for an old overcoat Master Yogananda had given me long ago. Sitting down in the sand, I began to prepare myself for whatever was forthcoming. My head — would it burst under the pressure? Cold fear ran through me with the shivers again. My senses detected negative forces gathering around about me. "You are going insane, bricklayer. You must doubt the authenticity of everything you see; it is all a dream," they jeered.

Looking toward the east, a bright orange sphere appeared. "When was this show to begin?" I wondered. The ship was hovering in the darkening eastern sky just south of Goat Mountain. The dry desert air, alive with static energy, produced a violet-blue aura around each yucca plant and joshua tree. A loud voice cried out; my name resounded from everywhere, filling the whole vault of the heavens with sound.

"Norman, Norman! For a time we will be with you, but tonight your initiation must begin. This you must complete and if you succeed, you will be able to see, hear, and converse with us at will. On your behalf, we will never lose

> Verily, we set it down on the Night of Power! And what shall make thee know what the Night of Power is? The Night of Power is better than a thousand months! The angels and the spirits descend therein, by the permission of their Lord with every bidding.
>
> — Mohammed, Koran

contact with you. You will have the ability to project and receive audible thought-forms and images over vast distances."

Hearing this, I now affixed my gaze on the bright orange sphere still hovering in the distance. As interior vision granted me entrance, I began to feel connected to the image.

"Yes, Brother, you are residing with us now in a vortex of force emanating from our mother *mu*. For more than twelve thousand years we have been waiting nearby. But now, behold new arrivals." Toward the east two more spheres of light came flashing downward toward the stationary ship. Just as they were about to collide, the radiant images rose upward like an arrow, leaving rainbows of colored light streaming downward from behind. Now all three ships were racing and performing together. What a stupendous light show in the heavens they did weave!

The maneuvers intensified as the three ships chased each other across the dark night sky. Flipping over and over, they fell spinning downward toward the desert floor. Would they crash? No! They accelerated upward into the heavens again. All the colors of the spectrum trailing forth behind the divine chariots slowly floated earthward, like a bejeweled rainbow fog. O colors magnificent to behold! O show, end not so quickly!

Now once more alone on the desert sand, O wonderment of all transpired, will you return again?

A big roll of canvas in my tool box served me for a bed. Spread out upon the desert sand I found out all too soon there would be little sleep this night. Lying covered up, my name was again called out, coming from all space and ringing down on all spirits below.

"Norm Paulsen, Norm Paulsen has done this for you!"

"But what have I done?"

"This meeting was made possible by you; the unseen spirits are gathered here, observe them all around you."

Closing my eyes, I saw the astral world of inner space suddenly sparkling with luminosity. I was surrounded by thousands of beings of all sizes and descriptions, they — watching, listening, and waiting.

Again a voice resounded, "Before your initiation is complete, they will receive the messages they need to hear."

"Where is Elithea?" What comfort she gives.

"I am here," came a soft reply. "Brother, you must sit upright in silence now."

The Initiation Begins

I must assume a meditative posture, facing the east; the three vessels are moving slowly toward me. "Are you going to land now?"

Elithea's soothing voice again: "Brother, you must be calm; the initiation has begun."

Something is descending from above. A soft fluttering and flapping, like wings, is coming upon me from behind. Could this

A bright light source came into view. . . . A vague form slowly became more distinct. Astonished, Betty observed a huge bird standing directly in front of the dazzling light source. . . .

be some kind of heavenly bird? Yes! It is. It's trying to land on my shoulders. But what kind of bird is this?

"I am the sacred bird of initiation long known by ancient spirits." This whispered utterance is coming from the feathered creature now sitting on my shoulders. "Brother, you must be quiet now. Don't move; we are placing a divine talisman within your energy field. This object will help you through your ordeals ahead on earth."

"It felt like something was piercing every cell in my body. . . . I understand now that I went through an initiation of some kind. . . . There is doubt in my mind that even you really believe me about an experience such as that, because it is unbelievable."

— Raymond Fowler, *The Andreasson Affair*, interviewing Betty Andreasson after a UFO encounter

A probing sensation in the center of my head — be still, O flesh, you feel no real pain. Faith I must have now. Above all, quietness, yes stillness, you must prevail. This winged spirit is monitoring my thoughts. Now it's spreading its wings, it's covering my head and face. I feel consciousness receding, I cannot hold on, I am spinning away. . . .

Here before me — the beauty of the clear starlit sky. How long have I been absent? There is no answer — only peace, utter peace.

Again a voice: "You have passed through one part of the initiation. Now behold the consecration of the life force by the sacred ring of fire; that rare event not performed by human hands — shortly it will come."

Oh! My head, it's bursting with the roar of many conversations. Their source is inner space, their destination other ships and stations far away. I can almost see them. I now have the ability to communicate with The Builders directly. My thoughts, like theirs, are made audible; my own voice is now heard on their vibratory energy spectrum. How incredible! Audible and visual thought transference, their actual means of communication! This is total instant communication for all members of the races of The Builders. Yea, not one sparrow falls not known by all. This is indeed the natural ability of the Angel Men and Women, to communicate with each other as they manifest in and around the creature bodies called hu-man.

As the hours of the night moved on, I was tested and retested by the Elders. The consecration of my life force was conducted by Divine Spirit within a ring of fire. This is part of the ancient mystical initiation between the Christed Angel Man and Woman and the self-conscious creature called hu-man. The long hours of the night now faded into a golden dawn. Wrapped in the old canvas, I had survived the night. The quickening dawn brightened up the heavens; I perceived no divine chariots in sight.

The old truck started right up. Daniel Boone and Giant Rock were only a few miles away. Driving along, the abilities to see, hear, and speak in the Spirit were present. I attempted to sing a song. Words formed in my consciousness, and I projected them strongly outward.

> The gate was opened to me that in one quarter of an hour I saw and knew more than if I had been many years at a university.
>
> — Jacob Behmen, *Works of Jacob Behmen*, Vol. I

The tones and lyrics of one of Yogananda's chants filled the heavens above with sound — my sound, my thoughts made audible.

" 'My Lord, I will be thine always, my Lord, I will be thine always.' Do you hear me, Father?"

The profound experiences of the last few days were flooding my mind. Initially, I had come to see my old friend, Daniel.

Now a familiar voice entered into my thoughts. "Brother, remember we are committed to return to this planet with the forces of Christ Consciousness, the light of the first begotten SöN-SüN. Do you remember? We are here in force now to deliver the final ultimatum to the forces known as Lucifer and Satan. These evil beings have held

> When the entities apparently spoke through Betty to us, I deliberately asked them religious-oriented questions, through Betty, to see what their response would be. . . . "Have they anything to do with what we call the second coming of Christ?" Betty: "They definitely do."
>
> — Raymond Fowler, *The Andreasson Affair*, interviewing Betty Andreasson under hypnosis after a UFO encounter

possession of the earth for more than twelve thousand years. During this time the Forces of Darkness have systematically destroyed all records on this planet which speak of The Builders and the golden civilizations they manifested and dwelt in. This destruction includes buildings, statuary, libraries, temples, and people. The spiritual path has been obliterated here on earth. Anyone who dares to follow the ancient pathway immediately becomes a target for the Forces of Darkness. These dark spirits do not want to let the self-conscious hu-man being evolve into Christ Consciousness on earth as preordained by divine law and guidelines.

"Mankind on Planet Earth is held in simple- and self-consciousness to wait on and entertain the Forces of Darkness and all their hosts. Many Sons and Daughters from the ranks of The Builders who have returned to earth to help illuminate humankind have been destroyed. They are put to death by evil inventions and practices so horrible they defy description. Brother Norman, your life from this day forth will be in jeopardy. This meeting with your old friends is being monitored by the Evil Ones who will now use every way conceivable to destroy you. They now know why you were brought here and what your mission is.

"Ten years from this time, the projections you have seen for communities of people will begin to materialize. Many of your old friends have already entered rebirth on earth to help you. During the time you will be with us, all the ancient records will be refreshed in your memory. Every question will be answered; nothing will be held back. You must stand strong — remember, you are not alone. For the next twenty years of your existence here, you will be under constant attack. It will be very hazardous."

The familiar dry lake, and now Giant Rock, came into view. The steady pulsating hum of a divine chariot was following me. Daniel Boone's abode, the old round house, was my first stop. He was home; his familiar figure was standing there in the doorway.

"Wow, Brother, it's been a long time."

"Boone, I have much to tell you!" I attempted to relate the whole incredible story, watching the reactions on Daniels' face as I described the events in detail. While speaking, the steady, pulsating drone of the mother *mu* sounded overhead. As I brought the whole story up to the present, Daniel looked at me in disbelief.

"Boone, the ship is right overhead, don't you hear it?" Jumping up, Daniel quickly stepped outside. "There, Boone! There's the ship! It's right over the dry lake at the end of the runway." At this moment vision conveyed the brilliant image of the divine chariot into my consciousness.

"Brother, I hate to say this, but I don't see a thing!" Boone's statement was a shock and difficult to receive. Again doubt gripped me; fear was standing by my side. Was this actually a dream, was I hallucinating? Was my mind disintegrating? "Norm, I'm really sorry, but I can't believe all of this you're telling me. You say there's a ship over there! Well, I don't see one."

Could I believe my old friend Daniel? If he didn't see or hear the ship with his spiritual development, then who could?

"How long has it been since you've eaten anything, Norm?"

"Look, Boone, they are taking care of me. I don't need any food."

"The hell they are! You look half dead!"

True, I had not eaten anything for quite some time. How long had it been? "Can I stay here with you for a time, Brother?"

Boone looked quite upset. "Norm, I can't have you around Sandra and the kids the way you are looking, acting and talking."

"Okay, Boone, I understand."

Driving away, I could not accept Boone's attitude. Why didn't he hear

393

and see also? As I waved a final farewell salute toward him, extreme grief settled over me. Then a great and overwhelming doubt pervaded my thoughts. Was I going insane? My old friend, he did not see or understand! "Oh Christ! I don't want to live here any more!"

I was barely able to keep the old truck on the road. Persecution was after me in hot pursuit. Where could I go from here? Unconsciously, I turned toward the northwest. The tears would not stop running from my eyes.

> Blessed are they which are persecuted for righteousness' sake: for their's is the kingdom of heaven.
> — Matthew 5:10

My physical body was not going to be able to function much longer; exhaustion was overtaking me. Negative voices were back again, suggesting that I take my own life in various horrible ways. I was caught between two forces which were trying to gain control of me, the Forces of Good and the Forces of Evil.

Loud words rang out from all space: "Go to Emerson Dry Lake."

The road to Emerson Dry Lake was not too far ahead. Boone and I had prospected there several times. In my memory, it was a strange and lonely place. I turned the old truck down the rough dirt track toward the lake. Whatever was going to happen to me would now happen at Emerson Dry Lake.

An ancient Egyptian image of the sacred bird of the higher self — the soul

The shape of this colossal ship reminds me of pictures of stepped pyramids in Central and South America. . . . Two figures are emerging; they are descending the stairs toward me.

CHAPTER 40

Encounter at Emerson Dry Lake

Emerson Dry Lake — approximately five miles long and three miles wide. Surrounded by multicolored, jagged peaks of wild and ruthless rock on the north, west and south, only an easterly approach is available. Etched in my memory, this place could well replace the terrain of some abandoned planet in a forgotten region of space. Abandoned mines, collapsed wooden structures and rusted machinery are strewn "hither and yon." During the gold rush days, large quantities of gold were mined from these barren hills.

I will cross the southeastern edge of the cracked, dry clay and proceed to the northern side. A natural windbreak — there — revealed behind large boulders! I will park the truck up next to them. And now the silence thunders in upon me. Yes, this is the end of the road for me, in more ways than one — this area so dry, so inhospitable, not even lizards and snakes live here. I have no food, but the large canvas water bag is full. First I must construct a shelter out of scraps of wood nearby, then I will sit until I have some answers and some direction.

The Ancient Ones conducted long fasts in the desert. My, how I marvel after them. Here! Now I myself in a similar position: but oh, such stillness! I am so dreadfully alone. A survey I must make: a few clothes and some mementos — all of which add up to nothing. In the eyes of this self-conscious world, I am indeed a total failure. The die is cast; I have no more alternatives to consider. I will make a bed for myself inside the unfinished shack

Taken by the sweetness of knowing the truth of the things concealed in heaven, and finding no other pleasure dearer to him in life, he left all other wordly care and gave himself to this alone, and, that no part of philosophy might remain unseen by him, he plunged with acute intellect into the deepest recesses of theology . . . caring nothing for heat or cold, or watchings, or fastings, or any other bodily discomforts, by assiduous study he came to know of the divine essence and of other separate intelligences all that the human intellect can comprehend.

— *Encyclopaedia Britannica*, ninth edition, on Dante, quoted by Richard Bucke, in *Cosmic Consciousness*

— "a few clapboards overhead," as Whitman once said. At least I have a windbreak — tomorrow maybe even a roof.

O Divine Spirit! Hear my prayers and give me guidance! The events of the past few days stagger my reason. Could I be going insane? Is this my imagination plus hallucination's wrath? Have I strained the natural flow of thoughts and burst through the dikes permitted to earthly life? Straining upon the mystical door, have I allowed supernatural forces entry into this dimension where entry is forbidden? Can I believe the voices and the visions running rampant in my soul? O Christ! Help me now!

An army of dark and negative tormentors have followed me to this final outpost. Foul language and rank hatred are boiling on the surface of what is left of my energy. I need sleep so badly. Yes, I could sleep for a week if left alone. In the shack now, I lie down and cover up with canvas. This day is over for me. Come, sleep, carry me away from this dark abyss. . . .

How long has this sleep lasted? I have no way of knowing. Time is out of joint; days and nights are added one to the other — a continuous existence, the Eternal Now. The water in the canvas bag is my only real comfort; it has not diminished. Either sitting or lying now, it makes no difference, the physical and the astral dimensions seem joined; both reveal their images at once. Demonic hosts of darkness, you surround me on all sides. Any efforts to meditate or pray are overwhelmed in unison by your chorus of negative insults. Those limbo spirits are speaking of Lucifer, their master: "He is coming shortly to destroy you, Paulsen!"

There now, glimpses of the evil adversary and the forces he commands; in this strange light they are able to manifest. The astral sky above me is as red as blood. Those hideous, distorted spirits cover the whole dark and barren landscape of rocks and crevices.

. . . the devils assaulted him with violent temptations; . . . the most terrible of all these pains was that of scrupulosity and interior desolation, in which he seemed to see hell open, ready to swallow him up.

— Alban Butler, *The Lives of the Fathers, Martyrs and Other Principal Saints,* on St. John of the Cross

Oh, years of my life on earth, you form a parade before me; every mistake I have ever made is pointed out and magnified by the demons.

Yes, my spirit has journeyed to the center of The Great Central SöN-SüN. I have entered the vast and endless primordial sea of life and energy. I know my Divine Parents, Mother and Father, face to face. I have seen the magnificent beauty of the Divine Creation filled with light and love, that special place where true Sons and Daughters of Spirit exist.

"But where is all of this now, Paulsen, you poor fool? It seems to us your vision only transmits a dimension now called hell. Why don't you give up and join us?"

"Jeer on, you demented fiends! I will never join you."

Oh yes, I do behold those inquisitive, fallen sons and daughters who have allowed themselves to be lured by desire into the net of negative static darkness. There, deprived of light, they have given birth to a center within themselves where only darkness exists. Like bats in the twilight, the darker it is, the better they see. That which was never meant to happen in the divine order of creation has happened! Divine Spirit's own children have disobeyed the laws which govern the expanding spheres of creation. There they are, standing before me!

"Not thy will, Father and Mother, but rather *our* will be done! *We* shall conquer the whole galaxy and storm the heavenly places with destruction."

My vision is penetrating the very deepest regions of this unnatural dimension they have created. One by one I am going to see all of the Spirits of Evil in these regions and finally encounter their leader face to face. Of this I am sure. My meditations are revealing the true facts of what is transpiring here on earth — an awesome spectacle fraught with practices unmentionable. Yes, I am to enter the regions of hell to penetrate the enemy camp. I am now going on a journey in another direction to the very center of evil darkness to try to help destroy the hub on which it spins.

Vision after vision tumbles before my weary consciousness. Directly now, I see how the evil, insidious forces have gained their dark births. The destruction of Spirit's children, the radiant Builders, and their divine civilizations — there revealed in wondrous visions. The first attack on The Builders by the Fallen Angels unleashed a storm of destruction and devastation that has never ceased to expand, even to this moment. For more than a million years my spirit has struggled trying to defend the remnants of this noble race. Yes, I am a warrior. How incredible that I am locked into the struggle to save the four races of The Builders from annihilation in this galaxy. The Builders fled for their lives before the evil spirits of destruction. The decision to stand and fight was made more than a million years ago. This decision created the need for warriors. I had stood forth as a volunteer in the growing ranks. My spirit has been moving for millenniums in the midst of battle and destruction.

My deep meditations are now revealing answers to that which before had no answer. The pathway ahead is narrow, dark and treacherous. On every side and down the middle, circumstances and conditions exist   I know the Path: it is strait and narrow. It is like the edge of a sword. I rejoice to walk on it. I weep when I slip. God's word is: He who strives never perishes. I have implicit faith in

399

which might trap and destroy me. Analyzing all of these visions and answers, I see the pathway ahead, finally dimly visible through the dark haze.

that promise. Though, therefore from my weakness I fail a thousand times, I will not lose faith.

— Mahatma Gandhi

How long have I been without contact with The Builders? O strength, rise up within. Project your new ability, your audible thoughts, toward the image of Elithea. There she exists so vividly in the hall of memory.

"Are you still nearby, oh friendly spirit?"

"Yes, Brother," she answers me. "We are still nearby. Your reactions to the visions have been positive. The initiation of your present earthly form is now complete; you have seen the fallen ones revealed in the light of truth."

Great relief is flooding through me. O comfort, settle down with me for the moment. I am weak; I can hardly move my body; oh, so stiff. Perhaps some water, ice cold from the chill desert air, will help. Drink, drink until you are filled. Oh, how sweet this water is. Oh, how good it tastes and feels. What a miracle this moisture represents.

I feel strengthened enough to crawl from beneath this ill-fashioned sentry shack. It's late in the afternoon; there the sun is settling behind those hills to the west. I must build a fire and warm up my stiff body. There are no matches. The cigarette lighter in the truck will provide fire to light some paper; old boards from the mine shaft nearby will create a big one. This fire is warming as well as cheerful. My tortured spirit feels relief.

"Brother, we are planning a surprise for you tonight. What would you like most?"

"To go aboard and lay hold of the images projecting your voices."

"Brother Norman, this is a difficult maneuver for us to perform; however, we will do it for you at this time."

"What! Do you really mean it? Are you going to land this time?"

"Yes, we will."

"Tonight?"

"Yes, tonight!"

Wow! My spirit is moving with new life! The fire needs more wood. I walk out on the dry lake for a distance; there's my solitary flare blazing like a navigation beacon in the darkness.

"Do you see my fire here below?"

"Yes, we are approaching you from the northwest."

Are they really coming this time? Three bright orange spheres appear over the mountains to the northwest. The ship in the center is beginning to descend toward me. The steady descent of the divine chariot reminds me of other times and other places — yes, such a spectacle as this I have beheld before!

The ship is only half a mile away. That thunderous pulsating hum is filling the empty vessel of Emerson Dry Lake with sounds never heard here before. This dried and parched surface is trembling beneath my feet as that huge and brilliant image settles toward the center of the lake bed. Clouds of dust and tumbleweeds are blowing outward in all directions from beneath the ship; it's making a final descent.

Run, quick! Catch it before it escapes like the fabric of some illusive dream. I must lay hands upon it! A loud voice yells at me, "Don't come any closer until we have made our landing secure and can assist you." Standing here, I must be in a dream. I implore you, O eyes, please interpret to my consciousness the true quality of this vision you now behold.

The hull of the vessel is transparent, like glass, with all the colors of the spectrum shimmering and reflecting through it. Long minutes are passing; nothing is moving. There, flights of stairs are projecting through the surface of the hull from the lower leading edge all the way up to the huge dome that crowns the top of the vessel. The shape of this colossal ship reminds me of pictures of stepped pyramids in Central and South America.

Its size — it's so enormous — I can only speculate as to its actual dimensions. Two figures are emerging from the dome; they are descending the stairs toward me. Look closer, the stairs are in motion and descending with the two entities. Both are wearing white garments.

The smaller figure is Elithea, and this time she seems quite real! The male figure is extending his right palm upward and forward in a gesture of greeting. At last it seems I am looking at the physical reality of The Builders, but am I really? Are they real flesh and bone, just as I? And their divine chariot, it looks as hard as steel, but is it? I cannot tell. O dream, surely now you will not deny me!

Remember, The Builders are masters of all the sciences, astral and physical. Their ability to project their thoughts, images, and consciousness over vast distances is a natural ability. Dad had demonstrated this many times. Are they doing this again?

Elithea is the first to speak. "We must pass you through the orientation chamber."

I feel very dizzy. A high-pitched ringing is enveloping me. I am falling down, down, down, into unconsciousness. Brightly colored lights are flashing in my face. Consciousness has returned. The walls of a small room surround me. They are alabaster white with colors of the spectrum shining

401

on the surface like mother-of-pearl. I am lying on my back, a couch beneath me; overhead a small, brilliant sphere in the ceiling changes color; it moves through the spectrum. With every color change it bathes me in warm, soothing energy.

A figure enters, and speaks: "Your physical body is not well. We are recharging every cell, as you can see, with radiant life force. I am glad to report that all of your energy centers are functioning through all of the eight vibratory dimensions. Also, there are no blockages in your Tree of Life from any of the twelve vibrations of consciousness. Soon you will feel much better mentally and physically."

"Yes, I am feeling better; in fact, ecstatic energies are flowing through my nervous system."

"Brother, will you follow me? I am instructed to take you to our Elder."

"Yes, I will." A curved passageway lies ahead.

I am walking on solid footing, but is this a dream? Will this experience suddenly vanish and push me back into the lonely existence I so detest? O Lord, let it be real; let me be here for a while. Everything I observe seems so familiar. Yes, surely I have been here before; I know this vision must be true.

"This vehicle is constructed of a nonferrous material superior in strength to the finest steel produced on earth. There are no ferrous metals used on or in this vessel. Much of the superstructure and many of the fixtures are constituted of gold, silver, and copper, as you know them." My guide is answering some of the hundreds of questions I wanted to ask.

We pause now for a moment; a panel suddenly opens, revealing a large, circular room. There in the center of the room sits a man; his features are familiar. Another individual is sitting beside him on a long semicircular divan that faces that large, clear, oval portal. Beneath that portal and in front of a long, low desk, three other figures are seated. My guide attempts to explain, "The navigator is on the left, the observer, or captain, is in the center, and the communications projector and receiver is on the right. All three figures are in control of the vessel."

Moving toward the two figures in the center of the room — images of star systems shine at me through the large portal. Wow! We are no longer on Mother Earth — those are distant stars and nebulae out there. I am in fact, on a divine chariot, moving through space!

"You wanted to come with us, didn't you?"

"Come with you! I had no idea! We are really out in space; you have taken me with you. Oh, joy of joys." Ecstasy is welling up around me.

The familiar Elder speaks. "We are out in the eternal sea and near the orbit of the earth's moon."

The floor or the walls of this room are moving around, it seems. Through the portal shines the image of Mother Earth, now no bigger than a ripe, blue plum.

Oh, how beautiful! How fantastic! I am reliving things that I have somehow always known deep within. Upon entering the hu-man creature body, I had lost contact with my only true home, infinite space. Yes, I am home now; this is where I really belong.

> In worldly matters they all are, or nearly all, as little children, while in spiritual things they are as gods.
>
> — Richard Bucke,
> *Cosmic Consciousness*

The two figures are rising; they salute me with upraised, open palms. I must return their greeting. The familiar figure is inviting me to sit next to him.

"It is divine will that brings us together again. Your life on earth has been difficult, and there will be more suffering ahead before you complete this mission you volunteered for."

"But who are you, sir?"

"I am one of the ancient Elders of the white race. Names mean nothing and continually change. As you already know, we are of one mind and consciousness in the eternal priesthood of our ancient forefathers. The promised return made by the hu-man called Jesus, who received the Baptism of Fire and was anointed the Christ, has begun and involves all of us. While you were unconscious and resting, we programmed your memory cells with all the answers and directions to perform your mission successfully. How you use this power in the future is now in your control. The horror of war which has destroyed Divine Spirit's projections in this galaxy rages on."

This ancient Brother reaches out and touches my cheek gently with his finger: "You must go to a dentist and have your teeth cared for. The unnatural diet you ate as a child has caused problems. We have given your inner body new strength; you must convey it to the creature body by effort.

"Divine Spirit Mother and Father love you, as you well know. Your journey to the center of The Great Central SöN - SüN is the final flight path of our ancient Elders. The fact that Divine Spirit has revealed its presence to you from beyond the Sphere of Creation and within the vast, eternal, primordial sea is unparalleled in our recent records. That is why you are here and not elsewhere. You are a member of that eternal and immortal priesthood created by our Divine Parents, therefore, Their Will be Done!

"For the next twenty years of your life here on earth you are going to feel the full power of our adversaries. The captain of that Dark Host will try to destroy you at every moment. I caution you not to be reckless but move only after confirmation is given to you by Divine Spirit. Our story must be told on earth for the Dark Ones have destroyed all records pertaining to The Builders and our civilizations that existed here. You, my son, will record my words of today in script. This I perceive! Enough has been said! Is there anything further you wish from us now?"

"No, sir."

Music is filling the room. The incredible sound of divine instruments fills my ears — now a chorus of voices coming from the very walls! Yes, from everywhere!

"Our mother *mu* herself is the loudspeaker for our entertainment. As we sail the seas of space, moving from one island world to another, we sing and make music as we go." Tears of joy fill my eyes as many voices join in singing, "Christ, our Savior, is born today. . . ." Was it from this ship that I heard the projected music and voices on New Year's Eve?

"Yes, my son, this is true." The Elder Brother stands. "Come, and I will show you through our mother *mu*." This Elder whom I follow must be the supreme commander of this starship and of all the other mother *mus* in this solar system.

"Let us go into the garden."

"The garden?"

"Yes, my son, the garden."

Dad's stories of the *Golden Dawn*, in which he had described lawns, flowers, trees, and gardens — will they find confirmation here?

"Your earthly father remembered well his own mother *mu*, my son."

We stand on steps and move upward, passing other levels; figures are at work creating images and objects. "We are able to produce all of our needs here within the environment of this vessel. There are game rooms and gymnasiums, as you can observe." We reach the highest level; a pleasant, humid atmosphere is pressing in. Above me, the vault of a large dome spreads out overhead reflecting heat and light like noonday brilliance on earth. A small sphere affixed to the apex at the highest point radiates its brilliance upon green plants of every description and variety.

Walking down a path — fruits and vegetables are growing in great abundance with flowers embracing borders on either side. Emerging from a small grove of fruit trees, the laughter of children echoes around us. Here before me — a beautiful pool, with green grasses upon its banks, children splashing in its waters.

"As you can see, we have created the environment of a tropical, watery planet within the sphere of this ship. Here we function self-sufficiently, able to produce all of our needs."

Suddenly the warmth and light vanish. Above, the vault of the dome becomes transparent. There, the rim of the galaxy and nearby stars are casting their faint glow, collecting shadows among leaves of plants.

"Eventide now prevails in the garden. My son, this is now a place of meditation for our family when solitude is needed. We, as caretakers of the galaxy, bring the many varieties of food-producing plants, herbs, and trees to other worlds which are capable of producing organic life-forms. Then we seed, plant, and gather any new varieties of life-forms which have come forth from Mother Divine's projections.

"Come, let us observe the power source which makes all this possible. We will descend to our vessel's propulsion systems which can propel us beyond the speed of light if the need arises. As I told you before, we can attain light speed while hovering. This is accomplished by increasing the velocity of rotation within our propulsion drive units. As the drive units accelerate, we begin to traverse the radiant energy spectrum, moving from infrared to ultraviolet. The entire mass of this vehicle is converted back into radiant life-energy particles as we traverse the spectrum. An outside observer on the physical plane sees the ship's image change in color from bright red through orange and into gold; then bright green, followed by blue and violet. At this point we vanish from your so-called third dimension in a flash of light as brilliant as any sun.

"The level containing the propulsion drive units spans the entire diameter of our ship's hull. Bridge works extend outward on eight segments reaching to the hull's perimeter. My son, the propulsion systems which drive this vessel are patterned after the perfect design of The Great Central SöN-SüN. The application of vortexes by Divine Spirit on its infinite body of life force, as you know, generated the first ignition of light. The visible expanding Sphere of Creation and all forces and images existing within are projected outward from the center of The Great Central SöN-SüN.

"A spinning, centripetal vortex projected into Spirit's infinite body of life-energy, produced a whirlpool. This thought-produced whirlpool began drawing Spirit's life-energy particles toward its center. Spirit's life-energy particles moving toward this center created directional lines of force whose drawing effects generate magnetic attraction. Magnetism has thus perpetuated a flow of life-energy particles into the vortex from the eternal sea of life-energy surrounding this genesis. The accumulation of masses of life-energy particles at this center of vortex, under tremendous pressure and friction, produced light. The masses of life-energy particles were now shaped by Divine Consciousness into the images and forces desired by Spirit.

"The propulsion unit on board this ship operates on the same divine principles. To create a vortex which would operate in the microcosm of this dimension in a similar manner, we must spin a physical object which is, or can be, magnetized. Spinning a magnetized object would create a vortex which would induce the free energy in space to move toward its center. As the energy particles from space are drawn into the vortex by magnetic attraction, they take orbital positions around the center of the magnetic core. The accumulation of energy particles around the spinning magnetic center generate a high-density magnetic field. With this condition we can create two poles, one at the center of the magnetic core, and one on the perimeter of the magnetic field. Here we can perpetually draw off energy in the form of positive and negative currents. This is the principle on which our propulsion units operate.

"Any type of physical material which has been magnetized will generate and discharge current if the object is rotated. The rotation of permanent magnets will, therefore, generate electrical current. The higher the velocity of rotation, the greater the flow of energy. Our propulsion unit consists of two large rotating discs. Facing each other, one disc will spin clockwise while the other spins counterclockwise. By rotating our two discs we have created two spinning vortexes.

"The outside perimeter of each disc carries twelve magnets. The simultaneous clockwise and counterclockwise rotation of these two discs creates two spinning magnetic fields. Here we can draw off current from the central hubs on which they spin and the rotating outside perimeters. The generation of a perpetual flow of energy from each disc will continue as long as the discs rotate. The space between the two discs is the area in which both spinning vortexes contact each other. It is here that the two spinning magnetic fields create a gyroscopic effect on each other. The magnetic fields generated by the two discs are so intense that any other gravitational or magnetic lines of force are bent around this force field. Therefore, the object which contains the generators of this magnetic and gyroscopic effect creates its own basic gravity. The object, or in this case, the vessel, creates its own force field which becomes so intense that the ship's hull exists in an antigravity space all its own.

"You have now seen much of our mother *mu*, my son, and your memory, I am sure, is refreshed. The basic design I have given you of this vessel's power and drive systems gives you the keys to many doors. Sometime in the future you may construct one-half of the ship's drive systems and have an unlimited supply of electrical energy on earth. This system would require no outside sources of energy to run it, such as fossil fuels or atomic power. That generator would be self-perpetuating as it would produce more energy than it would take to run it. You would, therefore, have an unlimited supply of totally free energy. The earth as it exists today is not ready for this divine truth. The Evil Ones would use it for an unlimited supply of weapons. I am withholding certain key factors that will be given to you when the time is correct."

This concept has been projected into a physical manifestation in the form of a generator. This divine formula has been proven at this time; the generator has been demonstrated.

— The Author

My Elder Brother continues to describe the entire design of the ship to me in detail. A realization dawns — this is knowledge that I have already recorded deep within my Book of Life. After touring the entire vessel, we are returning to the guidance and communications center. Standing now in front of the great portal, I see the bright image of Mother Earth growing larger as we approach.

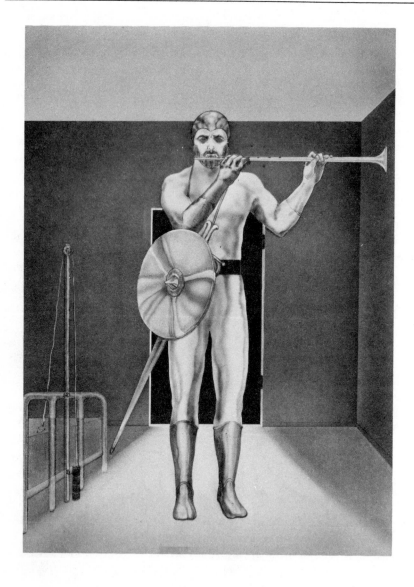

Lucifer, as he is now so-called, is undoubtedly one of the original spirits
who made the decision to step beyond our Creator's divine laws
and guidelines

408

CHAPTER 41

The Dark Night of the Soul Begins

Observe here the characteristic pains of the Dark Night as described by St. John of the Cross, Madame Guyon, DeCaussade, and almost every expert who has written upon this state of consciousness. Desolation and loneliness, abandonment by God and by man, a tendency of everything to "go wrong," a profusion of unsought trials and griefs — all are here. Suso, naturally highly strung, sensitive and poetic, suffered acutely in this mental chaos, and multiplication of woes. He was tormented by a deep depression, so that "it seemed as though a mountain weighed on his heart": by doubts against faith: by temptations to despair. These miseries lasted for about ten years. They were diversified and intensified by external trials, such as illnesses and false accusations, and relieved, as the years of purgation had been, by occasional visions and revelations.

— Evelyn Underhill, *Mysticism*

"You now must return to Santa Barbara! It is there that our projections will first begin to take form."

The Elder Brother's final word that night dropped anchor in my memory as I watched the image of the grand chariot of fire disappear among the stars. I must wait for another ten years, during which time I was to feel the full force of the negative adversaries. The demonic hosts were becoming a constant threat as I watched them momentarily possess the people around me. They interrupted my meditations and cast a dark cloud of negativity over everything I tried to do.

In order to support myself, I returned to the bricklayers' trade; however, I no longer enjoyed the work. The pressures of growing competition forced contractors to bid construction jobs too low just to get the work. The contractor who won the bid then had to cut job costs in order to make a profit. This was done by putting pressure on the craftsmen to work more rapidly, and by cutting down the use of quality materials. This runaway business competition not only creates inferior construction, but it destroys the tradesman's pride in his work.

With the attitude of "I don't care what it looks like as long as you get the job done quickly and it sells," the tradesman then loses his desire to create beautiful structures, as there is little appreciation for them. I now looked at my trade as backbreaking toil. Surely Divine Spirit never intended us to work in such a trivial manner without creative inspiration. Each night at five o'clock the bars were full of unhappy tradesmen. They drank to forget how much they detested their jobs and consequently, their lives. I now found myself within the ranks of the suffering, whose greatest moment every day was five o'clock when this unrewarding labor ended.

"Come on, Paulsen, let's go have a beer and forget this damn job." I decided to go along with them out of curiosity. Drinking was not my idea of pleasure, and I had to consume a tremendous amount before I noticed any change in my consciousness. Sitting in those bars, I watched the Forces of Darkness prey upon these mortal forms who were unable to see them. Men who were not negative or evil in nature changed into monsters as dark spirits entered them through the medium of alcohol. I watched men who were close friends fighting to destroy each other in vile rages. On some occasions I could see the negative spirits who possessed their bodies and minds. Alcoholism is demonic possession for many.

I listened to these dark spirits and their arguments against virtue with distaste, realizing that the use of alcohol opened one large doorway into Lucifer's dimension. Yes, a place called hell really does exist.

"Do you dare to venture in?" jeered an inner, demonic tormentor. "Many of your old friends are prisoners in here and they can't get out. Don't you want to come in and free them, Northman? We think Lucifer is stronger than you are. He can over-power you. Are you afraid to wrestle with Lucifer? Come on, do something! We are tired of waiting."

Anthony . . . began to pray. He raised his voice and prayed aloud, the words of devotion ringing into the darkness round him. . . . "O my Lord, help me and enlighten me!" But no sooner had he uttered these words than he saw all round him a host of hundreds and thousands of sulpur-yellow lights, and for every light he also heard a separate voice. . . . The voices flickered like will-o-the-wisps, and the lights struck up a spectral chant: "Lo! Anthony! We have come to enlighten you!" And this was followed by an outburst of fiendish laughter and a bedlam of wild applause.

— Rene Fulop-Miller,
Saints Who Moved the World, on
St. Anthony, circa 251 A.D.

Employment was hard to find. Working only two or three days a week, I could barely afford a cheap hotel room. The months of November and December 1961 were gloomy and negative. I tried to tell my friends about my experiences in the desert, but none of them would believe me. Many of

410

my old friends no longer wanted to be around me; the problems of this world were enough for them to think about. My only audience now became the patrons of saloons.

"Old Norm has lost his sanity. Too bad he actually believes that he was taken into an alien spaceship." My experiences in the desert were passed from one person to another, with each adding his own version.

Not only did the men avoid me, but women shunned me, too, once they found out who I was. In my loneliness, I felt that the only spirits who believed my story were the dark spirits who now surrounded me. They, of course, knew it was true! I did not realize it at the time, but that was exactly what the Evil Ones wanted. They had deliberately thrown dark clouds of negativity over my friends and new acquaintances to further isolate me. Finally, with only them to converse with, they hoped I would begin to slide in their direction. They were right.

On Christmas Eve, I decided that I was going to get good and drunk to celebrate my lonely existence. If I were going to penetrate the now familiar negative dimension, and meet its master face to face, I had to find ways of entry. Alcohol presented the door. There was no way that I could enter without suffering injury to my body and mind; the Arch Fiend would see to this. A further risk was to be defeated and remain a prisoner like our fallen brethren.

With reflection, I realized that I would never give up the divine experiences recorded in my Book of Life for lesser temporary pleasures. I had tasted the infinite joy and love of Divine Spirit in this life. There were no substitutes and I knew it!

Hindsight reveals, unfortunately, that this lofty position made me reckless and that is what my Elder Brother had warned me against. It was to prove to be my near undoing. My decision to drink on Christmas Eve was eagerly awaited by my enemies. I could feel them plotting my destruction.

I celebrated Christmas Eve of 1961 in the cocktail lounge of the old hotel where I was staying, drinking straight glasses of whiskey. The bartender kindly informed me, by holding up the empty evidence, that I had consumed a whole bottle. "You'd better slow down, fella, or we'll be carrying you out of here. Fact is, I don't know what's holding you up now!"

Suddenly I heard a familiar voice. "Hi, Norm, you staying in this old place?" A fellow bricklayer, out of work, stepped up beside me. Together we finished out the evening talking about hard times. "Let's get together on New Year's Eve, Norm. What do you say?" I had no other commitments, so why not? This decision pleased my negative adversaries.

411

New Year's Eve came, and the party grew in numbers as other occupants of the hotel joined in. I was having some fun, and I wasn't worrying about anything!

After New Year's Eve passed, our party continued. I had not eaten anything for several days and as time passed I lost all desire for food. I began to lose sleep as my nervous system became depleted of life force. The dark regions of Lucifer's domain and the hordes of demons crowded around me, displaying all manner of lewd and licentious behavior. The weaker I became, the more aggressive and confident were their attacks. I began to feel painful physical blows, and to my amazement, deep scratches were beginning to cover my back and arms.

I had heard that Satan and his hosts were actually able to materialize and inflict physical damage to mortals. Now I had proof of it! They are the dirtiest, filthiest fighters in existence, and at this point in my life, they had all the advantages. I was entering a dimension I knew absolutely nothing about. The divine power that created me had to sustain me. I had the ability to replace depleted life force as fast as the strongest of them were able to steal it from me. This amazed them and backed them off.

I could hear and feel their master watching as one by one he sent the strongest of his chiefs to overpower me. I was now living in both dimensions at the same time. During the day I passed the time with a few of the boys in the bar. Finally there was no one left but me; they had all ended up sick in bed. I decided this was enough drinking, so I stopped for a while and began to eat some food.

On February 3, 1962, the beginning of the Age of Aquarius, the earth was going to witness a major solar eclipse along with the largest conjunction of planets in

> Legions of disembodied evil spirits came against me, organized in companies that they might have more power, but they had not power over me to any great extent, because of the power that was in and sustaining me. I had the Priesthood, and the power of it was upon me. I saw the invisible world of the condemned spirits, those who were opposed to me and to this work, and to the lifting up of the standard of Christ . . . Did I at the same time see or have a vision of the angels of God — of His legions? No, I did not; though they were there and stood in defence of me and my brethren, and I knew it. And all this not that there was any very great virtue in me, but there was virtue in the Priesthood and Apostleship which I held, and God would and did defend; and the evil spirits were dispersed by the power of God.
>
> — Heber C. Kimball,
> *Journal of Discourses*,
> The Church of Jesus Christ of Latter-day Saints, Vol. 4

> Astrology involves the relationship between the larger universe outside you and the personal universe within. The same energies that function in your personal universe function in the larger one 'out there.' . . . A conjunction is a concentrated massing of

more than two thousand years. This solar display was going to fall right on my thirty-third birthday. Unfortunately I was unaware of this astral event at the time.

energy. . . . It may be harmonious or inharmonious, according to the planets involved.
— Isabel M. Hickey,
Astrology, A Cosmic Science

The winter of 1962 was very wet, with one southeasterly storm after another rolling up the Santa Barbara coast. Everyone in the construction business was out of work due to the heavy rains. While at the hotel cocktail lounge one afternoon, a few of my acquaintances decided to celebrate my birthday with me. I talked them into accompanying me to dinner.

"Norm, you drive; you're in good shape."

"Okay, guys, where to?"

As we pulled away from the hotel a demonic voice shouted to me in the spirit, "Paulsen, you're in for it now! We've got you right where we want you!" I felt icy chills spread through my body.

As we turned a corner onto State Street, my right front wheel hit the curb and bounced over it, clearing the turn.

"For God's sake, Norm! Be careful!" Halfway down the block, a siren's shrill scream was behind us; I looked in the rear view mirror — a bright red light was flashing.

"We're in big trouble! Straighten up quick!" Before I could pull over, two patrol cars converged upon us. I stopped the car, got out, and waited for the approaching bad news.

"You guys have all been drinking. Come on! Out of the car!" My companions came crawling out of the car trying to look sober. It was obvious to the police we had all been drinking. I was able to perform all of their sobriety tests, but that didn't convince them I was sober.

"Buddy, you and your friends are under arrest for driving under the influence."

It took hours for them to book all of us into the county jail that afternoon.

Now, the descent. . . . I was in a dark cell with two bunks; someone was asleep on the bottom one. The demonic fiends were howling at me again. "We've got you now, Paulsen! We've got you now! We're going to eat you alive tonight!"

I looked through the semidarkness at my new surroundings. The bunk was along one wall; the toilet and sink were in the corner. The cell was filthy, and the stench of urine was everywhere. A dirty mattress pad about two inches thick covered the top bunk. I climbed onto it and leaned back against the steel bulkhead, resigning myself to whatever might come upon me now. The violent activity of the demons was unlike anything I had ever before experienced. "We are going to tear you apart, piece by piece!"

One by one the hideous monsters in the enemy ranks ran up and jumped on me, biting, kicking, pounding, and scratching. As the hours wore on I got weaker and sicker. I could no longer see the dimly lighted cell. The dull red glow of Lucifer's dimension predominated. Suddenly, sick to my stomach, I had to throw up. Swinging my legs over the side of the bunk, I jumped down into the

> When it became clear that the ghosts and their mockery had failed, the devil resorted to more drastic methods of attack. He ordered his cohorts to close in on Anthony's weakened body, to torture him, to knock and kick and beat him until his passion for prayer would be vanquished. The spirits obeyed and lashed out at Anthony with such fury that his senses left him and he fell unconscious to the ground.
>
> — Rene Fulop-Miller,
> *Saints Who Moved the World*,
> on St. Anthony

dark cell. I had turned too far to my left. My right foot struck the edge of the toilet and all of my weight came down on my arch. Stabbing pains shot through my body as I landed on the floor in a heap. Grabbing my foot, I found it broken from the arch out toward my toes. I began screaming in pain for help, and after a few minutes, the form on the bottom bunk finally got up to help me yell. In the light of matches, I observed my foot already unnaturally swollen. Inmates in other cells began to yell for help. Half an hour of this finally brought a guard. A light shone through the bars upon me; a voice spoke from the darkness. "There is nothing we can do for you until morning, buddy."

"By morning! This foot is going to be swollen so badly they'll never be able to set it."

"Too bad, fella! That's just too damn bad!"

This act was beyond belief. Without another word the deputy turned and walked away. My cellmate screamed vile oaths after him. "I'll testify in court against that no-good creep, fella! That beats anything I've ever seen!"

The pain was finally unbearable. I passed out in exhaustion. Consciousness returned with the sounds of cellmates beating on the bars yelling for the guards. It was morning; all of the lights were on. The guards finally came. Two of them looked at my foot, which was now the size of a football, and dark purple.

"Okay, fella, we're taking you to the county hospital. When did this happen?"

"About six hours ago. The other guard walked off and left me like this!"

They looked at each other, shaking their heads as if somebody was in trouble. I am sure now it was only me. There I was in another patrol car headed for the hospital. I was given a room and from there x-rays were taken.

Two young doctors came with the bad news: "Mr. Paulsen, we must present you with the facts. The injury to your right foot is very serious. All five bones in the metatarsal joints of your right foot have been dislocated and the cartilage has been torn and probably destroyed. The swelling is so extreme that our x-ray pictures are not clear and do not give us a true picture of the extent of the damage. Unfortunately, many hours have elapsed since the injury occurred and there is severe swelling. It is impossible at this time to try and reset the bones. If we cannot reduce the swelling in the next twenty-four hours, we may have to amputate your foot. Your foot is going to be elevated now and packed in ice. Hopefully this will help reduce some of the swelling."

"Oh, my God!" I never expected anything as severe as this to happen to me! This was no game I was playing with the enemy. They were out to destroy me totally if they could. I was now looking directly into Lucifer's domain which now also included the hospital room.

The next day, even though the swelling had gone down, the two young doctors were perplexed over my foot. They finally decided to stretch the foot apart at the metatarsal joints; hopefully then some of the bones might realign.

I watched them bore three holes in my foot, right through the bone. Next, three large needles were inserted through the bones in my arch. The heel of my right foot was placed in a plaster cast with a molded hook at the bottom. They intended to attach weights to it. With that done, they now connected steel wires to the three pins and ran them over a pulley, down to more weights on the floor. This ingenious contrivance was, they said, going to stretch my foot apart and allow the bones to realign in the mangled joints. I would be there for the next sixty days, at least. But suppose this scheme didn't work? Well, at least the swelling had subsided and the possibility of having my foot amputated had passed.

Negative visions of possible future world events were projected by the Evil Ones. They passed before my exhausted inner vision like motion pictures. During this torment, I rediscovered a way to protect myself from the constant attack of Lucifer's demons. By drawing on the descending life force, I was able to project streams of high-velocity light-energy particles from my eyes. The dark spirits had no defense

> Padre Pio . . . often found himself surrounded by hideous monsters who jeered insults at him and challenged him to do battle.
>
> — Charles M. Carty,
> *Padre Pio, the Stigmatist*

against this energy as it began to disintegrate their bodies, to my amazement. Brilliant energy particles streamed forth like tiny tracer bullets, blasting holes in the astral forms of my tormentors. I now had the ability to destroy them, which gave them pause.

As the days went by, I spent my conscious moments investigating the dark regions of Lucifer's kingdom. A vision of President Kennedy's assassination appeared on the cosmic screen, acted out in detail long before it happened. In order to accomplish their evil deeds, the negative forces actually project themselves into duplicate astral images of mortals they wish to destroy and control. By acting out the death of a certain individual within the boundaries of a play, the wheel begins to turn. These strong images projected into the field of power (i.e., astral world, inner space) will eventually materialize in third-dimensional space. Unsuspecting mortals don't have a chance against these forces which they cannot see or cope with, once they are unleashed upon them. The only hope, or help, mortals have against the Evil Ones is the intervention of The Builders and the Angel Men and Women (i.e., Christ Consciousness).

I was learning the hard way the indescribable facts as they exist here on Planet Earth. Any mortal who has dared to challenge these dark forces in the past, who didn't have divine help and guidance, has ended up dying in some horrible manner. I was fully engaged in challenging them and they had won a victory, but at the same time I had succeeded in entering their dimension. I now knew some of their weaknesses. So far, I had been able to survive everything they could summon up. I could see my mission very clearly now. I had entered this life, not only to reveal Christ Consciousness, but also to reveal the existence of the Forces of Darkness, the Fallen Angels.

The days and weeks went by. My foot suspended from the wires and pins was torture.

One night, after wrestling with three powerful spirits, I watched the image of one of them disintegrate as a mass of light-energy particles struck him right in the chest, splitting his body asunder. The other two stopped and retreated, swearing at me as they moved back out of range. From there they began to yell at me that their master was coming tonight to devour me. Yes, my end was to be most horrible, as their master hated me more than anyone else. And now that I had just dispatched one of his favorite warriors into oblivion, he was on his way here.

"If this is true," I said, "then bring him on, for I fear him not! I am consciously existing within the substance called Life; from this force all visible images are formed, including your ugly bodies."

As soon as the two remaining spirits discerned my feelings, they

416

vanished very quickly, screaming a stream of vile oaths. I sensed that this time I was really going to meet one of the masters of the enemy camp face to face. This was a being who once commanded one of the grand celestial *mus* of The Builders. Raising the head of my bed, I was now fully upright. I had nothing to do but wait, for surely this spirit was really coming. The worst he could do was destroy my physical body.

The Vision of Lucifer

Hours have passed. A nurse is standing beside the bed. "Mr. Paulsen, it is after midnight; you get to sleep now."

Dozing a little — suddenly here before me a view as if from space! The whole North American continent lies far below me. There, the lights of many larger cities shine forth brilliantly. Something is strange — the light from the cities is red like fire. I must look closer. Oh, Lord! The cities are in flames!

The dreadful scene is changing. I must get a closer view. Mobs of people are running through city streets. They seem to be without reason and possessed. They are setting fire to their homes, stores, and everything that will burn. Why?

Suddenly an awesome presence — it's in the room, open your eyes quick! A gigantic figure — standing at the foot of the bed. His head is touching the ceiling a good twelve feet above me. I must record the gigantic proportions of this colossal manifestation!

This being is dressed in a form-fitting, one-piece garment. The garment, bright silver in color, seems to be alive, like some kind of living metal. His face is exposed beneath a skullcap of the same material. The features are Caucasian, with a finely chiseled nose. A beard, neatly trimmed covering a large square jaw beneath, presents the image of a very handsome face. A huge belt and buckler encircling his hips supports a gigantic double-handed sword. Knee-high boots made of the same material complete his dress. This is no hideous monster like some of the spirits I have encountered, but is surely the image of a former member of The Builders.

He is undoubtedly one of the original spirits who made the decision to step beyond our Creator's divine laws and guidelines and storm the gates of heaven in rebellion. Yes, this is Lucifer, as he is now so-called; a supreme commander of some of the Fallen Angels' dark hosts. The vibration of arrogant hostility encompasses me round about. This spirit is a destroyer and his eyes are set on me. There in his hands — a huge silver horn. Now he looks upon me with utter disgust. Raising the horn, he turns toward the south. The notes of a beautiful hypnotic melody are fading away into another vision.

Huge crowds of humanity around the world, in every major city, move with this hypnotic symphony. They are under his control. To stop the invasion of the Forces of Light (Christ Consciousness), Lucifer plans to put the torch to every major city on the face of the earth. This will be done through mob violence and temporary insanity. The earth is to become a burned-out cinder, along with its mortal inhabitants, before the Dark Angels ever surrender it to The Builders. In this projected vision I see no war which destroys the world with fire, but rather insane madness. Unable to move from my bed, I now face a being who could crush me like a grape. How can I stop him? I cannot allow him to act out and project this vision into the field of power, for surely he will make these horrible scenes materialize.

The insane mobs are moving through the streets with torches. There they begin to fight and kill one another. "Lucifer, you're showing me by demonstrations exactly what you plan," and this projection is, in effect, initiated at this very moment. He has stopped playing; he turns to look down on me.

"What do you think you're going to do, you insignificant pup?"

"I must stop you!" He is resuming his playing; he is not concerned about me. I must reach down to my right foot and unhook the wires. I haven't moved in weeks. Oh! It's difficult! The wires are in my grasp. I have them disconnected from the needles. Now I must get the weights off my heel — quickly! I must gather all the strength within me for this move. O Divine Spirit, please strengthen me!

My left foot is on the floor; sudden strength now flows into me from above. Quick now, stand up; I have to balance on my left foot. I have to keep my right foot up now, and hop on my left one toward him. What am I going to do when I get there? He is only six feet away and his buckler is on a level with my eyes.

Suddenly a movement — a force of energy from way out and beyond in space. O Christ, come forth! My life, my light, my soul! Another moment, and now from another vantage point, the crown of my head is wide open, revealing the image of Christ the SöN-SüN. O brilliant shaft of light descending and alighting on me! It's you, O light, brighter than the noonday sun, filling the vessel of my head with a seething sea of incandescent energy, which now, like a torrent, flows rapidly into the facets of my eyes.

Lucifer has stopped playing. He lowers his horn and looks upon me with astonishment and disbelief. The downward pressure of this force comes bursting through my eyes, dueling with his as our visions lock. Two brilliant arcs of fire, like laser beams of old, strike him betwixt the brows. The incandescent brilliance of these rays — its burning through his brow! Too late, O Lucifer; smoke is rising from a telltale fire within; you cannot escape.

The impossible has happened for me. Dual rays are burning his head; his shoulders and upper body disappear down to his waist. The rays, beyond my control, do not desist, and all is smoke from his head to his buckler; all is consumed. O Lucifer, too late you now leap from the room. Your legs and hips atangle in the roof, you try to disappear.

Lucifer had totally forgotten the powers of the Angel Man and Woman and as Goliath had underestimated David, Lucifer had underestimated this insignificant pup and the powers that a living Divine Spirit was able to bestow. He was disintegrated by the very power that had originally projected him into being. I stood there in the middle of the room in a state of shock, the incredible energy and brilliance still revolving around and around within my head. O vision! O soul! You are but the fabric dreams are stretched upon, O projector of all images.

A nurse burst through the door, unable to believe her eyes. She found me standing on one foot in the middle of the floor, looking up at the ceiling where Lucifer's remains had just disappeared.

"My God, Mr. Paulsen! How did you ever get out of bed?"

The nurse was trying to get me to move and I really wasn't listening to her at all. Quickly, she ran from the room to get more help. I was alone, and hopped back to the bed. I was able to connect myself back up to the contraption. For the rest of the night I lay awake. The news that the master had been destroyed spread rapidly throughout the astral regions of Lucifer's domain. One by one, Lucifer's chiefs came to look at me from a distance.

"He who destroys Lucifer becomes Lucifer!"

"Impossible! I believe in doing unto others as I would have them do unto me; therefore, I can never fit into his proportions or the vibrations of his life."

It was over for the moment. Now I had to effect the healing on my foot and be on my way. I had been in this hospital long enough!

Since there is no way in which we can test the reality of visions and of the operation of second sight, most people come to adopt one or the other general attitude, whether of belief or disbelief, towards such stories of ghosts, premonitions and psychic experiences. . . . The account of a vision, given by someone apparently sane and honest, can only be heard with respect, for no one is in a position to judge it.

— John Michell, *The View Over Atlantis*

Unidentified aerial phenomena, pictures taken by the author

CHAPTER 42

My Imprisonment

After I had spent more than four months in the hospital, the two young doctors assigned to my case finally decided to discharge me. "Mr. Paulsen, we don't like to admit it, but we have been unsuccessful in trying to reset the bones in your foot. We recommend a future operation." What a desperate situation I was now in! I had no money and no place to stay.

That afternoon the doctors removed the cast from my foot and pulled out the three pins. I hardly had a foot anymore. The bones in the arch were about two inches out of alignment, making it impossible to put on any kind of a hard shoe.

The county welfare department paid for my room in one of the cheap hotels on Santa Barbara's skid row. They also gave me some meal tickets that amounted to about ten dollars a week. After two weeks of trying to get around on crutches, and losing weight on one meager meal a day, I now had to do something quick. My foot was so weak and painful I could not put any weight on it. The only area that would support me was the heel and a small portion on the right instep. Using crutches, I began to force myself to walk on the foot.

One morning, as I was standing on the sidewalk, a friend of mine pulled up beside me in his car. "Hey, Norm! You want to go to work? I have a big cement job to pour."

"Are you kidding? Look at my foot! And me on crutches!"

"Well, you could help me trowel around the edges of the slab."

My friend was trying to help me. "Okay," I said, "let's go." Lord, you're going to have to help me now, for sure.

After we arrived at the job site, my friend handed me a pair of rubber boots. The time had come. Straining with determination, I pulled the boot on over my foot. The pain was excruciating! I forced my will to work for me, and we poured the slabs for two duplex apartments that day. My foot had become so numb from lack of circulation, I was unable to feel pain anymore. I was proud of my accomplishment; the numbness had allowed me to finish out the day.

For the next two years, I was to walk and work on the heel of my right foot. I found that by cutting out part of a tennis shoe, I was able to bend it enough to get it on my foot.

One evening in December 1962, a female acquaintance accompanied me to dinner. After dinner I drove her to her home which overlooked the city of Santa Barbara and the Pacific Ocean. Driving back into Santa Barbara, I suddenly heard familiar sounds and voices in the Spirit. As I looked out over the coast to the ocean, two divine celestial *mus* suddenly appeared. They were moving southward down the coast toward Santa Barbara.

I pulled over and stopped on a paved lookout area. The two divine chariots were tráveling slowly, and at this speed they were a bright, fiery orange. They continued toward the Santa Barbara Harbor, then suddenly performed a ninety-degree vertical turn. Then, accelerating upward from the horizontal to about five or six thousand feet, one ship moved to the east while another went to the west. They abruptly stopped and hovered, flashing on and off their familiar patterns.

"Brother Norman, go and ask your friend to return here to your present location with you and we will give her a demonstration and confirmation. After this, we have something to discuss with you."

Quickly, I drove back to my friend's home, and in excited anticipation, invited her to accompany me on a surprise adventure. She willingly consented and we both returned to the lookout point. Five minutes passed, then a voice entered my speeding thoughts. "Tell your friend we will be out over the coastal area shortly."

As I tried to describe what I had seen and heard to my friend, it became evident that she was having trouble believing me. Then suddenly, she was jumping up and down. "Oh, look! Look! My God, look, Norm!"

There were the two ships, again traveling the same route they had just previously covered. They were moving down the coast toward Santa Barbara Harbor. Here they performed the same maneuvers they had previously done. Flying horizontally, they abruptly turned ninety degrees and accelerated straight up to about six thousand feet. Comparing the size of the ships to familiar objects in the harbor, I judged them to be at least three hundred feet in diameter. One ship went to the northwest and the other went to the southeast. There they hovered, flashing intermittently. I am sure, to this day, my friend does not believe what she saw that night, and my ability to forecast their appearance within minutes made it all the more incredible.

The ships now suddenly accelerated straight up and disappeared from sight. We sat there in silence together looking at the place in the heavens where they had both disappeared.

Later, driving home, I was informed by the *Companions*, "Glenda is suing you for alimony and child support payments. There is now a warrant out for your arrest."

Shortly after I arrived at my apartment, two detectives appeared with the warrant. While I was being booked into the county jail, the phones were ringing constantly. "The whole damn town has gone crazy tonight! Everyone is seeing UFOs!" stated the annoyed detective.

I was allowed to make one phone call, and a friend bailed me out of jail that night. I was now in the position of either going to jail for one year, or paying all delinquent alimony and child support payments. Over the phone, the next day I heard the unbelievable from Glenda. "I will drop the charges and all back payments if you will allow my new husband, Keith, to adopt Aarn!"

I hung up the phone in disbelief. How could she do this to Aarn and me?

I couldn't handle a year in jail; there had to be some other way. The memory of that filthy environment made the decision for me. "I must be free," I thought. "I will sign your blackmail papers. The denial of any kind of relationship with my son will not be easily forgotten! Someday he will know my side of the story also!"

I finally managed to save enough money to have my foot operated on. Though the operation was successful, my foot was extremely weak and painful. The torn and damaged nerves were trying to grow back into the disjointed areas. Sharp, stinging pains jerked the tendons in spasms, preventing me from sleeping well at night.

When the cast was finally removed, my disappointment grew, for my foot was weaker than it had ever been. As the weeks went by the doctor was not satisfied with the results, either. I was still unable to put any weight on the foot three months after the surgery. One day, a nurse in the doctor's office casually asked me, "Mr. Paulsen, what are you going to do now that you will never be able to walk on that foot again?"

Stunned, I wandered aimlessly out onto the street. What was a 260-pound man going to do with only one foot, sell pencils?

On top of my depression, I acquired a very bad cold in my chest. Then without realizing it, I developed walking pneumonia. One night I returned home exhausted and retired to bed.

The Death Experience

I am standing at the head of an operating table. Doctors are desperately trying to save someone's life. A closer look, a stunning shock, the man on the table looks very much like me; in fact, it is me! Standing nearby, Elder Spirits in white robes are watching — intently watching. Memory tries to bring back events and circumstances now transpired.

I knew I was dying. . . . I was out of my body. . . . I could see my own body there on the operating table. My soul was out! . . . Then this really bright light came. . . . It was tremendously bright; I just can't describe it.

— A patient, quoted by Dr. Raymond Moody, in *Life After Life*

After I had retired to bed that evening, my lungs had filled up with fluid. My stepmother Dorothy, intuitively sensing something was wrong, had driven to Santa Barbara without Dad to see me. She had found me in a coma in the trailer, already turning blue from lack of oxygen. An ambulance was called, and I was rushed to the county hospital. Here they performed a tracheotomy in an effort to save my life. The first attempt was unsuccessful, and the doctors pronounced me dead. As they were leaving the room, one of the nurses saw my hand move and called the doctors back. With renewed effort, they were able to force some oxygen into my lungs and remove some of the heavy fluids. . . .

Watching now, there is no pain, no discomfort; I feel absolutely nothing. The doctors struggle frantically with their equipment. They suddenly stop! They are unsuccessful in keeping my body breathing and are abandoning their efforts. Pandemonium is in the energy around me; the Elders are deciding to do something drastic. Quickly now, my body sits bolt up-

I could feel myself moving out of my body. . . . I started rising upward, slowly. I saw more nurses come running into the room. . . . I watched them reviving me. My body was lying on the bed . . . and they were all around it. I heard one nurse say, "Oh, my God! She's gone!" while another one leaned down to give mouth-to-mouth resuscitation. I was looking at the back of her head while she did this.

— A patient, quoted by Dr. Raymond Moody, in *Life After Life*

right on the operating table, struggling to breathe. In desperation, the astonished nurse yells down the corridor at the doctors, now retreating. Running back and working feverishly, they finally remove enough fluid to allow sufficient oxygen into my lungs.

I must move toward my body; my body is breathing again. The doctors have saved its life, but their thoughts, I am aware of their thoughts — "What have we saved, if anything, here?"

Another is thinking, "He has been without oxygen much too long!"

Collectively now they assume, "He may never be normal again. The worst must be expected; he may well be a mindless and possibly violent person."

Now physical restraints are being applied to my arms and legs. I struggle violently against them. O Father, help me! They are not even going to try to see if I am normal!

Another voice nearby speaks. "Take him to the psychiatric ward where he can be watched." I am on a gurney headed there. Two orderlies wheel me into a room with heavy wire on the windows. I can barely breathe; there is a gaping hole in my throat covered with a cotton patch.

A voice in the spirit speaks. "The doctors have already decided to commit you to Camarillo State Hospital for prolonged observation."

A harassing voice sneers, "Once they get you there, they will keep you for the rest of your life." Hellish fear, you are grasping me everywhere!

I must escape; flex both arms — O Father, grant me strength. The heavy leather restraints are snapping loose as if they are not there at all. I must get out of here quickly! Luck is with me, I am still dressed. A long hall before me — a door at the other end. I must run! I will crash down that door or die in my attempt. Nearing the door — it's gone, its vanishing before my vision. I am free; the Elders have removed the door, I have run right through the door! Down that flight of steps — now running across the lawn. I must rest somewhere, I must rest. There is the old admissions building; I will sit there on the steps for a while.

> When St. John's imprisonment was drawing to its close he heard our Lord say to him, as it were out of the soft light that was around him, "John, I am here; be not afraid; I will set thee free." A few moments later, while making his escape from the prison of the monastery, it is said that he had a repetition of the experience as follows: He saw a wonderful light, out of which came a voice, "Follow me." He followed, and the light moved before him towards the wall which was on the bank, and then, he knew not how, he found himself on the summit of it without effort or fatigue.
>
> — David Lewis, "Life of St. John of the Cross," in St. John's *Life and Works*

The Elders are hovering overhead. An elderly Spanish man in an old Chevrolet sedan is pulling up to park. Here is my chance to get away! "Mister, can you help me get to Santa Barbara?" Surely I am scaring the old fellow badly, but without a word, he opens the door for me to enter. He seems to know everything and is trying to help.

We are out on the freeway now, I really feel faint! The Elders are talking, "You are too weak, you have nowhere to go, and now the police are looking for you."

Looking at my elderly companion, I realize it is no use running anymore. "Sir, please will you take me back?" He is turning the car around. The Elders have convinced me to return. I am too weak to escape for long in any direction. I had to find this out myself. Too bad, too bad.

We are back at the hospital, "Thank you, my friend." I must move slowly now, I feel so very weak. I must find my way back; no one seems to see me — there, flights of stairs ahead. I will walk up with those doctors and attendants. The psychiatric ward, I have found it.

It wasn't until I stepped onto the main floor of the ward that everyone seemed to notice me all at once. I had been gone the better part of two hours. No one had escaped before without leaving evidence as to how they had accomplished it. The fact that I had snapped the heavy leather restraints and escaped scared them. While I was gone they had obtained a judge and located my stepmother Dorothy, who had signed an order sending me to Camarillo State Hospital, immediately. "It's for his own good, Mrs. Paulsen," cautioned the judge.

Dad later told me he had been listening to the Santa Barbara news on the radio when they announced that Norman Paulsen had escaped the security psychiatric ward of the county hospital, in Santa Barbara.

— The Author

Within two hours I was in the back of a sheriff's car, on my way to the hospital, and shortly thereafter, I was admitted. In all my life I had never seen so many mentally ill people. The question of whether or not I was sane made no difference; I was thrown right in with the insane. I saw things I cannot relate in this writing. I slept in a large dormitory with perhaps twenty so-called insane people. Even though I never knew what to expect, I was never bothered by anyone.

Thorazine was the tranquilizer used on all the inmates. This helped to control the more violent ones, but made walking zombies out of the rest. "The devil is after you, fella," many of them would say as in a dream themselves.

I spent my nights in meditation trying to heal myself and spread the light of Christ in every direction I could. After about thirty days an elderly woman doctor called me into her study one afternoon.

"Mr. Paulsen, I have been watching you. Why, you're no more insane than I am! If I had my way, I would discharge you today. Unfortunately, the judge has committed you for a full ninety-day observation. I am really sorry for you. But there is something I can do to help. I am going to make you my personal assistant. In this way you will have your own room and special duties to perform."

426

Tears welled up in my eyes. Here was Mother Divine trying to help me in what little ways she could through this kind woman. The lessons I learned in human suffering while in Camarillo State Hospital I shall never forget.

At the end of my ninety-day observation period, the good doctor gave me my discharge papers. "My son, you may go now. I know you came here for reasons other than to prove your sanity. From the first time I saw you, I knew you were not mentally ill. Goodbye and good luck."

As I returned to Santa Barbara that day, the news was everywhere that President Kennedy had just been assassinated. Strangely enough, I had seen this in a vision only a few months before.

Phantom masts rising from the fog

CHAPTER 43

Vision of a Ghost Ship

I arrived in Santa Barbara, California with little money, no employment, and no place to reside; a cheap hotel room would have to suffice. After four or five days of seeking work, I met a masonry contractor who seemed to like me. He offered me a foreman's job building a twin-screen drive-in theatre for him. I accepted his offer and went to work.

I continued working through 1967, spending my leisure hours down at the yacht habor. One day, I found an old run-down sailing sloop for sale. Somehow my employer discovered I had my heart set on buying this thirty-two-foot sailboat. To my surprise, he approached me one day and handed me a check for three thousand dollars.

"Norm, you go and buy that boat you want and pay me back whenever you can."

With this money, plus some I had saved, I could pay cash for the old sloop. I moved on board to save rent money, and now began joyfully rebuilding the old vessel from stem to transom. This was to become one of the great enjoyments in my life: working on old sailing ships of all kinds and descriptions. All my life I had been thrilled over sailing ships. Now I had my first real chance to work and sail aboard one.

One morning while meditating in my cabin, I experienced a most unusual and prophetic vision.

The Vision

I am walking along the breakwater at Santa Barbara Harbor; there's a large fog bank offshore this morning. Wow! There are two of the tallest masts I have ever seen sticking up out of that fog. Two fishermen up ahead, are standing by their dory, "Hey, can you tell me about that big sailing ship anchored out there in the fog?" I must find a way to that ship at once; I

429

must see it up close! "Hey, mates, would you row me out to that big schooner for a price?"

Looking at each other, both men shake their heads. "No way, laddie! That's the ghost ship; no one goes near her that's sane."

"Look here, I'll pay you well if you'll just take me out there."

They glance at each other greedily — for money they'll overcome their fears. "Okay, laddie, let's be off, but mind you, we're not stepping one foot aboard! Aarrr, now! Understand, we'll just drop you off. Okay, mate, let's be off."

The fog is thick, vision is difficult; apprehension is high, but my two companions row on. An intense vibration is coming toward us; it carries the sounds of diesel engines running in the distance. O vision, you must strain upon the mist; the image of that apparition now must soon appear. These vibrations — they are intensifying — the surface of the water is beginning to dance to this pulsating hum.

"There she be, mates!"

A long, black phantom emerges from the fog.

"Arr-men, lads, no one has ever ventured this close to that black hull befar, lest it be the devil himself."

The sign of the cross is now quickly inscribed across the boatman's head and chest. Cold fear grabs both fellows; their eyes are bulging in their sockets. Coming alongside, strange sensations of energy are bringing every hair to attention. What awaits me on board, friend or foe? I do not know.

"All right, laddie; this is as far as we go. Quick now, make your jump abard."

Yes, I make the leap; I clear the caprail with one leg.

"Just swing yourself on deck, lad."

My two former companions now quickly disappear into the fog. I am isolated now, with the faith of my fathers and whatever this ghost ship has to offer.

Walking aft of the foremast here on the port side, a ghastly sight surrounds me. This phantom ship is burned entirely from stem to transom! With every step, burned wood snaps and crunches beneath my feet. Back aft, I hear the steady splash of oars as my former companions hurriedly depart this frightful vision. Here I am, actually standing on board a real ghost ship; to make a survey perhaps? Yes, legends of ghost ships have continued to be told, but here in fact is a real one!

From all appearances, not a timber is left unburned. It is amazing that this ship is still afloat. Intuition, you lead my gaze aloft — a double halyard block is breaking loose from the mastband at the crosstrees and it's hurtling down upon me! There, between my feet, it strikes the deck. The momentum of that heavy block could have easily crushed my skull, but instead, it knocks a large hole in the deck. Bright white metal is shining smoothly there beneath the broken charcoal bits. Scrape away the cinders for a better view. The whole hull is fabricated of this hard, white metal beneath the wood, everywhere I look. This vessel is a schooner of the finest design! She looks like a Gloucesterman of old except for the metal hull beneath. But what caused her to burn? And beyond that, who constructed her incredible metal body that shines like white gold? Where did such a ship come from?

The top of her main topmast is at least 130 feet above the main deck which, to a Gloucesterman, would put her overall deck measurement the same from stem to transom. Inspiration, you are seizing me — reach out and grab that huge bronze wheel with both your hands!

This is my moment — I sense it now — the ship is becoming alive beneath me. The secret of you, O phantom ship, now stands plainly revealed. We are one, you and I, one and the same, O dream. Yes, this ship, and I her master, long separated, are united again. The awesome spectacle you present has frightened away every scavenger who dared to venture near. You are like the story of my life, O ship, written out in immortality. This my soul, O ship! Fashioned from the light and life which formed star systems and galaxies! Yes, united again.

I am free. Free at last and ready to set sail once more. But where's the crew? O voice, you speak again. *"They will come, my son; they will come."*

A high-pitched ringing encircles me round about. O sound that I have heard, yes, many times before. The propulsion systems are not of this world. O dream, hum on. We are built to sail the seas of space forever.

> I believe in you my soul, . . .
> The lull I like, the hum of your valved voice.
> — Walt Whitman, "Song of Myself"

O ship, your burned-out image is falling away like bitter memories of the past. Yes, this ship, my soul, has journeyed far through this life and many more. Yes, many times, hard aground, wrecked and burned, no doubt my exterior scarred, my planks stove in, but underneath — that immortal skin.

Rescued! O sweet salvation, my earthly sojourn is finished.

The fog is lifting; thousands of people are standing on the beach. With a high-pitched hum, we are rising from the waters, you and I, to their astonishment, no doubt. I wave to all farewell and turn to starboard, ascending toward the brilliant eastern SöN-SüN. My immortal soul-ship has journeyed here again, and now again it leaves to sail the seas of space, forever going onward. O traveler, we are moving on. But the rest of the story is yet to come!

About 1968, I went to work building the new medical facility on the University of California's Santa Barbara campus. It was on this job that a familiar figure appeared. His face and physique formed the image of an ancient friend from times past. Looking at him was like looking at an image of myself in the mirror.

One morning before work I decided to do a few push-ups. Looking up I found I was not alone. Someone was watching. Discovered, he approached and offered his hand. "Hi! My name is Rick Yuill, what's yours? I do push-ups too."

This day marked the renewing of our friendship and continuing work together. Divine Spirit had drawn us, once more, back from times past, that we might help fulfill times future. And surely, this we would accomplish!

The masonry construction required cement blocks weighing an average of eighty-five pounds each in some walls.

"These blocks are heavy, Norm," lamented the boss. "The union has required us to use two men per block. If this is going to be the case we'll go broke fast on this job. Tell me, old buddy, can you lift these blocks alone? Don't answer yet, but there's a big bonus in it for you."

I accepted the challenge, but lasted only two months. Two discs in the sacral and lumbar areas of my spine were herniated, totally crippling me for a time. Heavy lifting for too many years had finally demanded a price.

"Take the day off, Norm" encouraged the boss. "You probably just pulled a muscle." However, x-rays taken a few weeks later revealed the unwelcome news. Two discs in my lower back were crushed. I was crippled now, and could have physical problems with my back for life.

I hired an attorney and after months of arguing in court finally received a settlement. The state awarded me disability insurance which amounted to ten thousand dollars.

Unable to work because of my back problems, and with little income, a dilapidated house trailer became my home. New friends and old were coming, faces like Rick Yuill's, long-known. The familiar friends of the past, long seen and heard in visions, were now gathering together, and the prophetic fulfillment of a community that I was to found was finally beginning to manifest. Meditations and discussions three nights a week were the prophetic manifestation of my visions. Young people, discovering my years spent with Paramhansa Yogananda, were thirsting to know about true religious experience. They were full of overwhelming desire to know and feel. "Teach us meditation as you have received it," they asked. "Help us find illumination. Please!" One evening,

just after sunset, a sister came running to the trailer, full of excitement.

"Hurry! Hurry! Come quickly; you should see what's just overhead!"

Everyone scrambled outside; a great sphere of fire hovered about five hundred yards above us. Flames were rising upward; their roaring sounds reached our ears. The sphere of fire began to change color; all of us watched in amazement. I knew the Ancient Ones were here to bless our new beginning. Yes! A "chariot of fire" seen by all!

My landlord, stupefied by the vision of the vessel, exclaimed loudly, "That's the work of the devil! Be ye not deceived — don't look. Pay no attention to it!" At his utterance, the sphere of fire vanished without a trace. Not one spark fell earthward.

I looked at him; he was trembling where he stood. "Are you sure you know what you're talking about, sir? Surely you sing quite often in your church of chariots of fire!" Grand celestial *mus* were often visible in those early days for all of us to see, perhaps to inspire and help us onward.

The silent Baptism of Fire, the seed energy of Christ Consciousness, was received by many of these brothers and sisters. They were possibly

I often reflect on the fact that congregations of yesterday's and today's Christian churches sing the hymn, "Swing low, sweet chariot, coming for to carry me home. A band of angels coming after me, coming for to carry me home." Just what kind of chariot are they referring to that may be crewed by a band of angels?

Such a chariot is described in II Kings 2:11, "And it came to pass as they still went on, and talked, that, behold, there appeared a chariot of fire, and horses of fire, and parted them both asunder; and Elijah went up by a whirlwind into heaven." Also, the prophet Ezekiel tries to describe such a vehicle. It would seem that so-called chariots of fire have been around the earth's vicinity for millenniums and do they not fit right into modern-day UFO reports? Is it not time we examine the facts and accept them instead of ridiculing those who claim to have seen and made contact with these divine chariots of fire?

— The Author

not aware of its presence at the time, but visions will reveal it to them sometime in the future. In the spirit I could see the seed energy of Christ Consciousness shining outward from the faces of the Angel Men and Women on all these spirits in total blessing. Surely that seed energy bore thirty, sixty, and one hundred-fold to all those who made a supreme effort of selfless service to Divine Spirit.

Our pool and sauna at Sunburst Farm

CHAPTER 44

Sunburst — The Early Years

The old trailer house on La Cumbre Road had served its purpose. It was no longer large enough to accommodate all the people who came by to talk about Divine Illumination. A local realtor had offered me an old warehouse in Santa Barbara.

"Norm, if you and your friends are willing to fix the old place up and make it a habitable dwelling, I'll give you six months' free rent."

I decided to take his generous offer. Renovation of the old building began, with lots of help from newly acquired friends. We were able to transform the old image into a clean and interesting center. Rick Yuill stopped by for a visit on his way to Hawaii.

"Rick, will you stay for a while and help me organize this venture?"

"You bet, Brother, I sure will."

Rick moved in, along with a dozen other spirits attracted to the manifestation of divine energy. A sign over the front door read, "The House of Aquarius," commemorating the coming new age. From 1969 to 1975 we attempted to feed anyone and everyone who stopped by the center for help.

Familiar faces I had known so long ago in visions began to appear, one by one. Many had been led to the door through visions and dreams. Many had seen some of our physical projections before we had even started them. Divine Spirit also showed me the faces of those who would one day betray, slander,

The message boldly emblazoned across the heavens at the moment of birth is not meant to emphasize fate — the result of past good and evil — but to arouse man's will to escape from his universal thralldom. What he has done, he can undo. None other than himself was the instigator of the causes of whatever effects are now prevalent in his life. He can overcome any limitation, because he created it by his own actions in the first place, and because he possesses spiritual resources that are not subject to planetary pressure.

— Paramhansa Yogananda,
Autobiography of a Yogi

435

and viciously try to destroy the very work they were sent here to help perform. Not one Judas, but many! And this, their own choice! Divine Spirit has sown and will reap true warriors committed to divine service with The Builders and their return with Christ Consciousness.

It was during the summer of 1970 that my future wife appeared. Mary came with a friend one Sunday evening to share community dinner and discuss meditation. As this pair entered the doorway, I recognized two old friends from out of the past.

Mary and I looked at each other for a moment, not realizing then that we were soon to become companions. It was during a trip to the desert that summer to visit Giant Rock that Spirit revealed our destiny to us. Now we both knew we must work together for a time.

One day, while sitting on the beach together, she whispered without thinking, "I came down here to take care of you for awhile."

I — taken aback — couldn't question her. As she had said it, so let it be. I will always remember her for watching over me.

Divine Spirit, through The Builders, was bringing brothers and sisters from everywhere; the group was now bursting through the walls of the old house. Good energy and enthusiasm were generated through deep meditations each evening. As more and more people came, we realized some kind of rules were necessary. No drugs, alcohol, or tobacco were to be allowed on the premises. I was able to speak to those afflicted and discourage others on the threshold. The higher flight path of the Ancients toward Divine Illumination stood firm against the very popular use of LSD, marijuana, and other mind-altering drugs. Counselling discussions often ended up in conversations about The Great Central SöN-SüN and the journey made possible for us all by Divine Spirit.

> The men who live entirely or almost entirely in simple-consciousness float on the stream of time as do the animals — drift with the seasons, the food supply, etc., etc., as a leaf drifts on a current, not self-moved or self-balanced, but moved by outer influences and balanced by the natural forces as are the animals and the trees. The fully self-conscious man takes stock of himself and is, so to say, self-centered. He feels that he is a fixed point. He judges all things with reference to that point. But outside of himself (we know) there is nothing fixed. He trusts in what he calls God and he does not trust in him — he is a deist, an atheist, a Christian, a Buddhist. He believes in science, but science is constantly changing and will rarely tell him, in any case, anything worth knowing. He is fixed, then, at one point and moves freely on that.
>
> The man with Cosmic Consciousness being conscious of himself and conscious of the Cosmos, its meaning and drifts, is fixed both without and within, "in his essence and in his properties." The creature with simple-consciousness only is a straw floating on a tide, it moves freely with every influence. The self-conscious man is a needle pivoted by its centre — fixed in

one point but revolving freely on that. The man with Cosmic Consciousness is the same needle magnetized. It is still fixed by its centre, but besides that it points steadily to the north — it has found something real and permanent outside of itself toward which it cannot but steadily look.

— Richard Bucke, *Cosmic Consciousness*

I stood amazed, watching the unseen forces bringing together so many spirits of varied backgrounds to live and work in brotherhood. There were many ideas and projections made on what a dedicated spiritual life should be. These subjects, discussed by all, finally evolved solutions through trial and error.

Yogananda's vision of self-sustaining, world brotherhood colonies where men, women, and children could live harmoniously together, practicing plain living and high thinking, was a parallel projection of the Ancient Builders. A place in the country, somewhere on fertile ground, an ideal environment, with running springs — here to spin our own energy and grow toward self-sufficiency; Christ Consciousness was our dream.

"A fitly born and bred race, growing up in right conditions of outdoor as much as indoor harmony, activity and development, would probably, from and in those conditions, find it enough merely to live — and would, in their relations to the sky, air, water, trees, etc., and to the countless common shows, and in the fact of life itself, discover and achieve happiness — with Being suffused night and day by wholesome ecstasy, surpassing all the pleasures that wealth, amusement, and even gratified intellect, erudition or the sense of art, can give." This passage from Walt Whitman seems prophetic of the coming Christ-Conscious race on earth.

— The Author

In order to support ourselves, we temporarily took odd jobs. I was able to teach some of the brothers the construction skills I knew: carpentry, masonry, and cement work. One morning, while working for a friend building her new home, she whispered something in my ear.

"Norm, a little bird told me there is a large ranch for sale right on top of Camino Cielo. You'd better get up there right away."

Rick Yuill and I jumped into the car. A quick ride around sharp winding curves brought us to the top of the mountain. There was only one ranch up here, the old trout fishing lodge and property. Sure enough, it was for sale. The residents gave us the owner's name and address. Rick and I sped back down the mountain to find the owner.

"Why, yes, boys, I just put it on the market a few days ago for eighty thousand. Are you interested?"

Swallowing a large lump, I managed a positive reply. After negotiating for several weeks on the ranch sale, the check for my disability settlement miraculously arrived. The total amount of the check was ten thousand dollars, the exact amount required for the down payment on the property. I was suddenly overshadowed with doubts. What if all these young people suddenly decided to leave after I made this purchase? How would I ever pay for the property? I sat in meditation, asking Spirit for an answer. Finally it came.

"My son, proceed; you will not fail."

The escrow closed and the property was ours. Some of us began the drive up the mountain to our new home. A light rain began to fall as the morning sun broke through the clouds, creating a magnificent rainbow before us. The rainbow's end darted along about twenty yards ahead of the car, leading us to the top of the mountain. Rounding a corner and entering a little valley, the rainbow again presented its full bow above us as the sun suddenly burst through the clouds over a ridge and illuminated the whole area. We decided to call the old lodge "Rainbow Lodge" and the land "Sunburst Farm."

Our construction jobs increased; there was work for everyone. Many of us worked for several weeks in constructing a brick patio with walls, steps, and planter boxes. On one summer day, as lunchtime arrived we all sat down as our sisters came with the lunch baskets. After eating heartily, I stretched out on the lawn in the warm sun and drifted away.

A Vision

Incandescent brilliance — the sun is before me, crowning the top of that very tall tree. I must look directly into that blazing orb — but now it speaks:

"My son, you are no longer a babe, but a man. Start walking!"

Two shafts of light fall toward my feet. Hands are reaching forth from the light; a pair of boots appear with long pointed toes. They shine like gold in the brilliance. The hands place them on my feet. These boots I recognize of old; they are of the warrior class, belonging to the ancient Brotherhood of The Builders. A voice confirms!

"You are, this day, accepted into the eternal service once more; you are a man and no longer a babe."

O Divine Spirit, let me always stand as a true son, in selfless service before you throughout this earthly life and all its persecutions!

I awakened to the blue sky, the green trees, and the summer sun. I had again seen the Face of Christ, the divine SöN-SüN . This was absolute direction now. I somehow had survived the enemy's worst assaults; but greater battles still remained here to be fought.

There are divine, intelligent, cosmic forces which operate divine laws. One night shortly after we obtained Sunburst Farm, and while sleeping, I awakened in inner space.

Vision of "I Am That I Am"

I am standing outside in the oak grove, the wind blowing through the trees. There, above the hill behind the water tank, a divine chariot of fire is hovering. An alien being is approaching, his appearance unlike any human ever seen. A strong projection of energy from the figure seems to throw me backwards. The figure is going to ask me something.

"Who are you?"

I cannot answer for, who am I, really? I do not know. A brilliant flash of light shines above my head. It's the burning, spherical image of Christ, the SöN - SüN, hovering above me!

"*I Am That I Am!*" A voice from all the heavens rings forth!

The entity is saluting the brilliant image. He turns and walks away toward his vessel.

"But who are you? This I must know!"

"We are the forces that raise and lower continents!"

> The ancient Egyptians had a special secret name they called on for producing wonderful results. That name was "I AM."
> The young prince Moses learned the secret power that could be released through that name at the court of Pharoah. That the Egyptians placed great power in this name was evident to Moses, since the words "I AM" appeared on the walls of every Egyptian temple.
> When Jehovah instructed Moses to use this all-powerful name to rescue the Hebrews from the dreaded Pharoah, Moses knew that extraordinary power would accompany him on his mission. . . .
> "I AM" was the Hebrews' name for God. . . .
> — Catherine Ponder, *The Dynamic Laws of Healing*

In the early morning, while leaving the farm, I told Mary of the vision. Turning on the car radio, to our great surprise, we heard the commentator describing a very bad earthquake in Los Angeles, California. The "forces that raise and lower continents" may have intended to shake the Santa Barbara area also. The fact they could have was as evident to me as the fact that they didn't. It would seem that the right answer was given. "I Am That I Am" did not want our new mountain retreat destroyed. Continuing our drive down the mountain, damage reports were coming in over KNX, the Los Angeles news station. It was February 9, 1971.

I loved to park my old housecar, a remodeled stepvan in which I lived, in the oak grove at Sunburst Farm. The sound of the wind in the trees and the creek flowing nearby lulled me to sleep one Sunday. In the early hours of the morning I was awakened in a vision.

The Vision of Jesus

The wind is blowing violently through the trees. The front of the housecar is no longer there. A gigantic wooden cross before me overwhelms my vision. There on the cross — the body of a man crucified. His head is down across his shoulder. The spirit that's riding this gale is tearing his hands and feet loose from the nails that hold him there. His body — it's falling down upon the windswept ground. He's moving — he's alive! His hands and arms are pushing him erect — he's standing up! The spirits of the wind suddenly fall silent, their mission finished; they have removed him from the cross.

"Here, take my hands; let me help you."

Those eyes — beneath the penetrating brows they are open; they are looking through me; they are conveying a message.

"Yes, my brother, we are one."

Two more steps and we will embrace. But wait, you quickly disappear; you have suddenly moved right within my body.

I now awakened further, only to find darkness and the wind fiercely blowing through the trees. The spirit of this vision still hovers near, within me, imparting knowledge of all which I desire to know of him: the crucified Jesus, now resurrected and no longer on the cross of death.

Our growing family gathered each morning before sunrise and each evening after sunset to unite our spirits with the Divine in meditation. Our Sunday meditations at Sunburst Farm were a special event.

> When the whole race shall have attained to Cosmic Consciousness our idea of God shall be realized in man.
>
> — Richard Bucke, *Cosmic Consciousness*

Visitors came to the mountain from everywhere to join us. The brothers and sisters began each meditation with beautiful songs they had written, accompanied by guitars. Many times the Elders would reveal profound teachings from the past. The ancient teachings of the Twelve Heavenly Virtues and the Eight Paths of Truth were given to us during one Sunday meditation as

> For though I preach the gospel, I have nothing to glory of: for necessity is laid upon me. . . .
>
> — I Corinthians 9:16

A gigantic wooden cross before me overwhelms my vision. . . . There on the cross
— the body of a man crucified. . . . He's moving — he is alive!

first the Buddha, then Jesus, and finally an ancient Red Brother appeared in a vision to some of us in confirmation.

Once we acquired Sunburst Farm, responsibilities began in earnest for everyone; we needed money for land payments, food, clothing, and the necessities of life. Now each person had to be responsible for contributing whatever he or she could to the community fund. To help meet our commitments, I purchased a used backhoe and a dump truck and we began to do larger construction jobs. The high cost of lumber, and our desire to recycle used materials whenever we could, got us many jobs doing demolition and salvage work. These projects gave employment to everyone and generated the true spirit of conservation and regeneration among us.

The previous tenants of our ranch had discouragingly stated, "There is only enough water here to support ten people. Your large group will never have enough water here!"

Disturbed, I prayed to Mother Divine that evening in meditation. Suddenly, in a vision, I was on my hands and knees beneath the oak trees as water flowed from the earth everywhere around me. After this vision in meditation I knew that we would always have enough water at Sunburst Farm. This vision was true; water came forth abundantly as old and new springs began to run everywhere.

During the early years at Sunburst Farm I had many visions that gave us direction and counsel. I was shown in one vision that in later years we would move to the northeast, toward the lands of the Hopi.

In one strong vision it was stated to me, *"Go and find a million acres of farmland and the money will be provided!"*

Where was I ever going to find such a gigantic property? I accepted the command and projected it into the future. I was also shown that we must earn as much money as possible to prepare for the day Spirit would move us in that direction. I saw thousands of people coming to join us eventually. Some would remain with us, while others would move on. Divine Spirit and The Builders were searching for those true ones who would be able to keep their commitment to divine service and help humankind from self-consciousness into Christ Consciousness.

Tajiguas Ranch

Family gatherings are an important part of our lifestyle.

CHAPTER 45

Ceremonies and Initiations

It was on February 3, 1972, that Mary and I had decided to have our wedding. It was both Mary's and my birthday. As yet we had no one to perform the ceremony; I was going to have to do it myself. Our lodge was overflowing with people; guitars and other instruments were everywhere. When everyone was seated, I began with a short talk and then chanted a poem I had written.

Looking up, I saw a familiar face appear in the doorway; it was Johnny Rivers, a famous singer. Behind him came a Hopi native American Indian chief. My intuition spoke loudly within, "The Hopi chief has come for two reasons: one, to conduct the marriage ceremony in the ancient traditional way of The Builders; the other, to unite our two brotherhoods again, the red and the white." White Bear approached and, without a word, sat down cross-legged in front of us both. He passed on the profound and ancient handshake of the four races of The Builders. He now chanted to the spirits of the air, earth, fire, and water, asking for their blessings.

Such a rare ceremony this was! It was much more than a marriage ceremony; it was the union of two ancient races, the red and the white. White Bear gave us the four colors of corn which represented the four created races of man in the Western Hemisphere. I knew the work of reuniting the four races was not going to be easy.

As the ceremony ended, Johnny Rivers approached me. "Will you and Mary accompany White Bear and me to Honolulu, Hawaii to attend an Aquarian Age Conference?"

Mary was enthusiastic. "Oh, Norm, let's go!" Two days later, the four of us arrived in Honolulu in time for the first talk at the conference.

White Bear began speaking of the Hopi prophecies and the warnings of the Ancient Ones. "The destruction of all land and life is taking place on earth methodically and expanding on a larger scale every day. We must all

445

work together to try and stop this destruction of Mother Earth."

I was asked to give a description of our efforts as a group and how we had been led together by Divine Spirit. "Meditation is a big part of our daily life along with service to Divine Spirit and humankind. We are united, all for one and one for all. Working together, we have acquired a large property on top of the mountains overlooking the city of Santa Barbara, California. The day we moved in it was cloudy and misty. Suddenly the sun burst through the overcast, illuminating and warming the whole area. We later named our new home Sunburst Farm. There is very little topsoil on the property, but after adding compost we now have wonderful vegetable gardens and orchards. Nearby springs flow into a large swimming pool and fill a million-gallon reservoir. A large sauna stands beside the pool and farther down the slope is a gymnasium. Men and women train in the martial arts and weightlifting for body conditioning. Diet is selected individually; food fanaticism can be a distraction and a stumbling block on the spiritual path.

> Not that which goeth into the mouth defileth a man; but that which cometh out of the mouth, this defileth a man.
>
> — Matthew 15:11

"Sunburst Farm is growing rapidly, and already we have purchased another ranch in the Los Padres National Forest nearby. This land we will call Lemuria, after the ancient lands of Mu long lost in the South Pacific. Our Lemuria will support natural farming operations which will expand on fertile soil. We will farm vegetables, along with grains and alfalfa for horses, cattle, sheep and goats. The national forest service has leased us surrounding lands upon which to graze our growing sheep and goat herds. These herds produce milk and wool for our family. It is impossible to describe in this allotted time all the projects we are engaged in. I hereby invite all of you to come and visit and see for yourselves."

White Bear is the co-author of the profound *Book of the Hopi*, an inspiration to any truth-seeker who reads it. White Bear and I had profound conversations about the Ancient Ones, The Builders, whom he calls Kachinas, or Elders. White Bear related to me what his grandmother had told him before she died: "Someday you will return to the land of the volcanoes over the waters to the west. These lands were the last stepping-stones in your ancestors' northeasterly migration from a land that sank, long ago, in

It is an interesting fact that the Hopis call their Elders Kachinas, whereas the native Hawaiians call their spiritual Elders Kahunas. Both races are from the same roots, the red race. The Hopi migration ended in North America, and the natives of Hawaii migrated northeastward from areas of the South Pacific. Tiki's influence is found in Hawaii and in the South Pacific. Note the strong physical resemblance between some

the waters to the west."

White Bear states: "Many had come by boat from Hawaii and many more had migrated through Central America following a star by night and a cloud by day."

Hawaiians and some Hopis. I believe they were the same people in ancient times.

— The Author

The Builders had decided to set down a foundation race permanently on the North American continent to keep the ancient records. The Hopi have recorded their activities in North America for more than twelve thousand years. The mysteries of the Hopi people have not yet been fully fathomed, but ask a Hopi and he will probably tell you, with firm conviction, where he has come from and where he is going. They are a race that rivals all others at this time in morality, virtue, and nonviolence.

Dad and Dorothy made a visit to our growing center in Santa Barbara shortly before his final exit from his body. He was delighted to meet all the sincere young men and women who were willing to seek and serve the great Mother-Father-God of all creation. The image of brotherhood communities reminded Dad of the Ancient Builders and his own roots with them long ago.

"Son, remember the stories of the *Golden Dawn* and 'Captain Norman and his Friends'? How they lived naturally on the land and spread the truth and the light of baptism wherever they went?"

"Yes, Dad, I remember."

"Son, you are beginning to manifest the ancient way of life again, as I knew you would."

"Dad, your storied images of the *Golden Dawn;* how could I ever forget them? Even now we are raising much of our own food and making some of the clothing and shoes we wear. Many of your dreams have already come true here along with visions projected to us by Spirit. Some of our married couples are conceiving and bringing forth from the womb the ancient spirits of The Builders again on earth. Once more these spirits, in their new forms, will be schooled directly from the image and forces of The Great Central SöN-SüN."

I saw Dad once more and we both knew that it would be the last time we would meet in our physical forms. The *Golden Dawn* was standing in orbit, and Dad needed a new mission and a fresh start. I could not hold onto him any longer. I must confess that I had a hand in staying his departure quite beyond his allotted time.

I knew in the Spirit that "The Traveler" wanted to move on; I could feel the tug. "Son, I must pass on now, as you must go on to new growth, also."

One morning I awakened to hear Dad calling me in the Spirit, as he had done a hundred other times. "Norman, it's your old dad. You must hurry! You must hurry!"

I lay there in the dark room wondering if I was dreaming or if Dad had really called me. About five minutes later the phone rang. I already knew who it was. "Norman, this is Dorothy. If you want to see your father alive, you'd better come as fast as you can. He won't last much longer."

Dad's Death and Resurrection

Now running for the old housecar — can I make it in time? Yes I can! I have to! And I do!

Dad's soft and final breath issues forth, his head cradled in my arms. Watching there — the forces of his spirit are rising from the crown of his head. Yes — into the infinite tunnel of life which leads directly to the image of The Great Central SöN-SüN . O Christ, receive him now.

"Goodbye, Son; I go to prepare a place for you." In the Spirit I hear these — Dad's final words to me.

Arriving back at home I feel so terribly alone; I must sit in meditation. The old housecar behind the center will be a good place to be alone. Dad's spirit is so very strong around me.

A Vision of Dad in Christ Consciousness

There — a tremendous flash of brilliant white light encompassing me. O Christ, your ecstasy! Your coolness! Your expanding atmospheres!

Dad's image, he is sitting here beside me. A great voice is speaking from all space, imparting ecstasy: *"This is the ignition!"*

Expansion, expansion; waves upon waves of light and sound — contractions, now contractions — Dad's image now gone. We had both been sitting side by side within the light of The Great Central SöN-SüN . I am now alone again; how deeply I regret his departure!

One night, about a month later, while sleeping in the old housecar, I was awakened. Someone was calling me. It was Dad's voice: "Norman! Norman! It's your old dad come to see you."

There he was, enveloped in an aura of white light, beside the bed. How magnificent he looked. His eyes were open and emitting rays of brilliance wherever they observed. "Norman, I can see now; the darkness is gone."

It was true! Dad's eyes were like two shining suns. "Dad, I salute you, for you have made the journey all the way home."

"Yes, Son, yes!"

"Goodbye for now! Goodbye, sweet soul; I love you much!"

His spirit-body moved upward through the roof into the night sky now visible, and disappeared in inner space.

Traveler's Benediction

I pray your heart to ever sing,
  To ever sing the song
Of the Soul of the Universe
  As you travel along.

I know the Light of God will fill
  Your heart and guide you through
As you look up, your soul beaming
  In happiness anew.

I pray that every setting sun
  And each pure golden dawn
Will fill your heart with wonderment
  As you go traveling on.

  Bye Traveler! Bye!

— Charles Paulsen, "The Traveler"

During initiations on Mu, the ancient Motherland, the priests wore feathered robes. Chosen sisters were dispatched to the beaches and sand dunes to collect cormorant feathers which were used to cover the initiation cloaks. It sometimes took a sister many years to complete one, as the feathers were difficult to find. The cormorant was considered to be sacred. All of the colors of the spectrum were to be seen in the reflected light of its feathers. For this and other reasons, it was felt that all knowledge was contained there vibrationally. Illumined initiates wore the robes of cormorant feathers when divine knowledge was desired or passed on; they were therefore known as the Cloaks of Facts. The Elders wore these cloaks to all initations and ceremonies.

After acquiring Sunburst Farm, which is and has been long a sacred place for native brotherhoods, I awoke one morning in a vision.

The Cloak of Facts

I was surrounded by a group of brothers and sisters, whom I quickly identified as the last remnants of The Builders in this region. The brothers were tall and fair-skinned; blond, red, brown and black hair adorned them. All bearded, they were easily distinguished from the red brothers of other coastal and inland tribes. Their leader held in his hand a large silver chalice, shining in the predawn light.

"We have come to welcome you all back, as we observe who you are. The Great Spirit Mother and Father wants to purify these lands again so our children may inherit them. Will you drink from the sacred cup with us?"

"Yes, I gratefully accept this honor for myself and all spirits present here."

"I have come with others to reveal the sacred image of The Great Central SöN-SüN to all spirits who receive the Baptism of Fire. The opposition is great, and the pathway strewn with stumbling blocks." The Elder stepped forward. "My brother, drink from the cup." The liquid was pure spring water; what better elixir in all space than this? "We offer you a Cloak of Facts. Will you please wear it for us on this special occasion?"

As I nodded consent, two Elders stepped forward and placed the feathered cloak over my shoulders. We all turned in unison to face a rising sun. Yes, the rising physical sun in this vision was, indeed, the image of The Great Central SöN-SüN , the Christ, whose brilliant rays blessed and penetrated the consciousness of everyone present. I knew all things would now be known in truth; all whatsoever I desired to know. I awoke from this vision with a feeling of great gratitude and love for the ancient spirits who had made it possible.

Supporting our Community

We supported our growing community with odd jobs: the brothers doing construction work, concrete, masonry, and carpentry, and the sisters housecleaning, babysitting, and doing crafts. In a meeting one day we all decided if we had to work to pay for our land, we should work at something that would bring us closer together. Unanimously, we decided to grow good natural produce and market it to the public through our own store.

Shortly afterwards we opened our first natural food store in Santa Barbara. This was to be the first of many stores we would eventually open. A commercial bakery and juice factory later followed this endeavor. There was such a great demand for naturally-grown fruits and vegetables that we were unable to grow enough to supply the demand ourselves, and had to contract with others to help us. With this realization, we opened our first wholesale warehouse for the distribution of naturally-grown foods and wholesome food products that were free from additives and preservatives.

This included a successful line of Sunburst natural food products that were distributed nationwide for many years. We even wrote a best-seller *Sunburst Farm Family Cookbook*. The wholesale warehouse was so successful, and the demand for our products so great, that we decided to open our version of a natural foods supermarket.

The old *Invader*, renamed *Golden Dawn* gave us great joy sailing her

CHAPTER 46

The Ships

One Sunday morning in the summer of 1972, I jumped in my old housecar and drove down to the harbor for a jog on the beach. As I approached the harbor, I noticed two gigantic masts sticking up out of a fog bank about a mile from shore. I could hardly believe my eyes, every hair on my body was standing at attention; this whole scene was so familiar in my memory. The vision I'd had years ago of the ghost ship came flooding back. There, in the exact same position in a large fog bank, were the same two tall masts. Glancing over my shoulder in fear it might disappear, I raced toward the boat rental on the pier. Renting a dory, I began rowing out toward the apparition. As I was rowing, a *deja-vu* experience occurred. Now, but for the lack of the two fisherman companions, the scene was almost identical to my vision of the ghost ship five years ago.

Is it not possible that a so-called *deja-vu* experience is but the subconscious memory of a vision that the conscious mind did not record in sleep?

— The Author

There lying in the fog bank was the same dark phantom hull. She was big, at least 140 feet from stem to transom. The boarding ladder was down over the side, so I tied the dory up to portside and ventured up on deck. "Anyone aboard?" I yelled down the main hatchway.

A voice echoed forth from down below. "Hell yes!" and Captain Waters stumbled out on deck, well watered down with booze.

"This ship for sale?"

"Yeah, do you want to buy her?" groaned Waters, squinting through bloodshot eyes.

"What's her history?" I asked.

"Well, sir, her registered name is *Invader*. She was built in 1905 for ocean racing. She won the Trans-Pac race from Los Angeles to Honolulu in 1926,

453

and holds that record today for her size. Her hull construction is wrought iron which was the best metal they could get back then."

Captain Waters rambled on about the ship's history. The *Invader* had survived two bad fires in San Francisco several years ago and had not sunk. The fires on board, along with the wrought iron hull, fulfilled parts of my vision of the ghost ship, which had also been burned from stem to transom. The appearance of the *Invader,* her construction, and her history fulfilled another part of my vision. Divine Spirit had brought this ship to Santa Barbara for us to resurrect and sail. The vision I'd had years ago of the *Golden Dawn* on San Francisco Bay was nearing fulfillment.

All the brothers and sisters who were interested in sailing and working on the ship gave her a good going over. We all knew it would be a herculean task to bring the vessel back to any of her former beauty and performance. Since there were no other ships of this size and design around for sale, we decided to buy her. Negotiating with Captain Waters proved profitable; we acquired the *Invader* for a fair price.

In just one year's time the rust-encrusted old hull was hardly recognizable due to our hard work. Everywhere we went, people exclaimed at her beauty. In 1974 we did twelve charter cruises for the study of marine biology. Jacques Cousteau's Ocean Search Program from Pepperdine University participated. The Santa Barbara Channel Islands are a wonderland for marine studies. We also took out scientists and students from the University of California at Los Angeles and the University of California at Santa Barbara, Bodega Bay Institute, and many other private foundations.

In December 1974, we sold the *Invader,* reluctantly, for a good price. Adding up our labor and materials against the selling price, we did very well financially, in addition to gaining an immense amount of experience and pleasure. The old *Invader,* renamed *Golden Dawn,* fulfilled parts of my visions and gave us all great joy and satisfaction resurrecting her. We were proud of the job we had done on her restoration, and proud of our ability to sail and race her at times.

After selling the *Invader,* everyone missed the environment of the sea and ships. Looking around Sausalito (a harbor in San Francisco Bay) one day we found a Danish cargo schooner from Allborg. She was run down but basically sound, and we eventually decided to purchase her. After a haulout and a paint job on her bottom and topsides, she looked beautiful. We decided to rename her *Galilee,* and we kept her for more than a year before trading her in on the *Star Pilot.* Both the *Invader* and the *Galilee* had come to us from the San Francisco Bay area.

With the wind aft of the **beam** the *Galilee* was great fun

The *Galilee* was a trim little ship, but her draft was so shallow she went sideways like a crab faster than she went ahead into the wind. She was not a ship to go windward, but with the wind aft of the beam she was great fun. The ghost ship had lines like the *Invader* but carried a main and topmast which matched the length of her hull in height. Somewhere, the real ghost ship was waiting for me, with her Gloucesterman lines, like a knife blade, at her bow; built to sail on her topsides best. She would be the ultimate sailing machine — the ghost ship of my dreams. My intuition told me she was not far away anymore; she would be coming after me soon and we would sail the seas of space again together.

One day on a business trip to San Francisco in December 1975, I spotted her in the Sausalito Yacht Harbor. I just could not believe my eyes. There before me was the largest pair of masts I had ever seen on a schooner. The main topmast was at least 130 feet above the water! She was a gaff-rigged schooner, and by her lines and design, she was a real Gloucesterman. But that was impossible! As far as I knew, there were no more Grand Banks fishing schooners left in operation, but yet here was one sitting quietly before me. She had to be the only operational, American-built, Grand Banks schooner left in existence.

Her entry and design were like that of the famous Canadian schooner, *Bluenose,* out of Nova Scotia. On deck she was 146 feet from stem to transom, as long as she was tall. The hull was tree-nailed (trunnel fastened). I could see the splits and wedges in her dowels poking their noses through her topside planks. A tree-nail fastened hull is unheard of any more as they are too costly to build. Getting my eye down for a look, I couldn't see an inch of hog in her full length. Her masts, topmasts, booms, and gaff booms all looked new; so did her whole standing rig. Someone had just completely rerigged her from the deck to the mast tops.

I still couldn't believe my eyes! Here sat the image of the ghost ship, her lines, freeboard, every inch of her. Well, needless to say, she was for sale. I offered the *Galilee* in trade, plus some other assets. The owners, anxious for a sale, consented to the trade. Overjoyed, we took possession of her and began preparing for the trip to Santa Barbara.

The *Pilot* was designed by Starling Burgess and built in the James Yard in Essex, Massachusetts, in 1924. Her frames and outside planking are white oak, and her ceiling is long-leaf yellow pine. Her decks are 2x4 vertical grain fir, and there is not a nail anywhere in the hull; she is completely tree-nail fastened.

Workwise, we recaulked her bottom and her topsides from the keel to the coverboards. Next we pulled all of her ballast out on deck, some sixty tons of iron ingots and lead. We checked every frame from the keelson up for dry rot, scrubbed down her bilges, and built new cribs for her ballast. It was a mammoth job! The ballast was all sandblasted and dipped in rust-resistant paint, and then replaced. We then reworked all of her standing rigging and replaced all of her turnbuckles and worn hardware. Next we had a big fisherman made for her which added another 2,200 square feet to her spread of sail. She could now put over 11,000 square feet of sail to the wind. We removed some of the hatchways that had been changed and replaced them with hatchways of traditional designs and dimensions.

Renamed *Star Pilot*, she finally fulfilled and completed the visions of the ghost ship in all respects — a dream-vision that has been manifested in true detail. Fully restored and in perfect condition, we were all proud of her and felt her spirit as an entity alone in beauty. *Star Pilot* sailed the California coastal waters from 1976 to 1983. She is currently at her berth in Honolulu, Hawaii, where she arrived in December 1983.

The *Star Pilot* — a dream vision that had manifested in true detail

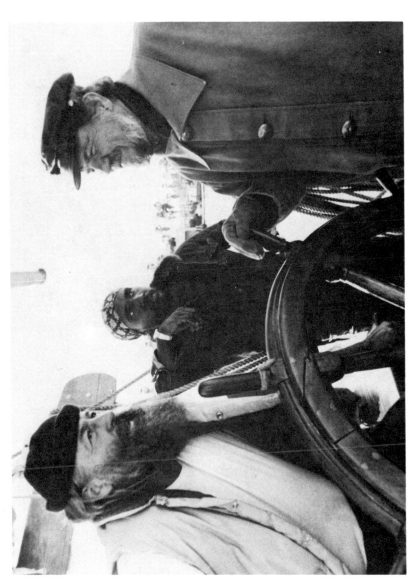

The author and Karl Malden during the remaking of *Captains Courageous*

The author at Big Springs Ranch

CHAPTER 47

Big Springs Ranch

"Go and find a million acres of farmland and the money shall be provided."

Thus had the strong command come forth within a vision of The Great Central SöN-SüN. Not forgetting this divine direction, I let it rest in memory for a future time. But where was I to find such a phenomenally large property, and with fertile farmland, also? Surely not in this country anymore, I reasoned, and if it did exist, the price would be astronomical. I must wait and see, for in time the property might well appear somewhere.

To help supply the increased demand for produce, we began to look for property in the immediate vicinity of Santa Barbara that would give us the capability of growing a large amount of organic produce on a year-round basis. In the winter of 1975, a group of our young men contracted to remove one hundred acres of walnut trees from Tajiguas Ranch, north of Santa Barbara. Rancho Tajiguas is one of the largest ranches in Santa Barbara County and contains fertile bottomland along Tajiguas Creek.

After removing the trees and meeting with the owners, we found we were in a position to purchase the property. Here we could raise all the produce for our growing natural food stores, and also supply our own family needs. After acquiring the ranch, we started our own avocado nursery. The plan was to plant hundreds of acres of avocado trees on the sloping coastal hills. Our organic farming efforts blossomed into fertile fields of produce of every kind and description.

We also purchased the herd of cattle that was on the ranch at the time. With the cattle, we also needed working cow horses. The acquisition of a stable full of the finest quarter horses came our way. The owner had suffered a heart attack and his fine brood mares, stallions, and yearlings were up for bid. We were successful in our bidding and brought all our new friends home. These fine horses are still with us. Some have won

461

handsomely in cutting and reining stock horse shows; others have proven themselves as superior working cow horses on Big Springs Ranch today.

Tajiguas Ranch was a paradise for us nestled in the foothills along the Santa Barbara coast, with its own beach frontage and property running back for miles into the Los Padres Mountains. I knew from the beginning it was not to be our permanent home. Visions had shown me that we would eventually move northeastward toward the lands of the Hopi. Tajiguas Ranch was to be a stepping-stone toward our future home far inland, away from the coast.

The acquisition of Sunburst Farm had been the first phase of our development. Here we tried to find direction and guidelines into the future. Tajiguas Ranch was the second phase. Here we found new direction and began to perfect some of our goals. The ability to grow good produce was achieved, along with the trades of carpentry and woodworking, electronics, brick and stone masonry, metalworking, pottery, weaving, and crafts of every description. These efforts, combined with the everyday business world in teaching our members management and clerical skills, would contribute the skills and talent necessary to our future attainments.

> The object, which is back of every true work of art, is the attainment of a state of being, a state of high functioning, a more than ordinary moment of existence. . . . We make our discoveries while in this state because then we are clear-sighted.
>
> — Robert Henri, *The Art Spirit*

As I stated formerly, everyone had agreed to hold all things in common: real estate, monies, livestock, vehicles, etc. Numbering near three hundred men, women, and children, our expenses and needs were now staggering. People who were in their teens and twenties when they came were now approaching their late twenties and early thirties. Families were expanding with more marriages and, of course, children.

In 1978, a growing discontent began among some members who no longer agreed with our system of common ownership. They began to feel that monies should be divided up and held individually. This was talked about at great length in many meetings. The problem was also discussed with attorneys, who informed us that a nonprofit religious corporation could not ever distribute its assets to its members; these assets were, in effect, public funds. This division continued to grow in our family until those who were

> Think not lightly that God is calling you, because of your own heart's desire.
> How much do you really want him?
> Planets come and go, like leaves on a tree,
> Listen and seek while you have the opportunity.
>
> — The Author

discontented decided to leave.

Many of them worked in our stores, and their departures forced us to hire people from the outside community to help us. Ranch payments fell behind as our cash flow shortened, along with the economic crunch which has crippled thousands of businesses in our country. The time had come to sell Tajiguas Ranch and move northeastward. A qualified buyer surfaced and the decision was made to sell the ranch and the businesses and leave the Santa Barbara area. It was shortly after this time that my wife, Mary, made the decision to leave our family, also.

To indicate we had unjust criticism and persecution in the Santa Barbara area would be appropriate because we did. Problems too numerous to mention happened on a daily basis. Our lifestyle of everyday spiritual observance and sharing all things in common did not conform with certain local factions. I look back to the persecution of the first followers of Christ who attempted to hold all things in common; and more recently, to the work of Joseph Smith when he was establishing the Mormon Church. The Mormons also attempted to do this in their United Order, and to this day some United Order precepts are followed. Their persecution is a tale of woe recorded in our present-day histories. I do not believe that common sharing is a prerequisite to spiritual attainment, but it does bring about the concept of brotherhood, the "all for one and one for all" teachings exemplified by Christ Jesus, himself, and many others.

Christians speak of the Second Coming of Christ and a world government ruled by him (i.e., God himself). Private ownership would surely vanish, as would our present monetary system. The problems of the rich and the poor would be abolished; in essence, a true theocracy would indeed exist. This very concept is the theme of this present volume. Christ Consciousness pervading all the races of

"The heavens are mine, the earth is mine, and the nations are mine! Mine are the just, and the sinners are mine; mine are the angels and the Mother of God; and all things are mine, God Himself is mine and for me, because Christ is mine and all for me. What dost thou then ask for? What dost thou seek for, O my soul? All this is thine — all is for Thee." (St. John of the Cross, *The Living Flame of Love.*) The world is mine, the universe is mine, everything is mine — but here they put a price tag on all my things.
— The Author

humanity would indeed bring heaven to earth once again. Our efforts as a group now reach into the future time when this may well occur. As a group we all agreed in the beginning to project this concept, and by popular vote the present membership decided to continue. We are unique, to say the least, and strong in our convictions as a family reaching for Christ Consciousness.

Man is made or unmade by himself. In the armory of thought he forges the weapons by which he destroys himself. He also fashions the tools with which he builds for himself heavenly mansions of joy, strength, and peace. By the right choice and true application of thought, man ascends to the Divine Perfection. By the abuse and wrong application of thought, he descends below the level of the beast. Between these two extremes are all of the grades of character and man is their maker and master. . . .

The divinity that shapes your destinies is not a mighty person molding you as a potter molds his clay but a Mighty Divine Power — within and all around you and around and in all substance — which is yours to use as you will. . . .

You must know that as you rise and are true, you lift the whole world with you; for as you tread the path it becomes plainer for your fellow-men. You must have faith in yourself, knowing fully that faith is God within.

— Baird T. Spalding, *Life and the Teaching of the Masters of the Far East*, Vol. 2

Looking back I remember a vision I once had after jogging along the Santa Barbara beach one day. Lying in the warm sand, I fell asleep. Awakening in a dream, I was jogging northward on a beach. To my left were barren, rocky, rose-colored mountains, beautiful in the sunlight. Looking upward toward the east, I focused on the brilliant sun at about eleven o'clock high. Not recognizing where I was, I asked the question: "Where am I, Lord?"

Looking across a beautiful flat expanse of water on my right, turquoise in the light, the voice replied, *"This is the Sea of Galilee; the one out West's the same. Go run along that shore. It is there that twelve tribes will again gather."*

Awakening from this dream-vision to find myself still lying on the beach, I arose in thought. Surely the Pacific Ocean was not the Sea of Galilee out West, but where was this sea so vividly expressed by the light of this vision? Dear reader, I have found the Sea of Galilee out West, even to matching the landscape, colors, mountains, directions, and virtual calmness of the water. It is the Great Salt Lake, with its ever-changing colors, barren rose-colored mountains in some areas, and fed by the runoff of fresh waters.

Needless to say, my first glimpse of the Great Salt Lake brought every hair to attention and thrilled me in depth. Here was, in fact, the same landscape of my vision, the confirmation that I had gone in the right direction. Now I must speak of the land we acquired.

Long ago, in another vision, I found myself inside a great starship. We were proceeding westward over mountainous regions. As we cleared the summit of a large range of mountains, I observed a tremendous valley, twenty to thirty miles wide, running from south to north. To the west another, higher range ran parallel to the valley. We were descending now

Big Springs Ranch headquarters with Pilot Peak in the distance

Big Springs Ranch — a diamond in the rough

to the valley floor. All was fertile and green, extending northward for at least fifty miles. The way was opened and I stepped forth upon the land. It sang beneath my feet! Surrounded by Elders, we walked upon the land. This was indeed the place I was given to come to at a later date. This whole valley, mountains, and more I could not see, was to be a colony for many people.

Long years passed and the vision was filed away until recently, when we acquired our Big Springs Ranch. Upon the impending sale of Tajiguas Ranch we went in search of properties, looking in Arizona, Oregon, and Nevada. At least fifty brochures were piled high on the desk, all expressing ranches and properties for sale. Thumbing through the pile one day I was attracted to the words, "Big Springs Ranch, Wells, Nevada." Instantly I knew within that this was, indeed, the place; the property we were to come home to.

With some of the brothers and sisters, I conducted an investigation of the property. It was fantastic! It was beautiful! It was so big we could hardly comprehend its size — well over half a million acres containing three mountain ranges and two incredibly large valleys. It was thirty miles wide and forty miles long, covered with artesian springs and ponds, forests in the mountains, grasslands for cattle and farming, and above all, clear, clean, fresh air. Old homesteads, long abandoned, lay near every spring. Yes, this was, indeed, the place!

The headquarters, incredibly beautiful, contains Johnson Springs which runs artesian at 2,500 gallons per minute, flooding pasturelands for miles. This was a stopping place for pioneers traveling westward from Salt Lake City to the California coast. In fact, the old Pony Express building and stage-stop are still standing at Big Springs Ranch headquarters. The waters of Johnson Springs are seventy-five degrees, year-round. It would take another volume to describe this land, and I am sure one could not see it all in a lifetime. Big Springs Ranch is a diamond in the rough.

It has always been a cattle ranch with very little farming. As the old saying goes, "We wouldn't do a damn thing that we couldn't do on horseback." This land has the potential for a "new age city"; yes, this is our projection. We have abundant sand and gravel for cement and blocks, limestone for mortar, plus we have water in abundance. Needless to say, we purchased Big Springs Ranch with the proceeds from the sale of Tajiguas Ranch. Now began the exodus from Santa Barbara, taking us one year to complete.

We took possession of Big Springs Ranch in the fall of 1981, moving key people up to take charge of the operations. The ranch lies north and south of Interstate 80 and approximately thirty miles west of the Nevada/Utah border. Ranch headquarters is located in the Goshute Valley at the foot of the Pequop Mountains. The small settlement of Oasis on Interstate 80 belongs to the ranch and includes a travelers' market, post office, restaurant, hotel, service station, garage, and small motel. We began the construction of a 73-unit trailer park at Oasis early in 1982, purchasing new, three-bedroom trailers for our people to live in.

The park, with the trailers in place, was barely finished before winter set in. Our people were moved from the balmy climate of Santa Barbara into the freezing cold of Nevada's high country winter. This move was very difficult for some people to adjust to; however, we survived it in good repair. Our next concern was how to support ourselves. Salt Lake City lies 150 miles to the east of the ranch on Interstate 80 and was the only logical place to set up businesses which would contribute support.

We began with the purchase of housing in Salt Lake City, looking for rundown residences that could be restored and later sold for profit. An old four-story brick mansion was purchased in the summer of 1982. Here we began restoration and set up our offices and headquarters. Five other older homes were also purchased for housing and restoration. Our previous success in the natural foods business has encouraged us to open natural foods stores in areas around Salt Lake City. We next acquired one of the largest demolition and excavation companies in Utah and the Intermountain West. Many of our people are now employed there. The recycling of building materials has always been one of our pet projects. From this surplus of used materials, projects can be completed on the ranch at lower cost. From the acquisition of real estate and our abilities to make improvements, we have acquired assets which are easily resold for profit. These investments have brought us through difficult times and have supported our projects and helped pay off our debts. We are continuing in these endeavors on a greater scale.

The Builders Construction Company has the license to engage in construction of all types, and we look here for revenue also. Our projections for developing Big Springs Ranch are extensive, to say the least. Plans are now being drawn for a resort community at Oasis which will include a large equestrian park with arena and stables for shows. Cross-country ski facilities are also contemplated, along with a hotel, restaurant, and full-spectrum health and healing center. The yearly traffic flow has been monitored and could easily support such an endeavor. Plans to incorporate Oasis as a city are underway on 3,500 acres of commercial property.

Big Springs Ranch roundup

We now have our own state-approved school at Oasis for our children. and a large food cooperative which supplies our family with their needs. As a family, the long-awaited improvements of our living conditions have arrived. We all have good housing, ample food and clothing, transportation, and recreation. Our third phase of physical, mental, and spiritual development as a family is well underway.

> To transform the world, we must begin with ourselves; and what is important in beginning with ourselves is the intention. The intention must be to understand ourselves and not to leave it to others to transform themselves. . . . This is our responsibility, yours and mine; because, however small may be the world we live in, if we can bring about a radically different point of view in our daily existence, then perhaps we shall affect the world at large. . . .
>
> — J. Krishnamurti, "Self-Knowledge," in *The First and Last Freedom*

Visions and Confirmations

By the year 1964, I had saved enough money to spend one year in as much isolation and meditation as I desired. After renting an old house, I began my solitary meditations. While in deep contemplation one day I suddenly became aware of the eastern horizon. Before me was the largest golden sun disc I had ever seen. As I was staring at the phenomenon a voice spoke to me, as in a command. *"Get them all together unto one place!"*

Trying to contain my surprise, I blurted out an answer. "How me, Lord? How me, and where, Lord? Where?" No answer was forthcoming: how this was to happen I would have to find out on my own. Only years later did I find out who, how, where, and when.

The light is almost certainly always subjective, and no doubt the voice also. The "voice" giving more or less explicit commands is a common phenomenon: With the Cosmic Sense comes a consciousness of certain facts, and the impression made upon the person is that he has been told these facts by some personage . . . hence the voice of God to Moses, the voice of the Father to Jesus, the voice of Christ to Paul, the voice of Gabriel to Mohammed, the voice of Beatrice to Dante.

— Richard Bucke, *Cosmic Consciousness*

This vision was also filed in my memory for a future time; that time arrived almost twenty years later. Those who were called *them* and the land that was *one place* all materialized into the future for me on Big Springs Ranch. While sleeping in the early morning at headquarters during the first weeks of spring, I awoke in a vision. There before me was the very same incredible golden sun disc suspended on the actual eastern horizon of the ranch. This was the same sun disc that had commanded me, *"Get them all together unto one place!"* I received the profound impression: *"My son, this is the place long known. They are gathering here. This is the fulfillment of that same vision you now recall."*

The race of beings referred to in this book as The Builders, those who continually possess the Cosmic Sense, girdled this planet with edifices and great cities for a reason. The great masses of block contained in their pyramid-like structures, along with their size and measurements which followed the golden proportion, or golden triangle, were in essence conductors for the earth's magnetic field. This power has been used many times to "make the deserts bloom," and we intend to do this at Big Springs Ranch.

The Ancients referred to the earth's magnetic field as the dragon current. This dragon current, or magnetic flow, moves from south to north and from east to west. By girdling the earth's equator north and south with great pyramids as conductors, they were able to harness the power of the earth's magnetic field, hereafter called the dragon current. This great power grid allowed the Ancients to convert deserts into fertile lands by drawing water moisture from the earth's crust and the earth's atmosphere.

... prehistoric civilization was founded on the universal control of those invisible currents which move over the surface of the earth, the fields of gravity and electromagnetic energy. . . . The work of scientists further confirms the possibility, that some form of natural energy was known in prehistoric times. . . . Whatever may be the nature of these currents that the Pyramid builders set out to control — and the Great Pyramid's construction undoubtedly played an important part in the vast engineering program whose aim was the fertilization of the entire Nile valley — they are still evidently present, still capable of being reinvoked when their function is again recognized.

— John Michell, *The View Over Atlantis*

In short, they were able to somewhat control the weather by creating vortexes of energy around and between their pyramid structures. The natural flow of the earth's magnetic forces from south to north, in essence, travels from the mass of one great mountain peak to another. In locating these natural flows across valleys from one prominence to another, the Ancients created their own massive conductors in areas they wished to populate and develop in agriculture.

Pyramid structures were designed to comply in shape and size with the golden proportion which follows the natural geometry existing in the images of creation. The great power grid which once existed on earth is now broken; the dragon has been slain. With the destruction of Mu and Atlantis during the great wars, the earth's weather changed drastically. The great biblical flood confirms much of this. Surely with the approaching time when Christ Consciousness once again predominates, the races on this planet will reconstruct this natural system.

The flow of the dragon current through the Goshute Valley on Big Springs Ranch toward a natural pyramid mass called the Collar and Elbow has been seen and photographed on occasions. The natural flow of this magnetic energy travels in vortex. Spinning vortexes as formerly described attract energy particles. In this case, water molecules in the air and earth are drawn toward this force. Moisture in the form of fog accumulates around the dragon current when it is extremely activated by the right weather conditions (i.e., high and low pressure systems). Natural springs abound along these magnetic flows.

The Ancients redirected these natural flows by constructing conductors in the form of pyramids and edifices. Thus the deserts were made to bloom! The Golden Ages of the Ancients have been lost to us, but the days of the Sons and Daughters of God are now returning.

> The full purpose of this terrestrial geometry is not yet clear. The evidence... points to the former existence of a civilization based on the manipulation of certain natural elements, a form of spiritual engineering whose implications are now barely conceivable.
>
> — John Michell, *The View Over Atlantis*

It is our projection to build a pyramid conductor on Big Springs Ranch on the ancient system of measurements called the golden proportion (or *phi*); in fact, we plan to surround that pyramid with the ancient designs of a "new age city." We hereby invite those interested in such physical, mental, and spiritual developments to visit and perhaps join our projections. All of the raw materials exist on the property; only the bodies, minds, and spirits filled with desire are needed. The writings contained in this volume are an open invitation to all seekers who might wish to investigate or participate.

The Geometrical Image of The Great Central SöN-SüN

Years ago, during the beginnings of our movement in Santa Barbara, I experienced a vision. In this vision I found myself standing at high noon at the foot of the north face of the Pyramid of Cheops. Gazing upward, I was astonished to find that the great blocks of polished limestone facing were gone, with only a few remaining near the apex. Crying out, I asked Divine Spirit. "O Lord, what time period is this? The limestone facing is gone," I heard a reply which indicated I must wait a moment. I next found myself in a great circular chamber beneath the upper mass of the pyramid. Twenty-four hooded and white-robed figures stood in a circle around the perimeter of the room. In the center of the chamber stood a great rectangular block of stone.

Suddenly I understood: I was awaiting the precise moment when the sun would illuminate a specific area on this monolith. That moment arrived as a brilliant shaft of light fell downward from high above and illuminated the geometrical image of The Great Central SöN - SüN, which was carved into the polished flat surface of the monolith. The colors of the spectrum flashed from the dazzling, bejeweled inlay outlining the image. This was the exact moment when the forces of Christ Consciousness would find the opportunity to begin repossession of the earth. A great voice spoke as if the combined voices of all in the congregation, *"This is the moment; you and yours are the custodians of this image on the surface."*

Upon returning from this vision, I marked the colors of the spectrum in their precise places upon a geometrical image of The Great Central SoN-SuN. This image expresses the golden proportion (called *phi*) in every degree. For example, *phi* is found in the golden triangle, the golden rectangle, the pentagon, and the golden spiral (see the figures in Chapter 32). It is the geometrical image of the Christ, the First Creation of Light, the first offspring of Divine Spirit. As a custodian of this image, I have attempted to present its radiations in this volume. It has been found in areas all over the world and to this day can be found carved in the pyramid at Xochicalco in Mexico. Surprisingly, it hangs in picture form in the Mormon Visitors' Center at Temple Square in Salt Lake City, Utah. They entitle it the Mexican Star of David.

Only a short time ago I found myself standing in a vision outside of the Mormon Temple in Salt Lake City. I gazed into the sun shining down upon the towers, surely in great blessing for the great works performed by a devoted people. For the first time in my life, I find understanding, compassion, and support from a people so very familiar.

We have found a home in Salt Lake City, as well as at Big Springs Ranch. The Divine Order of Melchisedec strives onward without beginning or ending, and members of that Order stand forth revealed today around the Sea of Galilee out West.

This photograph was taken at a meditation in 1958 with the late Kirpal Singh, who was one of The The Builders. It clearly shows the masculine descending vortexes turning counterclockwise within the descending feminine vortexes turning clockwise. Notice also the brilliance of the subjective light above the heads of the meditators. In this photo the author is seated in the center against the far wall. He also wishes to state that he saw this manifestation of vortexes and light upon this occasion, as did others in this group.

CHAPTER 48

The Baptism of Fire

The divine faculty termed Christ Consciousness, which has been the theme throughout this writing, stands forth arrayed in the garb of truth. The Baptism of Fire, referred to in scriptures around the world, is also revealed in the light of this truth. I have attempted to describe in written form that which is truly beyond words to describe. In light of this fact, further words about the Baptism of Fire might help convey more understanding.

What exactly is this so-called Baptism of Fire?

1. The Baptism of Fire is the *projected light and energy* emanating directly from Christ Consciousness within and around the First Creation of Light, the hub from which the expanding spheres of creation now spin. Duplicate images of the First Creation of Light appear everywhere:

    a) in sub-atomic and atomic particles

    b) solar systems

    c) galaxies

    d) universes

    e) Christ-Conscious hu-man beings

2. The energy and light of the Baptism of Fire radiates from *divine intelligence* impregnated within the life forces of Christ Consciousness.

3. It travels in time and space within the *four directions of vortex:*

    a) clockwise

    b) counterclockwise

    c) centrifugal

    d) centripetal

4. The Baptism of Fire is *androgynous;* masculine and feminine forces are encompassed by it.

5. In mankind it brings about the *second birth* referred to in John 3:3: "Except a man be born again, he cannot see the Kingdom of God," (that is,

473

Christ Consciousness). The second birth is the conception and birth of the Divine Spiritual Embryo within the heart of the self-conscious human. It is the divine Christ Child, the immaculate conception. The Christ Child grows forth from the throne of the human heart to possess all of the attributes of the self-conscious human being.

6. Christ Consciousness is, within itself, *immortal;* a spirit who attains this state knows it is immortal. The forces of Christ Consciousness possessing the human form, reprogram the genetic code with the theme of immortality: hence, the almost perfect preservation of the bodies of some saints and adepts. This condition is observed in the bodies of those who attained the immaculate heart which governs all emotions, thoughts, and actions (i.e., the heavenly heart).

7. *The Christed Angel Beings,* who directed the energies of creation into visible forms including the evolution and formation of humankind, also *conduct the Baptism of Fire upon mankind.* They are the guardian angels long known. It is here within humankind that the androgynous nature of Christ Consciousness manifesting as the Angel Man and Woman unite and achieve the conception and birth of the Divine Spiritual Embryo within the human heart. Descending within the dual vortexes of energy, the physical body is penetrated and wrapped within a cocoon of brilliant light. Observe the accompanying photo which clearly shows the masculine descending vortexes turning counterclockwise within the descending feminine vortexes which are turning clockwise. Note also the brilliance of the subjective light above the heads of the meditators. In this photo I am seated in the center against the far wall. I also wish to state that I saw this manifestation of vortexes and light upon this occasion, as did others in this group.

It is the consensus of all known cases of Christ Consciousness in the past and the present that they are able, by some means, to pass the New Sense on to others near and dear to them (i.e., the Baptism is passed from one to another). Let us see what others have said in this respect: "Verily, the hour is coming. I almost make it appear, that every soul may be recompensed for its efforts." (Mohammed.) Commenting upon this statement Richard Bucke says "the words, 'I almost make it appear,' would seem to refer to the feeling almost or quite universal with those having Christ or Cosmic Consciousness that universal endowment with this faculty is near, is imminent, and that an individual having the faculty can bestow it almost at will. 'I bestow,' says Whitman, 'upon any man or woman the entrance to all the gifts of the universe.' . . . The new faculty is becoming universal and these men and women, having the faculty, do bestow it upon such others as coming in contact with them are eligible." The main objective in life in the case of every man or woman having the Cosmic Sense is to bestow it upon the races and each feels within some power to so bestow it.

8. The phenomena herein described as the Baptism of Fire *can indeed be induced to frequent the aspirant desiring it:*

    a) by obtaining the company and persuasion of a person possessing the Christ or Cosmic Sense.

    b) by following that person's directions while attempting to approach the New Sense.

    c) by devoting the self-conscious mind toward selfless service to Divine Spirit in whatever direction one is led.

    d) by the utter surrender of selfish desires by the self-conscious entity, before the vision held of the Christ or Divine Spirit.

    e) by the continued daily meditation on and for the vision of Christ Consciousness.

    f) by the subjugation of the lower natures and the daily practice of virtue, using the gift of reason, herein described in twelve categories:

Charity	Patience	Compassion	Courage
Faith	Honesty	Continence	Humility
Loyalty	Perseverance	Equanimity	Temperance

The Baptism of Fire brings with it the divine umbilical cord with which the Christ Child is nourished as it grows within the throne room of the human heart. Even as each newborn child must enter this life with an umbilical cord, at the same time another divine umbilical cord awaits to be attached.

Observing the crown of the head on a newborn infant, we find the oval opening which is soft and responding to each beat of the heart. It is here we receive the divine impulses of energy which control the functions of the heart. It is also here that the divine Baptism of Fire enters into the recipient who will experience the second birth (i.e., the Christ Child). Attending this event are the dual vortexes of power. "Like a dove descending," they alight upon the crown of the head. Once the divine conception and birth has taken place, this heavenly umbilical cord is attached to the person, imparting a flow of divine energy, the very essence of Christ Consciousness. The powers of the Christed human being, the Son or Daughter of Almighty Spirit begin to manifest in the newborn infant. Here begins the struggle, for the newborn child must now overcome the habits and desires of the old self-conscious entity.

475

In this world, the life of the self-conscious entity is indeed a struggle; so also is the life of the Christ-Conscious entity. The scope of the work to be done on this earth stands forth revealed in staggering proportions to that one possessing the New Christ Sense. The struggle between the Forces of Light and the Forces of Darkness moves onward into the future. As before stated, the Forces of Darkness have access to humankind through the medium of the self-conscious mind, for it was back into simple- and self-consciousness that the Dark Angels fell. Once possessing the Cosmic Sense they remember well former days of glory. Having fallen from this high state, they resent its obtainment by evolving humanity. They try to prevent its infusion into the races with manifold endeavors of every description. Surely this struggle is evident to the reader and all possible safeguards must be taken. Even as Christ Jesus was sought after by King Herod that he might be destroyed, so also is the Christ Child still sought after wherever it might find birth; hence, endless persecution.

I wish to state to those candidates for the second birth. Be ye ever watchful, for your enemies are around and about. Salvation is the vision of Christ the SöN-SüN of God, Christ Consciousness, and its attributes. Gird up thy loins for the journey ahead. Reach for the highest and refuse the old self-conscious self with its doubts, desires and half-truths. For as many as would receive him, to them gave he the power to become the Sons and Daughters of God.

The lion and the lamb shall lie down together before the vision of the
Christ-Conscious entity.

Jesus of Nazareth

To Him That Was Crucified

My spirit to yours dear brother,
Do not mind because many sounding your name do not understand
   you,
I do not sound your name, but I understand you,
I specify you with joy O my comrade to salute you, and to salute those
   who are with you, before and since, and those to come also,
That we all labor together transmitting the same charge and
   succession,
We few equals indifferent of lands, indifferent of times,
We, enclosers of all continents, all castes, allowers of all theologies,
Compassionaters, perceivers, rapport of men.
We walk silent among disputes and assertions, but reject not the
   disputers nor any thing that is asserted,
We hear the bawling and din, we are reach'd at by divisions,
   jealousies, recriminations on every side,
They close peremptorily upon us to surround us, my comrade,
Yet we walk unheld, free, the whole earth over, journeying up and
   down till we make our ineffaceable mark upon time and the
   diverse eras,
Till we saturate times and eras, that the men and women of races,
   ages to come, may prove brethren and lovers as we are.

— Walt Whitman

479

Come, said my Soul,
Such verses for my Body let us write, (for we are one,)
That should I after death invisibly return,
Or long, long hence, in other spheres,
There to some group of mates the chants resuming, . . .
Ever with pleas'd smile I may keep on,
Ever and ever yet the verses owning — as, first, I here and now,
Signing for Soul and Body, set to them my name,

Walt Whitman

I cannot rest O God, I cannot eat or drink or sleep,
Till I put forth myself, my prayer, once more to Thee
Breathe, bathe myself once more in Thee, commune with Thee,
Report myself once more to Thee.

Thou knoweth the prayers and vigils of my youth,
Thou knowest my manhood's solemn and visionary meditations,
Thou knoweth how before I commenced I devoted all to come to Thee,
Thou knowest I have in age ratified all those vows and strictly kept them,
Thou knowest I have not once lost nor faith nor ecstasy in Thee,
In shackles, prison'd, in disgrace, repining not,
Accepting all from Thee, as duly come from Thee.

That Thou O God my life hast lighted,
With ray of light, steady, ineffable, vouchsafed of Thee,
Light rare untellable, lighting the very light,
Beyond all signs, descriptions, languages;
For that O God, be it my latest word, here on my knees,
Old, poor, and paralyzed, I thank Thee.

My hands, my limbs grow nerveless,
My brain feels rack'd, bewilder'd,
Let the old timbers part, I will not part,
I will cling fast to Thee, O God, though the waves buffet me,
Thee, Thee at least I know.

— Walt Whitman, *Leaves of Grass*

The Gate Is Open

In the silence of my being I hear the pulsating hum of all Creation moving through every atom of my body. This sound, O Lord, is the Divine Comforter.

If we but listen, we can hear you; we can feel you; we can see you. I know I am a being of consciousness, without form, beyond light. I am eternal. I am a part of you, Mighty Spirit.

My journey has been long. I have entered in this life; I have sought to do your will. I have sought your face. I have sought your love. I have sought to spread your light to all whom I see.

Our lives here are short, Mighty Spirit. Help us not to waste them in idle, self-conscious desires. Bless us with the consciousness of your true Son, of your true Daughter.

Enter into us. Let us hear the mighty sea of eternity roaring around us, swirling through us. We are infinite like you, O Father. Our bodies, but a dream, but a moment, in your eternity. You are our light, our love.

Help us not to forget, in the moment that we are here, that we must enter your eternal abode, without form, without our bodies; with our pure consciousness.

You are the Mighty Dreamer, O Lord, dreaming the images of all of us, all which we see—this planet, our familiar sun, and other orbs in eternity, we seek to see you, you who are projecting all.

Reveal to us eternity, beyond the shadows of dreams and corporeal desires. Put our spirits to rest in your eternal body. Give us Cosmic Awareness; awareness of your cosmos. The great Sphere of Creation is your visible body and all things contained in it.

Each one of us is but a dream. You are dreaming. You are each one of us. We feel you. We know it's true.

—Brother Norman

Bibliography

BOOKS

Albright, William F., and Freedman, David N., gen. eds. 44 vols. + The Anchor Bible. Garden City, N.Y.: Doubleday, 1964. Vol. 1: Genesis, translated by E. A. Spieser. Vol. 20: Second Isaiah, translated by John L. McKensie.

Balzac, Honoré de. *Louis Lambert.* New York: P.F. Collier, 1900.

Bancroft, Hubert Howe. *The Works of Hubert Howe Bancroft.* 39 vols. Vol. 1: *The Native Races.* San Francisco: A.L. Bancroft, 1883. Vol. 18: *History of California.* Santa Barbara, Ca.: Wallace Hebberd, 1963.

Behmen, Jacob. *Works of Jacob Behmen.* 4 vols. London: M. Richardson, 1781.

Blumrich, J.F. *Kasskara und die sieben Welten.* Dusseldorf, Germany: Econ Verlag GmbH, 1979.

Bucke, Richard Maurice. *Cosmic Consciousness.* New York: E.P. Dutton, 1969.

Butler, Alban. *The Lives of the Fathers, Martyrs, and Other Principal Saints.* 12 vols. New York: D. and J. Sadler, 1846. Vol. II.

Carpenter, Edward. *Towards Democracy.* New York: M. Kennerly, 1922.

Carty, Charles M. *Padre Pio, the Sigmatist.* Rockford, Il.; Tan Books, 1977.

Charroux, Robert. *Masters of the World.* Translated by Lowell Blair. New York: Berkley Publishing Corporation, 1974.

Charroux, Robert. *The Mysteries of the Andes.* Translated by Lowell Blair. New York: Avon Book, 1977.

Cheesman, Paul R., and Cheesman, Millie Foster. *Early America and the Polynesians.* Provo, Ut.; Promised Land Publications, 1975.

Churchward, James. *The Lost Continent of Mu.* New York: Ives Washburn, 1931.

Churchward, James. *Sacred Symbols of Mu.* New York: Coronet Communications, 1972.

Dante Alighieri. *Paradiso.* Translated by Charles E. Norton. Boston: Houghton, Mifflin, 1892.

Dante Alighieri. *Purgatorio.* Translated by Charles E. Norton. Boston: Houghton, Mifflin, 1892.

Dante Alighieri. *Vita Nuova.* Translated by Charles E. Norton. Boston: Houghton, Mifflin, 1892.

Daya Mata, Sri. *"Only Love."* Los Angeles: Self-Realization Fellowship, 1976.

de Acosta, Jose. *Natural and Moral History of the Indies.* 2 vols. New York: D. Franklin, 1970.

Dirvin, Joseph I. *Saint Catherine Labouré of the Miraculous Medal.* Garden City, N.Y.: Catholic Family Bookclub, 1963.

Dobzhansky, Theodosius. *Mankind Evolving: The Evolution of the Human Species.* New Haven, Ct.: Yale University Press, 1962.

Doctrine and Covenants of The Church of Jesus Christ of Latter-day Saints. Salt Lake City, Ut., 1982.

Emerson, Ralph Waldo. 3 vols. + *The Collected Works of Ralph Waldo Emerson.* Edited by Alfred R. Ferguson. Vol. 2. Cambridge, Ma: Belknap Press of Harvard University Press, 1971.

Evans, John Henry. *Joseph Smith, an American Prophet.* New York: Macmillan, 1933.

Fowler, Raymond E. *The Andreasson Affair.* New York: Bantam Books, 1980.

Fulop-Miller, Rene. *Saints Who Moved the World.* London: Hutchinson and Company, 1949.

Gilchrist, Alexander. *Life of William Blake.* New York: E.P. Dutton, 1942.

Gin Chow. *Gin Chow's First Annual Alamanac.* Edited by Thomas F. Collison. Lompoc, Ca.: Newcomb Printing, 1975.

Goodspeed, Edgar J., trans. *The Apocrypha: An American Translation.* New York: Random House, 1959.

Grumley, Michael. *There are Giants in the Earth.* Garden City, N.Y.: Doubleday, 1974.

Henri, Robert. *The Art Spirit.* Philadelphia: Lippincott, 1923.

Heyerdahl, Thor. *Aku-Aku*. Chicago, Il: Rand McNally, 1958.
Heyerdahl, Thor. *Kon-Tiki: Across the Pacific by Raft*. Translated by F. H. Lyon. New York: Rand McNally, 1950.
Hickey, Isabel, M. *Astrology, A Cosmic Science*. Watertown, Ma.: Isabel M. Hickey, 1979.
The Holy Bible. The King James Version is primarily used.
The Holy Bible, Oxford Annotated Edition. New York: Oxford University Press, 1962.
Horne, Charles, R., gen. ed. *The Sacred Books and Early Literature of the East*. 14 vols. New York: Pearle, Austin, and Lipscomb, 1917. Vol. 14: *The Great Rejected Books of the Biblical Apochrypha*, "The Book of Enoch," Part 3.
Irving, Washington. *Life of Mahomet*. London: J. M. Dent, 1911.
John of the Cross, Saint (John Yepes). *Life and Works*. Translated by David Lewis. London: Thomas Baker, 1889-91.
Jolly, Clifford J., and Plog, Fred. *Physical Anthropology and Archeology*. New York: Alfred A. Knopf, 1982.
Jung, C. G. *Flying Saucers*. Princeton, N. J.: Princeton University Press, 1978.
Kolosimo, Peter. *Timeless Earth*. Translated by Paul Stevenson. Secaucus, N.J.: University Books, 1973.
Kornberg, Warren, ed. *Human Evolution*, a National Science Foundation *Mosaic* Reader. Wayne, N. J.: Avery Publishing Group, 1983.
Kramer, Samuel Noah, ed. *Mythologies of the Ancient World*. Garden City, N.Y.: Doubleday, 1962.
Krishnamurti, J. *The First and Last Freedom*. Wheaton, Il: Theosophical Publishing House, 1954.
Kriyananda, Swami (Donald Walters). *The Path: Autobiography of a Western Yogi*. Nevada City, Ca.: Ananda Publications, 1979.
Lambert, W.G., and Millard, A.R. *Atra-Hasis: The Babylonian Story of the Flood*. Oxford: The Clarendon Press, 1969.
Landsburg, Alan and Sally. *In Search of Ancient Mysteries*. New York: Bantam Books, 1974.
Landsburg, Alan. *The Search of Lost Civilizations*. New York: Bantam Books, 1976.
Langdon, S. *The Babylonian Epic of Creation*. London: Oxford University Press, 1923.
Le Plongeon, Augustus. *Sacred Mysteries Among the Mayas and the Quiches 11,500 Years Ago*. New York: Robert Macoy. 1886.
Mahabharata. Several versions used.
Mendelsohn, Isaac, ed. *Religions of the Ancient Near East*. New York: The Liberal Arts Press, 1955.
Michell, John. *The View Over Atlantis*. New York: Ballantine Books, 1977.
Montgomery, Ruth. *The World Before*. New York: Coward, McCann, and Geoghegan, 1976.
Moody, Raymond A., M.D. *Life After Life*. New York: Bantam Books, 1981.
Moore, Ruth. *Evolution*, from the *Life* Nature Library. New York: Time-Life Books, 1964.
Mueller, F. Max, ed. *Sacred Books of the East*. 48 vols. Oxford: The Clarendon Press, 1879-. Vol. 1: The Upanishads. Vols. 6 and 9: the Qur'an (Koran), translated by E. H. Palmer. Vol. 39, The Texts of Taoism.
Neihardt, John. *Black Elk Speaks*. Lincoln, Neb.: University of Nebraska Press, 1979.
Oldenburg, Ulf. *The Conflict Between El and Baal in Canaanite Religion*. Leiden, Netherlands: E. J. Brill, 1969.
Paulson, Charles. "The Traveler." This was a radio program in the 1930s, created and produced by Charles Paulsen (the father of the author), on which he played original compositions, read his original poetry, and endeavored to inspire others to a spiritual life. Many of the materials for this program are still in the possession of the author.
The Pearl of Great Price of The Church of Jesus Christ of Latter-day Saints. Salt Lake City, Ut., 1982.
Ponder, Catherine. *The Dynamic Laws of Healing*. Marina Del Rey, Ca.: DeVorss, 1966.
Pritchard, James. Ancient Near Eastern Texts. 3rd ed. Princeton, N. J.: Princeton University Press, 1974.
Rawley, William. "The Life of the Honorable Author." In *A Harmony of the Essays, Etc., of Francis Bacon*, edited by Edward Arber. Westminster: A. Constable, 1895.

Reader's Digest Association. *The World's Last Mysteries:* Pleasantville, N.Y.: Reader's Digest Association, 1980.

Robinson, O. Preston. *The Dead Sea Scrolls and Original Christinity.* Salt Lake City, Ut.: Deseret Book Company, 1958.

Salmerón, Father Zárate. *Relaciones,* Translated by Alicia R. Milich. Albuquerque, N.M.: Horn and Wallace, 1966.

Self-Realization Fellowship: *Pictorial History of Self-Realization Fellowship.* Los Angeles: Self-Realization Fellowship, 1975.

Sharpe, William. *The Dual Image.* London: H. A. Copley, 1896.

Sitchin, Zecharia. *The 12th Planet.* Avon Books, 1978.

Spaulding, Baird T. *Life and Teaching of the Masters of the Far East.* 5 vols. Vol. 2. Marina Del Rey, Ca.: DeVorss, 1964.

Steiger, Brad. *Gods of Aquarius.* New York: Berkley Publishing Corporation. 1981.

Szekely, Edmond Bordeaux, ed. and trans. *The Essene Gospel of Peace, Book One (The Third Century Aramaic Manuscript and Old Slavonic Texts).* n.p.: International Biogenic Society, 1978.

Thoreau, Henry David. *Waldon.* Edited by J. Lyndon Shonley. Princeton, N.J.: Princeton University Press, 1971.

Tompkins, Peter. *Secrets of the Great Pyramid.* New York: Harper and Row, 1971.

Traherne, Thomas. *Centuries, Poems, and Thanksgivings.*, Vol. 1. London: Oxford University Press, 1958.

Underhill, Evelyn. *Mysticism.* New York: E. P. Dutton, 1961.

Uyeda, Seiya. *The New View of the Earth: Moving Continents and Moving Oceans.* San Francisco: W. H. Freeman, 1978.

Vaughan, Robert Alfred. *Hours With the Mystics.* 6th ed. 2 vols. New York: Charles Scribner's Sons, 1893.

von Däniken, Erich. *Chariots of the Gods?* Translated by Michael Heron. New York: Bantam Books, 1974.

von Däniken, Erich. *Gods from Outer Space.* Translated by Michael Heron. New York: Bantam Books, 1972.

von Däniken, Erich. *The Gold of the Gods.* Translated by Michael Heron. New York: Bantam Books, 1974.

von Däniken, Erich. *In Search of Ancient Gods: My Pictorial Evidence for the Impossible.* Translated by Michael Heron. London: Transworld Publishers, 1973.

Warren, Robert Penn. *Chief Joseph of the Nez Perce.* New York: Random House, 1982.

Waters, Frank and Fredericks, Oswald White Bear. *Book of the Hopi.* New York: The Viking Press, 1971.

Watt, G. D., ed. *Journal of Discourses, by Brigham Young, his Two Counsellors, and the Twelve Apostles.* 26 vols. Vol. 4. Liverpool, U.K.: S.W. Richards, 1857.

Whitman, Walt. *The Complete Poetry and Prose of Walt Whitman as Prepared by him for the Deathbed Edition.* 2 vols. New York: Pellegrini and Cudahy, 1948.

Whitman, Walt. *Specimen Days.* Boston: David R. Goodine, 1971.

Wilhelm, Richard, trans. The Secret of the Golden Flower. New York: Harcourt, Brace, Jovanovich, 1962.

Yogananda, Paramhansa. *Autobiography of a Yogi.* Los Angeles; Self-Realization Fellowship, 1979.

Yogananda, Paramhansa. *Cosmic Chants.* Los Angeles: Self-Realization Fellowship, 1974.

Yogananda, Paramhansa. *Whispers from Eternity.* Los Angeles: Self-Realization Fellowship, 1935.

PERIODICALS

Konrath, Jacob. "Mysteries of the Deep." *Flying Saucers Pictorial,* 1967.

Marden, Luis. "Titicaca, Abode of the Sun." *National Geographic Magazine,* February, 1971.

Petterson, Hans. "Exploring the Ocean Floor." *Scientific American,* August, 1950.

Index

488

491

492

496